33rd Edition

Railways Re

2012

The Best-Selling Guide to Heritage Railways

Edited by
Alan C. Butcher

HERITAGE
RAILWAY
ASSOCIATION

S

HASTE HILL

Ian Allan
PUBLISHING

Contents

Front cover: BR Standard Class 9F No 92203 *Black Prince* leaves Weybourne station bound for Holt. The locomotive is on loan to the North Norfolk Railway from the Gloucestershire Warwickshire Railway *ACB*

Previous page: Ruislip Lido Railway's sole item of steam motive power, *Mad Bess*, is seen at the head of a well-filled train. *RLRS*

First published 1980
Thirty third edition 2012

ISBN 978 0 7110 3694 9

Published by Ian Allan Publishing

an imprint of Ian Allan Publishing Ltd, Hersham, Surrey KT12 4RG.
Printed in England by Ian Allan Printing Ltd, Hersham, Surrey KT12 4RG.

Visit the Ian Allan Publishing website at www.ianallanpublishing.com

Distributed in the Unites States of America and Canada by BookMasters Distribution Services.

Code 1203/C3

The publishers, the railway operators and the Heritage Railway Association accept no liability for any loss, damage or injury caused by error or inaccuracy in the information published in *Railways Restored 2012* Train services may be altered or cancelled without prior notice, and at some locations diesel traction may be substituted for scheduled steam workings.

Railways ILLUSTRATED

The magazine with the best coverage of today's railway scene

ch issue of *Railways Illustrated* offers a nprehensive round-up of the latest news and cal events from the UK across the present day way, including heritage traction in operation on main lines.

pported by high quality photography and orial from experienced railway enthusiasts, *ways Illustrated* reflects the energy and vitality he present day railway scene.

oted to coverage of railway companies, train rators, infrastructure functions, main line m operations and principal modern traction tage sites, *Railways Illustrated* also presents a lar photographic overseas feature, some i-technical articles, and a popular practical es on digital photography.

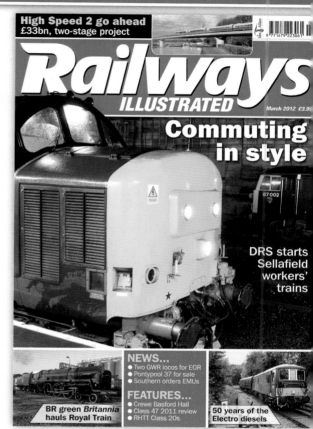

High Speed 2 go ahead
£33bn, two-stage project

Railways ILLUSTRATED March 2012 £3.9

Commuting in style

87002

DRS starts Sellafield workers' trains

NEWS...
● Two GWR locos for EOR
● Pontypool 37 for sale
● Southern orders EMUs

FEATURES...
● Crewe Basford Hall
● Class 47 2011 review
● RHTT Class 20s

BR green *Britannia* hauls Royal Train

50 years of the Electro diesels

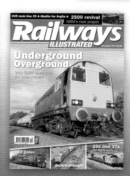

National Railway Heritage Awards

The Awards have been made annually since 1979 and were granted charitable status in 2004. The object remains the same: encouraging high standards of restoration of buildings, structures and signalling installations and of their environmental care, thus promoting public recognition and awareness of our historic railway and tramway heritage and its place in the environment. We aim to promote careful design and quality workmanship in restoration, modernisation, adaptation and maintenance, taking proper account of all relevant factors, particularly manpower and funding. In this way we encourage both public and heritage railways and tramways to present their operational premises as attractive 'shop-windows'. We also encourage owners and occupiers of former railway or tramway premises now used for other purposes to retain as much as possible of their original character.

The Awards are organised by the National Railway Awards Committee. Our main sponsors are Ian Allan Publishing together with Westinghouse Invensys, Network Rail, London Underground and the Railway Heritage Trust. Judging is done from the beginning of May through to the end of August and those shortlisted are notified at the beginning of October. The Awards are presented in early December at a prestigious location by a well-known public figure, with full media coverage.

1992 saw the inclusion of Ireland in the Awards initially with the addition of a special Premier Award and up to three Certificates of Commendation in each sector.

The Ian Allan Independent Railway of the Year Award

The Ian Allan Judges pay incognito visits to each of the heritage railways around the country, buy tickets and spend the day travelling as members of the public. The judges look at the quality of service, presentation and helpfulness of the staff, the stations, the catering, the toilets and the day as a whole.

The 2011 winner was the Gloucestershire Warwickshire Railway.

The HRA Annual Award

This, the premier award made by the HRA, is for a group or organisation making an outstanding contribution to railway heritage during the year of the Award.

The Award takes the form of a Royal Train Headboard from the London, Brighton & South Coast Railway, which is on loan to the HRA from the National Railway Museum. The Award is held for one year and the winning group also receives a commemorative plaque. The Award is announced and presented at the Association's Annual General Meeting which is held on the last weekend of January each year.

The following projects are eligible:

1 Any building, structure or signalling installation associated with railways or tramways since their inception in the United Kingdom, the Isle of Man and the Republic of Ireland.

2 An entry may comprise a whole station or any single structure or group of structures, which form, or once formed, part of railway or tramway premises.

3 Certain types of replica are eligible. These include:
- An historic building, structure or signalling installation re-erected at a new site
- An accurate reconstruction of a specfic building, structure or signalling installation, the original of which has been removed or demolished, rebuilt on or very close to its original site
- A completely new but authentic replica of a specific historic building, structure or signalling installation on a new site
- An entry comprising a combination of restored or adapted historic building, structure or signalling installation with modern additions
- Construction of a building in the general style of an historic building, structure or signalling installation with no specific or authentic basis for its design or location would not be eligible.

Who can enter?

Entries are invited from the following:

Train and tram operating companies.

Companies owning track, structures and stations.

Urban underground and passenger transport authorities and companies.

Operators of heritage, tourist and private railways and tramways.

Residual property owning bodies.

Owners of eligible infrastructure, whether or not still in railway or tramway use.

Architects, engineers and contractors involved in restoration, new or maintenance work.

Local Amenity groups.

Private individuals.

Any group in Great Britain and Ireland involved in the railway industry, whether as a private railway company or as a less formal organisation. Network Rail, Irish Rail, Northern Ireland Railways (NIR). Other public or commercial organisations.

For application forms apply to:
Robin Leleux
3 Sycamore Drive
Addington
Ilkley
West Yorkshire
LS29 0NY
Tel: 01943 839855
E-mail: robin.leleux@btinternet.com

On the following pages will be found a guide to well over 200 heritage railways, railway museums, preservation centres and miniature railways in Great Britain and Ireland. Information for visitors has been set out in tabular form for easy reference, together with a locomotive stocklist for most centres.

Many heritage centres and operating lines provide facilities for other groups and organisations to restore locomotives and equipment on their premises. It has not been possible to include full details of these groups, but organisations which own locomotives are shown under the centres at which they operate. In addition, a full list of member societies of the HRA is given elsewhere. In the case of most operating lines their length is given, but there is no guarantee that services are operated over the entire length.

Within the heading to each entry a heading block has been incorporated for easy reference as to what each site offers in the way of passenger service to visitors. These are as follows:

Timetable Service: Railways providing a passenger service between two or more stations with public access; eg Mid-Hants Railway.

Steam Centre: A railway or heritage site offering a passenger service on a short length of line, on a regular basis, with public access at only one point; eg Lavender Line.

Museum: A museum or site that does not offer a passenger service on a regular basis, if at all; eg Science Museum, London. Some sites may however offer rides on miniature railways.

Railway Centre: A catch-all for those centres which do not fall clearly into any of the other brackets. Generally those offering rides over short distances using non-steam motive power.

Attraction: Where the railway is an addition to the main attraction of the location; eg Bicton Woodland Railway.

There are a number of variations on this theme where the attraction warrants a different approach — Miniature Railway, Industrial Heritage Museum, etc.

As well as a guide as to what to expect on each site, *Railways Restored* shows what, if any, particular professional body the Companies or Societies belong to. These are:

HRA: Indicates that the organisation is a member of the Heritage Railway Association (HRA).

TT: Indicates that the organisation is a member of the Transport Trust (TT).

Membership of the HRA and TT is open to both organisations and private individuals. Private members are able to take advantage of concessions offered to them by the organisations that subscribe to these two bodies.

The concessions range from a discount on the admission price to free entry. The TT's Travel Back leaflet provides details.

Details given under **Access by public transport** should be checked beforehand to ensure services shown are operating. Unless the Heritage Railway, Steam Centre or Museum has identified the privatised train company operating the service, the phrases 'by rail', or 'main line', have been used to identify access by train.

Visitors wishing to see specific items of rolling stock or locomotives are advised to check before their visit that the exhibit is available for inspection. It should be stressed that not all items are usually available for inspection due to restoration, operating or other restrictions.

Above: During the summer of 2011 the Mid-Norfolk Railway was used for the running in of No 6023 *King Edward II* following its epic rebuild at the Didcot Railway Centre. The MNR also hired in this ex-LNER observation car from the Great Central Railway. It is seen here at Dereham awaiting unloading. *ACB*

Left: The history of miniature steam locomotives is as old as the full size versions. The two locomotives at the front of this line up at the Eastleigh Lakeside Railway date from the 1940s, older than a number of preserved standard gauge locomotives. *ELR*

AEC	Associated Equipment Co
AEG	Allgemeine Elektrizitäts Gesellschaft
A/Barclay	Andrew Barclay
A/Porter	Aveling & Porter Ltd
A/Whitworth	Armstrong Whitworth
B/Drewry	Baguley/Drewry
B/Peacock	Beyer Peacock & Co
B/Hawthorn	Black, Hawthorn & Co
BRCW	Birmingham Railway, Carriage & Wagon
BTH	British Thomson Houston
Buch	23 August Locomotive Works
D/Metcalfe	Davies & Metcalfe
E/Electric	English Electric Ltd
F/Jennings	Fletcher Jennings & Co
F/Walker	Fox Walker
G&S	G. & S. Light Engineering Co
G/England	George England & Co
GRCW	Gloucester Railway, Carriage & Wagon
H/Barclay	Hunslet Barclay
H/Clarke	Hudswell Clarke & Co Ltd
H/Hunslet	Hudson-Hunslet
H/Leslie	Hawthorn Leslie & Co
K/Stuart	Kerr Stuart & Co Ltd
L/Blackstone	Lister Blackstone
M/Cam	Metropolitan Cammell
M/Rail	Motor Rail Ltd
M/Vick	Metrovick (Metropolitan-Vickers)
M/Wardle	Manning Wardle & Co Ltd
N/British	North British Locomotive Co Ltd
N/Wilson	Nasmyth Wilson & Co Ltd
O&K	Orenstein & Koppel
P/Steel	Pressed Steel Co Ltd
RSH	Robert Stephenson & Hawthorn Ltd
R/Hornsby	Ruston Hornsby
R/Proctor	Ruston Proctor
S. F. Belge	Société Franco-Belge
S/Lamd	Severn Lamb
SMH	Simplex Mechanical Handling
YEC	Yorkshire Engine Co
W&M	Waggon & Maschinenbau
W/Rogers	Wingrove & Rogers

Company abbreviations

BR	British Railways
DB	German Federal Railway
DSB	Danish State Railways
GWR	Great Western Railway
JZ	Yugoslav Railways
LBSCR	London, Brighton & South Coast Railway
LMS	London, Midland & Scottish Railway
LNER	London & North Eastern Railway
LSWR	London & South Western Railway
MoS	Ministry of Supply
MR	Midland Railway
NLR	North London Railway
NS	Netherlands State Railways
NSB	Norwegian State Railways
RR	Rhodesia Railways
S&DJR	Somerset & Dorset Joint Railway
SAR	South African Railways
SECR	South Eastern & Chatham Railway
SER	South Eastern Railway
SJ	Swedish Railways
SNCF	French National Railways
SR	Southern Railway
USATC	United States Army Transportation Corps
WD	War Department

Other abbreviations

BE	Battery-electric
DE	Diesel-electric
DH	Diesel-hydraulic
DM	Diesel-mechanical
DMU	Diesel multiple-unit
E	Overhead electric
EMU	Electric multiple-unit
F	Fireless
G	Geared
GH	Gas-hydraulic
IST	Inverted saddle tank
LRO	Light Railway Order
ParM	Paraffin-mechanical
PH	Petrol-hydraulic
PM	Petrol-mechanical
PT	Pannier tank
R	Railcar
ST	Saddle tank
STT	Saddle tank and tender
T	Side tank
VB	Vertical boiler
WT	Well tank
4w	Four-wheel

Multiple-unit Type abbreviations

B	Brake
C	Composite (First/Standard class seating)
D	Driving
F	First class
K	Corridor
LV	Luggage Van
M	Motor
O	Open (seating arrangement)
P	Pullman (ex-'Brighton Belle')
R	Restaurant
S	Standard (or Second class)
T	Trailer

Added together these give the vehicle designation, for example: DMBS — Driving Motor Brake Second.

The addition of an L indicates that the vehicle has a lavatory (may not be operational on some vehicles).

Some lines operate a Standard class only policy and the First class facility is downgraded. This may result in some vehicles having a different designation to that originally applied.

Abbey Light Railway

Member: HRA, TT

The Abbey Light Railway was founded in 1976. It is a family-run operation supported by volunteers to restore and maintain vintage narrow gauge locomotives and stock. The railway takes visitors to the 11th century Cistercian monastery of Kirkstall Abbey

Proprietor: Mr P. N. Lowe

Location: Bridge Road, Kirkstall, Leeds LS5 3BW

Telephone: (0113) 267 5087

Internet address: *Web site:* www.abbeylightrailway.webs.com

Main station: Bridge Road (OS ref: SE 262356)

Other public station: Kirkstall Abbey

Car park: At Abbey House Museum with limited parking at Bridge Road

Access by public transport: By train to Headingley station. Buses from City Square

Refreshment facilities: At nearby

Industrial locomotives — 2ft gauge

Name	No	Builder	Type	Built
Loweco	1	Lister (20779)	4wDM	1942
Atlas	2	Hunslet (2465)	4wDM	1943
Odin	3	Simplex (5859)	4wDM	1934
Vulcan	4	R/Hornsby (198287)	4wDM	1942
—	5	R/Hornsby (235654)	4wDM	1946
Druid	6	Simplex (8644)	4wDM	1941
—	7	O&K (5926)	4wDM	1935
Go-Go	8	Hudson (39924)	4wPM	1924
—	9	Muir Hill (110)	4wPM	1925
—	10	Baguley (736)	0-4-0PM	1917
—	11	Baguley (760)	0-4-0PM	1917
George	12	Greenbat (2848)	4wBE	1957

Morrisons supermarket

Souvenir shop: Badges on sale on the train

Depot: Workshops at Bridge Road

Length of line/gauge: Quarter mile, 2ft gauge

Period of public operation: Sundays and Bank Holiday Mondays (13.00-17.00). Also open on the Saturday of the Kirkstall

Festival

Special events: Diesel gala — March; Kirkstall Festival — July; Diesel gala — October. See web site for details

Facilities for disabled: Toilets in the visitor centre in the abbey grounds. Unfortunately no means of carrying wheelchairs on trains

Membership details: As above

Abbey Pumping Station

Member: TT

Narrow gauge site railway (2ft gauge) formerly part of a sewage pumping station that now forms the museum site. Railway relaid in concrete by MSC scheme during early 1980s to original track layout. New track layout as an extension to original laid with 35lb rail on wooden sleepers. All the railway system is now run by volunteers. Original Simplex locomotive kept on site in operational condition. Line originally used for transferring solid material from screens to tip (about 100yd). Demonstration skip wagon trains as well as passenger trains are run when the railway is operating

Location: Abbey Pumping Station, Corporation Road, off Abbey Lane, Leicester LE4 5PX.

Next to the National Space Centre

Industrial locomotives — 2ft gauge

Name	No	Builder	Type	Built
Leonard	—	Bagnall (2087)	0-4-0ST	1919
—	—	M/Rail (5260)	4wPM	1931
—	—	R/Hornsby (223700)	4wDM	1944
—	—	SMH (40SD515)	4wDM	1979
New Star	—	Lister (4088)	4wPM	1931

Stock

3 new passenger vehicles based on Leicester & Swannington coaches.
10 skip wagons, 2 mine tubs, 2 flats, bomb wagon, various miscellaneous.
All locomotives are restored to working order; *Leonard* returned to service in 2005 when restoration work was completed

Operating group: Leicester City Council Museum, Leicester Museums Technology Association

Telephone: 0116 299 5111

Fax: 0116 299 5125

Internet address: *Web site:* www.leicester.gov/museums

Car park: Free on site

Access by public transport: Main line Leicester (London Road). First

Bus route 54 from city centre (alight at Beaumont Leys Lane)

Length of line/gauge: About 300yd, 2ft gauge. Passenger carrying on special event days and railway running days (small fare payable)

Period of public opening: Daily 1 February to 31 October, 11.00 to 16.30. Open for special

England

events only all year
On site facilities:
Museum/shop/toilets/car park.
Refreshments only on special event
days
Facilities for disabled: Access to
museum lower floor and grounds.
Lift to Engine House and
refreshments on event days.
Wheelchair access to railway
Volunteer contact: Tony Kendal,
c/o Abbey Pumping Station

Museum contact: Mr A. Simpson
(Curatoral), M. Patel (Operational),
c/o Abbey Pumping Station (Tel:
0116 299 5111)
Other attractions: Museum holds
various transport, steam navvy,
beam engines. Some items only
viewable by appointment or on
special event days
Special events: Hobbies &
Pastimes Steam Day — 15 April;
Recycling Railway Day — 5 May;

Teddies' 'Jubilee' Railway Day — 2
June; Leicester Vintage Festival —
23/24 June; Railway Gala Day —
7 July; Animal Rescue Railway Day
— 4 August; Seaside Special Steam
Day — 9 September; Scarecrow
Railway Day — 6 October; Ghostly
Engineer — Monday 29 October;
Diesel Railway Day — 3
November; Magnificent Meccano
— 13 January 2013; Steam Toys in
Action — 3 February 2013

Steam Centre — Amberley Museum & Heritage Centre — West Sussex

Member: HRA, TT

**Narrow Gauge & Industrial
Railway Collection (incorporating
the Brockham Museum of
Narrow Gauge Railways)**
The NG&IR Collection is part of an
open air industrial museum set in
36 acres of the former Pepper & Co
chalk pits. A 2ft gauge line has been
constructed and is used for carrying
passengers in genuine workmen's
vehicles
Location: Houghton Bridge,
Amberley, West Sussex (3 miles
north of Arundel) on B2139.
Adjacent to Amberley main line
station
OS reference: TQ 030122
Operating society/organisation:
Amberley Museum Trust, Amberley
Museum, Houghton Bridge,
Amberley, Arundel, West Sussex
BN18 9LT
Telephone: Bury (01798) 831370
(Museum office)
Internet addresses: *Web site:*
www.amberleymuseum.co.uk
e-mail (general museum enquiries):
office@amberleymuseum.co.uk
e-mail (specific railway enquiries):
info@amberleynarrowgauge.co.uk
Car park: Adjacent to Amberley
station
On site facilities: Shop and audio-

visual show. The 'Limeburners
Restaurant' opened in 2004 (event
booking details from 01798
839240)
Public opening:
23 March to 4 November —
Tuesday to Sunday, plus Bank
Holidays. 10.00-17.30 (last entry
16.30)
Special events: Spring Holiday
Crafts and Skills Day —
Wednesday 4 April; Vintage Car
Show — 8 April; Post Office
Vehicles and Industrial Trains Day
— 15 April; Veteran and Classic
Motorcycle Show — 6 May;
Vintage Agricultural Vehicles and
Woodland Crafts — 13 May;
Military Vehicle Show — 20 May;
Harrington Vehicle Gathering —
3 June; Mid Summer Steam
Weekend — 9/10 June; Printing
Weekend — 9/10 June; Dads Can
Do — 17 June; Electric Vehicle
Show — 17 June; Fire Show and
Commercial Vehicles — 24 June;
Railway Gala Weekend — 14/15
July; Classic Microcars and
Scooters — 22 July; Edwardian
Street Fair — 4/5 August; Harley
Davidson Day — 19 August; Bank
Holiday Story Book Day —
27 August; Ale at Amberley —
30/31 August, 1 September; Craft
and Food Fair — 1/2 September;

Bus Show and Riders' Day —
9 September; Miniature Steam
Weekend — 15/16 September;
Autumn Vintage Vehicle Show —
14 October; Autumn Industrial
Trains — 21 October
  Please refer to web site for further
details
Special notes: Displays include
working potter, blacksmith and
printer, stationary engines, historic
radio collection and vintage
Southdown garage and buses.
A 2ft gauge industrial railway
system is demonstrated when
possible, and a 3ft 2.25in gauge
line. In addition, a 2ft gauge 'main
line' has been constructed. The
500yd line was officially opened by
HRH Prince Michael of Kent on
5 June 1984. The railway is
operated every day the museum is
open (subject to mechanical
availability), with steam locomotive
haulage on certain days — for
details contact the museum office.
Wheelchairs can normally be
accommodated on the train.
  The 'Limeburners Restaurant'
features a timber frame, cedar
cladding and is floored with hand-
made clay tiles
Membership details: Friends of
Amberley Museum, c/o above
address

Locomotives — 2ft or 60cm unless otherwise indicated

Name	No	Builder	Type	Built	
Polar Bear	—	Bagnall (1781)	2-4-0T	1905	
Peter	—	Bagnall (2067)	0-4-0ST	1918	
—	—	Decauville (1126)	0-4-0WT	1947	
Townsend Hook	4	F/Jennings (172L)	0-4-0T	1880	(3ft 2.25in gauge)
Cloister	—	Hunslet (542)	0-4-0ST	1891	

10

Name	No	Builder	Type	Built	
Scaldwell	—	Peckett (1316)	0-6-0ST	1913	(3ft 0in gauge)
—	23†	Spence	0-4-0T	1921	(1ft 10in gauge)
Monty	(6)	O&K (7269)	4wDM	1936	(3ft 2.25in gauge)
The Major	(7)	O&K (7741)	4wDM	1937	
—	2	Ransomes & Rapier (80)	4wDM	1937	
—	—	H/Hunslet (3097)	4wDM	1944	
—	—	Hunslet (8969)	4wDH	1980	
—	2	R/Hornsby (166024)	4wDM	1933	
—	3101	M/Rail (Simplex) (1381)	4wPM	1918	(Armoured)
Peldon	—	John Fowler (21295)	4wDM	1936	
Redland	—	O&K (6193)	4wDM	1937	
—	—	Lister (35421)	4wPM	1949	
—	—	M/Rail (Simplex) (872)	4wPM	1918	
—	27	M/Rail (Simplex) (5863)	4wDM	1934	
—	—	M/Rail (Simplex) (10161)	4wDM	1950	(2ft 11in gauge)
Ibstock	—	M/Rail (Simplex) (11001)	4wDM	1951	
Burt*	—	Simplex (9019))	4wDM	1959	
CCSW	—	Hibberd (1980)	4wDM	1936	
Thakeham Tiles	No 3	H/Hunslet (2208)	4wDM	1941	
Thakeham Tiles	No 4	H/Hunslet (3653)	4wDM	1948	
—	—	Hudson (45913)	4wP/ParM	1932	(2ft 6in gauge)
—	—	H/Clarke (DM686)	0-4-0DM	1948	
Star Construction	—	H/Hunslet	4wDm	c1941	
—	18	R/Hornsby (187081)	4wDM	1937	
—	—	Lister (33937)	4wPM	1949	
—	—	Hibberd 'Y-type Planet' (3627)	4wPM	1953	
Jenny	—	Schoma (5239)	4wDH	1991	
—	—	B/Drewry (3751)	4wDH	1980	
—	WD 904	Wickham (3403/04)	2w-2PMR	1943	
—	2	W&R (5031)	4wBE	1953	
—	—	W&R (5034)	4wBE	1953	
—	—	W&R (4998)	4wBE	1953	
—	—	W&R (T8033)	0-4-0BE	1979	

* standard gauge
†includes hoist and 'haulage truck' for conversion to 5ft 3in gauge from Guinness Brewery

Stock
2 Penrhyn Quarry Railway 4-wheel coaches (2ft gauge, ex-1ft 10.75in gauge); RAF Fauld bogie coach (1940) (2ft gauge); 2 bogie coaches 382 and 384 ex-Lydd Ranges; Post Office Railway unit No 808 of 1930; 4 Groudle Glen Railway 4-wheel coaches (1896 and 1905) (2ft gauge); 60 other varied pieces of rolling stock of 12 different gauges ranging from 1ft 6in to 3ft 2.25in plus numerous miscellaneous exhibits including track, signals, etc

Owners
Cloister the Hampshire Narrow Gauge Railway Trust
Thakeham Tiles, Nos 3 and 4 owned by Peter & James Smith
Jenny owned by Chris Mann
B/Drewry (3751) owned by James Smith

Steam Centre	**Amerton Railway**	Staffordshire

The Amerton Railway is the home of the famous 1897-built Bagnall saddletank *Isabel*, the line having been built for it in the early 1990s. The railway has developed considerably over the years and now consists of a mile-long line run through the countryside via a passing loop at Chartley Road. At Amerton station there is the locomotive shed and workshop, where items of rolling stock can be seen under restoration, the carriage shed and yard, the former GNR station building from Stowe and the Leek & Manifold Railway signalbox from Waterhouses, now under restoration
Location: Amerton Railway, Amerton Farm, Stowe-by-Chartley, Stafford ST18 0LA (situated between Stafford and Uttoxeter, signposted off A51 at Weston)
Operating company: Staffordshire

Narrow Gauge Railway Ltd, c/o above address
Telephone: (Railway only) (01785) 254919; Farm (01889) 270294
Internet address: *Web site:* www.amertonrailway.co.uk
OS reference: SJ 993278
On site facilities: Car park at Working Farm. Licensed tea room and bakery (not operated by railway). Souvenir shop in railway ticket office. The railway is one of the main attractions at the farm, admission to most other attractions is free
Access by public transport: By rail to Stafford, then Stevenson's of Uttoxeter Ltd bus to Weston, then a mile walk to Amerton (no Sunday service)
Facilities for disabled: Wheelchairs can be accommodated in our 'Highland' coach where a wide door and access ramp are available
Period of public operation: Saturdays and Sundays from mid-March to end of October; Bank Holiday mondays. Weekdays during school holidays, see web site for details. Trains run 12.00 until 17.00. Subject to availability there will be steam on Sundays and Bank Holidays. Diesel haulage generally on Saturdays and weekdays
Special events: Summer Steam Gala (with visiting locomotives) — 16/17 June; Santa Specials — weekends in December
Membership details: Membership Secretary, c/o above address
Membership journal: *Isabel Gazette,* quarterly

Industrial locomotives — 2ft gauge

Name	No	Builder	Type	Built
Isabel	—	Bagnall (1491)	0-4-0ST	1897
No 1	—*	Bagnall (1889)	0-4-0ST	1911
Lorna Doone	—	K/Stuart (4250)	0-4-0ST	1922
	526	Henschel (14019)	0-8-0T	1916
Paddy	—	Wilbrighton (2)	0-4-0VBTT	2007
Jennie	—	Hunslet (3905)	0-4-0ST	2008
	746	M/Rail (40SD501)	4wDM	1975
—	—	M/Rail (7471)	4wDM	1940
Golspie	—	Baguley (2085)	0-4-0DM/SO	1935
Dreadnought	—	Baguley (3024)	0-4-0DM/SO	1939
—	Yard No 70	R/Hornsby (221623)	4wDM	1943
—	—	R/Hornsby (506491)	4wDM	1964
—	—	Jung (5869)	4wDM	1934
Gordon	—	Hunslet (8561)	4wDH	1978
—	—	Deutz (19531)	0-4-0DM	1937

*3ft gauge, to be rebuilt to 2ft

Rolling stock
4 toastrack coaches, 3 by Baguley, 1 ex-WHR, SNGRS-built passenger brake van and various wagons

Owner
Lorna Doone on loan from Birmingham Museum of Science & Industry

---

Steam Centre | **Apedale Valley Light Railway** | **Staffordshire**

Member: HRA
Postal address: 11 Ashwood Road, Disley, Stockport, Cheshire SK12 2EL
Site address: Apedale Heritage Centre, Loomer Road, Chesterton, Newcastle-under-Lyme, Staffs ST5 7RR
SatNav postcode: ST5 7LB
Telephone: 0845 094 1953
Internet address: *Web site:* www.mrt.org.uk
Period of public operation: Every Saturday from 31 March to 27 October. Additional trains operate on Bank Holiday weekend Sundays and Mondays. On the second complete weekend of each month steam locomotives are used, and trains are operated additionally on the Sunday. Santa trains will be operated during December
Length of line: Half mile round

Industrial locomotives (2ft gauge)

Name	No	Builder	Type	Built
Billet	1	W/Rogers (C6717)	4wBE	1963
Cable Mill	2	W/Rogers (C6716)	4wBE	1963
81A 186	3	M/Rail (8878)	4wDM	1944
Stanhope	4	K/Stuart (2395)	0-4-2ST	1917
—	5	K/Stuart (3014)	0-6-0WT	1916
—	6	M/Rail (7066)	4wPM	1938
—	—	M/Rail (9104)	4wPM	1941
—	7	Hunslet (1215)	4-6-0T	1916
—	7	M/Rail (8663)	4wDM	1941
—	9*	H/Clarke (1238)	0-6-0WT	1916
Electra	12†	Brook Victor (565)	4wBE	1970
—	13	M/Rail (11142)	4wDM	1960
Knothole Worker	14	M/Rail (22045)	4wDM	1959
Margaret	16	Hunslet (9056)	4wDH	1982
LCWW 81-03	18	H/Hunslet (6299)	4wDM	1964
—	20	M/Rail (8748)	4wDM	1942
—	21	M/Rail (8669)	4wDM	1941
—	23*	Lister (52031)	4wDM	1960
—	24	Hunslet (1974)	4wDM	1939
—	25	Hunslet (6007)	4wDM	1963
Twusk	26	H/Hunslet (6018)	4wDM	1961

England

Apedale Valley Light Railway

2'0" gauge steam and diesel trains. Newcastle-under-Lyme, Staffordshire – not far from J16 on M6.

Operating every Saturday from the end of March to October. Also bank holidays and some Sundays. Steam on selected dates. Gala weekend – September 8 & 9 plus Santa Specials.

www.avlr.org.uk

trip through Apedale Valley Community Country park.

2ft gauge

Special events: Santa Specials will be run in December — check web site for details

Facilities for disabled: Level access to majority of site. Wheelchair access to passenger train

Membership details: 11 Ashwood Road, Disley, Stockport, Cheshire SK12 2EL

Membership journal: *Moseley Matters* (quarterly)

Name	No	Builder Type		Built
Annie	27	R/Hornsby (198297)	4wDM	1939
—	28	Ruston (198228)	4wDM	1940
Vanguard	29	R/Hornsby (195846)	4wDM	1939
—	31	R/Hornsby (189972)	4wDM	1938
—	33	M/Rail (7033)	4wPM	1936
—	34	R/Hornsby (164350)	4wDM	1933
—	35	Wickham (4131)	4wPMR	1947
Commercial	36	R/Hornsby (280865)	4wDM	1949
—	37	R/Hornsby (260719)	4wDM	1948
Kenneth	38	R/Hornsby (223749)	4wDM	1944
—	39	M/Rail (1111)	4wPM	1918
Sludge	40	Simplex (40SD516)	4wDM	1979
—	41	M/Rail (5821)	4wDM	1934
—	42	M/Rail (7710)	4wDM	1939
—	43	Simplex (104063G)	4wDM	1976
Chaumont	44	Hudson (LX1002)	4wDH	1968
87008	45	R/Hornsby (179870)	4wDM	1936
—	47	M/Rail (1369)	4wPM	1918
R12/ND6458	48	R/Hornsby (235725)	4wDM	1943
—	50	Deutz (10050)	4wDM	1931
LAWR	52	Baguley (1695)	0-4-0PM	1928
—	53	Hibberd (2306)	4wDM	1940
Yard No 54	54†	Hibberd (2196)	4wPMR	1940
—	56†	Hunslet (9082)	4wDH	1984
—	57†	Hunslet (8827)	4wDH	1979
—	58	H/Clarke (D558)	4wDM	1938
—	59	O/Koppel (4588)	4wPM	1932
—	60	M/Rail (6035)	4wPM	1937

Name	No	Builder	Type	Built	
—	61	M/Rail (1320)	4wDM	1918	
MCWW P396	62	R/Hornsby (497542)	4wDM	1963	
—	64	R/Hornsby (256314)	4wDM	1949	
—	65	R/Hornsby (223667)	4wDM	1943	
—	66	Pikrose (B0366V)	4wBE	1993	
—	67	W/Rogers (D6912)	4wBE	1964	
—	69	Clayton (B0495)	4wBE	1975	
Crystal	70†	W/Rogers (K7070)	4wBE	1970	
—	71	Clayton (5843)	4wBE	1971	
Lady Anne	72	Clayton (B0922B)	4wBE	1975	
—	74	O/Koppel (3444?)	4wDM	1930	
—	78	M/Rail (5038)	4wPM	1930	
—	80	L/Blackstone (52610)	4wDM	1961	
(87004)	81	M/Rail (2197)	4wDM	1923	
—	82	Hibberd (3582)	4wDM	1924	
—	83	Rhiwbach Quarry	2-2wPM	c1935	
—	84	Howard (984)	4wPM	1931	
—	86	Hibberd (2586)	4wDM	1941	
—	89	R&Rapier (84)	4wDM	1938	
—	90	Drewry (3756)	4wDM	1982	
—	—	Clayton (B0495)	4wBE	1975	
—	—	Clayton (B1854)	4wBE	1979	
—	—†	Hunslet (8830)	4wDH	1979	
—	—†	Hunslet (8968)	4wDH	1980	

*stored off site
†2ft 6in gauge

Appleby Frodingham Railway Preservation Society

Steam Centre

North Lincolnshire

The society is pleased to be allowed to operate steam and/or diesel-hauled sightseeing rail tours within the Tata steelworks at Scunthorpe. It is one of Europe's major industrial complexes and Great Britain's premier iron and steelmaking site, covering approximately 12 square miles.
Headquarters: Tata Steelworks, Scunthorpe. *Please note that due to the enclosed and secure nature of the site casual visits to the steelworks or the society, are not permitted*
Address: Appleby Frodingham RPS, PO Box 44 Brigg, North Lincolnshire DN20 8XG
Telephone: Enquiries (excluding booking) (01652) 656661
Internet address: *Web site*: www.afrps.co.uk
Railtour bookings and enquiries:
Brigg Tourist Information Centre, 01652 657073, or e-mail:

Locomotives and multiple-units

Name	No	Origin	Class	Type	Built
—	D2853	BR	02	0-4-0DH	1960
—	D2128	BR	03	0-4-0DH	1960
—	07012	BR	07	0-6-0DE	1962
—	54207	BR	108	DTCL	1958
—	59245	BR	108	TSL	1958

Industrial locomotives

Name	No	Builder	Type	Built
Hutnik	—	Ferrum (3138)	0-6-0T	1952
—	—	Peckett (1438)	0-4-0ST	1916
—	—	Hunslet (3844)	0-6-0ST	1956
Arnold Machin	—	YEC (2661)	0-6-0DE	1958
Richard Clark	—	Bagnall (3151)	0-6-0DM	1960
—	—	H/Clarke (D1344)	0-4-0DM	1965
Cranford	—	Avonside (1919)	0-6-0ST	1924
Slough Estates No 5	—	H/Clarke (1544)	0-6-0ST	1924
Janus	1	YEC	0-6-0DE	

Note: from time to time those of the above locomotives that are privately owned may leave the site on a temporary or permanent basis

Stock
1 ex-BR Mk 1 coach No E4668; Director's saloon No DM395280;
3 20-ton brake vans, 6 former main line and internal wagons

14

brigg.tic@northlincs.gov.uk
All places on all tours MUST be pre-booked
Railtour platform: Frodingham Platform, via Tata Works Entrance/ Gate 'E', Main Approach, off Brigg Road, Scunthorpe (A1029) SatNav postcode: DN16 1XA
Other platform: Appleby, for access to the refreshment coach, toilets and depot — all only accessible to railtour participants
Vehicle parking: Via Tata Works Entrance/Gate 'E', Main Approach, off Brigg Road, Scunthorpe (A1029), opposite Frodingham House. Free for the duration of railtours
SatNav postcode: DN16 1XA
Access by public transport:
By rail — Scunthorpe station, 1 mile
By bus — Scunthorpe bus station 0.5 mile.
There is no public transport from either of these to or from Frodingham Platform
Souvenir shop: At the society's depot within the steelworks, only accessible to railtour participants
Length of line: There is approximately 100 miles of standard gauge track within the site. Nearly all of this is visible on tours but may not be suitable for access by coaching stock due to curvature,

Other locomotives and rolling stock
There is usually the opportunity to see a variety of Tata and main line locomotives and rolling stock during railtours

Owners
Slough Estates the Slough & Windsor Railway Society

production processes, Tata production rail traffic, clearances etc
Passenger trains: The tours cover some 8 miles (short tour) or 15 miles (long tour) of the Tata steelworks internal system. Every effort is made to provide an informed commentary throughout the tours which utilise coaching stock. Brake van tours, both timetabled and privately chartered, tend to cover areas not accessible to hauled coaching stock. The society cannot charge set fares but relies on donations which are collected at the end of each tour, except when private charters are operated.
Period of public operation:
Approximately Easter to the end of September for coaching stock; brake van trips throughout the year. Please note that brake van trips are *not* considered to be suitable for children under the age of 11 due to the nature of the vehicles
Special events: Occasional diesel days using a variety of locomotives

for haulage. These will be advertised as and when arranged. Footplate Experience Days on steam and/or diesel locomotives held on dates to suit participants, usually at weekends when there is no railtour scheduled
Facilities for mobility impaired visitors: Limited. Subject to notification at the time of booking wheelchair access can be provided to the departure platform and coaches. It is regretted that wheelchair access is not possible to the on-board toilet, the static refreshment coach and toilets at the depot.
Special note: Please note that Tata do not permit pets to be brought onto the site. The only animals permitted are fully trained assistance dogs
Membership details: Details available from Society Treasurer at the above address
Membership newsletter:
Approximately 4 times per year

| Miniature Railway | Ashmanhaugh Light Railway | Norfolk |

Formed in 2002, the line opened to the public in 2003. It is set in the Norfolk countryside within sight of the National Express East Anglian Bittern Line and within whistle distance of the Bure Valley Railway
Location/headquarters: East View Farm, Stone Lane, Ashmanhaugh, Nr Wroxham, Norfolk NR12 8YW
SatNav postcode: NR12 8YW
Tel: 01603 404263
Contact: Brian Mason
Internet addresses:
E-mail:
info@ashmanhaughlightrailway.co.uk
Web site:
www.ashmanhaughlightrailway.co.uk
Access by public transport:
By rail: Wroxham & Hoveton (2 miles

Locomotives — 7.25in gauge

Name	No	Builder	Type	Built
Thunderbox	1	D. King	4w+wPM	1989
The Shay	2	E. Peck	0-4-0+0-4-0	2000
Hotspur	3	Valentines	0-4-0	1997
The General	4	N. Duffield/R. Ives	4w+4BE	1992
The Sergeant	5	Tully	4wBE	1988
Lucille	6	A. Ruston	0-4-0ST	—

Rolling stock
10 coaches formed as one two-car and two three-car sets, and an additional two vehicles with two 4-wheel bogies (Mavis and Doris coaches). Two 4-wheeled open wagons

Car parking: On site
On site facilities: Toilets and light refreshments
Length of line: 900yd, 7.25in gauge
Period of public operation:

The first Sunday of each month from May to October, 14.00-17.00. Weather permitting
Special events: Birthday parties, driver experience courses

England

Astley Green Colliery Museum

The museum occupies some 15 acres south of the Astley Green colliery site. The low-lying landscape ensures that the museum's 98ft high lattice steel headgear can be seen for many miles. Apart from the steam winding engine and headgear the museum houses many exhibits, not least of which is the collection of over 20 colliery locomotives, the largest collection of its type in the UK. The museum is now run and maintained, on behalf of the community, by the Red Rose Steam Society Ltd, a registered charity based in Lancashire. A half-mile extension to the 2ft gauge railway will commence in the new year which will be to passenger-carrying standards

Location: Between the A580 and Bridgewater Canal in Higher Green Lane, Astley Green, Tyldesley

Operating company: The Secretary, Astley Green Colliery Museum, Higher Green Lane, Astley Green, Tyldesley, Manchester M29 7JB

Telephone: 01942 708969

Internet addresses: *E-mail:* info@agcm.org.uk

For school parties *e-mail*: school.visits@agcm.org.uk

For other groups *e-mail*: group.visits@agcm.org.uk

OS reference: SJ 705998

On site facilities: Car park, toilets

Access by public transport: Train to Atherton, buses 551, 654

Facilities for disabled: Toilet

Period of public operation:
Sundays — 13.30-17.00
Tuesdays — 13.30-17.00
Thursdays — 13.30-17.00.
Closed Christmas and Boxing Days

Membership details: Membership Secretary, Red Rose Steam Society, Higher Green Lane, Astley Green, Tyldesley, Manchester M29 7JB.
E-mail:
membership@rrss.agcm.org.uk

Industrial locomotives
(standard gauge)

Name	No	Builder	Type	Built
—	—*	R/Hornsby (244580)	4wDM	1946

(3ft gauge)

Name	No	Builder	Type	Built
—	17	H/Clarke (DM781)	0-6-0DMF	1953
—	—	Hunslet (4816)	0-6-0DMF	1955
—	11	H/Clarke (DM1058)	0-6-0DMF	1957
—	20	H/Clarke (DM1120)	0-6-0DMF	1957
—	18	H/Clarke (DM1270)	0-6-0DMF	1961
—	DM1439	H/Clarke (DM1439)	0-6-0DMF	1978

(2ft 6in gauge)

Name	No	Builder	Type	Built
—	—*	Hunslet (3411)	0-4-0DMF	1947
—	3*	E/Electric (7936)	4wBEF	1957
—	4	H/Clarke (DM1173)	0-6-0DMF	1959
—	5	H/Clarke (DM1352)	0-6-0DMF	1967
—	6	H/Clarke (DM1413)	0-6-0DMF	1970
—	7	H/Clarke (DM1414)	0-6-0DMF	1970
—	1-44-170	Hunslet (8575)	0-6-0DMF	1978
—	1-44-174	Hunslet (8577)	0-6-0DMF	1978
Foggwell Flyer	—	Hunslet (8567)	0-6-0DMF	1981
Bullfrogs Bullet	—	Hunslet (8568)	0-6-0DMF	1981

(2ft 4in gauge)

Name	No	Builder	Type	Built
—	6	H/Clarke (DM970)	0-6-0DMF	1957

(2ft 1in gauge)

Name	No	Builder	Type	Built
Kestrel	2	H/Clarke (DM674)	0-6-0DMF	1954

(2ft gauge)

Name	No	Builder	Type	Built
Stacey	—	H/Clarke (DM804)	0-6-0DMF	1951
—	T1	H/Clarke (DM840)	0-6-0DMF	1954
George	14	H/Clarke (DM929)	0-6-0DMF	1955
—	8	M/Vickers (892)	4wBEF	1955
Warrior	14	H/Clarke (DM933)	0-6-0DMF	1956
—	—	H/Clarke (DM1164)	0-4-0DMF	1959
—	—	Hunslet (6048)	0-4-0DMF	1961
Newton	—	Hunslet (8975)	0-6-0DH	1979
Sandy	—	M/Rail (11218)	4wDM	1962
Point of Ayr	—	R/Hornsby (497547)	4wDMF	1963
Roger Bowen	—	Hunslet (7373)	0-4-0DHF	1973
Calverton	—	Hunslet (7519)	4wDHF	1977
Mole	—	Hunslet (8834)	4wDHF	1978
Lionheart	—	Hunslet (8909)	4wDHF	1979
—	R4	H/Clarke (DM1443)	0-6-0DMF	1980

Rolling stock (standard gauge)
1 Smith & Rodley steam crane*, 1 Coles diesel crane*

*on display, remainder either sheeted over or stored in locomotive shed

Attraction — Audley End Railway — Essex

The Audley End Miniature Railway is a delightful ride on Lord Braybrooke's 10.25in gauge railway through estate woodland
Location: Audley End, Saffron Walden, Essex
Headquarters: (Postal address) Audley End Estate Office, Brunketts, Wendens Ambo, Saffron Walden, Essex CB11 4JL
Contact:
General Manager: H. T. White
Telephone: (01799) 541354 or 541956
Fax: (01799) 542134
Internet addresses: *E-mail:* estateoffice@aee.eclipse.co.uk
Web site: www.audley-end-railway.co.uk
Car parking: On site
Access by public transport: Rail to Audley End (1 mile)
On site facilities: Ticket office,

Locomotives — 10.25in gauge

Name	No	Builder	Type	Built
Lord Braybrooke	3548	D. Curwen	2-6-2	1948
—	4433	D. Curwen & Newbury	4-4-2	1965
Sara Lucy	489	D. Curwen	2-8-2	1977
Bruce	24	D. Curwen	2-6-2	1991
Loyalty	1980	D. Curwen	4-4-0	1994
Barbara Curwen	—	D. Curwen	2-4-2	1977
Saint Augustine	2914	N. Simkins	4-6-0	2004
Doris	682	D. Curwen	0-6-0PM	1982
Henrietta Jane	691	A. Crowhurst	0-4-0+0-4-0DH	1991

shop and light refreshments, toilets, large picnic area
Length of line: 10.25in gauge; 1.5 miles long
Period of public operation: 24 March to 21 October; Easter holidays — 31 March-15 April April; half term holidays — 2-10 June; summer holiday — 21 July-2 September
See web site for full information or

ring (01799) 541354 or 541956
Special events: Easter Bunny — 8/9 April; Road & Rail Steam Gala — 12/13 May; Autumn Steam Train Gala — 16 September; Halloween Specials (booking required) — 27-31 October; Santa Specials — 1/2, 8/9, 15/16, 22-24 December
Facilities for disabled: Carriage built in 2002 to enable wheelchair access

Timetable Service — Avon Valley Railway — South Glos

Member: HRA
The Avon Valley Railway runs on part of the Midland Railway which connected the cities of Bristol and Bath, and currently operates over three miles of relaid track between Oldland Common to the north and Avon Riverside to the south.

Avon Riverside station provides visitors with the opportunity to enjoy riverside walks, picnic areas and a local public house.

In 2011 the railway became only the second in the country to be awarded the Queen's Award for Voluntary Service; a Silver 'Green Tourism Business Scheme' award, the first heritage railway to receive such recognition; and the HRA Publication Award for the best heritage railway magazine — *Semaphore*
Headquarters: Avon Valley Railway Co Ltd, Bitton Station, Bath Road, Bitton, Bristol BS30 6HD

Locomotives

Name	No	Origin	Class	Type	Built
—	44123	LMS	4F	0-6-0	1925
—	D2994	BR	07	0-6-0DE	1962
The Royal Alex	73101	BR	73	Bo-Bo	1965
—	52006	BR	107	DMBS	1960
—	52025	BR	107	DMCL	1960

Locomotive notes: D2994, 52006, 52025 in service

Industrial locomotives

Name	No	Builder	Type	Built
Edwin Hulse	—	Avonside (1798)	0-6-0ST	1918
Karel	4015	Chrzanow (4015)	0-6-0T	1954
Littleton No 5	—	M/Wardle (2018)	0-6-0ST	1922
—	7151	RSH (7151)	0-6-0T	1944
—	—	Sentinel (7492)	0-4-0VBT	1928
Grumpy	WD70031	B/Drewry (2158)	0-4-0DM	1941
—*	Army 200	Barclay (358)	0-4-0DM	1941
Kingswood	—	Barclay (446)	0-4-0DM	1959
Western Pride*	D1171	H/Clarke (D1171)	0-6-0DM	1951
—†*	—	R/Hornsby (210481)	4wDM	1941
Basil*	—	R/Hornsby (235519)	4wDM	1945
—†*	—	R/Hornsby (252823)	4wDM	1947
—	429	R/Hornsby (466618)	0-6-0DH	1961
General Lord Robertson*	610	Sentinel (10143)	0-8-0DH	1961

Telephone: (0117) 932 5538 for general enquiries
(0117) 932 7296 for 24hr talking timetable .
Internet addresses: *E-mail:* info@avonvalleyrailway.org
Web site: www.avonvalleyrailway.org
Main station: Bitton
Other public stations: Oldland Common, Avon Riverside
OS reference: ST 670705
Car park: Bitton station
Access by public transport:
By rail: Main line train service to Keynsham.
By bus: First service No 332 (Bristol-Bath)
Access by bike: Bitton station is on the Bristol–Bath Railway Path (route 4 of the National Cycle Network)
Catering facilities: New café/restaurant opened in July 2008 with indoor seating in Mk 1 railway carriage. Hot and cold meals and food available, with daily specials. Confectionery and ice cream also available
On site facilities: Station and café/restaurant is open daily except Christmas Day. Toilets, picnic area, play area nearby
Public opening: Bitton station is open daily for viewing of its static collection of locomotives and rolling stock, except for Christmas Day.
Trains operate: 18, 25 March; 1, 3-12, 14*/15, 21*/22, 28*/29 April; 5*, 6/7, 12/13, 20, 26*/27 May; 2-8, 9*/10, 13, 17, 20, 24, 27 June; 1, 4, 7*/8, 11, 14*./15, 18, 21*/22, 24-26, 28*/19, 31 July; 1/2, 4*/5, 7-9, 11*/12, 14-16, 18*/19, 21-23, 25*, 23-31 August; 1*/2, 8*/9, 16, 23, 30 September; 6*/7, 14, 20/21, 25*/26*, 28, 31*/31* October; 1*/2, 4, 24/25 November; 1/2, 8-10, 15/16, 22-24, 26/27, 29/30 December; 1 January 2013

Name	No	Builder	Type	Built
—	—	Sentinel (7942)	0-4-0T	1928

*stored/undergoing restoration off-site
†chassis only

Locomotive notes: *Kingswood, Karel,* 70 and 7151 are in service

Stock
23 ex-BR Mk 1 coaches (5 stored off-site); 2 ex-BR Mk 1 Restaurant coach; 1 ex-BR Mk 3 sleeper; 3 cranes; 1 Wickham trolley; numerous assorted wagons

Owners
44123 the London Midland Society
52006 and 52025 on loan from Class 107 Ltd
73101 on loan from David Hurd (Dean Forest Railway)

*diesel-hauled
Special events: *Advance booking is essential for some of these events. Details from Bitton station — 0117 932 5538. Online booking is now available using the link from the railway's web site.*
Mother's Day Lunch — 18 March; Volunteer Day — 25 March; Easter Steaming — 3-12 April; Day out with Thomas — 12/13 May; Murder Mystery Evening — 19 May; 1940s Event — 2/3 June; 9th Bitton Beer Festival — 8/9 June; Father's Day Lunch — 17 June; Evening Fish & Chip Train — 20 June; Murder Mystery Evening — 23 June; Evening Fish & Chip Train — 11 July; Teddy Bears' Picnic — 15 July; Vintage Austin Car Rally — 29 July; Evening Fish & Chip Train — 18 August; Vintage Bus Rally — 12 August; Railway Relics Valuation Day — 2 September; Grandparents' Day — 9 September; Murder Mystery Evening — 22 September; Teddy Bears' Picnic — 23 September; End of Season Gala — 20/21 October; Murder Mystery Evenings — 27 October, 3 November; Half-Term Train Rides — 25/26, 28, 30/31 October;

Christmas Dining Train — 24 November; Santa Specials — 25 November, 1/2, 8/9, 15/16, 22-24 December; Sherry and Mince Pie Specials — 26/27, 28/29 December, 1 January 2013.
Steam 'N Cuisine (3-course dining trains) 18 march, 29 April, 27 May, 17 June, 22 July, 19 August, 16 September, 7 October, 24 November.
Bitton Bistro (2-course dining trains) 1 April, 1 July, 26 August, 2 September.
Driver Experience Courses — 17, 24, 31 March; 13 April; 19 May; 16, 23, 30 June; 13 July; 15, 22, 29 September; 13, 27 October; 3 November
Special facilities: Wedding licence. Carriage or train hire available for parties, staff outings or business functions
Facilities for disabled: Fully accessible disabled toilet at Bitton station. Coach converted for disabled use but no disabled toilet on train
Membership details: Membership Secretary, c/o Bitton station
Membership journal: *Semaphore* — every 6 months; *Ground Signal* newsletter every 2 months

Steam Centre	**Barrow Hill Roundhouse Railway Centre**	Derbyshire

NOTE: Various main line companies use Barrow Hill for overhaul, storage or stabling. These locomotives are not listed here

Member: HRA
In 1839 the North Midland Railway devised an arrangement of stabling locomotives around a turntable within a polygonal building with a

conical roof, hence roundhouse. In 1864 locomotives began to be housed in buildings of a square nature (retaining the name) and in 1870 Barrow Hill was built to this design. Retained following the end of steam, Barrow Hill remained in use until 1991. Saved from demolition at the 11th hour, the Grade 2 listed building is unique in Great Britain as the last surviving working roundhouse.

The roundhouse can accommodate up to 24 main line locomotives, and includes maintenance pits and ancillary services

Location/headquarters: Barrow Hill Roundhouse Engine Shed, Campbell Drive, Barrow Hill, Nr Staveley, Chesterfield, Derbyshire S43 2PR.

OS reference: SK 415754

Project manager: Mervyn Allcock

Contact address: Barrow Hill Engine Shed Society, address as above

Telephone: 01246 472450

Fax: 01246 472450

Internet address: *Web site:* www.barrowhill.org.uk

Car park: Adjacent to site

Access by public transport:

By rail: Nearest station is Chesterfield

By bus: Stagecoach service No 90 from Chesterfield (reduced Sunday

Locomotives (preserved)

Name	No	Origin	Class	Type	Built
Butler Henderson	506	GCR	'Director'	4-4-0	1920
—	1217	GER	J17	0-6-0	1905
—	1708	MR	1F	0-6-0T	1880
RAF Biggin Hill	45110	LMS	5MT	4-6-0	1935
Blue Peter	60532	LNER	A2	4-6-2	1948
—	61264	LNER	B1	4-6-0	1947
—	20096	BR	20	Bo-Bo	1961
—	26007	BR	26	Bo-Bo	1959
—	33108	BR	33	Bo-Bo	1960
—	37275	BR	37	Co-Co	1965
Viking	37057	BR	37	Co-Co	1962
—	37372*	BR	37	Co-Co	1963
Andana	D213	BR	40	1Co-Co1	1959
Sherwood Forester	45060	BR	45	1Co-Co1	1961
—	45105	BR	45	1Co-Co1	1961
Alycidon	D9009	BR	55	Co-Co	1961
Tulyar	55015	BR	55	Co-Co	1961
Royal Highland Fusilier	55019	BR	55	Co-Co	1961
—	56006	BR	56	Co-Co	1977
—	58016	BR	58	Co-Co	1984
—	73117	BR	73	Bo-Bo	1966
—	81002	BR	81	Bo-Bo	1960
—	82008	BR	82	Bo-Bo	1961
—	E3035	BR	83	Bo-Bo	1961
—	84001	BR	84	Bo-Bo	1960
Doncaster Plant 150 1853-2003	85101	BR	85	Bo-Bo	1961
—	89001	BR	89	Bo-Bo	1986

service). TM Travel also operate on Sundays

Access by road: Just off Jcts 29, 29A, 30 of the M1, follow A619 then follow brown tourist signs

On site facilities: Refreshments, souvenir shop and museum. Toilets

Refreshment facilities: Drinks and light refreshments

Public opening: Open most weekends — four major open weekends a year

Special events: Easter, summer, autumn and Christmas open weekends

Membership details: Martyn Brailsford, 18 Queen Street, Brimington, Chesterfield, Derbyshire S43 1HT

Society journal: *The Roundhouse* — three times a year

*for conversion to Class 23 'Baby Deltic'

Industrial locomotives (preserved)

Name	No	Builder	Type	Built
Henry	—	H/Leslie (2491)	0-4-0ST	1901
The Welshman	—	M/Wardle (1207)	0-6-0ST	1890
—	—	Peckett (2000)	0-6-0ST	1941
—	9	YEC	0-6-0ST	1952
Vulcan	—	V/Foundry (3272)	0-4-0ST	1918
Harry	—	Drewry (2589)	0-4-0DM	1956
—	4	Hunslet (6975)	0-6-0DH	1969
—	47	Hunslet (7181)	0-6-0DH	1970
—	RFS 10	E/Electric (D1228)	0-6-0DH	1967
Coalite 7	—	R/Royce (10279)	0-6-0DH	1970
Coalite 9	—	Vanguard	0-6-0DH	
—	1	GEC Kemira	0-6-0	—
—	—	RFS Valiant	0-6-0	—

Owners

45110 the Severn Valley Railway (Holdings) plc
45060 and 45105 the Pioneer Diesel Locomotive Group
Classes 81-9 locomotives the AC Locomotive Group
58016 the Class 58 Locomotive Group
The Welshman and 9 the National Mining Museum

Timetable Service | **The Battlefield Line Railway** | Leicestershire

Member: HRA, TT

A quiet country railway operated by the Shackerstone Railway Society Ltd

Headquarters: Shackerstone station (3 miles north of Market Bosworth in Leicestershire)

Address: Shackerstone Station, Shackerstone, Nuneaton CV13 6NW

Telephone: Timetable enquiries: (01827) 880754

Internet address: *Web site*: www.battlefield-line-railway.co.uk

Operating Manager: D. Weightman

Main station: Shackerstone

Other public station: Shenton

OS reference: SK 379066

Car park: Shackerstone (free), Shenton (council car park)

Access by public transport: Bus service from Nuneaton weekends only. Ring Traveline 0870 6082608 for details

Refreshment facilities: Tea rooms on Shackerstone station. Buffet/bar on most trains

Souvenir shop: Shackerstone

Locomotives and multiple-units

Name	No	Origin	Class	Type	Built
Mayflower	1306	LNER	B1	4-6-0	1948
Diane	D2867	BR	02	0-4-0DH	1961
—	11215	BR	04	0-6-0DM	1956
—	D2310	BR	04	0-6-0DM	1960
—	08528	BR	08	0-6-0DE	1959
—	08818	BR	08	0-6-0DE	1960
—	12083	BR	11	0-6-0DE	1953
—	D9529	BR	14	0-6-0DE	1965
—	20105	BR	20	Bo-Bo	1961
Brush Veteran	D5518	BR	31	A1A-A1A	1958
Calder Hall Power Station	31130	BR	31	A1A-A1A	1959
—	33008	BR	33	Bo-Bo	1960
Griffon	33019	BR	33	Bo-Bo	1960
—	33053*	BR	33	Bo-Bo	1961
—	37227	BR	37	Co-Co	1964
—	37905	BR	37	Co-Co	1963
Jimmy Milne	47635	BR	47	Co-Co	1964
University of Strathclyde	47640	BR	47	Co-Co	1964
—	56086	BR	56	Co-Co	1981
—	56098	BR	56	Co-Co	1981
—	73105	BR	73	Bo-Bo	1965
—	51131	BR	116	DMBS	1958
—	51321	BRCW	116	DMS	1959
—	55005	GRCW	122	DMBS	1958
—	59522	P/Steel	117	TC(L)	1959

20

England

Museum: Shackerstone
Depot: Shackerstone
Length of line: 4.75 miles (8km)
Passenger trains: Shackerstone-Shenton
Period of public operation: Shackerstone station is generally open weekends 11.45-17.00 and Bank Holiday Mondays 11.00-17.00.
Trains at weekends and Bank Holidays 3 March to 28 October. Selected Tuesdays and Wednesdays in July and August.
Special events: Battlefield Steam Gala — 17/18 March; Day out with Thomas — 21/22, 28/29 April; TRactor Weekend — 12/13 May; The World in Minature — 26/27 May; Pepper Pig & George Appearances — 9/10 June; 1940s Weened — 23/24 June; Rail and Ale Weekend — 14/15 July;
Facilities for disabled: Special car park and toilets
Special notes: Family tickets available. Scenic countryside views including Ashby Canal. Shenton station is adjacent to Bosworth Battlefield (1485) Country Park. 20 minute walk along 'Battlefield Trail' to visitor centre, return by later train
Operating company/ preservation society contact: The Secretary, Shackerstone Railway

*on long-term loan to Mid-Hants Railway

Industrial locomotives

Name	No	Builder	Type	Built
Waleswood	—	H/Clarke (750)	0-4-0ST	1906
Sir Gomer	—	Peckett (1859)	0-6-0ST	1932
Dunlop No 7	—	Peckett (2130)	0-4-0ST	1951
Richard III	—	RSH (7537)	0-6-0T	1949
Lamport No 3	—	Bagnall (2670)	0-6-0ST	1942
—	—	Barclay (422)	0-6-0DM	1958
—	19	Barclay (594)	0-6-0DM	1974
—	—	E/Electric (8431)	0-4-0DH	1963
—	890445	GEC (5402)	0-6-0DM	1975
—	47	T/Hill (249V)	0-6-0DH	1974
—	—	R/Hornsby (263001)	4wDM	1949
—	44	Hunslet (6684)	0-6-0DH	1968
—	—	R/Royce (10254)	0-4-0DE	1966
—	—	Simplex (9921)	4wDM	1955

Stock
8 ex-BR Mk 1 coaches (including Griddle Car), 2 ex-BR Mk 2 coaches, 1 ex-BR Mk 3 sleeper; 5 passenger-rated vans; 1 rail-mounted steam crane; 2 rail-mounted diesel cranes; 35 wagons (inc 3 goods brake vans SR, MR, BR)

Owner
20105, Barclay (594) and GEC (5402) on loan from Harry Needle Railroad Co

Society, Shackerstone Station, Shackerstone, Nuneaton CV13 6NW
Membership journal:
Shackerstone News — 2/3 times/year

Museum	Beamish	Co Durham

Member: HRA
The railway station, signalbox and goods shed have been completely re-created (originally from Rowley, near Consett) along with the other exhibits to show a way of life long past. There are some very old locomotives in the collection. Passenger rides are offered at weekends in the summer
Location: Beamish Museum, County Durham DH9 0RG
OS reference: NZ 214548
Telephone: 0191 370 4000
Fax: 0191 370 4001
Internet addresses: *E-mail:* museum@beamish.org.uk
Web site: www.beamish.org.uk
Car park: At museum
SatNav postcode: DH9 0RG

Locomotives

Name	No	Origin	Class	Type	Built
—	8088	LNER	Y7	0-4-0T	1923

On loan from North Norfolk Railway

Industrial locomotives

Name	No	Builder	Type	Built
Dunrobin	—	S/Stuart (4085)	0-4-4T	1895
Locomotion	1*	LE (1)	0-4-0	1975
Twizell	3†	Stephenson (2730)	0-6-0T	1891
South Durham Malleable Iron Co No 5	—††	Stockton Ironworks	0-4-0ST	1900
Coffee Pot	—§	Head Wrightson	0-4-0VB	1871
—	E1††	Black, Hawthorn (897)	2-4-0CT	1883
—	18**	Lewin (693)	0-4-0WT	1877
Steam Elephant	—*	Wallsend Colliery	0-6-0G	2000
—	17	Head Wrightson (33)	0-4-0VB	1873
Puffing Billy	—	A/Keef (71)	0-4-0	2005
—	E2	Siemens-Schucket (455)	4WE	1909

Access by public transport: Bus service from Eldon Square, Newcastle upon Tyne

On site facilities: This 300-acre open air museum vividly re-creates life in the North of England in the early 1800s and 1900s. The Town has dentist's surgery, solicitor's office, Co-op shops, garage, sweet shop and bank. The Colliery Village has pit cottages, village school and chapel, 'drift' mine and pithead. Home Farm with farm house, livestock and exhibitions. Railway station complete with goods yard and signalbox, rolling stock on static display. Pockerley Old Hall illustrates the lifestyle of a yeoman farming family in the early 1800s.

Early Railways — Pockerley Waggonway — a large stone engine shed with displays illustrating the development of railways in the early 1800s. Visitors take a short ride in re-created carriages of the period pulled by the replica *Locomotion, Steam Elephant* or *Puffing Billy*

Public opening:
Summer: April through October, 10.00-17.00.
Winter: November to March 2013, 10.00-16.00.
Closed Mondays and Fridays and Christmas Day.
Last admission always 15.00
  NB: A winter visit to Beamish is

†on long-term loan to Tanfield Railway
††on static display
§under repair
**undergoing major rebuild, due to be completed spring 2012
*replica

Locomotive notes: E1 not usually on display. Others usually on display.

Rolling stock includes Stockton & Darlington Railway coach, No 179 built in c1865, currently under restoration

Trams

No	Operator	Built
10	Gateshead	1926
16	Sunderland	1900
31	Blackpool	1901
51	Gateshead	1901 (in store)
114	Newcastle	1901
196	Oporto	1935
264	Sheffield	1907
513	Blackpool	1952
703 (101)	Blackpool (Sunderland)	1934
749	Blackpool (tower wagon)	1909 (in store)

centred on the Town, Tramway and Pit Village; other areas of the museum are closed and admission charges are, consequently, reduced
Length of line:
Pockerley Waggonway, ¼-mile — operational daily in summer. Rebuilt NER station 550yd line operational at weekends Easter to Christmas, colliery sidings operated on selected dates
Facilities for disabled: One carriage at 1825 Railway suitable

for wheelchairs. Advance notice for parties to Bookings Officer preferred
Notes: Demonstration trains will operate at both the NER railway station and in the Edwardian Colliery during 2012. Log on to www.beamish.org.uk for details.
  See transport collection latest news and download stocklists from: http://www.beamishtransport.blog spot.com

---

Miniature Railway	**Beer Heights Light Railway**	Devon

An extensive railway in the landscaped grounds of publisher and model railway manufacturing group
Location/Headquarters:
Pecorama, Underleys, Beer, Devon EX12 3NA
Managing Director:
C. M. Pritchard
Telephone: 01297 21542
Fax: 01297 20229
Internet addressed: *E-mail:* pecorama@pecobeer.com
Web site: www.pecorama.info
OS reference: SY 223891
Car parking: Ample on site, free for our visitors

Locomotives — 7.25in gauge

Name	No	Builder	Type	Built
Otter	1	WNG*	2-4-2	2004
Dickie	3	D. Curwen	0-4-2	1976
Thomas II	4	R. Marsh	0-4-2ST+T	1979
Linda	5	D. Clarke	2-4-0ST+T	1983
Jimmy	6	S/Lamb	Bo-Bo	1986
Mr P	7	Macdougall	2-4-2T	1997
Gem	8	Peco	0-6-0T+T	1999
Claudine	9	Macdougall	2-4-4†	2005
Alfred	10	Macdougall / Nation	Bo-Bo Tram	2003
Yeo	—	J. Milner§	2-6-2T	1979
Samastipur	—	ESR§	0-4-2T	1999

*built by Western Narrow Gauge, privately owned
†single Fairlie
§privately owned

England

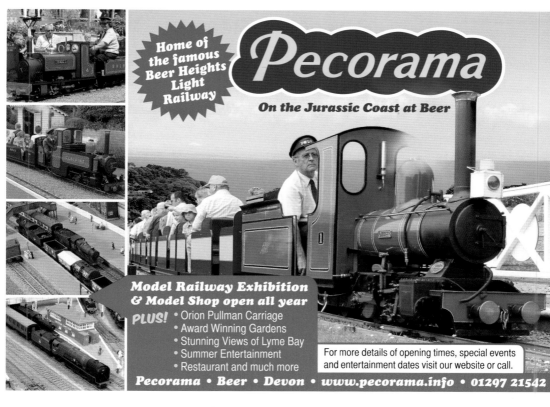
Access by public transport:
By rail — to Axminster station, then Axe Valley Bus to Beer; or rail to Exeter station, then First Bus to Weymouth via Beer
On site facilities: Restaurant, shop, model railway exhibition and fully restored Pullman car 'Orion', extensive gardens, children's activities
Length of line: 1 mile, 7.25in gauge
Period of public operation:
2 April to 2 November — Monday to Friday 10.00-17.30 plus all day Saturdays and Sundays 7-15 April, 5/6 May and 26 May-9 September. Peco Model Railway Exhibition and Model Shop open all year. Please ring or refer to web site for opening times
Special events: Spring Art Week — 30 April to 5 May; PECO Annual Vintage/Classic Vehicle Rally — 27 May; Father's Day — 17 June

Rolling stock — coaches
9 x 4-seat bogie open 'Pullman' coaches built by BHLR, 16 x 4-seat quad-articulated coaches built by BHLR
Rolling stock — wagons
6 x 4-wheeled wagons; 1 bogie open wagon; 2 x 4-wheel bolster wagons, 2 x 4-wheeled tipper wagons; 1 generator wagon

Note:
Some locomotives and rolling stock are not on permanent display

(Free entry for dads accompanied by one or more children); National Garden Scheme Open Garden Days for charity — 30 June/1 July; PECO Open Gardens Day for charity — 15 July; PECO Bank Holiday weekend of special events — 25-26 August; Kit Car Display — 9 September; FREE entry to gardens 10 September to 27 October; Rides on the Beer Heights Frights Ghost Train — 29 October-3 November
Facilities for disabled: All toilet blocks with facilities for disabled, wheelchair access to Model Exhibition, gardens and restaurant (Note: some paths in the gardens are steep and wheelchair users will need assistance)
Special facilities: Driver Experience Courses available on a 1:1 or 2:1 basis 09.30-16.30 (please refer to web site for further details
Membership details: Season ticket to Pecorama available, apply to above address

| Miniature Railway | Bickington Steam Railway | Devon |

Location/headquarters: Trago Mills Shopping & Leisure Park, Nr Newton Abbot, Devon, TQ12 6JD
Postal address: Charles Robertson Developments Ltd, Twowatersfoot, Liskeard, Cornwall PL14 6HY
OS reference: SX 822743
SatNav postcode: TQ12 6JD
Tel/Fax: 01626 82111
Contact: Malcolm Sandbach, Managing Director
Internet addresses:
E-mail: pa4trago@btconnect.com,
Web site:
www.miniaturerailwayworld.co.uk/bickington
Main station: Riverside
Other public stations: Central,

Locomotives — 10.25in gauge

Name	No	Builder	Type	Built
Blanche of Lancaster	750	Curwen	4-4-2	1948
E. R. Calthrope	1	Coleby Simkins	2-6-4T	1974
Alice	—	Simkins & Vere	2-6-0	1984
(Sandy River)	24	Coleby Simkins/Allcock/Vere	2-6-2T	1991
—	D5910	D. Nicholson	4w-4wDH	1987

Goose Glen Halt
All stations within the leisure complex
Access by public transport:
By rail: Newton Abbot, then taxi
By bus: No bus service
Access by car: Just off the A38, follow brown signs to Trago Mills at Newton Abbot turn off
On site facilities: Car parking, refreshments and shops
Souvenir shop: Adjacent to Central station
Length of line: 2.25 miles, 10.25in gauge
Period of public operation: Weekends, plus local school holidays, 11.00-17.00
Facilities for disabled: Very limited

| Attraction | Bicton Woodland Railway | Devon |

A passenger-carrying line of 18in gauge with stock mainly from the Woolwich Arsenal Railway and of World War 1 vintage
Location: Bicton Park, near Budleigh Salterton
OS reference: SY 074862
Operating society/organisation: Bicton Woodland Railway, Bicton Park Botanical Gardens, East Budleigh, Budleigh Salterton, Devon EX9 7BG
Telephone: Colaton Raleigh (01395) 568465
Fax: (01395) 568374
Internet addresses:
E-mail: info@bictongardens.co.uk
Web site: www.bictongardens.co.uk
Car park: On site
SatNav postcode: EX9 7BG
Access by public transport:
By bus: Buses pass half-hourly

Locomotives — 1ft 6in gauge

Name	No	Builder	Type	Built
Bicton	2	R/Hornsby (213839)	4wDM	1942
Clinton	4	H/Hunslet (2290)	0-4-0	1941
Sir Walter Raleigh	—	Keef	4wDM	2000

Stock
5 closed bogie coaches

from Exeter, Exmouth, Sidmouth in season
By train: Nearest station is Exmouth
Access by road: Follow brown tourist signs from M5, Jct 30, or from A30 at Daisymount Jct
On site facilities: Indoor and outdoor play areas, Glass Houses, Palm House, Grade 1 gardens, museum and restaurant
Length of line: 1.5mile (2.4km), 18in gauge. 25min ride
Public opening: Open all year (except 25/26 December), winter 10.00-17.00, summer 10.00-18.00
Trains operate: Winter 12.15 and 14.30, summer 6-8 trains a day. 25min trips
Facilities for disabled: Toilets, wheelchairs available. Special carriage for wheelchairs

The Blackpool & Fleetwood Tramway is the sole surviving traditional street tramway system in the United Kingdom. During the autumn the streets are illuminated and tours are available by historic or illuminated tram

Operating organisation:
Blackpool Transport Services Ltd, Rigby Road, Blackpool, Lancashire FY1 5DD
Telephone: (01253) 473001
Managing Director:
Trevor Roberts
Engineering Director:
Dave Hislop
Customer Services Co-ordinator:
Bryan Lindop
Length of line: 11.5 miles, standard gauge
Period of public operation: Daily throughout the year, except Christmas Day, Boxing Day and New Year's Day

*BTS heritage fleet
§reserve fleet
†feature tram
±out of service
**on loan

Owners
5 the Stockport 5 Trust
40 the Tramway Museum Society
66 the Bolton 66 Group
304 the Lancastrian Transport Trust

Trams

No	Trucks	Builder	Date (Rebuilt)
Boat Cars			
*600	E/Electric	E/Electric	1934
*602	E/Electric	E/Electric	1934
§604	E/Electric	E/Electric	1934
Brush Cars			
§631	EMB	Brush	1937
Centenary Cars			
*648	Blackpool	East Lancs	1985
Towing Cars			
§675	E/Electric	E/Electric / Blackpool	1958
§676	E/Electric	E/Electric / Blackpool	1958
Trailer Cars			
§685	Maley & Taunton	MCW	1960
§686	Maley & Taunton	MCW	1960
Balloon Cars			
700	E/Electric	E/Electric	1934
§701	E/Electric	E/Electric	1934
*706	E/Electric	E/Electric (open top)	1934
707	E/Electric	E/Electric	1934 (1998)
709	E/Electric	E/Electric	1934 (2000)
711	E/Electric	E/Electric	1934
713	E/Electric	E/Electric	1934
*717	E/Electric	E/Electric	1934 (±)
718	E/Electric	E/Electric	1934
719	E/Electric	E/Electric	1934
720	E/Electric	E/Electric	1935 (±)
723	E/Electric	E/Electric	1935
724	E/Electric	E/Electric	1935 (2004)
Illuminated Trams			
†733/734	E/Electric	from Pantograph 174	1962 (±)
†736	E/Electric	from Pantograph 170	1965 (2004)
±†737	EMB	from Brush 633	2001
Engineering Vehicles			
260	EMB	Blackpool	1973
750	MRCW	Blackpool	1907 (2004)
754	E/Electric	Blackpool	1992
Preserved Trams			
5	?	D/Kerr	1901
**40	Preston McGuire	United Electric Co	1914
**66	Brill	Electric Railway & Carriage	1901
*147	Preston McGuire	Hurst Nelson	1924
**304	Maley & Taunton	Hurst Nelson	1952
*660	Maley & Taunton	Charles Roberts	1953

New Flexity 2 BombardierTrams

No	Trucks	Builder	Date
001	Bombardier	Bombardier	2011
002	Bombardier	Bombardier	2011
004	Bombardier	Bombardier	2011
005	Bombardier	Bombardier	2011

England

Member: HRA, TT

This famous steam railway was the first standard gauge passenger line to be taken over by enthusiasts. It derives its name from the bluebells which proliferate in the woodlands adjoining the line. A strong Victorian atmosphere pervades this branch line which has a large collection of Southern and pre-Grouping locomotives and coaches

Operations Manager: Mr Chris Knibbs

Headquarters: Bluebell Railway plc, Sheffield Park Station, A275, East Sussex TN22 3QL

Telephone:
For travel information (24hr talking timetable): Uckfield (01825) 720825.
General enquiries etc during office hours: (01825) 720800.
'Golden Arrow' Pullman, reservations and Catering Department: (01825) 720801.
Shop: (01825) 720803

Internet address: *Web site:* www.bluebell-railway.com

Locomotives and multiple-unit

Name	No	Origin	Class	Type	Built
Stepney	55	LBSCR	A1X	0-6-0T	1875
Fenchurch	72	LBSCR	A1X	0-6-0T	1872
Birch Grove	32473	LBSCR	E4	0-6-2T	1898
—	27	SECR	P	0-6-0T	1910
—	65	SECR	O1	0-6-0	1896
—	263	SECR	H	0-4-4T	1905
—	323	SECR	P	0-6-0T	1910
—	592	SECR	C	0-6-0	1902
—	1178	SECR	P	0-6-0T	1910
—	96	LSWR	B4	0-4-0T	1893
—	488	LSWR	0415	4-4-2T	1885
—	27505	NLR	2F	0-6-0T	1880
Earl of Berkeley	9017	GWR	90	4-4-0	1938
—	541	SR	Q	0-6-0	1939
—	847	SR	S15	4-6-0	1937
Stowe	928	SR	V	4-4-0	1934
—	1618	SR	U	2-6-0	1928
—	1638	SR	U	2-6-0	1931
—	30064	SR	USA	0-6-0T	1943
Blackmoor Vale	21C123	SR	WC	4-6-2	1946
Sir Archibald Sinclair	34059	SR	BB	4-6-2	1947
Camelot	73082	BR	5MT	4-6-0	1955
—	75027	BR	4MT	4-6-0	1954
—	78059†	BR	2MT	2-6-0	1956
—	80064	BR	4MT	2-6-4T	1953

Main station: Sheffield Park
Other public stations: Horsted Keynes and Kingscote
Car parks: Sheffield Park, Horsted Keynes
OS references:
Sheffield Park TQ 403238,
Horsted Keynes TQ 372293
Access by public transport: Bus service 473 between main line East Grinstead and Kingscote (2 miles). See timetable brochure for details of operation
Refreshment facilities: Sheffield Park restaurant/bar/self-service; Horsted Keynes – 1930s bar/ buffet. The line's 'Golden Arrow' Pullman operates a dinner service most Saturday evenings and luncheon service most Sundays.
Telephone (01825) 720800 during normal office hours for details
Souvenir shops: Sheffield Park, Horsted Keynes
Museum: Sheffield Park (currently closed for major rebuilding works). Small display of memorabilia at Horsted Keynes station
Depots: Sheffield Park (locomotives), Horsted Keynes (stock)
Length of line: 9 miles
Passenger trains: Sheffield Park-Horsted Keynes-Kingscote
Period of public operation:
Weekends all year round;
daily 11-19 February (half term), daily 31 March to 4 November. Santa Specials weekends in December, daily 27-31 December. Closed 25 December.
Museum. Locomotive sheds, buffet and shop at Sheffield Park open daily except Christmas Day
Special events: Spring Specials — 16-20, 23-27 April; Toy and Rail Collectors' Fair — 28 April; Bluebell Specials — 30 April, 1-4, 8-11 May; Southern at War — 12/13 May; Sussex Food Fair (at Horsted Keynes station) — 23/24

June; Victorian Picnics (evening event) — 30 June/1 July; Songs of Praise Evening — 15 July; Toy and Rail Collectors' Fair — 21/22 July; Vintage Transport Weekend — 11/12 August; Autumn Tints Observation Car Specials— 1-5, 8-12, 15-19, 22-26 October; Sussex Branch Line Weekend — 20/21 October.Santa Specials — selected dates in December. Further details of events available on request
Special facilities: Private charters available. Horsted Keynes and

Sheffield Park stations are licensed for wedding ceremonies and civil partnerships
Facilities for disabled: All station facilities are on the level and ramps available for placing wheelchair visitors into trains. Special toilets in buffet at Sheffield Park and at Kingscote, 'multi-purpose vehicle' for use by groups, please telephone to confirm availability
Membership details: Membership Secretary, c/o above address
Membership journal: *Bluebell News* — quarterly

Name	No	Origin	Class	Type	Built
—	80100	BR	4MT	2-6-4T	1954
—	80151	BR	4MT	2-6-4T	1957
—	92240	BR	9F	2-10-0	1958
—	D3023	BR	08	0-6-0DE	1953
—	11201*	BR	4COR	DMBSO	1937

†purchased without tender, for conversion to tank engine, work in hand
*on static display at Horsted Keynes

Industrial locomotives

Name	No	Builder	Type	Built
Baxter	3	F/Jennings (158)	0-4-0T	1877
Stamford	24†	Avonside (1972)	0-6-0ST	1927
Sharpthorn	4*	M/Wardle (641)	0-6-0ST	1877
Britannia	—	Howard (957)	4wPM	1936

*On static display
†On long-term loan to Rocks by Rail (Rutland Railway Museum)

Stock
Substantial collection of pre-Nationalisation coaches including SECR, LSWR, Bulleid, Maunsell and Chesham vehicles. Also freight stock and engineers' vehicles plus 45-ton steam crane

Owners
592 the Wainwright C Class Preservation Society
541, 847, 928 and 1618 the Maunsell Locomotive Society Ltd
96 and 21C123 the Bulleid Society Ltd
263 the H Class Trust
73082 the Camelot Locomotive Society
80064 the 80064 Group
80151 the 80151 Group
D3023 on loan from the Heritage Shunters Trust
11201 the Southern Electric Group

Bodmin & Wenford Railway

Member: HRA

The Bodmin & Wenford Railway typifies the bygone branch railways of Cornwall. The terminus at Bodmin General, close to Bodmin town centre, has an interesting collection of standard gauge locomotives and rolling stock, and the operating line winds down to a junction with main line rail services at Bodmin Parkway, where cross-platform interchange is available. Passengers can alight at the intermediate Colesloggett Halt from where a footpath (not suitable for wheelchairs or the infirm) leads to Cardinham Woods (FC) with waymarked trails, picnic areas and a café. From the train there are scenic views across the beautiful valley of the River Fowey. The line, which is 6.5 miles in total, also runs from Bodmin General to Boscarne Junction where it meets the Camel Trail, a recreational path

Locomotives and multiple-units

Name	No	Origin	Class	Type	Built
—	30120	LSWR	T9	4-4-0	1898
—	30587	LSWR	0298	2-4-0WT	1874
—	4612	GWR	5700	0-6-PT	1942
—	4247	GWR	4200	2-8-0T	1916
—	5552	GWR	4575	2-6-2T	1928
—	6435	GWR	6400	0-6-0PT	1937
Triumph	50042	BR	50	Co-Co	1968
—	33110	BR	33	Bo-Bo	1960
—	37142	BR	37	Co-Co	1963
The Sapper	47306	BR	47	Co-Co	1964
—	D3452	BR	10	0-6-0DE	1957
—	08444	BR	08	0-6-0DE	1958
—	51947*	BR	108	DMBS	1960
—	52054	BR	108	DMCL	1960
—	50980	BR	108	DMBS	1960

*for spares

Industrial locomotives

Name	No	Builder	Type	Built
—	—	Bagnall (2766)	0-6-0ST	1944
—	19*	Bagnall (2962)	0-4-0ST	1950
Judy	—	Bagnall (2572)	0-4-0ST	1934

for cyclists and walkers. A visit can be made to the nearby Camel Valley Vineyard (July and August only). The majority of trains are steam-hauled

Location: Bodmin General station, on B3268
General Manager: Richard Jones
Operating society/organisation: Bodmin & Wenford Railway, Bodmin General Station, Bodmin, Cornwall PL31 1AQ
Telephone:
Enquiries (01208) 73555
Fax: 01208 77963
Internet addresses: *e-mail:* enquiries@bodminrailway.co.uk
Web site: www.bodminrailway.co.uk
SatNav postcode: Bodmin General Station — PL31 1AG
Car park: Bodmin General, free
Access by public transport:
By rail: Interchange at Bodmin Parkway arrivals by main line train; through tickets available from most stations. Tel: 08457 484950
By bus: Local services to Bodmin (Western Greyhound services 555, 529, 593). Tel: 01637 871871
Access by road: Half mile from Bodmin town centre, signposted from A30, A38, A389
Refreshment facilities: Buffet at Bodmin General (open every day when trains are running). Café in the old signalbox at Bodmin Parkway (open daily). Bar and buffet on most trains
On site facilities: Railway giftshop, small display of historic artefacts, toilets (including disabled), workshop viewing area. New Exhibition coach (opens late May)
Length of line: 6.5 miles
Passenger trains: 10/11, 14, 18, 21, 25, 28 March; 1-15, 18, 20-22, 24/25, 28/29 April; 1/2, 5-9, 13, 15/16, 20-31 May; daily — 1 June-30 September; 1-5, 7, 9/10, 12-14, 16/17, 21, 23/24, 28-31 October;

Name	No	Builder	Type	Built
Alfred	—	Bagnall (3058)	0-4-0ST	1953
—	—	Bagnall (3121)	0-4-0F	1957
Peter	—	Fowler (22928)	0-4-0DM	1940
Lec	—	R/Hornsby (443642)	4wDM	1960

*on hire to Pontypool & Blaenavon Railway during 2012

Stock
12 BR Mk 1 coaches; 1 Mk 3 Sleeper; 6-wheel 10-ton steam crane; 3 GWR coaches; 1 GWR Siphon G; various freight wagons

Owners
120 and 30587 on loan from the National Railway Museum
37142, 47306 and 50042 the B&W Main Line Diesel Group

2, 8/9, 15/16, 22-24, 26, 30/31 December; 1/2, 5/6 January 2013
Special events: Half-Price Weekend — 10/11 March; Easter Egg-travaganza — 6-9 April; Spring Steam Spectacular — 20-22 April; Spring Diesel Day — 28 April; Steaming Thru' the 40s — 5/7 May; Bodmin Branch 125th Anniversary Gala — 25-27 May; Peppa Pig — 3/4 June; Heritage Transport Festival — 16/17 June; China Clay Weekend — 14/15 July; Paddington Bear — 3-5 August; Fireman Sam — 26/27 August; Steam Gala and Real Ale Festival — 7-9 September; Autumn Diesel Day — 29 September; Railmotor Weekend — 12-14 October; Postman Pat — 28 October; Half-Price Weekend — 3/4 November; Santa by Steam — 2, 8/9, 15/16, 22-24 December; Winter Steam Up — 5/6 January 2013.
Murder Mystery Specials: 19, 26 June; 3, 10, 17, 24, 27, 31 July; 3, 7, 10, 14, 17, 21, 28 August; 4, 11, 18 September; 30 October, 7 December.
Steam Beer and Jazz: 21 April, 5 May, 16 June, 21 July, 8 September.
Disco Train: 29 June.
Fish & Chip Quiz Night: 8 June, 31 August

Luxury Dining Train: 18 March (Mothering Sunday), 15 April, 20 May, 10 June, 7, 28 July, 11, 25 August, 16 September, 21 October, 2, 9, 16, 23 December
Driving Experience Courses: Courses held in spring and autumn. Please apply for details
Facilities for disabled: Parking on station forecourt at Bodmin General. Level access to booking hall, platform, toilets, giftshop and buffet. Disabled toilet. Facilities for wheelchairs available on most trains, with purpose-built accommodation and a ramp to ease boarding from the platform. Registered disabled travel at child fare, carers (from a recognised organisation) carried free
Membership details: BRPS Membership, c/o above address
Special notes: Reduced fares for families. Bicycles and dogs conveyed *free*. Groups and parties welcome. Generous discounts available on many trains for pre-booked parties of 10+, with 25% discount for groups of 25 or more. Train/carriage available for private hire — please enquire for details
Membership journal: *Bodmin & Wenford News* — 3 issues/year

Bowes Railway

The railway includes the only preserved rope-hauled standard gauge inclines, whose operation requires considerable skill and dexterity. You should not miss the opportunity of inspecting the inclines and winding house and haulage engine when you can. The Engineering Workshop has just been restored.

The whole railway including the buildings, machinery and rolling stock is now a Scheduled Ancient Monument and is managed by the Bowes Railway Co ltd on behalf of the current owners, Sunderland City Council and Gateshead Council

Chairman: Phillip Dawe
Location: Bowes Railway, Springwell Village, near Gateshead (on B1288)
OS reference: NZ 285589
Operating society/organisation: Bowes Railway Co Ltd
Telephone: (0191) 416 1847
Internet address: *Web site:* www.bowesrailway.co.uk
Car park: Springwell
Access by public transport: Northern Buses services Nos 184 Washington/Birtley, 187/188 Gateshead Metro/Sunderland, 189 Washington (Brady Sq)-Gateshead 638 Ryton/Sunderland
On site facilities: Exhibition of the railway's history, wagon exhibition, workshop displays. On operating days — shop, refreshments and guided tours. One of the last operational Strowger mechanical telephone exchanges still in daily use. Steam-hauled brake van rides. Rope haulage demonstration trains. Tarmac car park available for helicopter visitors (prior permission required, phone site)
Public opening: Site open Mondays to Saturdays for static viewing. Trains operate selected Sundays and special days. Santa Specials week prior to Christmas. Guided tours Saturdays, out of season can be accommodated with prior notice (not trains)
Length of line: 1.25 miles of rope haulage incline railway.

Industrial locomotives

Name	No	Builder	Type	Built
WST	—	Barclay (2361)	0-4-0ST	1954
—	22	Barclay (2274)	0-4-0ST	1949
—	20/110/709	Barclay (613)	0-6-0DH	1977
—	—	Hunslet (6263)	0-4-0DH	1964
—	503	Hunslet (6614)	0-6-0DH	1965
—	101	Planet (3922)	4wDM	1959
—	2207/456†	E/Electric (2476)	4wBE	1958
Victoria	2216/286†	H/Clarke (DM842)	0-6-0DMF	1954
BO3	20/122/514*	Hunslet (8515)	Bo-BoDMF	1981
—	—*	EIMCO (LD2163)	Rockershovel	1959
—	—§	Clayton (5921)	4wBE	1971
—	—§	Clayton (B3060)	4wBE	1983

†2ft gauge
*2ft 6in gauge
§3ft gauge

Owners
WST on loan from British Gypsum Ltd and loaned to National Railway Museum
Barclay 0-6-0DH on loan from Mr P. Dawe

Stock
20 ordinary 10-ton wooden hopper wagons (Springwell built); 16 other wooden hopper wagons (of various pedigrees); 3 steel 14-ton hopper, 2 steel 16-ton hopper wagons; 7 wagons; 7 steel 21-ton hopper wagons; 1 reel bogie (for rope replacement); 1 drift bogie (for shunting by rope); 1 loco coal wagon; 7 material wagons; 2 tool vans; 3 brake vans; 4 flat wagons; 1 18-ton wooden hopper (ex-Ashington); 1 21-ton wooden hopper (ex-Seaham); 2 steel ballast hopper wagons; 1 tank wagon; 1 wooden side door coal wagon; 3 Londonderry Chaldron wagons, 2ft gauge 4-wheel manrider, 2ft 6in gauge R. B. Bolton-type bogie manrider, Easington Colliery weights wagon, 1 Pontop & Jarrow Railway flat bogie, 1 Dandy cart

Stationary haulage
Met-Vick/Wild, 300bhp electric (Blackham's Hill) 1950
BTH/Robey, 500bhp electric (Black Fell) 1950
Clarke Chapman, 22hp electric (Springwell Yard)
14ft diam, Gravity Dilly Wheel (Springwell)

1.5 mile line used for passenger trains as the Wreckenton extension is now open
Special notes: Preserved section of the Pontop & Jarrow Railway; designed G. Stephenson; opened 1826; largest collection of colliery wagons in country, the only preserved standard gauge rope-hauled incline railway in the world; railway's own historic workshops preserved, with examples of all of the railway's wagon types

Facilities for disabled: Toilet and refreshment room
Membership details: John Young, Railway Secretary, c/o above address
Disclaimer: The Bowes Railway Co Ltd wish to point out that all advertised facilities are subject to alteration without prior notice. The company can therefore not be held responsible for any loss or expense incurred

England

Brading Station Visitor Centre and Railway Heritage Centre

Heritage Centre

Isle of Wight

The station and signalbox was the 2010 winner of the national Railway Heritage Conservation Award
Location/headquarters: Brading station
Postal address: Brading Station, Station Road, Brading Isle of Wight PO36 0DY
SatNav postcode: PO36 0DY

Tel/Fax: 01903 401770 (or during opening hours 01983 401222)
Contact: Cathy Mills
Internet addresses:
E-mail: townclerk@brading.gov.uk
Web site:
www.bradingtowncouncil.org.uk
Access by public transport:
By rail: 'Island Line' from Ryde/Shanklin to Brading

By bus: Stagecoach
On site facilities: Visitor centre shop open for refreshments, gifts and local tourist information. Guided tour around the recently restored signalbox on certain days
Period of public opening: Daily April to September 10.00-16.00

Bredgar & Wormshill Light Railway

Steam Centre

Kent

Member: HRA
A short, 2ft gauge, private railway constructed and operated to a very high standard
Location/headquarters: The Bredgar & Wormshill Light Railway, The Warren, Bredgar, Nr Sittingbourne, Kent ME9 8AT
Contact: Bill Best, David Best
Telephone: (01622) 884254
Internet addresses: *E-mail:* williambest@btinternet.com
Web site: www.bwlr.co.uk
Access by public transport: Main line trains to Sittingbourne (5 miles) and Hollingbourne (3.5 miles). No taxis from Hollingbourne
OS reference: TQ 868579
Car park: On site (300 places)
On site facilities: Souvenir shop, museum, light refreshments, toilets, picnic sites, traction engines, 7.25in and 15in gauge model locomotives, working beam engine, model railway. Steam-hauled train rides from Warren Wood to Stony Shaw (2km).
Public opening: First Sunday in each month May to October

Industrial locomotives — 2ft gauge

Name	No	Builder	Type	Built
Bronhilde	1	Schwartzkopf (9124)	0-4-0WT	1927
Katie	2	Arn Jung (3872)	0-6-0WT	1931
Armistice	4	Bagnall (2088)	0-4-0ST	1919
Bredgar	5	B/Drewry (3775)	0-4-0DH	1983
Eigiau	6	O&K (5668)	0-4-0WT	1912
Victory	7	Decauville (246)	0-4-2ST	1897
Helga	8	O&K (12722)	0-4-0WT	1936
Limpopo	9	Fowler (18800)	0-6-0T	1930
Zambezi	10	Fowler (13573)	0-4-2T	1912
Bicknor	12	Simplex (DM9869)	4wDM	1953
Wormshill	11	Huwood/Hudswell (DM1366)	0-6-0DM	1965
Lady Joan No 1 (2ft 6in gauge)	—	Hunslet (1429)	0-4-0ST	1922
Siam	105	Henschel (29582)	0-6-0WT	1956

Stock
4 bogie coaches, 1 four-wheel coach, 6 four-wheel wagons, 1 four-wheel tank wagon, 4 four-wheel works trucks, 1 4-wheel guards van, 4 tipping skips

(11.00-17.00). Also Easter Sunday. Enthusiasts' Day 28 October
Admission: Adults £10, children £4, family £25 (2 adults + 3 children
Special events: Steam locomotive driving courses. Private hire

available
Facilities for disabled: Generally good, including toilets
Note: A private site with no 'out of hours' access, but groups by arrangement

Member: TT

Five miles of various gauges of railway running through extensive gardens, and a collection of well-maintained and impressive main line locomotives. All the fun of the fair, with something for everyone, a great day out for all the family

Location: Two miles west of Diss, and 14 miles east of Thetford on the A1066

OS reference: TM 080806

General Manager: Alastair Baker

Operating society/organisation: Bressingham Steam Preservation Co Ltd, Thetford Road, Diss, Norfolk IP22 2AA

Charity number: 266374

Telephone:
General enquiries and bookings (01379) 686900.

Fax: (01379) 686907

Internet addresses: *E-mail:* info@bressingham.co.uk

Web site: www.bressingham.co.uk (includes online bookings)

Car park: Plant Centre (free).

Access by public transport: Diss main line station (3 miles)

On site facilities: 10.25/15/24in and standard gauge lines, totalling nearly 5 miles. Museum, steam roundabout, souvenir shop and restaurant, extensive gardens and plant centre. 'Dad's Army' permanent exhibition

Public opening: Open every day between Easter and end of October, 10.30-17.30. Steam every day with narrow gauge rides and the Gallopers. Education services for schools are available with pre-booking in March-October period

Special events: Please telephone (01379) 686900 for details

Special facilities: The corporate hospitality venue is available for events, from parties to conferences. Please telephone (01379) 686900 for details

Facilities for disabled: Wheelchair access to majority of site including toilets. Able to take wheelchairs on Nursery Line Railway and Waveney Line

Special notes: Reduced rates for coach parties. Prices on application

Locomotives and multiple-unit

Name	No	Origin	Class	Type	Built
Martello	662†	LBSCR	A1X	0-6-0T	1875
—	87	GER	J69	0-6-0T	1904
Thundersley	80	LTSR	3P	4-4-2T	1909
Granville	102	LSWR	B4	0-4-0T	1893
—	490	GER	E4	2-4-0	1894
Henry Oakley	990	GNR	C2	4-4-2	1898
—	54347	Met/Cam	101	DTC	1958
Peer Gynt	5865	RB	52	2-10-0	1944
King Haakon VII	377†	NSB	21c	2-6-0	1919

†may be out on hire during 2012

Industrial locomotives

Name	No	Builder	Type	Built
Beckton	25	Neilson (5087)	0-4-0ST	1896
William Francis	6841	B/Peacock (6841)	0-4-0+0-4-0T	1937
Millfield	—	RSH (7070)	0-4-0CT	1942
Bluebottle	—	Barclay (1472)	0-4-0F	1916
County School	GET 1	R/Hornsby (497753)	0-4-0DE	1963

2ft gauge locomotives

Name	No	Builder	Type	Built
Gwynedd	—	Hunslet (316)	0-4-0ST	1883
George Sholto	—	Hunslet (994)	0-4-0ST	1909
Bevan	—	BSM	0-4-0PTT	2010
Toby	—	M/Rail (22120)	4wDM	1964
—	—	BEV	0-4-0BE	

15in gauge locomotives

Name	No	Builder	Type	Built
Rosenkavalier*	—	Krupp (1662)	4-6-2	1937
Mannertreu*	—	Krupp (1663)	4-6-2	1937
Works Loco	—	Diss	0-4-0DM	1992
Replica	6353	—	Bo-Bo	—
St Christopher	—	Exmoor (311)	2-6-2T	2001

*dismantled for overhaul

10.25in gauge locomotive

Name	No	Builder	Type	Built
Alan Bloom	1	BSM	0-4-0ST	1995

Owners
80, 87, 490 and 990 on loan from the National Railway Museum
GET 1 the Great Eastern Traction Group

Steam Centre — Bristol Harbour Railway — Bristol

Member: HRA

Note: The new 'M' Shed museum opened in 2011. The railway operates from Princes Wharf to the SS *Great Britain* and Create Centre on advertised weekends — see Bristol City Council's Museums web site

Location: Princes Wharf, Bristol

OS reference: ST 585722

Operating society/organisation: Bristol Museum Galleries & Archives, Princes Wharf, Bristol BS1 4RN

Telephone: (0117) 903 1570

Fax: (0117) 929 7318

Internet addresses: *E-mail*:

Industrial locomotives

Name	No	Builder	Type	Built
Portbury	34	Avonside (1764)	0-6-0ST	1917
Henbury	—	Peckett (1940)	0-6-0ST	1937
—	3*	F/Walker (242)	0-6-0ST	1874
—	—	R/Hornsby (418792)	0-4-0DM	1958

*not on public display

general.museum@bristol.gov.uk

Web site: www.bristol.gov.uk/museums

Car parks: Available nearby

Access by public transport: Buses to centre of city, 1km from Temple Meads station

Length of line: One mile

Facilities for disabled: Reasonable access

Special notes: Operation of railway on advertised weekends only, 11.30-17.00

Membership details: Officer in charge — D. Martin, Bristol Harbour Railway c/o above address

---

Miniature Railway — Brookside Miniature Railway — Cheshire

Member: Britain's Great Little Railways

A large extension opened in 2007

Location: Brookside Garden Centre

Headquarters: Brookside Garden Centre Ltd, London Road North, Poynton, Cheshire SK12 1BY

Contact: Chief Executive Mr C. Halsall

Telephone: (01625) 872919

Fax: (01625) 859119

Internet address: *Web site:* www.brooksideminiaturerailway. webs.com

Car parking: On site

SatNav postcode: SK12 1BY

Access by public transport: Main line stations: Hazel Grove (2.5 miles), Poynton (2 miles). Bus No 191 stops outside the Centre

On site facilities: Full restaurant/café facilities. Extensive museum of railwayana, large display of totems (c200) and advertising enamels

Locomotives – 7.25in gauge

Name	No	Builder	Type	Built
Jean	—	Exmoor	0-4-2T	2000
Jane	—	Exmoor	0-4-2T	2002
Amy Louise	—	Exmoor	0-4-2T	2004
Billy May	—	Exmoor	2-4-2	1999
Mighty Max	—	Greatex	Bo-Bo	2000
Annie	—	D McFarlane	Co-Co	1997
Sir Richard	—	Greatex	Bo-Bo	2009
Miss Katie	—	Greatex	Bo-Bo	2010

Rolling stock

10 Cromar White sit-astride coaches, 8 assorted covered coaches, 2 Pullman coaches, 'Toad' guard's van, 3 ICI hoppers, 'Saxa Salt' covered van, 2 open coal wagons, 'Palethorpes' sausage van, well wagon, oil tank wagon.

Depots: On site and visits may be made by prior arrangement

Length of line: 7.25in gauge, half mile

Period of public operation: Weekends throughout the year, plus Wednesdays April to September; every day mid-July and August. All school holidays. Summer — 11.00-16.30 (Sundays 11.00-16.00); winter — 11.00-16.00

Special events: Santa Specials — weekends in December

Facilities for disabled: Disabled toilet facilities and access to all parts

Fare: Adult/child: £1.40; under 2s free; 10-ride ticket £10

Buckinghamshire Railway Centre

Member: HRA

The Buckinghamshire Railway Centre is situated at Quainton Road on the freight-only Aylesbury-Calvert line, once part of the Metropolitan and Great Central line from London to Verney Junction. Quainton Road station is also the old junction for the Brill Tramway closed in 1935. The Centre is now home to the former LNWR Rewley Road station moved brick-by-brick from the centre of Oxford. Opened in 1851, this Grade 2* listed building is built in the same manner as the Crystal Palace Great Exhibition building of 1881 destroyed by fire in the 1930s. It is unique in its construction and provides a superb setting in which the pick of the Centre's locomotives and carriages are now displayed

Location: Adjacent to goods-only line to Aylesbury. Turn off A41 at Waddesdon 6 miles NW of Aylesbury, Bucks

OS reference: SP 738190

Operating society/organisation: Quainton Railway Society Ltd, The Railway Station, Quainton, Nr Aylesbury, Bucks HP22 4BY

Telephone: Quainton (01296) 655450

Internet address:

Web site: www.bucksrailcentre.org

Car park: Quainton Road — Free parking

Access by public transport: Main line Aylesbury station. Local bus Monday-Saturday only

On site facilities: Souvenir bookshop, light refreshments, toilets, steam-hauled train rides. Museum of small relics, secondhand bookshop, miniature railway

Catering facilities: Hot snacks and light refreshments available

Length of line: Two half-mile demonstration lines

Public opening: Open Wednesday to Sunday inclusive from April to October. Steaming days each Sunday and Wednesdays during school holidays, plus Bank Holidays.

Locomotives and multiple-units

Name	No	Origin	Class	Type	Built
—	1	Met Rly	E	0-4-4T	1898
—	0314	LSWR	0298	2-4-0WT	1874
Defiant	5080	GWR	'Castle'	4-6-0	1939
Wightwick Hall	6989	GWR	'Hall'	4-6-0	1948
—	7200	GWR	7200	2-8-2T	1934
—	7715	GWR	5700	0-6-0PT	1930
—	9466	GWR	9400	0-6-0PT	1952
—	D2298	BR	04	0-6-0DM	1960
—	3405*	SAR	25NC	4-8-4	1958
—	51886	BR	115	DMBS	1960
—	51899	BR	115	DMBS	1960
—	59761	BR	115	TCL	1960

*3ft 6in gauge

Industrial locomotives

Name	No	Builder	Type	Built
Scott	—	Bagnall (2469)	0-4-0ST	1932
—	—	Baguley (2161)	0-4-0DM	1941
Swanscombe	—	Barclay (699)	0-4-0ST	1891
—	GF3	Barclay (1477)	0-4-0F	1916
—	—	Barclay (2243)	0-4-0F	1948
Osram	—	Fowler (20067)	0-4-0DM	1933
—	3	H/Leslie (3717)	0-4-0ST	1928
Sir Thomas	—	H/Clarke (1334)	0-6-0T	1918
—	—	H/Clarke (1742)	0-4-0ST	1946
—	—	Hunslet (2067)	0-4-0DM	1940
Arthur	—	Hunslet (3782)	0-6-0ST	1953
—	65	Hunslet (3889)	0-6-0ST	1964
—	66	Hunslet (3890)	0-6-0ST	1964
—	26	Hunslet (7016)	0-6-0DH	1971
Redland	—	K/Stuart (K4428)	0-4-0DM	1929
Coventry No 1	—	NBL (24564)	0-6-0ST	1939
—	—	Peckett (1900)	0-4-0T	1936
Gibraltar	—	Peckett (2087)	0-4-0ST	1948
—	—	Peckett (2104)	0-4-0ST	1948
—	—	Peckett (2105)	0-4-0ST	1948
—	T1	Hibberd (2102)	4wD	1937
Tarmac	—	Hibberd (3765)	0-4-0DM	1955
—	11	Sentinel (9366)	4wVBTG	1945
—	7	Sentinel (9376)	4wVBTG	1947
—	—	Sentinel (9537)	4wVBTG	1947
Chislet	9	Yorkshire (2498)	0-6-0ST	1951

Stock: *Coaches* —
1 LCDR 1st Class 4-wheeler; 1 MSLR 3rd Class 6-wheeler; 4 LNWR coach bodies; 2 GNR 6-wheelers; 3 LNWR; 3 LMSR; 1 BR(W) Hawksworth brake 3rd; 2 BR Mk 1; 1 BR Mk 2; 1 BR Suburban brake; 3 LNER; 1 LNWR full brake 6-wheeler; 1 LMSR passenger brake van; 1 GWR passenger brake van; 1 GCR Robinson brake 3rd

Wagons —
A large and varied collection including 1 LNWR combination truck; 1 LSWR ventilated fruit van; 1 SR PMV; 1 BR(W) Siphon G; 1 BR horse box; 1 BR CCT

3 ex-London Underground coaches

34

England

Opening times: 10.30-16.30
Special events: Steam Enthusiast's Day — 6 May; Miniatures Day — 7 May; 1940s Weekend — 19/20 May; Bus Rally — 4 June; Historic Commercial Vehicle Rally — 17 June; Bucks Herald Steam Train — 8 July; Rover Veteran Vintage Car Rally — 26 August; Traction Engine Rally — 22/23 September; Spooky Halloween — 28 October; Santa's Magical Adventures — 1/2, 8/9, 15/16, 22, 24 December; Mince Pie Specials — 27/28 December
Facilities for disabled: Access to

1 2ft gauge post office mailbag car 803
Sentinel/Cammell 3-car steam railcar unit 5208 (ex-Egyptian National)
Numerous goods vehicles/wagons/vans

Owners
9466 the 9466 Group
Defiant on loan from Tyseley Locomotive Works

most of site including special toilets
Special notes: One of the largest collection of standard gauge locomotives, together with a most interesting collection of vintage coaching stock, much of which was built in the 19th century

General: The public area of the centre covers some 25 acres of land with views across the Buckinghamshire countryside. A picnic area is available at the miniature railway

---

Timetable Service	**Bure Valley Railway**	Norfolk

Member: HRA, TT
Opened in 1990, the BVR runs over the old Great Eastern Wroxham-Aylsham line. It is paralleled throughout the entire 9 miles by the Bure Valley Walk and cycle path which offers excellent photographic opportunities
Headquarters: Bure Valley Railway (1991) Ltd, Aylsham Station, Norwich Road, Aylsham, Norfolk NR11 6BW
Chairman: Giles Margarson
General Manager: Andrew Tunwell
Marketing: Susan Munday
Bookings contact: Judith Harvey
Telephone: (01263) 733858
Fax: (01263) 733814
Internet addresses: *E-mail:* info@bvrw.co.uk
Web site: www.bvrw.co.uk
Main public station: Aylsham (Norwich Road, NR11 6BW); Wroxham (Coltishall Road, NR12 8UU)
Other public stations: Coltishall, Brampton and Buxton
Car and coach parks: Aylsham and Wroxham
OS reference:
Aylsham — TG 195264
Wroxham — TG 303186
GPS co-ordinates:
Aylsham — 52°47.29 (52.7913) North, 1°15.17 (1.2547) East
X(619500) Y 326500)
Wroxham — 52°42.994 (52.7168) North, 1°24.624 (1.4076) East

Locomotives — 1ft 3in gauge

Name	No	Builder	Type	Built (rebuilt)
Wroxham Broad	1	G&S/Winson	2-6-4T	1992
2nd Air Division USAAF	3	BVR	4w-4wDH	1989
—	4	H/Hunslet	0-4-0DH	1996
—	5	Lister	4wDM	
Blickling Hall	6	Winson*	2-6-2	1994 (2004)
Spitfire	7	Winson*	2-6-2	1994 (2006)
John of Gaunt	8	BVR/Winson†	2-6-2T	1997 (2008)
Mark Timothy	9	Winson/Keef§	2-6-4T	2003

*based on Indian Railways 2ft 6in gauge 'ZB' class
†based on Vale of Rheidol Railway design
§based on Leek & Manifold Railway design

Stock
19 fully enclosed saloons, 2 fully enclosed compartment coaches, 6 enclosed saloons designed to carry wheelchairs, 1 fully enclosed brake saloon, 2 guard's vans, generator car. Former Green-Bat vehicle, re-gauged to 15in, currently being converted into a p-way flat bed vehicle with cab for guard's brake area. Miscellaneous wagons including a rail-mounted flail and weedkilling unit and purpose-built p-way tool vehicle arrangement

Owners
1 the Wroxham Broad Preservation Group
3, 5, 6, 7 and 8 the Bure Valley Railway
4 the Friends of the Bure Valley Railway
9 is privately owned

X(630200) Y(318700)
Access by public transport:
By rail: Wroxham station is adjacent to main line Hoveton & Wroxham station (Norwich-Cromer/Sheringham line).
By bus: First and Sanders buses run between Norwich and Aylsham or Norwich and Wroxham
Refreshment facilities:

Whistlestop Café at Aylsham with picnic area, light refreshments at Wroxham.
   Aylsham's Whistlestop Café is open every day even when the railway does not operate trains
Souvenir shops:
Aylsham and Wroxham
   Aylsham shop is open every day even when the railway does not

operate trains

Model shop: Aylsham station is home to 'Bure Valley Models' and stocks a wide selection of model railway items, many of which can be purchased by mail order. Please see the web site

Journey time: Approximately 45min each way plus turnround time

Length of line: 9 miles; 15in gauge

Passenger trains: Frequency depends on time of year, maximum frequency one per hour

Period of public operation: Daily 11-19 February, then weekends in February and March. Daily 31 March to 4 November. Daily 10-18 and weekends in November

Exhibit availability: The workshops at Aylsham are open to the public at most times of year for viewing

Facilities for disabled: Toilets at Aylsham and Wroxham. Main stations are all on one level, special rolling stock to carry wheelchairs; advance notice would be appreciated

Special events: Please contact for full details.
Teddy Bear Express — 11-19 February; Volunteers' Open Day — 4 March; Mothers' VIP Day — 18 March; Easter Eggspress — 6-9 April; Macmillan Charity Walk — 21/22 April; Calling Junior Trainspotters — 5-7 May; Everything Goes — 2-5 June; Fathers' VIP Day — 17 June; Strawberries and Steam — weekends in July; History Down The Line — (40th anniversary of closure of the standard gauge line) — 29/30 September; Model Railway Express — 6 October; Spooky Express — 27 October-4 November; Santa Specials 24/25 November, 1/2, 7-9, 14-16, 21-24 December (advance booking essential); Mince Pie Specials 27 December 2012 to 6 January 2013

Special notes: Steam locomotive driving courses. Group discounts available. Frequent Travellers' Railcards. Children's Birthday Parties. Private charters by arrangement. Special combined train and Broads boat excursions run most operating days

Membership details: Friends of the Bure Valley Railway, Membership Secretary, c/o above address

---

The passenger-carrying line which opened at Bursledon Brickworks Industrial Museum in April 2010 has been extended to 450yd and will be operated by *Wendy* on a regular basis. The railway is operated by the Hampshire Narrow Gauge Railway Trust (please see HNGRT web site)

Location/headquarters: Bursledon Brickworks Industrial Museum, Coal Park Lane, Swanwick, Southampton, Hants SO31 7GW

SatNav postcode: SO31 7GW

Tel/Fax: 01489 576248 (not manned regularly)

Contact: Mrs Margaret Fairhead (HNGRT)

Internet addresses:
E-mail: Via web site or admin@bursledonbrickworks.org.uk
Web site: www.bursledonbrickworks.co.uk or www.hngrt.org.uk

Access by public transport:
By rail: Bursledon main line station, short walk
By bus: First Group

Locomotives — 2ft gauge

Name	No	Builder	Type	Built
Wendy	—*	Bagnall (2091)	0-4-0ST	1919
Agwi Pet	—*	M/Rail (4724)	4wPM	1939
Bambridge Hall	—*	M/Rail (5226)	4wPM	1931
Beccy	—	M/Rail (8694)	4wDM	1943

*property of the Hampshire Narrow Gauge Railway Trust

Rolling stock
Ramsgate Tunnel Railway coach, brake van

Access by car: Junction 8 of M27, then A3024 to A27 (Bridge Road) turn left to Swanwick Road

On site facilities: Café and gift shop. 7.25in gauge railway. Traction engine rides available for public in a 4-wheeled wagon

Souvenir shop: On site

Length of line: Passenger-carrying 450yd, 2ft gauge

Period of public operation: Open Thursdays (January-November) 10.00-16.00) plus special events

Facilities for disabled: Yes

Special events: Spring Steam Up & Country Fair — 15 April; Vintage Car Event — 13 May; Beer & Jazz — 10 June; Victorian Day — 15 July; Railway Event — 19 August; Heritage Open Day (free admission)— 6 September; Big American Wing Ding — 23 September; Traction Engine Event — 21 October; Winter Festival — 25 November

Membership details: Friends of Bursledon Brickworks, c/o above address

Museum membership journal: *Brickbats* — 3 issues/year

Cambrian Heritage Railways

Member: HRA

The Cambrian Railways Trust currently operates about two-thirds of a mile of the former Cambrian Railways main line from Llynclys South to Penygarreg Lane, Pant. A platform has been completed at Penygarreg Halt to enable passengers to alight and explore the adjacent Montgomery Canal and the surrounding countryside.

At long last Network Rail has sold the mothballed Gobowen–Oswestry–Llynclys Junction–Blodwell line to Shropshire County Council, leases have been agreed with the Trust and the Cambrian Railway Society, and the two bodies have combined as Cambrian Heritage Railways Ltd.

Part of the platform at Oswestry is also in the process of being rebuilt, and a brake van shuttle service will be operating from Easter — the first to carry passengers since 1966

Location: Llynclys is situated on the B4396 about 5 miles south of Oswestry, just off the A483 Welshpool-Oswestry road

Telephone: 01691 679007

Internet addresses: *E-mail:* admin@cambrianrailwaystrust.com

Web site: www.cambrianrailwaystrust.com

OS reference: SJ 284239

Operating society: Cambrian

Locomotives and multiple-units

Name	No	Origin	Class	Type	Built
—	D3019	BR	08	0-6-0DE	1953
—	51187	Met-Cam	101	DMBS	1958
—	51205	Met-Cam	101	DMBS	1958
—	51512	Met-Cam	101	DMC	1959
—	54055	Met-Cam	101	DTSL	1957

Industrial locomotives

Name	No	Builder	Type	Built
Cyril	322	Planet (3541)	4wDM	1952
Kimberley	—	E/Electric (D1230)	0-6-0DH	1969
—	11517	R/Hornsby (458641)	0-4-0DE	

Rolling stock

8 ex-BR Mk 1 coaches plus RMB buffet car (static), 4 ex-GWR coaches/bogie vans, 20 goods wagons

Railways Trust, Llynclys South Station, Llynclys, Oswestry, Shropshire SY10 8BX

Access by public transport: Bus approx hourly from Oswestry to White Lion Inn, Llynclys crossroads (200yd from site), with connecting buses from Gobowen station and Shrewsbury. Also buses from Welshpool and Llanfyllin (Arriva Midlands / Tanat Valley Coaches)

On site facilities: Buffet, shop, station facilities including disabled

Period of public opening: Trains running Sundays from 6 April to 28 October, Saturdays from 7 April to 22 September, and all Bank Holidays between March and November.

Visitors welcome at other times

Special events: Santa Specials — 9, 16 December

Disabled facilities: Level access to platforms, ramps onto trains

Membership details: c/o above address

Membership journal: Quarterly newsletter

Special note: Special trains can be arranged for parties at any time. Footplate experience days available, see web site or phone 01691 679007

Chasewater Railway

Member: HRA, TT

Founded in 1959 as the Railway Preservation Society (West Midlands District), the Chasewater Railway was re-formed in 1985 as a Registered Charity. The railway operates as 'The Colliery Line' to reflect its origins and location in the heart of the Cannock Chase coalfield. A regular timetabled service operates between Brownhills West station and Chasetown (Church Street), with

intermediate stations at Norton Lakeside (which adjoins Chasewater's Wildfowl Reserve) and Chasewater Heaths

Location: Chasewater Park, Brownhills (off A5 southbound, nr jct A452 Chester Road). Brown tourism signs are provided on A5

OS Reference: SK 034070

SatNav postcodes:
Brownhills West WS8 7NL
Chasewater Heaths WS7 3PG

Operating society/organisation:

Chasewater Light Railway & Museum Co

Telephone: 01543 452623

Internet addresses: *E-mail:* info@chasewaterrailway.org

Web site: www.chasewaterrailway.com

Car park: Ample free parking, coaches welcome by appointment

Access by public transport: *Nearest railway stations —* Walsall and Birmingham New Street. *Bus services from Walsall Bus*

Station (St Paul's Street) —
Mondays to Saturdays: 33, alight at Poole Crescent; National Express West Midlands 10A to Rising Sun Inn.
Sundays: Arriva 63A to Brownhills West (Rising Sun Inn).
Bus services from Birmingham (Carrs Lane)
Diamond: 56 and 56A to Brownhills West (Rising Sun Inn).

Visitors travelling by bus are advised to contact the operators to confirm service times.

Brownhills West station is approx 15min walk from the Rising Sun Inn, 10min walk from Poole Crescent.
For timetable information and details of services, contact Traveline 0870 608 2608
On site facilities: Accredited museum, heritage centre, standard and narrow gauge lines, model railway, gift shops and tea rooms. Guided tours by request
Catering facilities: Hot and cold buffets at Brownhills West and Chasewater Heaths stations
Length of line: Approx 2 miles
Public opening: Sundays 5 February to 18 November; Saturdays Easter-end of October; Bank Holidays and Tuesdays and Thursdays during most local school holidays.
Tea rooms at Bank Holiday weekend open Tuesday-Sunday. Chasewater Heaths station is open most mid-week days except Wednesday, for booking and information: 01543 452623.

Check web site for fares, running days and timetable
Special events: Spring Gala — 17/18 March; Easter week running — 6-9, 12 April; Road and Rail Steam Traction — 2-4 June; Summer evening special (includes

Locomotives and multiple-units

Name	No	Builder	Class	Type	Built
—	D3429	BR	08	0-6-0DE	1958
—	W59444	BR Derby	116	TS	1958
—	W59522	Pressed Steel	117	TCL	1960
—	W59603	Pressed Steel	127	TSL	1959

Industrial locomotives

Name	No	Builder	Type	Built
Colin McAndrew	3	Barclay (1223)	0-4-0ST	1911
British Gypsum No 4	—	Barclay (2343)	0-4-0ST	1953
Linda	—	Bagnall (2648)	0-4-0ST	1940
Sheepbridge No 15	—	H/Clarke (431)	0-6-0ST	1895
Whit No 4	—	H/Clarke (1822)	0-6-0T	1949
Asbestos	4	H/Leslie (2780)	0-4-0ST	1909
Darfield No 1	—	Hunslet (3783)	0-6-0ST	1953
Alfred Paget	11	Neilson (2937)	0-4-0ST	1882
—	6	Peckett (917)	0-4-0ST	1902
Nechells No 4	—	RSH (7684)	0-6-0T	1951
Sentinel	5	Sentinel (9632)	4wVBT	1957
Bass No 5	—	Baguley (3027)	0-4-0DM	1939
Hem Heath	—	Bagnall (3119)	0-6-0DM	1956
Dealer	—	Brush (3097)	0-4-0DE	1956
—	—	Fowler (4100013)	0-4-0DM	1948
Toad	37	Fowler (4220015)	0-4-0DH	1962
—	462	Hibberd (1891)	4wDM	1934
—	6678	Hunslet (6678)	0-4-0DH	1968
—	21	Kent Constr (1612)	4wDM	1929
—	D2911	NBL (27876)	0-4-0DH	1958
Ryan	—	R/Hornsby (305306)	0-4-0DM	1952
—	—	R/Hornsby (544998)	0-4-0DE	1969
Marston Thompson Evershed	—	Baguely (3410)	0-4-0DM	1955

Rolling stock
A variety of passenger and freight vehicles are housed on site, including a number of considerable historical importance, together with an ex-LNER steam crane

meal) — 16 June; Coal Train Day — 17 June; Summer Evening Special Symphony Concert — 30 June; Model Railway Weekend — 7/8 July; Annual Charity Day — 12 August; Industrial Gala — 27 October; Halloween Specials — 27 October; Santa Specials —2, 4, 6, 8/9, 11, 13, 15/16, 18, 20, 22/23,

27 December
Facilities for disabled: Disabled access to stations, trains and buffet
Membership details: Membership Secretary, Brownhills West Station, Chasewater Country Park, Pool Road, Nr Brownhills, Staffs WS8 7NL

Chinnor & Princes Risborough Railway — 'The Icknield Line'

Steam Centre | Oxfordshire

Member: HRA
The Chinnor & Princes Risborough Railway runs from Chinnor station, close to the beautiful Chiltern Hills and to the Vale of Aylesbury.

Originally built in 1872 to connect the towns of Watlington in Oxfordshire to Princes Risborough in Buckinghamshire, the line was closed to all traffic by British

Railways in 1989. Since then a team of volunteers has rebuilt Chinnor station to its Victorian glory. The railway operates the 3.5-mile ex-Great Western Railway branch line as a tourist attraction for both families and railway enthusiasts. A regular steam-hauled service is provided every Sunday from Mother's Day to Halloween. Special events are a feature of the programme including Teddy Bear Days and Santa Specials. Cream teas are served on some standard Sunday afternoon trains and on some special events

Location: M40 junction 6 then B4009 north 4 miles towards Princes Risborough to village of Chinnor. Once in village follow brown tourist signs to station

Operating society/organisation: Chinnor & Princes Risborough Railway Co Ltd, Chinnor Station, Station Road, Chinnor, Oxon OX39 4ER

Telephone: Talking Timetable 01844 353535. Santa Booking Line: 01844 354117 (Weekends 10.00-15.00 only)

Internet addresses: *E-mail:* enquiries@chinnorrailway.co.uk *Web site:* www.chinnorrailway.co.uk

OS reference: SP 756003

Access by public transport: Nearest main line station — Princes Risborough (4 miles) Chiltern Railways

By car: M40 junction 6 then B4009 north towards Princes Risborough to village of Chinnor, then follow brown tourist signs to station

Length of line: 3.5 miles

Journey time: 45min, steam and heritage diesel trains

On site facilities: Souvenir shop, small buffet on Chinnor station. Bar/buffet on most trains (cream teas generally available on standard timetable Sunday afternoons). Toilets, free car park, picnic area

Passenger trains: Chinnor-Thame Junction-Chinnor

Public opening: Every Sunday and

Locomotives

Name	No	Origin	Class	Type	Built
—	1369	GWR	1366	0-6-0PT	1934
—	9682	GWR	57xx	0-6-0PT	1948
Haversham	13018	BR	08	0-6-0DE	1953
—	D8568	BR	17	Bo-Bo	1964
—	D5581 (31163)	BR	31	A1A-A1A	1960
Sister Dora	37116	BR	37	Co-Co	1963
—	55023	BR	121	DMBS	1960

Industrial locomotives

Name	No	Builder	Type	Built
Iris	459515	R/Hornsby (459515)	0-6-0DH	1952

Stock - coaches

1 ex-LNWR Mess coach, 1 ex-BR Mk 1 TSO, 1 ex-BR Mk 1 RMB, 2 ex-BR Mk 1 BSK, 16 various wagons, 1 Coles self-propelled crane

Owners

D8568 the Diesel Traction Group
1369 on loan from South Devon Railway
9682 on loan from Southall Railway Centre

Bank Holiday from 18 March until the end of October. Saturday and Sundays in December for Santa trains

Special events: Mother's Day — 18 March; Easter Specials — 6-9 April; Railway Open Day — 19 May; Teddy Bear Days — 6-7 May; Father's Day — 17 June; Senior Citizens' Day — 15 July; Steam and Diesel Gala — 5 August; Annual Gala Day — 9 September; Teddy Bear Days — 26/27 August; Senior Citizens' Day — 7 October; Halloween Spooks Express — 28 October; Santa Specials —1/2, 8/9, 15/16, 22/23 December; Mince Pie Specials — 29-31 December. *Evening events:* Murder Mystery Dining Train — 12 May, 7 July, 18 August, 15 September. Fish and Chip Quiz Evenings — 21 April, 26 May, 9 June, 2 July, 1, 29 September. Carol Evening — 15 December

Evening events start at 19.00 For details or to book phone 07979 055366

Special note: Group charter hire and film and photographic facilities available, contact: 07979 055366. Advance booking is necessary for Santa Specials

Driver Experience Courses: The railway will be offering steam and diesel driver experience days throughout the year. Gift vouchers are available for these courses. Please telephone 07784 189322 or visit the web site for details

Facilities for disabled: Ramp, toilet, accessible parking area. All public areas accessible and special area for wheelchair disabled on board the train. Guide dogs welcome

Membership details: Mr Brian West, 10 Coombe Hill Crescent, Thame, Oxon OX9 2EH

Membership journal: *The Watlington Flyer* — quarterly

Timetable Service — Cholsey & Wallingford Railway — Oxfordshire

Member: HRA

Location: Hithercroft Road, Wallingford, Oxfordshire

Sales: Mrs P. Goodenough

Marketing: Mrs S. Harington,

Mr C. Young

Operating Society: Cholsey & Wallingford Railway Preservation Society, 5 Hithercroft Road, Wallingford, Oxon OX10 9GQ

Telephone: (01491) 835067 (24hr information line)

Internet addresses: *E-mail:* cwrail@yahoo.co.uk *Web site:* www.cholsey-wallingford-railway.com

Disabled access: Access direct to Wallingford station from adjoining car park, access ramp to shop, platform and train. No disabled access at Cholsey station
Access by public transport:
By bus — Thames Travel Buses — X39 from Oxford, X40 from Reading.
By rail — First Great Western trains from Didcot and Reading to Cholsey station
Public opening: Trains depart every hour from Wallingford, 11.05 to 16.05; and from Cholsey 11.35 to 16.35 (platform 5)
Length of line: 2.5 miles
Journey time: Approximately 14min (one way), 40min (round trip)
On site facilities: Souvenir shop, café and museum
Special events: Ivor the Engine — 7-9 April; Spring Bank Holiday — 6/7 May; Two-day plant sale — 12/13 May; Blues and Beer Festival — 2-4 June; Father's Day — 17 June (fathers go free if accompanied by children); Senior Citizen Weekend — 23/24 June (OAP goes free with full fare paying adult); Ale on Rail Weekend — 7/8 July; Guiness Weekend — 28/29 July; Teddy Bears' Weekend — 26/27 August (under 8s free if accompanied by a teddy); Trains on a summer Bank Holiday — 26/27 August; BunkFest (singing trains) — 1/2 September; Agatha Christie Mystery Weekend — 15/16 September; Halloween Trains — 27/28 October (dress up if you care, be there if you dare); Santa Specials — 8/9, 15/16, 22/23 December

Special notes: Whilst it is intended to operate as advertised all services, events and fares may be altered due to prevailing circumstances with or without notice.

The railway crosses Wallingford bypass (A4130) at a level crossing and runs into Cholsey main line station
Membership details: Jenny Beckley, at above address
Membership journal: *The Bunk* — 3 issues/year

Locomotives

Name	No	Origin	Class	Type	Built
Unicorn	D3074	BR	08	0-6-0DE	1953
Lion	D3030	BR	08	0-6-0DE	1953
George Mason	D3190	BR	08	0-6-0DE	1955

Industrial locomotives

Name	No	Builder	Type	Built
Carpenter	3271	Planet (3270)	0-4-0DM	1949
—	803	Alco (77777)	Bo-Bo	1950

Rolling stock — coaches: GWR BSK, 2 BR Mk 1 TSOs

Timetable Service	Churnet Valley Railway	Staffordshire

Member: HRA

This heritage railway is situated deep in the heart of the Staffordshire moorlands. Begin your journey at either Cheddleton, a Victorian country station set in picturesque countryside complete with riverside parking and picnic island or Kingsley & Froghall with the impressive NSR-style station complete with award-winning tea rooms, souvenir shop and picnic area. The 10.5 mile return journey takes you to the idyllic hamlet of Consall Forge and incorporates Leekbrook tunnel
Main station/location: Kingsley & Froghall Station, Froghall, Staffs ST10 2HA
OS reference: SJ 983519
Operating society/organisation: Churnet Valley Railway (1992) plc
Telephone: 01538 360522
Fax: 01538 361848
Internet addresses: *E-mail:* enquiries@churnetvalleyrailway.co.uk

Locomotives and multiple-units

Name	No	Origin	Class	Type	Built
—	5197	USATC	S160	2-8-0	1942
—	6046	USATC	S160	2-8-0	1945
—	48173	LMS	8F	2-8-0	1943
—	92134	BR	9F	2-10-0	1957
—	D2334	BR	04	0-6-0DM	1961
Tamworth Castle	D7672	BR	25	Bo-Bo	1967
—	33102	BR	33	Bo-Bo	1960
—	37075	BR	37	Co-Co	1962
—	37407	BR	37	Co-Co	1965
—	47524	BR	47	Co-Co	1967
—	53455	BRCW	104	DMBS	1957
—	53437	BRCW	104	DMBS	1957
—	53494	BRCW	104	DMCL	1957
—	53517	BRCW	104	DMCL	1957
—	59137	BRCW	104	TSL	1957

Industrial locomotives

Name	No	Builder	Type	Built
Brightside	—	YEC (2672)	0-4-0DH	1959
Janus	—	YEC (2805)	0-6-0DE	1960

Stock
Ex-BR Mk 1 coaches: CK (1), BSK (2), SO (3), TSO (2), FK (3), RMB (2), RK (1) and BG (2); ex-BR Mk 2 coaches: BFK (1); ex-BR suburban

Web site:
www.churnetvalleyrailway.co.uk
Other stations: Cheddleton and Consall
Souvenir shops Kingsly & Froghall
Car parks: Adjacent to Cheddleton and Froghall stations
Access by public transport: Main line Stoke-on-Trent (10 miles). A regular bus service (No 16) runs from Hanley and Leek to Cheddleton village
On site facilities: Refreshment facilities at Cheddleton and Froghall
Souvenir shop: Cheddleton and Froghall
Museum: Small relics museum at Cheddleton
Length of line: 5.25 miles
Tickets: Day rover tickets available
Public opening: Steam trains Sundays — March-October. Saturdays April-end September.
  Bank Holidays and Wednesdays in Bank Holiday weeks, plus certain other dates (see timetable). Wednesdays in July and August.
Special events: 1940s Weekend — 28/29 April, Wednesday 2 May; Volunteers' Weekend — 19/20

coaches: S (1), BS (2), SLO (1); 1 ex-NSR coach body; 1 ex-LMS 6-wheel full brake; 2 ex-LMS goods brake vans; 1 ex-LMS 6-wheel CCT; 2 ex-LMS box vans; 3 ex-BR box vans; 2 ex-LMS five-plank wagons; 1 ex-LMS hopper wagon; 1 Esso tank wagon; 1 ex-BR standard brake van; 1 ex-BR Oyster; 5 ex-BR General Utility Vans; 2 ex-BR Medfits; 2 ex-BR Catfish; 1 ex-GWR bogie bolster; 2 Flatrols; 1 Lowmac; 7-ton diesel rail-mounted crane; 75-ton rail-mounted diesel crane; 3 ex-BR QQX tool vans; 1 ex-BR QPX staff and dormitory

Owners
33102 and D7672 the North Staffordshire Railway Co
37075 the 5C Group
47524 the Staffordshire Type 4 Ltd

May; Jubilee Street Party — Tuesday 5 June; Alf Tunstall Classic Bus Rally & Swap Meet — 9/10 June; Consall Garden Party — 1 July; 12th National Railway Velocipede Rally — 8 July; 2nd Rail Ale Trail Beer Festival — 20-22 July; Day out with Thomas — 25-27, 29 August; Diesel Gala — 22/23 September; Folk Festival and Classic Cars — 7 October; Ghost Train — 27 October; Santa & Steam — selected dates in December; Mince Pie Specials — 29/30 December
Facilities for disabled: Access to

station areas is possible by wheelchair, train travel by arrangement. Disabled toilet facilities at Consall and Froghall
Membership details: North Staffordshire Railway Co (1978) Ltd, Membership Secretary, c/o above address
Special facilities: Party bookings by arrangement, footplate experience courses, wine & dine dates on application. Licensed for weddings and civil partnerships at all three stations

Timetable Service	Cleethorpes Coast Light Railway	North East Lincolnshire

Member: HRA
The East Coast's award-winning seaside 15in gauge light railway. Built in 1948 as a 10.25in line, it was converted in 1972 to 14.25in and then to 15in gauge in 1994. The railway now has a two-mile stretch of line along the Humber estuary coastline, from Kingsway station at the south end of Cleethorpes Promenade, through the attractive boating lake, and onwards to the current southern terminus at North Sea Lane in Humberston.
  The railway has a good reputation for galas and events, and facilities continue to improve year on year. In 2005 a 'Griffon Hall' museum was officially opened, and is now open on most running days, showcasing the history of the 'Sutton Collection' as well as providing a home for other historic railway equipment, including the

Locomotives — 15in gauge

Name	No	Built/rebuilt	Type	Date
—	7	Lister	4wDH Tram	1944
The Cub/John	3	Minirail/CCLR	4w+4DM	1993
—	24	Fairbourne	2-6-2	1989
Battison	5	Battison	2-6-4DH S/O	1958
Yvette	111	—	2-6-0	1946
Efie	—	Great Northern Steam	0-4-0	1999
—	6284	Crome & Loxley	2-8-0	2009

Rolling stock
13 coaches, 2 x 4-wheel wagons, 2 x 4-wheel box vans, 2 x 4-wheel goods brake vans, 3 bogie flat wagons, 1 x 4-wheel ballast/coal wagon

Locomotives (18in gauge) Not viewable by public

Name	No	Built/rebuilt	Type	Date
Crompton	—	Curwen	4-4-2	1951

15in gauge Sutton Collection

Locomotives

Name	No	Built/rebuilt	Type	Date
Sutton Belle	1	BL/Cannon Ironfoundries/Hunt	4-4-2	1933
Sutton Flyer	2	Bassett Lowke/Hunt	4-4-2	1950
Mighty Atom/ Prince of Wales	BL1 SMR3	Bassett-Lowke/G. Llewellyn	4-4-2	1908

England

'Little Titan' steam crane.

The railway is supported by the Light Railway Supporters' Association, whose members assist in running the line, undertaking a wide range of duties from track work to driving the trains.

2012 features a wide range of events, including the annual 'Works Outing' gala and Oktoberfest events. The web site is continually updated with the latest timetable and event details

Operating society/organisation: Cleethorpes Coast Light Railway, Lakeside Station, Kings Road, Cleethorpes, Lincolnshire DN35 0AG

Telephone: (01472) 604657
Fax: (01472) 291903
Internet addresses: *E-mail:* office.cclr@btconnect.com
Web site: www.cleethorpescoastlightrailway. co.uk

Access by public transport: By rail to Cleethorpes station (First Trans-pennine Express). Local bus service Stagecoach services 8 and 9 operate all year round, additional No 17 operates over the summer season. 'Lollipop Express' road train from the pier connects with CCLR services at Kingsway station
Access by road: Kings Road is the resort main road with access

Name	No	Built/rebuilt	Type	Date
—	4	G&S Light Engineering	Bo-Bo	1946

Rolling stock
6 closed coaches, 4 open coaches, 1 x 4-wheel coal truck

15in gauge Bushmills Railway Collection
Locomotives

Name	No	Built/rebuilt	Type	Date
Mountaineer	—	van Heiden/Severn-Lamb	0-4-0	1985
—	DA1	BMR	4wDM	1986

Rolling stock
5 closed coaches, 2 drop-side 4-wheel wagons

Also resident
'Little Titan' steam crane, replica of NER steam crane to quarter scale. With scale train including a bogie well wagon, 4-wheel box wagon and 4-wheel match truck. Built by E. Cheeseman, 1975

Note
During the year visiting locomotives are based on the CCLR, and locomotives and rolling stock are under repair for other operators

directly from the M180, A180 and A46, brown tourist signs direct to 'Lakeside'. There is a large 500 space council-operated pay & display car park directly adjacent to Lakeside station
On site facilities:
Kingsway station — Station Master's gift and model shop. Lakeside station — Brief Encounter Tea Room, Griffon Hall museum, Signal Box Inn, public toilets

(including disabled and baby changing)
Period of public opening: Weekends throughout the year, daily during school holidays, contact or visit the web site for details. Please note that not all services are suitable for disabled passengers, please contact in advance of visit so that advice can be given

---

Steam Centre — **Colne Valley Railway** — **Essex**

Member: HRA, TT
A completely reconstructed country station and railway within sight of a 12th century castle and specialising in entertainment and education
Location: Castle Hedingham Station, Yeldham Road, Castle Hedingham, Halstead, Essex CO9 3DZ
OS reference: TL 774362
Operating society/organisation: Colne Valley Railway Preservation Society Ltd
Telephone: Hedingham (01787) 461174
Internet address:
Web site: www.colnevalleyrailway.co.uk
Car park: At the site (access from

Locomotives and multiple-units

Name	No	Origin	Class	Type	Built
Blue Star	35010	SR	MN	4-6-2	1942
—	45163	LMS	5	4-6-0	1935
—	45293	LMS	5	4-6-0	1936
—	D2041	BR	03	0-6-0DM	1959
—	D2184	BR	03	0-6-0DM	1962
—	08670	BR	08	0-6-0DE	1960
—	20035	BR	20	Bo-Bo	1959
—	20063	BR	20	Bo-Bo	1961
—	31255	BR	31	A1A-A1A	1961
—	47771	BR	47	Co-Co	1966
—	54287	P/Steel	121	DTS	1961
—	55033	P/Steel	121	DTC	1960
—	E79978	AC Cars	—	Railbus	1958
—	55508	BR	141	DMS	1983
—	55528	BR	141	DMS(L)	1983

plus various Class 08s between hire contracts

A1017 road between Castle Hedingham and Great Yeldham)
Access by public transport:
By bus: Eastern National bus services 88 Colchester-Halstead, 89 Halstead-Hedingham and Hedingham Omnibuses 4 Braintree-Hedingham, 5 Sudbury-Hedingham. No Sunday service.
Special bus link from Braintree railway station on selected Sundays
By rail: Braintree (7 miles)
On site facilities: Depot, museum, souvenir shop, buffet, 4-acre riverside picnic area, toilets, video carriage, exhibition centre, Travelling Post Office, model railway
Catering facilities: Buffet carriage when trains operating. Pullman on-train service on selected days for Sunday lunch, private hire and evening wine and dine (pre-booking essential for all Pullman services)
Length of line: 1 mile
Public opening: Steam trains operate every Sunday 18 March to 21 October, also Wednesdays and Thursdays during school summer holidays, every Bank Holiday (except Christmas & New Year), Wednesdays during other school holidays. Diesel railcar on many other days. Phone for free timetable or visit web site
Special events: Diesel Gala — 25 March; Vintage Vehicle Rally — 21/22 April; CV&HR 150 Weekend — 26/27 May; Model Railway Exhibition — 24 June; Colne Valley at War — 8 July; Bus and Commercial Vehicle Rally — 22 July; Craft Fair — 16 September; Victorian Sunday — 14 October; Wizard's Evening — 27 October
Educational events: Diesel trains available every day for school visits (steam on certain days).

Industrial locomotives

Name	No	Builder	Type	Built
Victory	8	Barclay (2199)	0-4-0ST	1945
—	WD190	Hunslet (3790)	0-6-0ST	1952
Jupiter	60	RSH (7671)	0-6-0ST	1950
Barrington	—	Avonside (1875)	0-4-0ST	1921
—	1	H/Leslie (3715)	0-4-0ST	1928
—	—	Barclay (349)	0-4-0DM	1941
—	YD43	R/Hornsby (221639)	4wDM	1943
—	—	Hibberd (3147)	4wDM	1947
—	—	Unilok (2109)	4wDM R/R	1982
—	—	Lake & Elliot (1)	4wPM	1924
—	—	R/Hornsby (281266)	4wDM	1950

Locomotive notes: Operational locomotives will be WD190, *Victory* and *Isabel*, Hunslet w/n 3437 0-6-0ST, (on loan from Epping-Ongar Railway)

Stock (some vehicles may be at Yeldham Transport Museum for restoration)
2 ex-Pullman cars, *Aquila* and *Hermione;* 9 ex-BR Mk 1 coaches (2xTSO, SO, 2xCK, SK, 2xBSK); 1 ex-BR Mk 3 SLEP; 10 BR NPCCS (including Travelling Post Office set), 2 ex-LNER — 1xBTO (16551) 1xTK (42240); 1 LMS BG, 1 GER BTK;
4 goods brake vans (GWR, LNER & 2 BR), 3 oil tank wagons, BR steam crane, LT ballast wagon, BR Sturgeon, BR Conflat, GER van, BR van, BR Medfit, LNER tube wagon, BR diesel crane, BR Flatrol, BR Lowmac

Owners
35010 and 45293 the British Engineman's Steam Preservation Society
54287 and 55033 Pressed Steel Heritage Ltd
31255 the Colne Valley Railway Diesel Group
47771 the Class 47 Preservation Project
45163 the 45163 Preservation Group

All educational events must be pre-booked
Family tickets: Available — 2 adults and up to 3 children, giving unlimited train rides except on special events
Facilities for disabled: Access to most areas with disabled parking available. Ramps to trains (including Travelling Post Office), staff will help. Special carriage and toilets available
Special notes: The railway has been completely rebuilt on part of the original Colne Valley & Halstead Railway trackbed. It offers much of educational value specialising in school party visits by appointment at any time of the year. 12-month season tickets available
Special facilities: Private or corporate hire of Pullmans is available. Driver Experience Courses (steam and diesel) available throughout the year
Membership details: Membership Secretary, c/o Castle Hedingham Station

Crewe Heritage Centre

Steam Centre — Crewe Heritage Centre — Cheshire

Location: Crewe Heritage Centre, Vernon Way, Crewe CW1 2BD
OS reference: SJ 709552
Operating society/organisation: Crewe Heritage Trust Ltd
Telephone: (01270) 212130
Internet address: *Web site:*

www.creweheritagecentre.co.uk
Car park: On site, town centre, Forge Street, Oak Street
Access by public transport: Main line Crewe
Refreshment facilities: Adjacent Tesco superstore

On site facilities: Gift shop, picnic area, weekend train rides, standard gauge and miniature railway, exhibition hall, main line viewing area, 3 working signalboxes with 'hands-on' visitor operation, model railway layouts, also preserved buses

44

Public opening: Weekends and Bank Holidays only, Easter to end of September 10.00-16.30 (last admission 15.30). Family tickets available. Please contact for details of events.

Weekday visits by prior arrangement with the manager
Facilities for disabled: Toilets
Membership details: Friends of the Crewe Heritage Centre, c/o above address
Notes: Steam locomotives passed for use over main line tracks are stabled between duties from time to time

Locomotives

Name	No	Origin	Class	Type	Built
Thornbury Castle	7027	GWR	Castle	4-6-0	1950
—	03073	BR	03	0-6-0DM	1959
—	37108	BR	37	Co-Co	1963
Ixion	D172	BR	46	1Co-Co1	1962
—	D1842	BR	47	Co-Co	1965
—	73006	BR	73	Bo-Bo	1962
Robert Burns	87035	BR	87	Bo-Bo	1974

Rolling stock
APT vehicle Nos 48103, 48106, 48404, 48602, 48603, 49002; various ex-BR coaches and passenger brake vans from time to time for repairs

Owners
7027 and D172 the Waterman Heritage Trust
37108 and 73006 are privately owned

Tram Service — Crich Tramway Village — Derbyshire

Member: HRA, TT
An experience of living transport history with vintage horse-drawn, steam and electric trams running through a re-created townscape of authentic buildings, stone setts, iron railings and historic street furniture. The heart of the Museum is its collection of over 70 vintage trams and you can enjoy the thrill of travelling on the scenic mile-long track
Location: Crich, Nr Matlock, Derbyshire DE4 5DP
OS reference: SK 345549
Manager: Vacant
Operating society/organisation: Tramway Museum Society
Telephone: 01773 854321
Internet addresses: *E-mail:* enquiries@tramway.co.uk
Web site: www.tramway.co.uk
Car park: On site; coach parking also available
Access by public transport: By rail, nearest main line stations: Cromford or Alfreton then by bus; or Whatstandwell and steep uphill walk
On site facilities: Souvenir shop, play areas, bookshop and picnic areas. 1-mile electric tramway. Tramway period street, depots, displays, exhibitions and video theatre. Large exhibition hall with new interpretive display depicting the history of the tram and Turn of the Century Trade Exhibition plus other exhibitions/displays
Refreshment facilities: Hot and

Locomotives

Name	No	Builder	Type	Built
—	—	B/Peacock (2464)	0-4-0VB tram loco	1885
—	—	E/Electric (717)	4wE	1927
Rupert*	—	R/Hornsby (223741)	4wDM	1944
GMJ*	—	R/Hornsby (326058)	4wDM	1952
—*	—	R/Hornsby (373363)	4wDM	1954

*not on display

Trams

No	Operator	Built
1	Derby	1904
1	Douglas Head Marine Drive	1896
1	Leamington & Warwick	1881
1	London Transport	1932
2	Blackpool & Fleetwood	1898
4	Blackpool Corp	1885
5	Blackpool	*1972
5	Gateshead & District	1927
7	Chesterfield	1904
8	Chesterfield	1899
9	Oporto	1873
10	Hill of Howth	1902
14	Grimsby & Immingham	1915
15	Sheffield	1874
21	Dundee & District	1894
22	Glasgow	1922
35	Edinburgh	1948
40	Blackpool & Fleetwood	†1914
40	Blackpool	1926
45	Southampton	1903
46	Sheffield	1899
(47)	New South Wales Govt	1885
49	Blackpool	1926
52	Gateshead & District	*1901
59	Blackpool	*1902
60	Johannesburg	1905
68	Paisley & District	1919
74	Sheffield	1900

England

45

cold snacks and meals
Public opening: Daily February half term (10.30-16.00). Weekends in March (10.30-16.00). Daily 31 March until 31 October (10.00-17.30). Weekends from November to 15 December (10.30-16.00).
Special events: Easter 1940s Weekend* — 8/9 April; Morris Minor Event — 13 May; Classic Motorbike Weekend — 19/20 May; Beside the Seaside — 3/4 June; 1950s Weekend* — 23/24 June; London 60 — 8 July; Edwardian Weekend* — 14/15 July; Mini Meet — 29 July; Emergency Vehicles Day — 5 August; 1940s Weekend* — 11/12 August; Alice in Woodland* — 26/27 August; Classic Ford Day — 9 September; Enthusiasts' Tram Event / Glasgow 50 — 15/16 September; Models Weekend — 20/21 October; Red Oktober Day — 21 October; Starlight Halloween* — 27 October.
*Premier event
Family tickets: Available
Facilities for disabled: Access to all public facilities, Braille guide book available, 1969 Berlin tram specially adapted to lift and carry people in wheelchairs. Also a 'wheelway', a smooth path routeing around and through cobbled areas
Special notes: Crich houses the largest collection of preserved trams in Europe and has a 1-mile working tramway on which restored electric trams are regularly operated. Special events are arranged at weekends and Bank Holidays throughout the season. Part of tram line occupies route of narrow gauge mineral railway built by George Stephenson
Membership details: From above

No	Operator	Built
76	Leicester	1904
102	Newcastle	1901
106	London County Council	1903
132	Kingston-upon-Hull	§1910
166	Blackpool	1927
167	Blackpool	1928
180	Leeds	1931
180	Prague	1908
189	Sheffield	1934
264	Sheffield	1937
273	Oporto	—
298	Blackpool	*1937
331	Metropolitan Electric	1930
345	Leeds	*—
399	Leeds	1926
510	Sheffield	1950
600	Leeds	1931/54
602	Leeds	1953
607	Blackpool & Fleetwood	1934
674	New York 3rd Avenue Transit	1939
712	Blackpool & Fleetwood	1935
812	Glasgow	1900
869	Liverpool	1936
902	Halle	
1100	Glasgow	1928
1105	Glasgow	1929
1147	Hague	1957
1282	Glasgow	1940
1297	Glasgow	1948
1622	London Transport	1912
3006	Berlin	1969
—	London Tramways	c1895

*stored off-site †on loan to Blackpool
§on loan to Hull Museum of Transport

Note: In addition to the trams (including examples from Czechoslovakia, Germany, The Netherlands, Portugal, USA and South Africa) — about a third of which have been restored to working order — there are a number of Works Cars not listed

address
Membership journal: *The Journal* — quarterly

Dartmoor Railway

Timetable Service — Devon

Member: HRA
Following its unexpected closure in 2008, the Ealing Community Transport (ECT) sold its interest to Iowa Pacific Holdings (IPH). IPH have created a new company, British American Railway Services, to operate both Dartmoor and Weardale Railways.

The Dartmoor Railway is a very young railway as far as tourism is concerned, although the railway has been in existence for 140 years as the Southern Railway main line from Waterloo to Plymouth. The line only survived because of ballast supplies from Meldon Quarry. The railway offers a unique experience which encompasses access to Dartmoor National Park for everyone including the disabled and cyclists. Views of Meldon Quarry and workings from the cycle route. Far reaching views at Meldon of Dartmoor, Exmoor and surrounding areas. Meldon visitor centre shows a history of the railways and tramways of Dartmoor. Okehampton station has been restored to the 1950s style

Headquarters: Dartmoor Railway, Okehampton Station, Okehampton, Devon EX20 1EJ
Telephone: 01837 55164
Fax: 01837 55927
Internet addresses: *E-mail:* info@dartmoorrailway.co.uk
Web site: www.dartmoorrailway.co.uk
General Manager: Graham Isom
Main station: Okehampton, access by road, rail (very restricted service), bus or National Cycle Route 237 and other footpaths. Ample free parking, including coaches
Other public stations: Meldon for Meldon Viaduct and Dartmoor National Park, access only by rail and National Cyclepath. Sampford Courtenay has access by road or rail, limited free parking
Access by public transport: Bus all year, check with Traveline 0870 6082608 for availability.
Trains from Exeter (Sunday Rover) late May to late September
Refreshment facilities: Okehampton buffet open Friday and weekends, plus all week in high season
Model & Gift shops: Extensive model and gift shop (West Country Models) at Okehampton, some gifts also available at Meldon buffet (tel: 01837 55637)
Depot: Meldon Quarry, no public access. Viewing only from National Cyclepath
Length of line: 15.5 miles, Coleford Junction-Meldon Quarry
Passenger trains: Fridays and weekends Easter to November, plus Tuesdays in high season
Special events: Santa Specials, Mince Pie Specials and Dining Specials. Contact for details
Special notes: Visits for special interest groups and education tours

Locomotives and multiple-units (some in use as hauled stock)

Name	No	Origin	Class	Type	Built
Bluebell Mel	08937	BR	08	0-6-0DE	1962
Waverley	47701	BR	47	Co-Co	1966
unit 205028	60146	BR	205	DMBS	1957
unit 205028	60673	BR	205	DMBS	1957
unit 205028	60827	BR	205	DTC	1957
unit 205032	60150	BR	205	DMBS	1957
unit 205032	60677	BR	205	DMBS	1957
unit 205032	60831	BR	205	DTC	1957
—	70273	BR	411	TSOL	1958
unit 412	76301	BR	438 / 4TC	DTSO	1967
unit 412	76302	BR	438 / 4TC	DTSO	1967
—	69332	BR	423 / 4VEP	TRB	1970
—	69310	BR	422 / 4BIG	TRBS	1966
—	61742	BR	411 / 4CEP	DMBSO	1961
—	61743	BR	411 / 4CEP	DMBSO	1961
—	76812	BR	421 / 4CIG	DTCSOL	

Industrial locomotives

Name	No	Builder	Type	Built
—	S103*	H/Clarke (1864)	0-6-0T	1952
Flying Falcon	MSC 0256*	Fowler	0-6-0DE	

*undergoing restoration, expected to enter service in

Stock
ex-BR Mk 1s RBR: 1691; FO *Rosemary*
ex-BR Mk 2s TSO 5920, 6002, 6181; FO 3353, 3354, 3387, 3402, 3411, 3425; RBR 1213; BSO 9492, 9501
ex-BR Mk 3 sleeping cars 10518, 10595, 10611
Selection of maintenance vehicles including horsebox S96300 converted to Generator coach for 'Dartmoor Belle'

Owners
Class 205 units stored on behalf of Porterbrook Leasing Co
08937 and MSC 0256 Aggregate Industries
76301, 76302, 76812 and 70826 Rolltrack Trains
Groups and individuals own some of the rolling stock

may be arranged. Trains are available for private hire or corporate functions. Trains have facilities to carry bicycles free, dogs also carried free
Facilities for disabled: Full disabled facilities and access at Okehampton, partial access to inside Meldon buffet. Toilets at Okehampton and Meldon are RADAR key operated
Membership details: Friends of Dartmoor Railway c/o Okehampton station. Various discounts available
Membership journal: Quarterly, also available to purchase

Dartmouth Steam Railway & Riverboat Co

Member: HRA
The Dartmouth Steam Railway & Riverboat Co is the holiday line with steam trains running for seven miles in Great Western tradition along the spectacular Torbay coast to Churston and through the wooded slopes bordering the Dart estuary to Kingswear. The scenery is superb, with seascapes right across Lyme Bay to Portland Bill on clear days. Approaching Kingswear is the beautiful River Dart, with its fascinating craft, and on the far side, the 'olde worlde' town of Dartmouth and Britannia Royal Naval College, Butterwalk, Bayard's Cove and Dartmouth Castle

General Manager: Andrew Pooley
Headquarters: Paignton Queen's
Park Station, Paignton, Devon
TQ4 6AF
Telephone:
Paignton (01803) 555872
Internet address: *Web site:*
www.dartmouthrailriver.co.uk
Main station: Paignton Queen's
Park (TQ4 6AF)
Other public stations:
Goodrington, Churston, Kingswear
(for Dartmouth)
SatNav postcodes:
Goodrington — TQ4 6LN
Churston — TQ5 0LL
Kingswear — TQ6 0AA
(for Dartmouth — TQ6 9BH)
OS reference: SX 889606
Car parks: Paignton municipal car
park, Goodrington, Dartmouth
(ferry to Kingswear)
Access by public transport:
Adjacent to both Paignton main line
station and bus station
Refreshment facilities: Paignton
and Kingswear
Workshops: Churston (TQ5 0LN).
No public access
Length of line: 7 miles
Passenger trains: Paignton-
Kingswear, views of Torbay
and Dart estuary, 495yd tunnel,
3 viaducts
Period of public operation:
1 April to 30 October and Santa
Specials in December.
NOTE: no service on 29 April
Facilities for disabled: Limited,
special ramp to take wheelchairs
onto trains. Disabled toilets at
Paignton and Kingswear
Special events: Heritage Weekend
(150th anniversary of trains to
Churston) — 28-30 May; Day out
with Thomas — 22-25 October.

Locomotives and multiple-units

Name	No	Origin	Class	Type	Built
Hercules	4277	GWR	5205	2-8-0T	1920
Warrior	4555§	GWR	4500	2-6-2T	1924
Trojan	4588†§	GWR	4575	2-6-2T	1927
Goliath	5239	GWR	5205	2-8-0T	1924
Lydham Manor	7827	GWR	7800	4-6-0	1950
Braveheart	75014±	BR	4MT	4-6-0	1951
Titan	D2192	BR	03	0-6-0DM	1962
Samson	D3014	BR	08	0-6-0DE	1954
Mercury	D7535	BR	25	Bo-Bo	1965
—	59003*	BR	116	TS	1957
—	59004*	BR	116	TS	1957
—	59488*	P/Steel	117	TCL	1959
—	59494*	P/Steel	117	TCL	1959
—	59503*	P/Steel	117	TCL	1959
—	59507*	P/Steel	117	TCL	1959
—	59513*	P/Steel	117	TCL	1959
—	59517*	P/Steel	117	TCL	1959

*converted to locomotive-hauled vehicles

Note: Locomotives out of service are not available for viewing
†may not be on site for all of 2012
§stored out of service
±undergoing major overhaul

Stock
11 ex-BR Mk 1 coaches; 1 Pullman observation coach

Also Dining Trains, and Santa
Specials — please see timetable and
press for details. Combined river
excursions available
Special facilities: Private charters,
details on request. Timeline
exhibition coach at Kingswear
station (no disabled access).
Churston station is a registered
location for civil wedding
ceremonies (see
www.dartmouthwedding.co.uk
for a truly unique wedding day)
Special note: The railway also
operates combined excursions.
Train ride and ferry to Dartmouth
(plus 1-hour circular cruise option)
The Round Robin — train, ferry
river cruise (Dartmouth-Totnes),
bus (Totnes-Paignton). Start
anywhere on the route.
The Round Robin Gold — as above
but starting in Torquay, bus
Torquay-Paignton.
The Sea Train — sea cruise
(Totnes-Dartmouth) ferry, train and
bus (Paignton-Torquay)
New from 2011 — circular tour
starting in Teignmouth, sea cruise
(Totnes-Dartmouth), ferry, train
(Kingswear-Paignton), bus
(Paignton-Teignmouth)

Timetable Service — Dean Forest Railway — Glos

Member: HRA, TT
Passenger services operate between
Norchard and Lydney Junction
(Severn & Wye Joint), and
Norchard and Parkend. The line
boasts five level crossings, three of
which are manually operated.
 A new station is being
constructed at Whitecroft and is
anticipated to be open for public
use in the spring of 2012. Please
check web site for further details
Location: Headquarters at
Norchard station on the B4234.
Signposted off the A48 Lydney
bypass to town centre whence
B4234 commences
SatNav postcodes:
Norchard GL15 4ET
Lydney Jct GL15 5ET
Lydney Town GL15 5HJ
Parkend GL15 4JA
OS reference: SO 629044
Operating society/organisation:
Dean Forest Railway Society in
conjunction with owning company,
Forest of Dean Railway Ltd
Telephone: (01594) 843423
information line; (01594) 845840
(daytime — 11.00-16.00)

England

Internet address: *Web site:* www.dfr.co.uk

Car park: Norchard only, adequate for cars and coaches. No parking at other stations

Access by public transport: Main line station at Lydney. Stagecoach buses (service 73 Monday-Saturday) Gloucester-Lydney; James Bevan buses (service 755 Monday-Saturday) Chepstow-Lydney

On site facilities: Shop at Norchard with accredited museum, riverside, lineside and forest walks

Catering facilities: Hot and cold meals at Platelayer's Buffet on Norchard platform on service days. Parties catered for by appointment. Sunday lunchtime service by 'Royal Forester' first class dining car service, runs on selected Sundays in season, also evening supper trains, advance booking essential

Length of line: 4.25 miles

Public opening: Daily for static display — shop and museum, open 11.00-16.00, extended hours on running days.

Steam train days (some days DMUs and diesels). All Sundays 25 February to 10 November; Good Friday, Easter Saturday and all Bank Holiday Sundays and Mondays (Christmas excepted). Wednesdays June to October. Thursdays in late July and August.

Heritage DMU or main line diesel service operates alone some Saturdays in June and July and all Saturdays in September, plus Thursdays in August

Special events: Day out with Thomas — 14/15 April, 9/10 June, 17-19 August; Bygone Branchline Days — 11 March, 6 April, 5 May, 2 June, 21 July, 4, 11, 25, 29 August, 1 September; Great Western Branchline Days — 28 April, 30 June, 1 July; Diesel Gala — 19 May, 14/15 September; Mixed Traction Weekend — 28/29 July; Milirtary Weekend — 22/23 September; Santa Specials — 9, 15/16, 22-24 December (advance booking essential)

Special facilities: Branchline Experience Days available throughout the year. See web site (www.dfr.co.uk) for details and dates

Facilities for disabled: Norchard — access to museum, shop, toilets

Locomotives and multiple-units

Name	No	Origin	Class	Type	Built
—	1450	GWR	1400	0-4-2T	1932
—	5521	GWR	4575	2-6-2T	1927
—	5541†	GWR	4575	2-6-2T	1928
—	9681	GWR	5700	0-6-0PT	1949
Charlie	08238	BR	08	0-6-0DE	1956
Gladys	D3937	BR	08	0-6-0DE	1960
—	D9521	BR	14	0-6-0DH	1965
—	D9555	BR	14	0-6-0DH	1965
—	D7633	BR	25	Bo-Bo	1965
—	27066	BR	27	Bo-Bo	1962
—	31466	BR	31	A1A-A1A	1959
—	D5634	BR	31	A1A-A1A	1960
—	37263	BR	37	Co-Co	1965
—	E6001	BR	73	Bo-Bo	1962
—*	73002	BR	73	Bo-Bo	1962
—	E6005	BR	73	Bo-Bo	1962
—	E6006	BR	73	Bo-Bo	1962
The Royal Alex	73101	BR	73	Bo-Bo	1965
—	50619	BR	108	DMBS	1958
—	51566	BR	108	DMSL	1959
—	51914	BR	108	DMS	1960
—	56492	BR	108	DTC	1960
—	59387	BR	108	TS	1958
Unit 1499	62364	BR	421	MBSO	1970
Unit 1392	62378	BR	421	MBSO	1970
Unit 1881	71080	BR	421	TS	1967
Unit 11499	76726	BR	421	DTCSoL	1970
Unit 1392	76740	BR	421	DTCSoL	1970
Unit 1499	76797	BR	421	DTCSoL	1970
Unit 1392	76811	BR	421	DTCSoL	1970

E6006 is on loan to Severn Valley Railway
73101 is on loan to Avon Valley Railway
*mobile stores vehicle
†undergoing restoration

Industrial locomotives

Name	No	Builder	Type	Built
—	—	Barclay (2221)	0-4-0ST	1946
Uskmouth No 1	—†	Peckett (2147)	0-4-0ST	1952
Wilbert	—*	Hunslet (3806)	0-6-0ST	1953
Warrior	—†	Hunslet (3823)	0-6-0ST	1954
—	—	Hunslet (2145)	0-4-0DM	1940
Salty	—	Hunslet (6688)	0-4-0DH	1968
—	—	Fowler (4210127)	0-4-0DM	1957
—	—	Hibberd (3947)	4wPM	1960

†undergoing restoration
*Due to re-enter service in 2012

Stock

2 ex-GWR coaches; 10 ex-BR coaches; 1 DFR constructed Cafeteria coach, 3 Wickham trolleys; 1 steam crane Thos Smith (Rodley) TS 5027 (10-ton); Booth 15-24 tonne diesel-hydraulic crane

Owners

5541 the Forest Prairie Fund
9681 the Dean Forest Locomotive Group
08238, D3937, 27066, 31466, D5634, D7633, E6001, 73002, E6005, E6006 and 73101 the Dean Forest Diesel Association
37263 the 37263 Locomotive Group
Class 108 DMUs the Dean Forest DMU Group

and trains. Lydney Jct — access to toilets and trains. Lydney Town and Parkend — access to trains
Membership details: Mr R. F. Bramwell, 8 Nodens Way, Lydney,

Glos GL15 5NP
Membership journal: *DFR Magazine* — 6 per year
Marketing name: The Friendly Forest Line

Derwent Valley Light Railway

Railway Centre

North Yorkshire

Member: HRA, TT

The most notable fact about the DVLR'S history is that it was never nationalised. Private from its inception until the final section was closed in the early 1980s. The line was mothballed until 1989 when part of the line (York Layerthorpe to Osbaldwick) was transformed into a cycleway by Sustrans. A half-mile section adjacent to the Yorkshire Museum of Farming was donated to the museum along with the most necessary Light Railway Order; trains began running again in 1990

Location: Murton Park, Murton Lane, Murton, York YO19 5UF
Operating society/organisation: Derwent Valley Light Railway Society
Telephone: (01904) 489966
Internet addresses: *E-mail:* dvlr@hotmail.com
Web site: www.dvlr.org.uk
OS reference: SE 651537
On site facilities: Refreshments, souvenir shop (Yorkshire Museum of Farming)
Car park: Free, on site
Length of line: Half-mile
Access by public transport: York-Stamford Bridge and York-Hull bus services from York main line station. (Tel: 0870 608 2608 or www.yorkshiretravel.net)

Locomotives

Name	No	Origin	Class	Type	Built
—	03079	BR	03	0-6-0DM	1960
—	D9523	BR	14	0-6-0DH	1964

Industrial locomotives

Name	No	Builder	Type	Built
—	8	A/Barclay (2369)	0-4-0ST	1955
—	—	Fowler (4200022)	0-4-0DM	1948
Churchill	—	Fowler (4100005)	0-4-0DM	1947
Pluto	—	Hibberd (3777)	4wDM	1955
Jim	—	R/Hornsby (417892)	4wDM	1959
—	97088	R/Hornsby (466630)	4wDM	1962
British Sugar York	—	R/Hornsby (327964)	0-4-0DM	1953
James	—	YEC (2675)	0-4-0DH	1960

Rolling stock

1 BR Mk 1 TSO (No E3805 on loan from North Yorkshire Moors Railway). 1 NER coach, 1 NER coach body, 1 Swiss-style coach (built in 2003), 11 various freight wagons, and 1 steam rail crane

Souvenir shops: Within the Yorkshire Museum of Farming, and a railway souvenir shop within the station (open when trains running). Once the entrance fee to the Yorkshire Museum of Farming has been paid train rides are free
Facilities for disabled: Toilets, ramped ways, etc
Public opening: Open daily mid-February-end October, for the Yorkshire Museum of Farming, Danelaw (Viking) Village and the Derwent Valley Light Railway.

Trains operate Sundays and Bank Holidays Easter-end September and for Santa Specials
Special events: Santa Special — weekends and certain weekdays in December. See announcements for extra events on web site
Membership details: Christine Bailey, Membership Secretary, Derwent Valley Light Railway Society, Murton Park, Murton Lane, Murton, York YO19 5UF
Society journal: *DVLR News* (quarterly)

Devon Railway Centre

Railway Centre

Devon

The Devon Railway Centre features a lovingly restored Victorian Great Western Railway station together with historic locomotives, carriages and wagons as featured on TV. Unlimited passenger rides can be taken on the 2ft gauge railway and

miniature railways. There is also a large model railway exhibition featuring 15 working layouts including Polchester and Chiltern Green. Edwardian Model Village and outdoor play area. All-inclusive admission price

Location: Alongside Bickleigh Bridge over the River Exe on the A396, four miles south of Tiverton and 10 miles north of Exeter
General Manager: Matthew Gicquel
Contact address: Devon Railway

England

Centre, Bickleigh, Nr Tiverton, Devon EX16 8RG
Telephone: 01884 855671
Internet address: *Web site:* www.devonrailwaycentre.co.uk
OS reference: SS 938074
Car park: On site
Access by public transport: Regular bus service from Tiverton and Exeter, routes 55 and 55A
On site facilities: Passenger-carrying line, large model railway exhibition, restored GWR station, standard gauge static display, historic narrow gauge collection, miniature railway, refreshments and souvenirs, crazy golf, drive your own miniature railway. Model village and outdoor play area
Length of line: Half mile, 2ft gauge; half mile 7.25in gauge, 200yd standard gauge demonstration line; 100yd 7.25in gauge drive your own train
Opening times: 10.30-17.00. 31 March until 4 Novemberber. Daily 31 March to 15 April, 30 May to 9 September, 27 October to 4 November, (closed Mondays in June).
Wednesday to Sunday 2-27 May, 12-30 September. Weekends in October.
Special events: Steam Gala — 18/19 August; Everything Goes — 22/23 September; Santa Specials — 15/16, 22/23 December
Timetable: Narrow gauge line operates every 30min, miniature railway runs as required. Both lines operate whenever the Centre is open whatever the weather

Industrial locomotives — 2ft gauge

Name	No	Builder	Type	Built
Rebecca	—	O&K (5744)	0-4-0WT	1912
Horatio	—	R/Hornsby (217967)	4wDM	1942
Pen-yr-Orsedd	—	R/Hornsby (235711)	4wDM	1945
Ruston	—	R/Hornsby (418770)	4wDM	1957
Claude W. Lane	—†	R/Hornsby (435398)	4wDM	1959
Planet	—	Planet (2201)	4wDM	1939
Lister	—	Lister (6299)	4wPM	1935
—	—§	Lister (34025)	4wDM	1949
Ivor	—	M/Rail (8877)	4wDM	1944
—	—	M/Rail (20073)	4wDM	1950
Sir Tom	—	M/Rail (40s273)	4wDM	1966
—	—*	M/Rail (105H006)	4wDM	1919
—	—§	BEV	0-4-0BE	c1970

†2ft 9in gauge
*3ft gauge
§off site for restoration

Industrial locomotives (standard gauge)

Name	No	Builder	Type	Built
Boris	1	Baguley (3357)	0-4-0DM	1952

Locomotive notes: During 2012 passenger trains will be hauled by either *Rebecca, Ivor*, *Ruston* or *Horatio*

Rolling stock: All 2ft gauge unless indicated. Two Alan Keef bogie passenger coaches, 1 Hudson bogie passenger coach, Dinorwic Yellow Coach, 2 slate slab wagons, 7 skip wagons, 4 mine tubs, RAF bomb wagon, Hudson 3-plank wagon, 2 bogie coach chassis. Lochaber incline wagon (3ft gauge), copper mine tub (20in gauge), Cattybrook brickworks wagon (2ft 10in gauge), assorted works wagons.
Standard gauge — 3 ex-BR Mk 1 coaches, 4 ex-BR Mk 1 BGs

Miniature railway locomotives (7.25in gauge)

Name	No	Builder	Type	Built
—	D7011*	Cromar White	Bo-BoBE	1969
(Intercity)	—	—	Bo-BoBE	c1995
—	—	Pfeiferbahn	4wPH	1993
—	—	Chandler	4wBE	1978
—	7	Parkside	4WBER S/O	2002

*rebuilt from petrol to battery power by DRC during 2002
7 is a drive-your-own train operated by coin in the slot

Rolling stock: 3 sit-in coaches built by DRC/Roanoake, 1 bogie wagon

Steam Centre — Didcot Railway Centre — Oxfordshire

Member: HRA, TT
The Great Western Railway was incorporated in 1835 to build the railway from Bristol to London and it was designed and engineered by Isambard Kingdom Brunel to be the finest in the land. At Didcot, half way between Bristol and London, members of the Great Western Society have created a living museum of the GWR. It is based around the original engine shed and depot, to which has been added a typical branch line with a country station, signalling demonstrations and re-creation of Brunel's broad gauge trackwork and a replica of the locomotive *Fire Fly* dating from 1840. There is a large collection of GWR steam locomotives, carriages and wagons. On steamdays the locomotives come to life and you can ride in the 1930s trains on one or both of the demonstration lines. The present Didcot engine shed was built in 1932 and was taken over by the Great Western Society in 1967 when it arrived with just three locomotives, the start of what was to become the Didcot Railway Centre
Operations Manager: Roger Orchard
Location: Adjacent to main line

England

station, Didcot, Oxfordshire. Access via station subway
OS reference: SU 525907
Operating society/organisation: Great Western Society Ltd, Didcot Railway Centre, Didcot, Oxon OX11 7NJ
Telephone: Didcot (01235) 817200
Internet address: *Web site:* www.didcotrailwaycentre.org.uk
Car park: Didcot station
Access by public transport: Entry is at Didcot Parkway rail station served by First Great Western trains from London (Paddington), the Thames Valley, Oxford, Birmingham, Bristol, etc.
   On the A4130 road signed from the M4 motorway (jct 13) and A34
Refreshment facilities: Refreshment room open all days centre is open (lunches, snacks). Picnic area
On site facilities: GWR locomotive depot, replica GWR station, museum and broad gauge demonstration. Souvenir sales. Rides are available on the demonstration lines on Steamdays.
   Admission prices vary according to events and include train rides on Steamdays. Party rates available for more than 15 persons, guided tours, evening visits and special menus for lunch or tea can be arranged. Private steamings when visitors can try their hand at driving locomotives can be arranged
Length of line: 1,000yd
Public opening: Every Saturday, Sunday and Bank Holidays. Daily from 11-19 February, 1-15 April, 2 June-16 September, 27 October-4 November, 27 December-1 January 2013. See web site for details of running days.
 Gate opening times: on running days 10.30-16.30 between 1 March to 12 October, all other times 10.30-15.30.
Running days: 11/12, 15 February; 6-9 April; 5-7 May; 2-5, 9/10, 16/17, 23/24, 30 June; 1, 7/8, 15/16, 21/22, 25, 28/29 July; 1, 4/5, 8, 11/12, 15, 18/19, 22, 25-27, 29 August; 15/16, 27/28, 31 October; 29/30 December; 1 January 2013
Train rides: On Steamdays there is normally continuous operation of the passenger train, interrupted by Travelling Post Office demonstrations and turning of the locomotives on some days
Special events: Day out with

Locomotives

Name	No	Origin	Class/Builder	Type	Built
Fire Fly	—†	GWR	'Fire Fly'	2-2-2	2005
—	22	GWR	Diesel Railcar	1A-A1	1940
(Steam Railmotor)	93	GWR	—/GWS	0-4-0	1908/2011
County of Glamorgan	1014§	GWR	'County'/GWS	4-6-0	
—	1338	GWR	Kitson (3799) (Cardiff Rly)	0-4-0ST	1898
Trojan	1340	GWR	Avonside (1380)	0-4-0ST	1897
—	1363	GWR	1361	0-6-0ST	1910
Lady of Legend*	2999	GWR	'Saint'/GWS	4-6-0	1929
—	3650	GWR	5700	0-6-0PT	1939
—	3738	GWR	5700	0-6-0PT	1937
—	3822	GWR	2884	2-8-0	1940
Pendennis Castle	4079	GWR	'Castle'	4-6-0	1924
—	4144	GWR	5101	2-6-2T	1946
—	4866	GWR	4800	0-4-2T	1936
Earl Bathurst	5051	GWR	'Castle'	4-6-0	1936
—	5322	GWR	4300	2-6-0	1917
—	5572	GWR	4575	2-6-2T	1927
Hinderton Hall	5900	GWR	'Hall'	4-6-0	1931
King Edward II	6023	GWR	'King'	4-6-0	1930
—	6106	GWR	6100	2-6-2T	1931
—	6697	GWR	5600	0-6-2T	1928
Burton Agnes Hall	6998	GWR	'Hall'	4-6-0	1949
—	7202	GWR	7200	2-8-2T	1934
Cookham Manor	7808	GWR	'Manor'	4-6-0	1938
—	D3771	BR	08	0-6-0DE	1959
—	18000	BR	Gas Turbine	A1A-A1A	1950
Shannon	5	Wantage Tramway		0-4-0WT	1857

†broad gauge reconstruction of 1840 design
*under construction using frames of No 4942 *Maindy Hall*
§under construction using frames of No 7927 *Willington Hall*

Industrial locomotives

Name	No	Builder	Type	Built
Bonnie Prince Charlie	1	RSH (7544)	0-4-0ST	1949
—	26	Hunslet (5238)	0-6-0DH	1962
King George	—	Hunslet (2409)	0-6-0ST	1942

Locomotive notes: Locomotives available in 2012 should be: *Fire Fly*, 22, 93, 3650, 3738, 5322, 6023. Locomotives under restoration include: 1363, 4144, 4079, 7202. 4079 was repatriated from Australia in 2000

Stock
Over 40 ex-GWR coaches are preserved along with numerous ex-GWR freight wagons

Owner
5 on loan from the National Railway Museum

Thomas — 3/4 March; Enhanced Running Days — 6-9 April; Gala — 5-7 May; Enhanced Running Days — 3/4, 30 June; Enhanced Running Days — 1, 28/29 July; Enhanced Running Days — 25-27 August; Gala — 15/16 September; Day out with Thomas — 6/7 October; Days out with Thomas to visit Father Christmas — 1/2, 8/9, 15/16, 22/23 December
Facilities for disabled: Visitors are advised that there is an awkward flight of steps at the entrance, with level access within the centre (help can normally be given with prior advice)
Special facilities: Railway Experience Days offer the chance to be an engine driver for a day, and a

Day at Didcot offers a guided tour on normal Steamdays. Special steamings can be arranged for group and party visits

Membership details: Charles Roberts, at above address
Membership journal: *Great Western Echo* — quarterly

Note: Children under 12 must be accompanied by an adult

Operating Museum — East Anglia Transport Museum — Suffolk

Member: HRA, TT

The East Suffolk Light Railway is the title given to the 2ft gauge railway, which winds its way 300yd or so along the northern perimeter of the museum site, between the stations of Chapel Road and Woodside. The railway commenced operation in 1973 and aims to re-create a typical passenger-carrying light railway of years gone by. Many aspects of railway interest can be found along its length. The track came from Leziate sand quarry and Canvey Island, as well as from the Southwold Railway, and signals from various local locations; all of which help to set the overall scene

Location: Carlton Colville, three miles south-west of Lowestoft in Suffolk

OS reference: TM 505903

Operating society/organisation: East Anglia Transport Museum Society Ltd, Chapel Road, Carlton Colville, Lowestoft, Suffolk NR33 8BL

Telephone: (01502) 518459

Internet address: *Web site:* www.eatm.org.uk

Car park: Adjacent

Access by public transport:
By bus: First Eastern Counties 103 and X2 and Anglian 525 from Lowestoft or X2 from Norwich.

Industrial locomotives

Name	No	Builder	Type	Built
Aldeburgh	2	M/Rail (5912)	4wDM	1934
Leiston	4	R/Hornsby (177604)	4wDM	1936
Orfordness	5	M/Rail (22209)	4wDM	1964
Thorpeness	6	M/Rail (22211)	4wDM	1964

Trams

No	Trucks	Body	Date	Operator
11	Maley & Taunton	E/Electric	1939	Blackpool Corp
14	Brill	Milnes	1904	Lowestoft Corp
159	Preston McGuire	Blackpool Corp	1927	Blackpool Corp
313	Maley & Taunton	Roberts	1950	Sheffield Corp
474	Beijnes	Beijnes	1929	Amsterdam
1858	EMB	E/Electric	1930	London Transport

Stock

Locally designed and built covered coach, plus combined coach and brake van, suitable for wheelchairs. Small selection of wagons. Van body ex-Southwold Railway.

By rail: Oulton Broad South (1.5 miles) no connecting bus service

On site facilities: Refreshments, picnic areas, souvenir and bookshop, toilets (including disabled), working transport museum, including trams, narrow gauge railway, trolleybuses, steamrollers and other commercial and public transport vehicles. Unlimited free rides

Public opening: Sundays and Bank Holidays (11.00-17.00) April until end of September. Also Thursdays and Saturdays (13.00-17.00) June to September. More frequently during school holiday periods (see web site or leaflet).

Last admission 1 hour before closing

Special events: Please phone for details

Special notes: Limited facilities for the disabled. Pre-booked party rates

Membership details: From the above address

Steam Centre — East Anglian Railway Museum — Essex

Member: HRA, TT, AIM, EETB, EATL

Adjacent to Chappel Viaduct which is the most spectacular railway structure in East Anglia

Location: Chappel & Wakes Colne Station, near Colchester

OS reference: TL 898289

Operating society/organisation:

East Anglian Railway Museum, Chappel & Wakes Colne Station, Station Road, Wakes Colne, Essex CO6 2DS. Registered charity No 1001579

Telephone: Colchester (01206) 242524

Internet addresses: *E-mail:* information@earm.co.uk

Web site: www.earm.co.uk

Car park: On site

Access by public transport:
By rail: National Express East Anglia Chappel & Wakes Colne station.

By bus: First/Hedingham Omnibus service No 88 Colchester-Halstead (hourly). Sundays Network

Colchester No 88 Colchester-Halstead (every 2 hours)
On site facilities: Refreshments, bookshop, museum, signalboxes, souvenir shop, picnic area, visitor interpretation centre, miniature railway and toilets
Public opening:
Daily 10.00-16.30 or dusk
Special events: Steam Day — 25 March; Day out with Thomas — 6-9 April; Vintage Transport Weekend — 6/7 May; Railway Experience — 2 June; Fifties Day — 3 June; Railway Experience — 4 August ; War on the Line with Dad's Army — 5 August; Day out with Thomas — 25-27 August; 26th Chappel Beer Festival — 4-8 September; Small Engines Event — 6/7 October; Day out with Thomas and Santa — 2, 9, 16, 23 December. Some additional events are planned but not as yet confirmed
Family tickets: Available on all days (unlimited rides on steam days)
Special notes: Steam days as in Special Events list. Driver Experience Courses available on a number of dates throughout 2012; please phone for details or book online at http://www.earm.co.uk
  Three restored signalboxes, large goods shed and restoration shed. Original Victorian country junction station. Schools days and Santa steamings. Disabled visitors

Locomotives and multiple-units

Name	No	Origin	Class	Type	Built
A. J. Hill	69621	GER	N7	0-6-2T	1924
—	D2279	BR	04	0-6-0DM	1960
—	51213	BR	101	DMBS	1959
—	51505	BR	101	DMC	1959
—	56358	BR	101	DTC	1959
—	54365	BR	101	DTCL	1958
—	65217	BR	306	DMSO	1949
—	65417	BR	306	TBSO	1949
—	65617	BR	306	DTSO	1949

Industrial locomotives

Name	No	Builder	Type	Built
Jubilee	—	Bagnall (2542)	0-4-0ST	1936
—	11	Barclay (1047)	0-4-0ST	1905
Jeffery	2039	Peckett (2039)	0-4-0ST	1943
Penn Green	54	RSH (7031)	0-6-0ST	1941
—	AMW144	Barclay (333)	0-4-0DM	1938
—	23	Fowler (4220039)	0-4-0DH	1965
—	2029	Simplex (2029)	0-4-0PM	1920

Stock
4 ex-BR Mk 1 coaches (TSO, BCK, SK, BS), 1 ex-LNER TSO coach; 1 fully restored GER 6-wheel full brake; 1 GER fully restored 4-wheel coach; 1 ex-GER bogie coach; 1 SR PMV; 1 ex-BR 13-ton open wagon; 2 ex-BR 16-ton mineral wagons; 1 Lowmac wagon; 1 ex-LMS 12-ton open wagon; 1 Wickham trolley; 1 GWR Toad brake van; 1 ex-BR brake van; Somersham 'pump' trolley, 1 Grafton steam crane, 1 LMS 5 plank wagon, 1 BR cattle van (on loan ex-NRM), 1 BR special cattle van, 1 tube wagon, 1 Pooley van, 1 LNER fish van, 1 BR box van, 2 tank wagons, 1 Molasses tank wagon

welcome — prior notification appreciated. Guided tours by prior arrangement. Light refreshments daily

Membership details: Membership Secretary, c/o the museum
Membership journal: *Stour Valley Steam* — 3 times/year

Timetable Service	East Kent Railway	Kent

Member: HRA
The East Kent Light Railway Society was formed in 1985 with the aim of preserving the remaining 2-mile section of the Colonel Stephens light railway which originally ran from Shepherdswell to Wingham. Passenger-carrying operations between Shepherdswell and Eythorne started during 1995, and 1996 saw the first steam on the line for over 30 years. The railway became a charitable trust in 2003
Location: Station Road, Shepherdswell, Dover, Kent CT15 7PD
Internet address: *Web site:* www.eastkentrailway.co.uk

Locomotives and multiple-units

Name	No	Origin	Class	Type	Built
—	09025	BR	09	0-6-0DE	1961
—	50256	M/Cam	101	DMBS	1957
—	56343	M/Cam	101	DTC(L)	1958
—	65373*	BR	2EPB/416	DMBS	1956
—	77558*	BR	2EPB/416	DTS	1956
—	68001	BR	MLV/419	DMLV	1959
—	68002	BR	MLV/419	DMLV	1959
—	68008	BR	MLV/419	DMLV	1961
—	68009	BR	MLV/419	DMLV	1961
—	61229†	BR	412/CEP	DMSO(A)	1958
—	61230†	BR	412/CEP	DMSO(A)	1958
—	69013†	BR	412/BEP	TSRB	1959
—	70235†	BR	412/CEP	TBCK	1958
—	60154§	BR	205	DMBS	1957
—	60800§	BR	205	DTCL	1957
—	68008†	BR	ML 419	DMVL	1961

England

OS reference: TR 258483
Operating organisation: East Kent Railway Trust
Car park: Shepherdswell and Eythorne stations
Access by public transport: Main line trains to Shepherdswell station (adjacent) tel: 08457 484950
On site facilities: Shepherdswell — buffet, visitor centre, 5in miniature railway, model railway carriage (3 gauges), souvenir shop, Picnic area and toilets.
Eythorne — Signalbox, shop and toilets
Length of line: 2 miles
Public opening: Pre-season special day 25 March, then 1 April to 30 September on Sundays and Bank Holidays, also Saturdays on most special events and throughout August. First train leaves Shepherdswell at 11.00 on special event days, 11.30 on other dates
Special events: Travel for a pound — 25 March; Easter Bunnies — 6-9 April; Kids Go Free — 28/29 April; Classic Car Rally — 20 May; Members' Day — 27 May; Teddies' Weekend — 2-4 June; Buses and Commercial Vehicles (with Dover Transport Museum) — 17 June; Kids Go Free — 7/8 July; Classic Car Rally — 15 July; Kids Go Free

Name	No	Origin	Class	Type	Built
—	10096	SR	4COR	TTK	1938
—	11161	SR	4COR	MBT	1937
—	11825	SR	4COR	TCK	1937

§unit No 1101
*unit No 5759
†unit No 7105

Industrial locomotives

Name	No	Builder	Type	Built
Richborough Castle	—	E/Electric (D1197)	0-6-0D	1967
The Buffs	—	R/Hornsby (466616)	0-6-0DH	1961
Snowdown	—	Fowler (416002)	0-4-0DM	1952
St Dunstan	—	Avonside (2004)	0-6-0ST	1927

Rolling stock
LMS brake third, LMS full brake (BG), BR Mk 1 TSO, BR Mk 2 TSO and a selection of freight vehicles including an SR GUV

Owners
St Dunstan and diesel multiple-units the East Kent Railway Trust
LMS brake third the Walmer Model Railway Group
EMU vehicles the EPB Preservation Group
4COR vehicles the Southern Electric Group

— 11/12 August; Beer Festival — 25-27 August; EMU Weekend — 15/16 September; Ghost Trains — 27/28 October; Santa Specials — 1/2, 8/9, 15/16, 22-24 December (Santa hotline: 01634 856228)
Facilities for disabled: Disabled access to buffet at Shepherdswell, ramp to platforms at Eythorne, disabled toilets at Eythorne
Membership details: EKR Membership Secretary, Shepherdswell Station, Dover, Kent CT15 7PD
Membership journal: *East Kent Railway News,* 3 times a year

Timetable Service		East Lancashire Railway		Lancashire

Member: HRA, TT
A very popular railway run by the East Lancs Railway Society in close co-operation with local authorities, the line won the 1987 ARPS award. Visit the line to find out the cause of the line's popularity and success
Location: Bolton Street Station, Bury, Lancashire BL9 0EY
OS reference: SD 803109
Publicity Director: Graham Vevers
Operating society/organisation: East Lancashire Railway Preservation Society
Telephone: (0161) 764 7790
Internet address: *Web site:* www.east-lancs-rly.co.uk
Access by public transport: Main line services to Manchester, Bolton,

Locomotives and multiple-units

Name	No	Origin	Class	Type	Built
—	3855	GWR	2884	2-8-0	1942
—	7229	GWR	7200	2-8-2T	1935
—	42765	LMS	5P4F	2-6-0	1927
—	44871	LMS	5MT	4-6-0	1945
—	45337	LMS	5MT	4-6-0	1937
The Lancashire Fusilier	45407	LMS	5MT	4-6-0	1937
—	46428	LMS	2MT	2-6-0	1948
—	47324	LMS	3F	0-6-0T	1926
249 Squadron	34073	SR	BB	4-6-2	1948
Shaw Savill	35009	SR	MN	4-6-2	1945
British India Line	35018	SR	MN	4-6-2	1945
Duke of Gloucester	71000	BR	8P	4-6-2	1954
—	80097	BR	4MT	2-6-4T	1954
—	11506	BR	01	0-4-0DM	1956
—	D2062	BR	03	0-6-0DM	1959
—	D3232	BR	08	0-6-0DE	1956
—	08479	BR	08	0-6-0DE	1958
—	08700	BR	08	0-6-0DE	1960

Rochdale and Burnley. Metrolink from central Manchester to Bury Interchange. Various bus services also operate to Bury, Ramsbottom or Rawtenstall from the main line stations listed

On site facilities: Refreshments normally available when trains are running. Buffet car service on most trains. Souvenir shop, transport museum

Length of line: Approximately 12 miles

Public opening: Steam- and diesel-hauled services operate on Saturdays, Sundays and Bank Holidays throughout the year. Wednesday to Fridays 4 April to 28 September, Santa Specials (advance booking only) in December

Special events: Diesel Weekend — 3/4 March; DMU Theme Day — 17 March; Residents' Weekend — 24/25; Kids' Workshop at Bury Transport Museum — 4, 11 April; Classic Bike Rally — 8 April; Day out with Thomas — 5-7 May; 1940s Wartime Weekend — 2-4 June; Kids' Workshop at Bury Transport Museum — 6 June; Summer Diesel Weekend — 6-8 July; Kids' Workshop at Bury Transport Museum — Wednesdays during school summer holiday; 25th Anniversary of Re-opening — 25 July; Day out with Thomas — 3-5 August; Teddy Bears' Picnic and Treasure Hunt — 27 August; Vintage Transport Gathering — 9 September; Day out with Thomas — 6-7 October; Diesel Gala — 13/14 October; Autumn Steam Gala, Lancashire and Yorkshire Bus Gathering and Transport Collectors Fair — 20/21 October; Kids' Workshop at Bury Transport Museum — 24 October; Halloween Ghost Trains — 27/28 October; Diesel Theme Day — 3 November; Santa Specials — 1/2, 8/9, 15/16, 20-24 December. Irwell Valley Diner, Wine & Dine Trains (advance booking only — please apply for details)

Special notes: The Society re-opened the Bury-Summerseat-Ramsbottom section in 1987 and the Ramsbottom-Irwell-Rawtenstall section in 1991 with the Bury-Heywood section following in September 2003

Membership details: Stephen Lawton

Name	No	Origin	Class	Type	Built
—	08944	BR	08	0-6-0DE	1962
—	D9531	BR	14	0-6-0DH	1965
—	D8233	BR	15	Bo-Bo	1959
—	20087	BR	20	Bo-Bo	1961
—	D5054	BR	24	Bo-Bo	1960
—	D5705	BR	28	Co-Bo	1958
—	33109	BR	33	Bo-Bo	1960
—	33117	BR	33	Bo-Bo	1960
—	D7076	BR	35	B-B	1963
—	37109	BR	37	Co-Co	1963
—	37418	BR	37	Co-Co	1965
—	37518	BR	37	Co-Co	1962
—	37901	BR	37	Co-Co	1963
—	D335	BR	40	1Co-Co1	1961
—	D345	BR	40	1Co-Co1	1961
Onslaught	D832	BR	42	B-B	1961
3rd Carabinier	45135	BR	45	1Co-Co1	1961
—	D1501	BR	47	Co-Co	1962
Valiant	50015	BR	50	Co-Co	1967
Western Prince	D1041	BR	52	C-C	1962
Gordon Highlander	55016	BR	55	Co-Co	1961
Royal Scots Grey	55022	BR	55	Co-Co	1961
—	51192	M/Cam	101	DMBS	1958
—	56352	M/Cam	101	DTC (L)	1959
—	51485	Cravens	105	DMBC	1958
—	51532	BR	108	DMC	1959
—	51922	BR	108	DMBS	1960
—	56121	Cravens	105	DTC	1956
—	55001	BR	122	DMBS	1958
—	56289	BR	121	DTS	1961
—	60130†	BR	207	DMBS	1962
—	60904†	BR	207	DTS	1962
—	65451	BR	504	DMBS	1958
—	70549	BR	207	TS	1958
—	77172	BR	504	DTS	1958

†unit 207202

Industrial locomotives

Name	No	Builder	Type	Built
Sapper	WD132	Hunslet (3163)	0-6-0ST	1943
Earl Davies	—	Hunslet (2183)	0-6-0ST	1945
Gothenburg	32	H/Clarke (680)	0-6-0T	1903
	1	Barclay (1927)	0-4-0ST	1927
MR Mercury	1	Hibberd (3438)	4wDM	1950
Winfield	—	M/Rail (9009)	4wDM	1948
	4002	H/Clarke (D1076)	6wDM	1959

Stock

45 BR Mk 1 coaches; 19 BR Mk 2 coaches, 1 BR Mk3 coach; 1 GWR coach; 1 Bogie guard's coach; Cravens 50-ton steam crane RS1013/50 (1930), NER 5-ton hand crane DB915390 (1880) and Smiths 5-ton diesel crane (1939) plus over 80 goods vehicles

Owners

D335 and D345 the Class 40 Preservation Society
D5705 the Pioneer Diesel Locomotive Group
65451 and 77172 the Class 504 Group
35009, 44871, 45407 and 37518 Riley & Sons (Railways)
D5054 the East Lancs Type 2 Group
D1501 the Waterman Heritage Trust
Class 101 on loan from the National Railway Museum
D8233 the Class 15 Preservation Society

England

Membership journal: *The East Lancashire Railway News* — three copies yearly
Marketing name: East Lancs

50015 the Bury Valiant Group
55022 by Martin Walker

East Somerset Railway

Somerset

Member: HRA

The ESR seeks to portray a country branch line, and offers a warm personal welcome to all visitors, giving them a wonderful experience of the sights and sounds of steam travel. Cranmore is still one of the few preserved railways offering only steam-hauled trains

Contact: Booking Office
Headquarters: East Somerset Railway, Cranmore, Shepton Mallet, Somerset BA4 4QP
OS reference: ST 664429
Telephone: Cranmore (01749) 880417
Fax: (01749) 880764
Internet addresses: *E-mail:* info@eastsomersetrailway.com
Web site: www.eastsomersetrailway.com
Main station: Cranmore
Car park: Cranmore — free
Refreshment facilities: The Whistlestop Restaurant at Cranmore offers lunches, snacks, teas, etc. Group catering by arrangement. Picnic areas at Cranmore. Public and private Wine & Dine trains
Souvenir shop: Cranmore
On site facilities: Station shop. Signalbox. Children's play area. Engine shed and workshops open for viewing. Small railway museum and miniature railway
Depot: Engine shed and workshop at Cranmore West (0.25-mile from Cranmore)
Length of line: 2.5 miles
Passenger trains: Cranmore to Mendip Vale via Cranmore West and Merryfield Lane. Return trip takes c35min. Ticket allows unlimited travel on normal operating days. All trains are steam-hauled
Period of public operation: Weekends and Bank Holidays early April to end October. Weekends and

Locomotives

Name	No	Origin	Class	Type	Built
—	5637	GWR	5600	0-6-2T	1924
—	B110	LBSCR	E1	0-6-0T	1877

Industrial locomotives

Name	No	Builder	Type	Built
Lady Nan	1719	Barclay (1719)	0-4-0ST	1920
Meteor	1	RSH (7609)	0-6-0T	1950
Moorbarrow	47	RSH (7849)	0-6-0T	1955
Cattewater	—	Sentinel (10199)	4wDH	1964
—	39	Sentinel (10204)	0-4-0DH	1965

Stock
Numerous ex-BR Mk 1 coaches; 25 assorted wagons, mostly LMS and SR

Owners
5637 the 5637 Locomotive Group
Sentinel (10204) Stratford Railway Society

Wednesdays in June and July. Weekends, Wednesdays and Thursdays in August. Note: Sundays only in October. Open for Santa special trips in December (see timetable and web site). Shop and restaurant open on steaming days. Shop and office open April-December 09.30-15.30 Tuesdays to Fridays. Shop and office open January to March 09.30-14.30.
Engine sheds: Open throughout the year to visitors. On non-steaming days a suggested £2 donation to help with operational costs
Special events: Online booking available for some events.
Easter Family Fun — 6-9 April; Day out with Thomas — 5-7 May; Teddy Bears' Picnic — 2-4 June; Models and Miniatures — 28/29 July; Day out with Thomas — 10-12 August; The Way We Were 1930s-1950s— 25-27 August; Mendip Steam Dream — 8/9 September; Spooky Specials — 27/28, 31 October; Santa Specials — 2, 8/9, 15/16, 22-24 December
Wine & Dine trains

Lunch on the Mendip Belle — 18 March (Mother's Day), 22 April, 20 May, 17 June (Father's Day), 22 July, 5 August, 16 September, 21 October, 14 December
Murder Mystery on the Mendip Belle — 18 August, 22 September. Booking required for all Wine & Dine services. Booking available online at above web site
Facilities for disabled: All public areas and trains are accessible to mobility impaired visitors, please ask for help if required
Special notes: Footplate experience courses available, both half day and full day. Please call for availability, prices and brochure. School groups, children's parties, private parties and Wine & Dine by arrangement — please call to discuss your requirements
Membership details: Membership available online or call 01749 880417 for details
Membership journal: *Cuttings* — 4 per year

Location: Lakeside Country Park, Eastleigh
Headquarters: Eastleigh Lakeside Steam Railway, Lakeside Country Park, Wide Lane, Eastleigh, Hants SO50 5PE
Contact: Clive Upton
Telephone: 023 8061 2020
Internet addresses: *E-mail:* elr@steamtrain.co.uk
Web site: www.steamtrain.co.uk
Car parking: On site, free
On site facilities: Lakeside café open daily (except Christmas Day) 09.00-16.00
Length of line: 1.25 mile, 7.25in and 10.25in gauges
Period of public operation: Every weekend through the year, all school holidays and daily from 21 July to 16 September. 10.00-16.30 (16.00 in the winter)
Special events: Spring Locomotive Steam Gala — 18 March; Easter Egg Hunt — 8 April; Day out with Thomas — 26/27 May; Summer Locomotive Steam Gala — 24 June; Day out with Thomas — 7/8 July; Visiting Locomotives Weekend — 21/22 July; Day out with Thomas — 15/16 September; Super Power Weekend — 29/30 September; Big Four Weekend (GWR/LMS/LNER/SR) — 13/14 October; Small Engines Miniature Steam Gala — 28

Locomotives — 10.25/7.25in gauge

Name	No	Builder	Type	Built
Sandy River	7		2-4-2	1982
			rebuilt ELR	2008
The Monarch	1001	Bullock	4-6-2	1932
The Empress	1002	Bullock	4-6-2	1933
Edward VIII	2006	Bullock	4-6-2	1936
Coronation	6200	Dove	4-6-2	1946
Rob Roy	70055	Pullen	4-6-2	1948
Sir Nigel Gresley	4498	Kirkland	4-6-2	1964
Sir Arthur Heywood	7	Williamson	2-6-2*	1990
Ernest Henry Upton	1908	G&S Engineering	4-4-2	1937
William Baker	4789	Baker	4-4-2*	1947
Royal Scot	6100	Carling	4-6-0	late 1940s
Francis Henry Lloyd	3	Guest	4-8-4*	1959
Taw	—	Horsfield	2-6-2T	1999
Florence	92	ELR	0-6-0DH	1999
Blundells	932	Moody	4-4-0*	2000
Saint-Leonard	1A	Marshall	0-4-0-0-4-0*	2001
Lord Nelson	850	Moody	4-6-0	2007
Eastleigh	—	ELR	B-B	rebuilt 2008
Eurostar	3221	ELR	Bo-Bo	rebuilt 2008
Channel Packet	21C1	Moody	4-6-2	2011
Sanjo	—	Battle	0-4-0*	
Sgt Murphy	—	Marshall	0-6-0T*	
David Curwen	—	Curwen	2-6-0	

*7.25in gauge, remainder 10.25in

October; Santa Specials — 15/16, 22/23 December
Facilities for disabled: Toilet, wheelchair access to platform
Fares: *Standard class* — Single: £1.80 (all ages)
Return: Adults — £3.00; Children — £2.50.

First Class tickets available, three Return Ride tickets also available Children under 2 travel free. Children under 8 must be accompanied by an adult

Member: HRA
In 2011 the railway opened its whole line, some five miles north of Derby, to the market town of Wirksworth together with a further short branch from Wirksworth to Ravenstor. The Ravenstor line incorporates grades of 1 in 27 and provides a link to the High Peak Trail, National Stone Centre and Steeple Grange Light Railway.

Duffield station is adjacent to East Midlands Trains' Duffield station which is served by hourly, on weekdays, Nottingham, Derby and Matlock trains. Through tickets to Wirksworth can be purchased at any Network Rail station.

During 2012 it is hoped to re-open the one remaining wayside station along the line at Shottle
General Manager: Martin S. Miller
Headquarters: Wirksworth Station, Coldwell Street, Wirksworth, Derbyshire DE4 4FB

Telephone: 01629 823076
Internet addresses: *E-mail:* wirksworth_station@wyvernrail.co.uk
Web site: www.e-v-r.com
Main station: Wirksworth
Other stations: Ravenstor, Idridgehay, Shottle (opening 2012)
OS references: Wirksworth (SK 290541), Ravenstor (SK 287548), Gorsey Bank (SK 288533), Idridgehay (SK 290489),

Shottle (SK 304469),
Hazelwood (SK 319449),
Duffield (North) (SK 337439)
Car parking: Ample parking is available at Wirksworth but there is no car parking available at Ravenstor, Idridgehay or Shottle. Limited pay & display parking is available at Duffield main line station
Access by public transport:
By rail – to Duffield
By bus – to Wirksworth and Idridgehay, Derby/Belper/Idridgehay/Wirksworth/Matlock/Bakewell
Location of refreshment facilities: Wirksworth station
Souvenir shops & museum: Wirksworth station
Length of line: 9 miles. 200metre 2ft gauge line at Wirksworth
Opening times: Wirksworth station – daily March to November 10.00-16.00
Public operation: Weekends and Bank Holidays March to November, with Tuesdays mid-June to end September
Facilities for the disabled: Specially equipped toilets, fully accessible Museum Coach and all trains have wheelchair access
Special facilities: Up to 80 covers for meals in the splendid Ecclesbourne Pullman coaches located at Wirksworth. Charter trains can be run at anytime and the web site has details of prices. The web site also has links to steam and diesel experiences together with a popular Day with a Driver offer
Membership details: Ecclesbourne Valley Railway Association, 530 Kedleston Road, Derby DE22 2NG
Membership Journal:
Ecclesbourne Express – quarterly

Locomotive and multiple-units

Name	No	Origin	Class	Type	Built
—	20001	BR	20	Bo-Bo	1957
—	31414	BR	31	A1A-A1A	1961
—	33035	BR	33	Bo-Bo	1961
—	50170	Met/Cam	101	DMC(L)	1957
—	50599	BR	108	DMBS	1958
—	51073	Gloucester	119	DMBC	1958
—	51188	Met/Cam	101	DMBS	1958
—	51360	P/Steel	117	DMBS	1959
—	51505	Met/Cam	101	DMCL	1958
—	55006	Gloucester	122	DMBS	1958
—	59303	Met/Cam	101	TSL	1956
—	68500*	BR	489	GLV	1959
—	68506*	BR	489	GLV	1959
—	72501*	BR	491	FO	1973
—	72617*	BR	491	TS	1973
—	79900	BR	—	DMBS	1959

*former Gatwick Express hauled-stock

Industrial locomotives

Name	No	Builder	Type	Built
The Duke	—	Bagnall (2746)	0-6-0ST	1944
Henry Ellison	—	Barclay (2217)	0-4-0ST	1947
Brian Harrison	3	Barclay (2360)	0-4-0ST	1954
Cathryn	—	H/Clarke	0-6-0ST	1955
—	11520	R/Hornsby (319284)	0-4-0DM	1952
Sir Peter & Lady Hilton	—	R/Hornsby (402803)	0-4-0DE	1956
L. J. Breeze	—	Sentinel	0-6-0DE	1969
—*	—	Lister (29688)	0-4-0DM	1944

*2ft gauge

Stock
1 BR Newspaper van (used as DMU support vehicle); 1 Taylor Hubbard crane and runner wagon. Around 25 wagons for use in maintaining the line, including examples of Grampus and Dogfish hopper wagons, plus 5 Road/Rail vehicles

Owners
DMUs by Railcar Enterprises
20001 the Class 20 Association
33035 the Pioneer Diesel Group

Railway Centre	Eden Valley Railway	Cumbria

Member: HRA
The Eden Valley Railway plans to re-open all of the 6-mile railway which still connects with the famous Settle & Carlisle line at Appleby. This year's service is from Warcop to Dingley Dell, a distance of 2.25 miles.

Please contact or see web site for further details
Headquarters:
Eden Valley Railway Co and Eden Valley Railway Trust, Warcop Station, Warcop, Appleby, Cumbria CA16 6PR
Internet addresses: *E-mail:*

enquiries@evr-cumbria.org.uk
Web site: www.evr-cumbria.org.uk
Main station: Warcop
OS reference: NY 753156
Car park: Appleby
Access by public transport:
By bus: Grand Prix Coaches route 563 services from Penrith to

Brough (stops at Warcop station) (0870 6082608 for details). Timetable available online at http://www.cumbria.gov.uk/elibrary/content/internet/544/931/1099/4059 10948.pdf
By rail: Appleby on the Settle & Carlisle line.
By road: M6 jct 40, A66 east to Warcop (18 miles); M6 jct 38, A685, B6260 to Appleby (10 miles); A1 Scotch Corner, A66 west to Warcop (40 miles).
Period of public operation: Every Sunday 10 April to 18 September; Saturday 23 April; Mondays 25 April, 2, 30 May, 29 August; daily 25-30 July, 22-27 August. Train departures 11.00-16.00
Refreshment facilities: Light refreshments available on open weekends, picnic area
Membership details: Membership Secretary, 41 Firshill Walk, Firshill, Sheffield S4 7BR
Membership journal: *Eden Valley Railway Magazine* — 4 times/year

Locomotives and multiple-units

Name	No	Origin	Class	Type	Built
—	37042	BR	37	Co-Co	1962
—	37250	BR	37	Co-Co	1964
—	60108†	BR	205	DMBS	1957
—	60658†	BR	205	DMBS	1957
—	60808†	BR	205	DTC	1957
—	61798§	BR	412	DMSO	1961
—	61799§	BR	412	DMSO	1961
—	61804*	BR	412	DMSO	1961
—	61805*	BR	412	DMSO	1961
—	68003	BR	419	MLV	1960
—	68005	BR	419	MLV	1960
—	70229§	BR	412	TSOL	1958
—	70539*	BR	412	TSOL	1960
—	70354§	BR	412	TBCK	1959
—	70607*	BR	412	TBCK	1961

†unit 205009, *unit 2311, §unit 2315

Industrial locomotives

Name	No	Builder	Type	Built
—	21	Fowler (4220045)	0-4-0DH	1967
Darlington	1	RSH	0-6-0DH	1965
—	226	V/Foundry (5262)	0-4-0DM	1945
—	ND 3815	Hunslet (2389)	0-4-0DM	1941
—	—	Fowler (22971) rebuilt T/Hill (130C/1963)	0-4-0DH	1942
—	—	Drewry (2181) built by V/Foundry (5262)	0-4-0DM	1945

Stock
3 ex-BR Mk 1 coaches; 4 passenger-rated BR Mk 1 vans; 1 rail-mounted 15-ton diesel crane (DRT81343); selection of wagons for maintenance work including a snowplough and Wickham trolley and trailer

Museum	Electric Railway Museum	Warwickshire

Member: HRA
Originally commenced in 1983 as the Coventry Steam Railway Centre which was (and still is) the only standard gauge line in the county of Warwickshire, the Centre has been developed on a six acre greenfield site with no prior railway use. In 2000 the Suburban Electric Railway Association (SERA) bought controlling interest in the operating company and used the site to locate its collection of vintage electric multiple-units (EMUs); with the SERA collection and some privately owned EMU vehicles and electric locomotives on site it has become home to the largest collection of dc electric traction in preservation. This prompted a change of name and direction in 2006 for the

Electric multiple-units (complete)

Unit Nos	No	Origin	Class	Type	Built
4732	12795	BR	4SUB / 405	DMBSO	1951
	12354	BR	4SUB / 405	TS	1948
	10239	BR	4SUB / 405	TOS	1948
	12796	BR	4SUB / 405	DMBSO	1951
—	28690	LMS	503	DMBSO	1938
	29298	LMS	503	DTTO	1938
	29720	LMS	503	TCO	1938
5791/93	65321	BR	2EPB / 416/2	DMBSO	1954
	77112	BR	2EPB / 416/2	DTC	1954
4311	61287	BR	2HAP / 414	DMBSO	1959
	75407	BR	2HAP / 414	DTCL	1959
6307	14573	BR	2EPB / 416/3	DMBSO	1959
	16117	BR	2EPB / 416/3	DTS	1959
	61183	BR	501	DMBSO	1957
	75186	BR	501	DTBSO	1957
309616	977962	BR	309	BDTC	1962
	977963	BR	309	MBSO	1962
	977966	BR	309	DTSO	1962
309624	977963	BR	309	BDTC	1962
	977966	BR	309	MBSO	1962
	977967	BR	309	DTSO	1962

England

development of the site as the UK's only Electric Railway Heritage Centre. The site has witnessed some extensive development over the last couple of years

Location: At the boundary of Coventry Airport, south of the city centre and adjacent to the East Midlands Air Museum. Reached via Rowley Road, junction with A45/A46, Coventry Eastern Bypass — M6/M69/M1 link road. Follow signs to Coventry Airport and the entrance is on Rowley Road

Internet addresses: *E-mail:* chairman@electricrailwaymuseum.co.uk
Web site: www.electricrailwaymuseum.co.uk

OS reference: SP 349750

Access by public transport: National Rail services to Coventry, West Midlands bus route 1 from overbridge at north end of station to Tollbar End — 10-15min walk up Rowley Road to site

Operating society/organisation: Electric Railway Museum Ltd / Suburban Electric Railway Association

Length of line: Third of a mile (under construction)

Public opening: Due to ongoing construction work at the site there is no regular opening, but groups or parties can be accommodated by prior arrangement. Please check web site and railway press for details of other public opening/events.

Confirmed 2012 open days are: 14/15 April, 9/10 June, 8/9 September (Heritage Open Weekend)

Other dates to be added, please check web site for details

Please note that many items are tarpaulined for protection

Car park: On site, at main access gate

Facilities for disabled: Site is relatively flat, assistance will be given if requested by prior notice. There are no toilets on site

Electric multiple-units (from incomplete units)

From Unit No	No	Origin	Class	Type	Built
—	(7)	LOR*	—	TFO	1895
5176	15345	BR	415 / 4EPB	TSO	1954
—	RDB975386§†	BR	—	—	1958
7001	67300	BR	457	DMSO	1981
308136	75881	BR	308	BTSL	1961
321792	78037	BR	312/1	DTCOL	1976
312792	71205	BR	312/1	TSO	1976
307123	75023	BR	307	BDTS	1955
370001	49006	BR	370 / APT	PC	1983

*Liverpool Overhead Railway, built by Brown Marshall & Co
§built Eastleigh as a Hastings DEMU buffet car and converted to Lab 4 *Hastings* as a test vehicle for the APT project in the 1970s
†departmental unit number
49006 on loan from the National Railway Museum

Electric locomotives

Name	No	Builder	Type	Built
—	(1)	E/Electric (EE905)	4wBE/WE	1935
—	1	H/Leslie	Bo-Bo	1928
Doug Tottman	1	RSH	Bo-Bo	1945

Diesel locomotives

Name	No	Builder	Type	Built
Mazda	—	R/Hornsby (268881)	0-4-0DE	1950
(Crabtree)	—	R/Hornsby (338416)	4wDM	1953

Petrol locomotives

Name	No	Builder	Type	Built
(C. P. May)	—	Hibberd (2895)	4wPM	1944

Rolling stock

Coaches — Ex-City & South London Railway trailers Nos 135, 163
Wagons — 1 bogie tool van (converted from Maunsell Ironclad coach). High speed freight vehicle 1 (HSFV1), built Derby RTC 1966
Rail-mounted cranes — 1 steam crane, 1 hand crane

Steam Centre — Elsecar Heritage Railway — South Yorkshire

Member: HRA
The Elsecar Railway runs between Elsecar Heritage Centre and the canal basin at Hemingfield, through a scenic conservation area alongside the Elsecar branch of the Dearne & Dove Canal

Location/headquarters: Elsecar Heritage Centre, Wath Road,

Elsecar, Barnsley, South Yorkshire S74 8HJ
Telephone: (01226) 746746
Internet address: *Web site:* www.elsecarrailway.co.uk
Main station: Elsecar
Length of line: 1-mile, 20min journey
Car park location: On site, free

Access by public transport: Main rail line Elsecar from Sheffield, Huddersfield, Leeds
Refreshment facilities: On site
Souvenir shops: On site
On site facilities: Refreshments, antiques centre, crafts and souvenir shop, toilets
Museum: Attractions include

Educational Workshops, 'Playmania', Living History Centre, Bottle Collection, Hot Metal Press, Newcomen Beam Engine, working crafts people, various special events. Antiques centre open 7 days a week

Facilities for disabled: There are four disabled persons' toilets at different locations on the site. All buildings are fully wheelchair-accessible at ground floor level

Public opening: Site open daily 10.00-17.00. The railway operates a public service on Sundays 12.00-16.00 all year, also Halloween and Christmas events, special event days and Bank Holidays

Special events: Include Thomas the

Industrial locomotives

Name	No	Builder	Type	Built
Earl Fitzwilliam	1917	Avonside (1917)	0-6-0ST	1923
—	1	Avonside (1945)	0-6-0ST	1926
Gervase	—	Sentinel (6807)	0-4-0VBT	1928
—	—	Sentinel (9376)	4wVBT	1647
William	—	Sentinel (9656)	4wVBT	1956
Earl of Strafford	2895	YEC (2895)	0-6-0DH	1963
Mardy Monster	2150	Peckett (2150)	0-6-0ST	1954
Louise	—	Hunslet (6950)	0-6-0DH	1967

Stock

4 ex-BR Mk 1 coaches, 1 Wickham trolley

Tank Engine, Vintage Weekend, 1940s Weekend (and Saturday evening wartime dance) Christmas Fair, Halloween Hauntings and Santa Specials on the railway

Special notes: Free admission to site except for some special events when a charge will be made. Charges apply to railway and special events

---

Timetable Service	**Embsay & Bolton Abbey Steam Railway**	North Yorkshire

Member: HRA, TT

Yorkshire's 'Friendly Line' operates from Embsay station built in 1888. The railway is very family-orientated with many events for children. The enthusiast is not forgotten, with one of the finest collections of ex-industrial tank engines in Britain. The railway is currently constructing a new museum and workshop complex, and the line's extension to Bolton Abbey opened in 1997. Bolton Abbey station has been built to the original Midland Railway style. An atmosphere of the rural branch line prevails, which is operated by ex-industrial locomotives

Operating Committee: N. Hubbs

Business & Marketing Manager: Stephen Walker. Tel: 01756 710614 (ext 3). Fax: 01756 710720

Internet address: Web site: www.embsayboltonabbeyrailway. org.uk

Location: Bolton Abbey Station, Bolton Abbey, Skipton, Yorkshire BD23 6AF

OS reference: SE 007533

Operating society/organisation: Yorkshire Dales Railway Museum Trust

Telephone: 01756 710614, 24hr Talking Timetable 01756 795189

Car parks: Embsay and Bolton Abbey

Locomotives and multiple-units

Name	No	Origin	Class	Type	Built
—	6619	GWR	5600	0-6-2T	1928
—	D2203	BR	04	0-6-0DM	1952
—	08054	BR	08	0-6-0DE	1953
—	08700	BR	08	0-6-0DE	1960
—	08773	BR	08	0-6-0DE	1960
—	NCB 38 (D9513)	BR	14	0-6-0DH	1964
—	D5600	BR	31	A1A-A1A	1960
—	31119	BR	31	A1A-A1A	1959
—	D5600	BR	31	A1A-A1A	1960
—	37294	BR	37	Co-Co	1965
—	47004	BR	47	Co-Co	1963
—	3170	NER railcar	—	4w-4PE	1903

Industrial locomotives

Name	No	Builder	Type	Built
Annie	9	Peckett (1159)	0-4-0ST	1908
Gladiator	8	H/Clarke (1450)	0-6-0ST	1922
Slough Estates No 5	—	H/Clarke (1709)	0-6-0ST	1939
Ann	—	Sentinel (7232)	4wVB	1927
Beatrice	7	Hunslet (2705)	0-6-0ST	1945
Airedale	3	Hunslet (1440)	0-6-0ST	1923
Wheldale	—	Hunslet (3186)	0-4-0ST	1944
York No 1	—	Yorkshire (2474)	0-6-0ST	1949
Illingworth	—	H/Clarke (1208)	0-6-0ST	1916
—	140	H/Clarke (1821)	0-6-0T	1948
Spitfire	S112	Hunslet (2414)	0-6-0ST	1942
Wheldale	S134	Hunslet (3168)	0-6-0ST	1944
Sir Robert Peel	8	Hunslet (3776)	0-6-0ST	1952
—	69	Hunslet (3785)	0-6-0ST	1953
—	—	Hunslet (3788)	0-6-0ST	1953
Monkton No 1	—	Barclay (2320)	0-4-0ST	1952
—	22	RSH (7086)	0-6-0ST	1943
Norman	—			

Access by public transport:
Pennine bus from Skipton, National Park bus from Ilkley

On site facilities: Souvenir shop at Bolton Abbey and Embsay — transport and industrial archaeological bookshop at Embsay

Catering facilities: Buffet and bar on most trains. Buffet at both Bolton Abbey and Embsay stations. Special charters can be arranged, meals for parties can be arranged on normal service trains, subject to advance booking, please write for further details

Length of line: 4.5 miles

Public opening: Steam trains run every Sunday throughout the year, weekends from April to October, Tuesdays in May, June, early July, daily 21 July to 1 September

Special events: Volunteering Open Day — 25 March; Day out with Thomas — 6-9 April; Branchline Weekend / Mixed Traffic Event — 5-7 May; Day out with Thomas — 2-5 June; Day out with Thomas — 25-27 August; 1940s Weekend — 8/9 September; Santa Trains — 25 November, 1/2, 8/9, 15/16, 22/23 December; After Christmas Running — 26, 30 December

Special notes: Steam rides are on the 4.5-mile line to the new station and picnic area at Bolton Abbey. Old Midland Railway buildings, fine collection of industrial locomotives

Membership details: Membership

Name	No	Builder	Type	Built
—	68005	RSH (7169)	0-6-0ST	1945
Thomas	4	RSH (7661)	0-4-0ST	1950
H. W. Robinson	—	Fowler (4100003)	0-4-0DM	1946
—	—	Fowler (4200003)	0-4-0DM	1948
—	MDE15	B/Drewry (2136)	4wDM	1938
—	887	R/Hornsby (394009)	4wDM	1955
—	—	Wickham (7610)	2w-2PMR	1957
—	—	R/Hornsby	4wDM	1957
—	—	R/Hornsby (394009)	4wDM	1955
Meaford	—	Barclay (440)	0-4-0DH	1958
—	36	H/Clarke (D1037)	0-6-0DM	1958

The following are 2ft gauge

—	—	Lister (9993)	4wPM	1938
—	—	Lister (10225)	4wPM	1938
—	—	R/Hornsby (175418)	4wDM	1936
—	—	R/Hornsby	4wDM	—
—	—	M/Rail (8979)	4wDM	1946
—	—	M/Rail (5213)	4wDM	1930
—	—	Simplex (60SD754)	4wDM	1980
—	—	Simplex (60SD755)	4wDM	1980

Stock
18 ex-BR Mk 1 coaches (SK, CK, 2xBCK, 5xTSO, 2xRMB, 1xBSO(T), 1xRBR and 1xSLS), 4 ex-LNER coaches; 2 SR parcels vans; Freight stock and service vehicles, SR and GW brakes. NER autocoach No 3453 Stephen Middleton collection of vintage coaches

Note
Items on display may vary

Owner
3170 and 3453 the NER Autocar Trust (www.electricautocar.co.uk)

Secretary at above address
Membership journal: *Dale Steam YDR News* — 4 times/year

Timetable Service — Epping-Ongar Railway — Essex

Member: HRA

A preserved section at the northern end of the former London Underground Central Line. The line has been closed to the public for improvement works and should re-open in 2012. Please check web site for updates

Operating society/organisation:
Epping Ongar Railway, Ongar Station, High Street, Ongar, Essex CM5 9BN

Contact: Simon Hanney
Telephone: 01277 365200
Internet address: *Web site:* http://eorailway.co.uk
Main station: Ongar

Locomotives and multiple-units

Name	No	Origin	Class	Type	Built
Pitchford Hall	4953	GWR	Hall	4-6-0	1929
—	4141	GWR	5101	2-6-2T	1946
—	03119	BR	03	0-6-0DM	1959
—	03170	BR	03	0-6-0DM	1960
—	D3462	BR	08	0-6-0DE	1957
—	D7523	BR	25	Bo-Bo	1963
—	31438	BR	31	A1A-A1A	1959
—	D6729	BR	37	Co-Co	1961
—	51342	P/Steel	117	DMS	1959
—	51384	P/Steel	117	DMS	1959
—†	60110	BR	205	DMBS	1957
—†	60810	BR	205	DTS	1957
—	76773	BR	421 (3-CIG)	DTC	1971
—	76884	BR	421 (3-CIG)	DTC	1971
—	62411	BR	421 (3-CIG)	MBSO	1971

Other station: North Weald
OS references: Ongar TL 551035;
North Weald TL 496036
Access by public transport: Use London Underground Central Line to Epping, then local bus service to Ongar or North Weald. Local buses also available from Harlow and Brentwood
Length of line: 6.5 miles (4.5 miles operational)
Public opening: Please see web site for details
Special events: Please see web site
Facilities for disabled: Level access to platforms. Ramp available for wheelchair access to guard's compartment
Membership details: Epping Ongar Railway Volunteer Society, c/o above address
Membership journal: *Mixed Traffic* — quarterly

Name	No	Origin	Class	Type	Built
—	(1008)	Finnish*	Hr1	4-6-2	1948
—	1060	Finnish*	Tr1	2-8-2	1954

†unit 205 205
*1,524mm gauge, on static display
Class 421 unit is named *Farringford*

Industrial locomotives

Name	No	Builder	Type	Built
Isabel	—	H/Leslie (3437)	0-6-0ST	1919
—	—*	R/Hornsby (398616)	4wDM	1956
—	—	R/Hornsby (512572)	4wDM	1965

*for spares only

Stock
3 BR Compartment coaches, 5 BR Mk1 coaches, 8 BR Mk 2 coaches, 5-ton crane with matching jib runner, Shark brake van, 38-ton Rectank, Macaw B wagon, Fruit D van, Dogfish ballast hopper Twin-bin mechanically powered ballast hopper and box/ferry vans, Tamper-liner 73241, 1 Finnish Railway wooden-bodied carriage (1,524mm gauge being converted to static gift shop facility)

Evesham Vale Light Railway

Steam Centre | Worcestershire

Member: BGLR
The Evesham Vale Light Railway takes you through the old apple orchards to a picnic and viewing area overlooking some of the most picturesque scenery in the Vale of Evesham. Steam locomotives are used on most days and it is possible to break your journey and walk to the river, returning on a later train. The railway is situated within Evesham Country Park, 1 mile to the north of the historic town of Evesham. Enjoy a day out and stroll around the 130 acre estate, including a mile and quarter of the River Avon. Visit the Ark Animal Sanctuary, browse in the relaxed atmosphere of the courtyard shops or try some of the freshly prepared lunches and snacks in the licensed Apple Barn restaurant
Location/headquarters: Evesham Vale Light Railway, Evesham Country Park, Twyford, Nr Evesham, Worcestershire WR11 4TP
Contact: Adrian and Sandra Corke
Telephone: 01386 422282
Internet addresses: *E-mail:* enquiries@evlr.co.uk
Web site: www.evlr.co.uk
Main station: Twyford (adjacent to

Locomotives — 15in gauge

Name	No	Builder	Type	Built
John	103	B/Lowke	4-4-2	1921
Count Louis	32	B/Lowke	4-4-2	1924
St Egwin	312	Exmoor Steam Rly	0-4-0T+T	2003
Dougal	3	S/Lamb	0-6-2T	1970
Sludge	JGF4	Lister (41545)	4wDM	1955
R. H. Morse	712*	Morse	0-4-0	1950
Prince William	5751*	G&S	4-6-2	1949
Bessie	—	Eddy/Nowell	4wDM	2002
—	359	Morse (82)	4-4-0PM	1939

*in syorage awaiting overhaul

Note: Engines can be viewed, by prior arrangement, on days when the railway is operating. No access when the railway is closed

Evesham Country Park car park)
Other station: Evesham Vale (in the country park)
OS reference: SP 0446
On site facilities: Large car and coach park, licensed restaurant within park shopping complex. Small souvenir shop at Twyford station
Length of line: 1.25 miles, 15in gauge
Locomotive and carriage depots: Adjacent to Twyford station — viewing available on request
Access by public transport: By train to Evesham main line station

then bus — Stagecoach No 28 — from Evesham bus station, hourly service will stop close to park entrance, then 15min walk to Twyford station
Public opening: Every weekend throughout the year plus Bank Holidays and main school holidays. Phone 24hr information line 01386 422282 or visit web site (www.evlr.co.uk) to check dates and for special events. Trains run every half-hour from 10.30 to 17.00 (16.00 November to March)
Facilities for disabled: Wheelchair facilities on all trains

England

Exbury Gardens Railway

Steam Centre | **Hampshire**

Member: BGLR, HRA
A comparatively new line with purpose-built locomotives and rolling stock around part of Exbury Gardens. Train fare is in addition to entrance fee
Location/headquarters: Exbury Gardens, Exbury, Southampton SO45 1AZ
Contact: Ian Wilson (railway foreman). Tel: 023 8089 2898
Telephone: 023 8089 1203
Internet address: *Web site:* www.exbury.co.uk
Access by public transport: Main line trains to Brockenhurst. New Forest Explorer bus calls into Gardens during summer holidays. Visit: www.newforesttour.info
Car park: On site, free
On site facilities: Souvenir shop, with railway memorabilia (including prints and DVDs), refreshments and toilets adjacent to main car park
Length of line: 1.25 miles, 12.25in gauge

Locomotives — 12.25in gauge

Name	No	Builder	Type	Built
Rosemary	—	Exmoor (315)	0-6-2T	2001
Naomi	—	Exmoor (316)	0-6-2T	2002
Eddy	—	Exmoor	0-4-0DH	2001
Mariloo	—	Exmoor	2-6-0	2008

Stock 10 coaches

Public opening: 10 March to 4 November. Limited winter opening for Santa Steam Specials.
Visitors are able to enter the locomotive shed to see Exbury's locomotives and railway memorabilia
Special events: Easter at Exbury — 7-9 April; The Glory of the Garden — 14 April-10 June; Festival of Autumn Colour — 1 October-4 November; Exbury Ghost Train — 27 October-4 November; Exbury Santa Steam Specials — 8/9, 15/16, 22/23 December
Facilities for disabled: Yes, access to 4 coaches

Tickets:
£4.00 per person (includes voluntary Gift Aid donation), Rover Ticket (unlimited rides) available. Garden tickets, adults £10.50, seniors/concessions £10.00, children under 16 free.
Season tickets available
Special facilities:
Engine shed licensed for civil weddings and partnerships and for private hire.
Railway available for private charter (£4 per person, or a minimum 'steam-up' fee of £100)

Foxfield Steam Railway

Timetable Service | **Staffordshire**

Member: HRA
The railway was built in 1893 to carry coal from Foxfield Colliery to the North Staffordshire Railway at Blythe Bridge. Following closure of the colliery in 1965 the line was rescued for preservation. The Society is working towards rebuilding the railway a further 0.75 mile down the famous Foxfield Bank to the site of Foxfield Colliery as part of a half million pound lottery grant
Chairman: S. Turner
Headquarters: Foxfield Steam Railway, Blythe Bridge, Stoke-on-Trent

Industrial locomotives

Name	No	Builder	Type	Built
Bellerophon*	—	Haydock Foundry (C)	0-6-0WT	1874
—	1827	B/Peacock (1827)	0-4-0ST	1879
—	6	R/Heath	0-4-0ST	1886
—	4101	Dübs (4101)	0-4-0CT	1901†
Henry Cort	—	Peckett (933)	0-4-0ST	1903††
Millom	—	Avonside (1563)	0-4-0ST	1908†
Moss Bay	—	K/Stuart (4167)	0-4-0ST	1920††
Cranford	—	Avonside (1919)	0-6-0ST	1924†
Helen	—	Simplex (2262)	4wDM	1924
Marston No 3	—	H/Leslie (3581)	0-6-0ST	1924†
—	—	K/Stuart (4388)	0-4-0ST	1926•
Lewisham	—	Bagnall (2221)	0-6-0ST	1927
Rom River	—	K/Stuart (4421)	6wDM	1929
Boots No 1	—	Barclay (1984)	0-4-0F	1930††

Postal address: PO Box 1967,
Stoke-on-Trent ST4 8YT
Telephone:
(01782) 396210 or (01782) 259667
Fax: (01782) 396210
Internet address: *Web site:*
www.foxfieldrailway.co.uk
Main station: Blythe Bridge
(Caverswall Road)
OS reference: SJ 957421
Car park: Blythe Bridge
Access by public transport: Main
line railway Blythe Bridge (400yd).
PMT bus service to Blythe Bridge
Refreshment facilities: Buffet and
real ale bar at Blythe Bridge
Souvenir shop: Blythe Bridge
Passenger trains: Steam-hauled
trains operate from Blythe Bridge
(Caverswall Road) to Dilhorne Park
and return
Family ticket: Available (2 adults
+ 2 children or 1 adult + 4 children)
Length of line: 3.5 miles. Current
operation over 2.5 miles of line
Period of public operation: Steam
trains operate Sundays and Bank
Holiday Mondays Easter-end
October inclusive, also Wednesdays
in July and August. Trains run
between Blythe Bridge and
Dilhorne Park
Special events: Recruitment
Weekend — 14/15 April; Steam
Cream Landcruise Train —
22 April, 20 May, 24 June, 11 and
29 July, 15 and 18 August,
23 September, 28 October;
Miniature Railway Weekend —
5/6 May; Local Residents' Day —
7 May; Beer Festival — 2-5 June;
Fathers Day Morris Minor Rally —
17 June; Wickham Rally Weekend

Name	No	Builder	Type	Built
Ironbridge No 1	—	Peckett (1803)	0-4-0ST	1933††
Spondon No 2	—	E/Electric (1130)	4wBE	1939††
Roker	—	RSH (7006)	0-4-0CT	1940††
Hawarden	—	Bagnall (2623)	0-4-0ST	1940
—	WD820	B/Drewry (2157)	0-4-0DM	1942
(Hercules)	242915	R/Hornsby (242915)	4wDM	1946
—	11	Peckett (2081)	0-4-0ST	1947•
Whiston	—	Hunslet (3694)	0-6-0ST	1950
—	9535	Sentinel (9535)	4wVBGT	1952•
Florence No 2	—	Bagnall (3059)	0-6-0ST	1953†
—	—	Hibberd (3716)	4wDM	1955
Wimblebury	—	Hunslet (3839)	0-6-0ST	1956
(Gas-oil)	88DS	R/Hornsby (408496)	4wDM	1957†
Wolstanton No 3	—	Bagnall (3150)	0-6-0DM	1960
B. R. C. (Megan)	—	Thomas Hill (103C)	0-4-0DH	1957
Rachel	—	R/Hornsby (423637)	0-4-0DE	1958
(Roman)	165DS	R/Hornsby (424841)	0-4-0DE	1960
Ludstone	—	YEC (3207)	0-4-0DH	1961
Leys	—	Bagnall (2868)	0-6-0DE	1962
Meaford No 4	—	Barclay (486)	0-6-0DH	1964

†under overhaul
††static exhibit
•awaiting overhaul
*on loan for ten years

Stock
3 ex-BR Mk 1 CK coaches; 1 ex-BR Mk 2a TSO coach; 4 other coaches;
3 scenery vans (converted for other uses); 79 assorted wagons, 16-ton
mineral wagons; 1 rail-mounted self-propelled diesel-electric crane

Owner
Bellerophon the Vintage Carriages Trust

— 14/15 July; Teddy Bears Day —
8, 26 August; Eastern European Car
Rally — 8/9 Septemberber; Autumn
Steam Gala— 20/21 October; Santa
Specials — 1/2, 8/9, 15/16, 22-24
December
Facilities for disabled: Access to
majority of Caverswall Road station
is on the level; disabled toilets.
Advance notice essential for those
wishing to travel on the train.
Induction loop
Membership journal: *Foxfield
News* — quarterly

Timetable Service	Gartell Light Railway	Somerset

Owned and operated by three
generations of the Gartell family,
the Gartell Light Railway offers
visitors the chance to travel by
train along the route of the old
Somerset & Dorset Joint Railway.
A half-mile section of the line from
Pinesway Junction to Park Lane
runs along the old S&D trackbed,
while work has started on an
extension northwards from
Pinesway Junction along the S&D
formation towards Templecombe.

Locomotives — 2ft gauge

Name	No	Builder	Type	Built
Amanda	1	GLR	Bo-BoDH	2003
Andrew	2	Baguley-Drewry	4wDH	1973
Alison	5	A/Keef (10)	4wDH	1983
Mr G	6	N. Dorset Loco Wks	0-4-2T	1998
Jean	9	N. Dorset Loco Wks	0-4-0T+T	2009

Rolling stock — coaches: 9 fully enclosed bogie coaches

Rolling stock — wagons: goods guard's van, tool van, beer van, milk
tanker, open wagon, bogie p-way gang/tool van, bogie hopper, bogie open,
bogie well, bogie flat and bogie crane

England

A flyover has been constructed to carry the extension over the existing line to the terminus at Common Lane and tracklaying has begun. On most open days a three-train service is operated, with departures every 15min and trains crossing at Pinesway Junction. The GLR is fully signalled using a variety of upper and lower quadrant, colour light and shunt signals controlled by two full size signalboxes. The GLR's first steam locomotive, a locally built 0-4-2T, specially designed to cope with the steep gradients and sharp curves of the section from Common Lane up to Pinesway Junction, entered service in 1998. The line's newest locomotive, an 0-4-0 tender tank engine, again built specially for the line, entered service at the beginning of the 2009 season

Location/headquarters: Gartell Light Railway, Common Lane, Yenston, Nr Templecombe, Somerset BA8 0NB

Telephone: 01963 370752

Internet address: *Web site:* http://www.glr-online.co.uk

General Manager: John Gartell

Main station: Common Lane

Other stations: Pinesway Junction, Park Lane

Car park: Large free car park at Common Lane

OS reference: ST 718218

Access by public transport: 1.5 miles south-east of Templecombe railway station

Refreshment facilities: Refreshment room at Common Lane serving a range of hot and cold snacks and drinks. Lakeside picnic area at Pinesway Junction and trackside picnic area at Common Lane

Visitor centre: Common Lane

Souvenir shop: Common Lane

Depot: Common Lane (not open to public)

Length of line: 0.75-mile

Facilities for disabled: Two of the three trains in service have accommodation for a disabled visitor in a wheelchair

Special facilities: Clean, well-maintained independent caravan site with running water close to the railway.

The Pines function suite available for outside hire, with entertainment licence, licensed bar and seating for 200; ideal for weddings, anniversaries, classic car and motorcycle rallies, children's parties, etc. Train rides can be arranged

Period of public operation: Last Sunday of the month, April-October, Bank Holiday Mondays and every Sunday in August. 10.30-16.30

Special events: Steam & Vintage Show (vintage lorries, classic cars and motorcycles, miniature traction engines, live steam model railways etc) — 30/31 July

Museum — Gloucester Waterways Museum — Glos

Location: Gloucester Docks — signposted 'Historic Docks'

OS Reference: SO 826183

Operating society/organisation: Gloucester Waterways Museum, The Waterways Trust, Llanthony Warehouse, Gloucester Docks, Gloucester GL1 2EH

Tel: (01452) 318200

Fax: (01452) 318202

Internet addresses: *E-mail:* bookingsnwm@thewaterwaystrust.org

Web site: www.gloucesterwaterwaysmuseum.org.uk

Car parks: Pay & display outside museum. Free coach parking

Access by public transport: Main line Gloucester station, 1 mile

On site facilities: Tea room, souvenir and specialist bookshop (canal-related with some railway literature). School room/children's holiday activities. Working demonstrations vary. Trip boats and other museums in docks

Industrial locomotive

Name	No	Builder	Type	Built
—	1	A/Barclay (2126)	0-4-0F	1942

Ex-Gloucester Corporation, Castle Meads Power Station, Gloucester Docks, now on static display

Rolling stock

William Balmforth of Rodley crane, c1880. Sharpness Docks open wagons and Gloucester-built flat wagon, Manchester Ship Canal (ex-GWR) Toad brake van

Facilities for disabled: Full facilities, lifts, ramps, toilets. All indoor displays, quaysides and tea room accessible. Floating exhibits not accessible

Public opening: Summer (April-October) — daily, 10.00-17.00, Winter (November-March) — daily, 11.00-16.00. Closed 25/26, 31 December and 1 January

Special events: Preservation, modellers' & craft events; leisure learning courses (send for further information)

Membership details: 'Friends' support organisation. Membership Secretary, c/o museum address, Volunteers active in restoration/fundraising. Winter meetings programme

Membership journal: *Llanthony Log* — quarterly

Gloucestershire Warwickshire Railway

Member: HRA

Part of an ambitious project to link Cheltenham with Stratford, much has been done to re-create the railway and buildings that made up this cross-country route. The railway is home to many owners of private locomotives and rolling stock, so from time to time the items on display may vary. The extension from Gotherington to Cheltenham Racecourse opened in April 2003 with the extension to Broadway in hand.

Location: Toddington station, Toddington

OS reference: SO 050322

Operating society/organisation: Gloucestershire Warwickshire Steam Railway plc, The Station, Toddington, Cheltenham, Glos GL54 5DT

Telephone: Toddington (01242) 621405

Internet addresses:
E-mail: enquiries@gwsr.com
Web site: www.gwsr.com

Main station: Toddington

Other public stations: Winchcombe, Cheltenham Racecourse, Gotherington (request halt)

Access by public transport: Hourly service from Cheltenham to Greet for Winchcombe station. Local bus service Castleways will answer timetable queries on (01242) 602949. Regular Stagecoach service to Cheltenham station. Racecourse park & ride (approx half mile to GWR station)

Car park: All stations, except Gotherington Halt

On site facilities: Sales, catering, narrow gauge rides, toilets, new children's play area

Length of line:
Standard gauge 10 miles
Narrow gauge 1 mile

Public opening: On non-operating mid-weekdays the station is closed. Public services: weekends, Bank Holiday Mondays, between March and November, some summer weekdays

Special events: Mothering Sunday — 18 March; Easter Eggspress — 9 April; Spring Ale & Steam

Locomotives and multiple-units

Name	No	Origin	Class	Type	Built
—	2807	GWR	2800	2-8-0	1905
—	4270	GWR	4200	2-8-0T	1919
Kinlet Hall	4936	GWR	6959	4-6-0	1929
Raveningham Hall	6960*	GWR	6959	4-6-0	1944
Owsden Hall	6984	GWR	6959	4-6-0	1948
Foremarke Hall	7903	GWR	6959	4-6-0	1949
—	7069	LMS	—	0-6-0DE	1939
Peninsular & Oriental SNCo	35006	SR	MN	4-6-2	1941
—	45160†	LMS	8F	2-8-0	1941
—	76077	BR	4MT	2-6-0	1956
Black Prince	92203§	BR	9F	2-10-0	1959
—	03069	BR	03	0-6-0DM	1959
—	D2182	BR	03	0-6-0DM	1952
—	08927	BR	08	0-6-0DE	1962
—	D9553	BR	14	0-6-0DH	1965
—	D8137	BR	20	Bo-Bo	1966
—	24081	BR	24	Bo-Bo	1960
—	26043	BR	26	Bo-Bo	1959
—	37215	BR	37	Co-Co	1964
Clydebridge	37324	BR	37	Co-Co	1962
Phaeton	45149	BR	45	1Co-Co1	1961
—	47105	BR	47	Co-Co	1963
Freightliner 1995	47376	BR	47	Co-Co	1965
—	73129	BR	73	Bo-Bo	1966
—	51950	BR	108	DMBS	1960
—	52062	BR	108	DMC	1960
—	51339	P/Steel	117	DMBS	1959
—	51363	P/Steel	117	DMBS	1959
—	51382	P/Steel	117	DMS	1959
—	51405	P/Steel	117	DMS	1959
—	55003	P/Steel	122	DMBS	1958
—	59510	P/Steel	117	TCL	1959

*on loan to West Somerset Railway for 2012
†built as LMS No 8274, used by War Department and sold to Turkish State Railways (TCDD) post war, carries TCDD livery as 45160
§on loan to North Norfolk Railway

Industrial locomotives

Name	No	Builder	Type	Built
Wemyss Private Rly	15	Barclay (2138)	0-6-0ST	1945
—	19	Fowler (4240016)	0-6-0DH	1964
—	21	Fowler (4210130)	0-4-0DM	1957
John	—	Peckett (1976)	0-4-0ST	1939
—	1	Drewry/RSH (2573/7859)	0-6-0DM	1956
—	2	Drewry/RSH (2574/7860)	0-6-0DM	1956
—	—	Hunslet (5511)	0-6-0DM	1957
—	372	YEC (2760)	0-6-0DE	1957

Stock

4 ex-GWR coaches; 59 ex-BR coaches; 4 ex-LMS coaches; Baguley/Drewry inspection vehicle; 2 Wickham trolleys; plus over 150 wagons (including 12 brake vans, 45-ton steam crane, 18-ton diesel crane)

Weekend — 19/20 May; Day out with Thomas — 26/27 May; Jack Boskett Photographic Exhibition — 31 May to 31 July; Classic Vehicle Day — 10 June; Midsummer Murder Mystery — 16 June; GWR Sponsored Walk — 17 June; Walkers' Sunday — 15 July; Classic Bus Rally — 22 July; GWR C&W Dept Open Weekend — 18/19 August; Autumn Ale & Steam Weekend — 15/16 September; Classic Vehicle Day — 16 September; Day out with Thomas — 22/23 September; Race the Train — 13 October; Steam & Scream — 27 October; Santa Specials — selected dates in December; Mince Pie New Year Specials — 26 December-2 January 2013
Special notes: The site is being developed as the headquarters of the railway between Cheltenham and Stratford. The GWR owns the railway land between Cheltenham and Broadway and operates over 10 miles from Toddington to Cheltenham Racecourse with an intermediate station at Winchcombe.

No public access to restoration area or sheds except on guided tours. Please ring for details.

A major landslip at Gotherington closed the line from Gotherington to Cheltenham Race Course in May 2010. This section should re-open in during 2012 along with an extension northwards to Laverton.

Guest locomotives will be operating during the year. Long-term restoration projects GWR No 2807 and LMS '8F' No 45160 returned to steam during 2010.

Round-trip tickets give unlimited travel on day of purchase.

Family tickets available

Owners
2807 the Cotswold Steam Preservation Ltd (www.gwr2807.co.uk)
35006 the P&O Locomotive Society
45160 (8274) and 7069 the Churchill (8F) Locomotive Co
92203 David Shepherd
26043 and 45149 the Cotswold Mainline Diesel Group
D9553 Cotswold Diesel Preservation Group
37215 and 37324 the Growler Group
47105 and 47376 the Brush Type 4 Fund
D8137 the English Electric Type 1 Group
51363, 51405, 55003 and 59510 the Cotswold Diesel Railcar Ltd

North Gloucestershire Railway
Industrial narrow gauge locomotives (2ft gauge)

Name	No	Builder	Type	Built
Isibutu	5	Bagnall (2820)	4-4-0T	1946
George B	—	Hunslet (680)	0-4-0ST	1898
Chaka	—	Hunslet (2075)	0-4-2T	1940
Justine	—	Jung (939)	0-4-0WT	1906
Brigadelok	—	Henschel (15968)	0-8-0T	1918
—	2	Lister (34523)	4wDM	1949
—	3	M/Rail (4565)	4wPM	1928
Spitfire	—	M/Rail (7053)	4wPM	1937
—	1	R/Hornsby (166010)	4wDM	1932
—	L5	R/Hornsby (181820)	4wDM	1936
—	—	R/Hornsby (354028)	4wDM	1953

Stock
3 coaches; 11 wagons

Facilities for disabled: Visitors with impaired mobility welcomed, please inform staff in advance if possible. Wheelchairs can be accommodated in specially converted carriages. The platform at Racecourse is reached via a steep slope which may be difficult for some visitors. Disabled toilets and parking at all stations
Special facilities: Steam and diesel experience courses. Hire of train (steam or diesel). Children's parties on-train or in Flag & Whistle tea rooms.

Wine & Dine train 'Elegant

Excursions' at www.elegantexcursions.net — the 'Cheltenham Flyer' fish and chip specials run on selected Saturdays April to September (pre-booking essential).

Special trains to March and November race meetings at Cheltenham Racecourse. Contact Classic Hospitality 08456 528 888 or www.classichospitality.co.uk (advance booking essential).
Membership details: From above address
Membership journal: *The Cornishman* — quarterly

Timetable Service — Great Central Railway — Leicestershire

Member: HRA, TT
The original Great Central Railway's extension to London in 1899 was the last main line to be built in this country, most of which was closed in the 1960s. Steam-hauled services operate through attractive rolling Leicestershire countryside, crossing the

picturesque Swithland reservoir. The railway's aim is to re-create the experience of British main line railway operation in the days of steam. The images of a main line are backed up by a double track line with trains hauled by large locomotives
Headquarters: Great Central

Railway plc, Loughborough Central Station, Great Central Road, Loughborough, Leicestershire LE11 1RW
Telephone: Loughborough (01509) 230726
Fax: 01509 239791
Internet addresses: *E-mail:* sales@gcrailway.co.uk

Web site: www.gcrailway.co.uk
Main stations: Loughborough Central
Other public stations: Quorn & Woodhouse, Rothley, Leicester North
OS reference: SK 543194
Car park: Quorn, Rothley
Access by public transport: Loughborough Midland station (0.75-mile). Arriva, Kinch, Nottingham City and Trent Buses serve Loughborough Baxtergate (0.5 mile). Arriva Nos 126/7 pass end of Great Central Road (A6 Leicester Road, 300yd)
Refreshment facilities: Licensed Griddle Car with hot and cold drinks on selected trains and at Loughborough Central station. Ellis's tea-room at Rothley opens daily except Fridays. Light refreshment facilities available weekends at all other stations. Luxurious First Class Restaurant Car, for which advance booking is obligatory, is provided on 13.15 train every Saturday and Sunday. Also provided on 19.30 train most Saturdays. Private charter trains available, along with more details of all the above, on request

Locomotives and multiple-units

Name	No	Origin	Class	Type	Built
Witherslack Hall	6990	GWR	'Hall'	4-6-0	1948
Sir Lamiel	30777	SR	N15	4-6-0	1925
Boscastle	34039	SR	WC	4-6-2	1946
Alderman A. E. Draper	45305	LMS	5MT	4-6-0	1936
—	46521	LMS	2MT	2-6-0	1953
—	47406	LMS	3F	0-6-0T	1926
—	48305	LMS	8F	2-8-0	1943
—	8624	LMS	8F	2-8-0	1943
—	63601	GCR	O4	2-8-0	1912
—	69523	GNR	N2	0-6-2T	1921
Oliver Cromwell	70013	BR	7MT	4-6-2	1951
—	73156	BR	5MT	4-6-0	1956
—	78019	BR	2MT	2-6-0	1954
—	07005	BR	07	0-6-0DE	1962
—	D3101	BR	08	0-6-0DE	1955
§—	D4067	BR	10	0-6-0DE	1961
—	D8098	BR	20	Bo-Bo	1961
—	20142	BR	20	Bo-Bo	1966
—	D5185	BR	25	Bo-Bo	1960
Harlech Castle	25265	BR	25	Bo-Bo	1963
—	27056	BR	27	Bo-Bo	1962
—	D5830	BR	31	A1A-A1A	1962
—	33116	BR	33	Bo-Bo	1960
—	37198	BR	37	Co-Co	1954
—	37255	BR	37	Co-Co	1965
†—	D123	BR	45	1Co-Co1	1961
Sparrowhawk	D1705	BR	47	Co-Co	1965
—	51427	BR	101	DMBS	1959
—	51616	BR	127	DMBS	1959

England

Souvenir shop: Loughborough
Museum: Loughborough
Depot: Loughborough
Length of line: 8 miles
Passenger trains: Loughborough-Leicester North
Period of public operation: Weekends and Bank Holidays throughout the year. Certain weekdays April to September with additional services at times of peak demand
Special events: Mothering Sunday Luncheon — 18 March; 1960s Steam Weekend — 30 March-1 April; Diesel Gala — 19/20 May; Easter Vintage Festival — 6-9 April; Toy & Train Fair — 27 May, 5 August; Swapmeet — 3 June, 2 September; Wartime Event — 8-10 June; Father's Day Sunday Luncheon — 17 June; Beer Festival — 21-23 September; Family Fun Weekend — 29/30 September; Autumn Steam Gala — 4-7 October; Halloween Fright Night — 31 October; Bonfire Night — 5 November; Rememberance Service — 11 November; Steam Enthusiasts Event — 17/18 November; Santa Specials — 24/25 November-1/2, 8/9, 15/16, 21-24 December; Christmas Day Trains — 25 December; Christmas Holiday Trains — 27-30 December
For additional information phone 01509 230726
Facilities for disabled: Disabled lift at Loughborough along with toilet facilities. Special carriage for wheelchair/disabled persons

Name	No	Origin	Class	Type	Built
—	51622	BR	127	DMBS	1959
—	53193	BR	101	DMC	1959
—	53203	BR	101	DMBS	1957
—	53266	BR	101	DMC	1957
—	53321	BR	101	DMC	1958
—	59276	BR	120	TS	1958
—	W79976	AC Cars	—	Railbus	1958

§named *Alfred Thomas & Margaret Ethel Naylor*
†named *Leicestershire and Derbyshire Yeomanry*
Note: 6960 on loan to West Somerset Railway during 2012

Industrial locomotives

Name	No	Builder	Type	Built
Robert	—	H/Clarke (1752)	0-6-0ST	1943
—	3809	Hunslet (3809)	0-6-0ST	1954
Duke of Edinburgh	28	Barclay (400)	0-4-0DM	1956
(Arthur Wright)	D4279	Fowler (4210079)	0-4-0DE	1952

Owners
6990 the David Clarke Railway Trust
30777, 63601, 70013 and 33116 on loan from the National Railway Museum
34039 the Boscastle Locomotive Syndicate
45305 and D123 the 5305 Locomotive Association
46521 and 78019 Loughborough Standard Locomotives Group
D3101 and D4067 private
69523 the Gresley Society
73156 the Bolton Steam Locomotive Co
D5830, D8098 and D1705 the Type One Locomotive Co
Class 101s Renaissance Railcars

(advance notice required). Wheelchair access good at Quorn, Rothley and Leicester North. Boarding ramps at all stations
Share details: Company Secretary, Great Central Railway plc
Special facilities: Director's saloon, beavertail observation car or complete train for hire. Drive a locomotive experience packages available.
Membership: Membership Secretary, Friends of Great Central Railway, c/o above address

---

Great Cockcrow Railway

Surrey

The origins of the GCR can be traced back to a private address in Walton-on-Thames in 1946. However in 1968 a move was made to the small village of Lyne near Chertsey. The layout has continued to develop since moving to its present site.

The miniature railway is one of the most extensive of its kind in the country and authentic operation is evident.
Headquarters: Hardwick Lane, Lyne, Chertsey, Surrey KT16 0AD

Locomotives — 7.25in gauge

Name	No	Prototype	Builder	Type	Built
—	1239	NER R1	Baldwin Bros	4-4-0	1913
Eureka	1947	Freelance	L. Shaw	4-6-2	1927
River Itchen	1803	SR U	Schwab/J. Davis	2-6-0	1970s
—	837	SR S15	D. Curwen	4-6-0	1947
Longmoor	73755	WD 2-10-0	J. Liversedge	2-10-0	1951
City of London	46245	LMS Duchess	W. Miller	4-6-2	1950
Mere Hall	7915	GWR Hall	Rowe	4-6-0	1952
—	206	LNER K5	D. Simmonds	2-6-0	1956
—	1401	GWR 14xx	R. Sills	0-4-2T	1980
Sister Dora	5000	LMS 5P5F	A. Glaze	4-6-0	1981
North Foreland	2422	LBCSR H2	J. Lester	4-4-2	1983
Lord Nelson	850	SR LN	Scarret	4-6-0	1985

Telephone:
Sun (01932) 565474
Internet addresses: *E-mail:*
admin@cockcrow.co.uk
Web site: www.cockcrow.co.uk
Main station: Hardwick Central
Car parking: On site
Access by public transport:
Chertsey railway station (1.25
miles); Abellio 446 and 461
Guildford Road (half-mile)
On site facilities: Toilet, light
refreshments, picnic area
Depots: Hardwick Central
Length of line: 1.75 miles,
7.25in gauge
Period of public operation:
Sundays 6 May to 21
October13.30-17.00 and
Wednesdays in August, 13.00-
16.00
Special events: Gala in September
and Halloween in October (check
web site for times)
Journey time: About 15-20min
Facilities for disabled: Limited,
but staff are happy to co-operate
Special note: Sponsored by Ian
Allan Group. Send second class
SAE for brochure to Terminal
House, Shepperton, TW17 8AS.
Fare £3.50 adult, £3 child.
Gladesman £5.50 per person

Name	No	Prototype	Builder	Type	Built
—	1249	NER T2	R. Sills	0-8-0	1986
Scots Guardsman	6115	LMS 6P	P. Almond	4-6-0	1989
—	1442	NER C1	Parkinson/ Hammond	4-4-2	1989
Grand Parade	2744	LNER A3	R. Warren	4-6-2	1990
—	5145	LMS 5P5F	Axon/N. Sleet	4-6-0	1991
General Steam Navigation	21C11	SR MN	N. Sleet	4-6-2	1993
—	8374	LMS 8F	Glaze, Hancock & York	2-8-0	1993
The Glasgow Highlander	45157	LMS 5P5F	D. Grant	4-6-0	1997
—	30541	SR Q	J. Butt	0-6-0	2000
—	45440	LMS 5P5F	J. Clarke/ N. Sleet	4-6-0	2003
Alison	—	Bridget	H. Parsons/ N. Trower	0-4-2T	2006
Buttercup	10	H/Leslie	A. Stobbs	0-6-0ST	
Wensleydale	684	Holmside	N. Trower	0-6-0ST	2011
Lulubelle	1	Freelance		0-4-0	
Faraday	11	BR Class 08	Jennings/ A. B. McLeod	0-6-0P	1958
A. B. McLeod	—	BR Class 35	A. Glaze	Bo-Bo	1982
Pillar	1	BR Class 60	N. Sleet	Co-Co	2008

Attraction — **Great Whipsnade Railway** — Bedfordshire

Member: HRA
Location: Whipsnade Wild Animal
Park, Dunstable, Bedfordshire
LU6 2LF
Telephone: (01582) 871332
(extension 2270)
Fax: (01582) 873748
Internet address: *E-mail:*
whipsnade-operations@2sl.org
Railway Engineer: Kevin Edwins
Main station: Whipsnade Central
Length: 2 miles (2ft 6in gauge)
On site facilities: Car park
(100yd), souvenir shop,
refreshments (30yd)
Period of public operation:
January — no trains; February —
weekends; March — weekends

Locomotives — 2ft 6in gauge

Name	No	Builder	Type	Built
Chevallier	1	M/Wardle (1877)	0-6-2T	1915
Excelsior	2	K/Stuart (1049)	0-4-2T	1908
Superior	4	K/Stuart (4034)	0-6-2T	1920
Victor	—	Fowler (4160004)	0-6-0DM	1951
Hector	—	Fowler (4160005)	0-6-0DM	1951
—	3	B/Drewry	4wDH	1973

Rolling stock: 10 carriages, 10 wagons

only; daily April to end of
September — steam trains; October
— weekends only; November — no
trains; December — no trains.
Subject to availability, steam all
year

Facilities for disabled: Carriage
designed for wheelchairs

England

Haig Colliery Mining Museum

Member: HRA
Haig Colliery Mining Museum, Whitehaven, is an educational and informative museum under development based on local and social mining history. The museum is situated in Cumbria's last deep coal mine that closed in March 1986. It houses the world's only Bever Dorling & Co Ltd winding engines, one of which is restored and operated daily
Location: Kells, half-mile south of Whitehaven, take the road to St Bees and follow brown tourist signs

OS reference: NX 967176
Operating society/organisation: The Haig Colliery Mining Museum Ltd, Solway Road, Kells, Whitehaven, Cumbria CA26 9BG
Charity number: 1050534
Telephone/Fax: 01946 599949 (general information)
Internet addresses:
E-mail: root@haigpit.com
Web site: www.haigpit.com
Car park: On site
Access by public transport:
By rail: Whitehaven is on the Barrow-Carlisle line

By bus: No 01 bus from bus station (opposite railway station) — 9min journey
On site facilities: Small gift shop, gardened area suitable for picnics. Toilets. Meet and Greet by museum guides. Locomotives viewable on request to the guides
Public opening:
Daily (09.30-16.30). Free entry
Facilities for disabled: Parking area, toilets, wheelchair access to all areas

Hayling Seaside Railway

There are three stations on the line: Beachlands, the main station/storage/workshop building located seaward of the funfair; Eastoke Corner, 1-mile to the east, is the other end of the line; Mengham Road with passing loop between
Headquarters: 20 Jasmond Road, Cosham, Portsmouth PO6 2SY
Managing Director: Bob Haddock
Telephone: 023 9237 2427 or 07775 696912
Internet address: *Web site:* www.haylingseasiderailway.com
Main public station: Beachlands (postcode: PO11 0AG)
Other public stations: Eastoke Corner, Mengham Road
Car parks: Pay & display at all stations. Free parking during November, December, January and February
Access by public transport: Regular buses from Havant railway station
Refreshment facilities: At all stations
Journey time: Departures every 45 minutes. First train 11.00 from

Locomotives — 2ft gauge

Name	No	Builder	Type	Built
Jack	—	A/Keef (23)	0-4-0DH s/o	1988
Alister	—	Ruston (201790)	4wDH	1940
Alan B	—	M/Rail (7199)	4wDM	1937
—	—	EHLR	0-4-0T	*
Edwin	—	R/Hornsby (1002-0967-5)	4wDH	1967

*under construction

Stock
1 enclosed bogie coach built 2004,
3 toastrack bogie coaches built 2004/5/6. All built by East Hayling Light Railway in its own works

Beachlands, half hour return journey (possible to break journey and return later)
Length of line: 1 mile, 2ft gauge
Period of public operation: Every weekend and Wednesday (market day) all year round, plus school holidays
Facilities for disabled: All platforms and coaches built to latest mobility standards
Special events: Please contact for full details; Pirates of Beachlands — May half term; Two-train

running, Santa Specials. Plus visiting steam locomotives
Special notes: On display are the original BR station signs Hayling Island and Havant for Hayling
Special facilities: A train may be hired for birthday parties or other special occasions
Membership details:
Madeline Burden 023 9263 7596
Membership journal: *The Hayling Billy* — quarterly

Museum

Head of Steam /
Darlington Railway
Museum

County
Durham

Member: HRA

The site as a whole is known as the Head of Steam, and is owned by Darlington Borough Council. Within the site are four separate buildings. The former North Road Station is run as a museum by the council. Darlington Railway Preservation Society occupies the former Stockton & Darlington Railway North Road Goods and the former S&DR Hopetown Carriage Works is divided between the A1 Steam Locomotive Trust and the North Eastern Locomotive Preservation Group. Darlington Model Railway Club occupies the museum first floor.

All organisations except the Model Railway Club are members of the HRA.

The Ken Hoole Study Centre houses a collection of reference material on the railways of north-east England including the library of the North Eastern Railway Association (access by appointment).

Northern train services provide a link to Darlington's main line station and to Shildon, for 'Locomotion' and the Timothy Hackworth Museum

Museum Manager: David Tetlow
Location: North Road Station, Darlington, County Durham DL3 6ST. Approximately three-quarters of a mile north of town centre, off North Road (A167)
OS reference: NZ 289157
Telephone: (01325) 460532
Internet address: *Web site:* www.drcm.org.uk
Car park: At museum site
Access by public transport: Rail services to Darlington North Road station. Local bus services along North Road
Catering facilities: Snacks and light refreshments
On site facilities: Souvenir and bookshop, toilets, meeting room
Public opening:
October to March: Closed Monday to Thursday. Friday to Sunday 11.00-15.30.
April to September: Closed Monday. Tuesday to Sunday 10.00-16.00.
Special events: Contact for details, details will appear on the web site, or write or telephone
Facilities for disabled: Access to main museum building for wheelchairs. Disabled person's toilet. Parking spaces for disabled in forecourt
Membership details: Friends of

Locomotives

Name	No	Origin	Class	Type	Built
Locomotion	1	S&DR	—	0-4-0	1825
Derwent	25	S&DR	—	0-6-0	1845
—	1463	NER	1463	2-4-0	1885
—	901	NER	Q7	0-8-0	1919

Name	No	Builder		Type	Built
—	—	Bagnall (2898)		0-4-0F	1948

Stock

1 North Eastern Railway coach body (c1860)
1 Chaldron wagon

Owner

Locomotion, Derwent, 901 and 1463 are all on loan from the National Railway Museum, along with the coach body

Darlington Railway Preservation Society

Member: HRA
Internet address: *Web site:* www.drps.visit.ws

Locomotives

Name	No	Origin	Class	Type	Built
—	78018	BR	2MT	2-6-0	1954

Industrial locomotives

Name	No	Builder	Type	Built
—	2	RSH (7925)	0-4-0DM	1959
—	1	Peckett (2142)	0-4-0ST	1953
David Payne	185	Fowler (4110006)	0-4-0DM	1950
Smiths Dock Co Ltd	—	Fowler (4200018)	0-4-0DM	1947
—	—	GEC	4wE	1928
—	—	R/Hornsby (279591)	0-4-0DE	1949
—	—	R/Hornsby*	4wDM	—
—	—	R/Hornsby*	4wDM	—
—	—	R/Hornsby*	4wDM	—
—	—	RSH	0-6-0T	1938

*1ft 6in gauge

Stock Various wagons, steam and diesel cranes

Darlington Railway Museum, Darlington Railway Preservation Society and North Eastern Locomotive Preservation Group. All can be contacted via the museum. Members of these organisations and members of the Museums Association and holders of HRA InterRail passes all receive free admission except on Thomas and Santa days
Note: The Goods Shed and part of the Carriage Works are occupied by

the North Eastern Locomotive Preservation Group for the overhaul of its locomotives. The workshop is open only by appointment. Visitors are welcome at all buildings on the site, but are strongly advised to make arrangements in advance for all buildings other than the main station itself

Heatherslaw Light Railway

Timetable service — **Northumberland**

Location/headquarters:
Heatherslaw Light Railway Co Ltd,
Ford Forge, Heatherslaw, Cornhill
on Tweed, Northumberland
TD12 4TJ
OS reference: NT 933384
SatNav postcode: TD12 4TJ
Tel: 01890 820244
Tel/Fax: 01890 820317
Contact: Mr P. Smith
Internet addresses:
E-mail:
info@heatherslawlightrailway.co.uk
Web site:
www.heatherslawlightrailway.co.uk
Main station: Heatherslaw
Other public stations: Etal Castle
Access by public transport:
By bus: Local bus services
Access by car: On the B6354
between Ford and Etal villages.

Locomotives — 15in gauge

Name	No	Builder	Type	Built
The Lady Augusta	—	B. Taylor	0-4-2	1989
Bunty	—	HLR/Keef	2-6-0TT	2010
Clive	—	N. Smith	4w-4wDH	2000

Rolling stock
Coaches are being upgraded to match the two new coaches built in 2010. All coaches are built or renovated on site and are finished in blue livery to match *Bunty*. This process is ongoing with at least one renovated every winter.

Free parking at Heatherslaw and Etal
On site facilities: Ticket office and railway shop. Railway Society room with G gauge model layout
Souvenir shop: On site
Length of line:
2 miles (3.25km), 15in gauge

Period of public operation:
End March to end October. Trains operate hourly from 11.00-15.00, extra trains on Bank Holidays and in high season
Facilities for disabled: Yes
Special notes: Party bookings welcome

Helston Railway

Railway Centre — **Cornwall**

Member: HRA
The society was set up in 2006 to re open as a heritage railway as much of the old Helston branch line as possible. The long-term aim is to re open the 3-mile Nancegollen-Water-ma-Trout section. A half-mile section has been cleared and the track laid; a further half-mile towards Truthall Halt is currently in hand
Location/headquarters: Trevarno Gardens, Crowntown, Helston, Cornwall TR13 0RU.
Please note that the admission fee to Trevarno Gardens is payable for visitors to the HRPS site
Postal address: Helston Railway Preservation Society, 149 Polwithen Drive, Carbis Bay, St Ives, Cornwall TR26 2SW
Tel: 01736 796456
OS reference: SW 642304
Internet addresses:

Multiple-units

Name	No	Origin	Class	Type	Built
—	50413	P/Royal	103	MBS	1957
—	56196	P/Royal	103	DTCL	1957

Industrial locomotives

Name	No	Builder	Type	Built
—	—	R/Hornsby (395305)	0-4-0DM	1953
—	—	R/Hornsby (327497)	0-4-0DM	1956

Rolling stock
BR 20-ton brake van, RES 'Super GUV'

Owners
Class 103 unit — the Helston Railway Diesel Group
R/Hornsby locomotives — the Helston Shunter Group

E-mail:
chairman@helstonrailway.co.uk
Web site: www.helstonrailway.co.uk
Access by public transport:
By rail: Camborne, Hayle and St Ives stations, each about 6 miles away
By bus: Nearest bus service is Travel Cornwall / Summercourt Travel service 445 between

Camborne and Helston, which serves Crowntown (30min walk from Trevarno)
Traveline: 0871 200 2233
Access by car: Trevarno Gardens is signposted off the B3303

Camborne-Helston Road
On site facilities: Shop and information point at Trevarno station. Other facilities within Trevarno Gardens
Length of line: Half mile

Period of public operation: Please see Trevarno Gardens web site: www.trevarno.co.uk
Membership details: Membership Secretary, 37 Gwithian Towans, Hayle, Cornwall TR27 5BT

Miniature Railway — Hills Miniature Railway — Cheshire

Opened in 2000, the railway runs through the landscaped grounds of Hills Garden Centre
Location: Hills Garden Centre, London Road, Allostock, Knutsford, Cheshire WA16 9LU
Contact: Mr C. Halsall
Telephone: 01565 722567
Fax: 01565 723818
Internet address: *Web site:* www.hills-miniature-railway.co.uk
Car parking: Space for 80 cars on site. One coach space available
Access by public transport: Holmes Chapel main line station is 4 miles away, as is the nearest bus station
Access by car: Exit M6 at Jct 18 and follow A54 to Holmes Chapel.

Locomotives — 7.25in gauge

Name	No	Builder	Type	Built
Amy Louise	—	Exmoor	0-4-2	2005
Sir Richard	—	Greatrix	Bo-Bo	2005
—	—	N/k	4-4-0	1990
Peter the Great	—	J. Horsfield	0-4-0	2001

In Holmes Chapel turn left onto A50 London Road, follow for 5 miles. Hills Garden Centre is on the left-hand side
On site facilities: Souvenir shop, light refreshments
Length of line: 600yd, 7.25in gauge
Period of public operation: Weekends and Bank Holidays throughout the year. Trains operate

10.45-16.30. All trains weather permitting
Special events: Santa Specials — December weekends up to Christmas Eve
Facilities for disabled: Disabled toilet. level site, wheelchair loan and plenty of seating. Designated disabled parking space

Steam Centre — Hollycombe Steam Collection — West Sussex

Member: HRA, TT
An extensive collection of working steam, including railways, traction engines, fairground rides, Bioscope, organs, the oldest Burrell Showman's engine *Emperor*, sawmill and engine from the paddle steamer *Caledonia*, set in woodlands and gardens
Location: Iron Hill, Hollycombe, near Liphook, Hants
OS reference: SU 852295
Operating society/organisation: Hollycombe Working Steam Museum, Iron Hill, Midhurst Road, Liphook, Hants GU30 7LP
Telephone: Liphook (01428) 724900 (24hr answerphone)
Fax: (01428) 723682
Internet address: *Web site:* www.hollycombe.co.uk
Car park: On site
Access by public transport:

Standard gauge industrial locomotives

Name	No	Builder	Type	Built
Commander B	50	H/Leslie (2450)	0-4-0ST	1899
—	3	YEC (2679)	0-4-0DH	1962
Yvonne	—	Cockerill (2945)	0-4-0VBT	1920

Narrow gauge locomotives — 2ft gauge

Name	No	Builder	Type	Built
Caledonia	70	Barclay (1995)	0-4-0WT	1931
Jerry M	38	Hunslet (638)	0-4-0ST	1895
—	16	R/Hornsby	4wDM	1941

Liphook main line station (1 mile)
On site facilities: Shop and refreshments, toilets, car park, *dogs allowed in car park only*
Length of lines: Standard gauge – quarter mile
2ft gauge 'Quarry Railway' – 1.5 miles
7.25in gauge – quarter mile
Public opening:
Sundays and Bank Holidays:

6 April to 21 October.
Daily: 6-8 June (local school half term week), 1-27 August (not Mondays or Tuesdays apart from 27th)
Normal opening times 11.00-17.00.
Train rides from 12.00.
Fair from 13.00
Special events: Steam in Miniature Weekend — 12/13 May;
Hollycombe Steam Weekend —

26/27 May; Local Locomotion Club Rally — 9/10 June; Railway Weekend — 16/17 June; Bus Rally — 24 June; MG Car Club Rally — 15 July; Fairground Weekend — 21/22 July; Fairground at Night (19.00-22.00) — 15, 22, 29, September, 6 October; Halloween Fairground at Night (19.00-22.00) — 13, 20 October. Please phone or check web site for these and other events

Irchester Narrow Gauge Railway Museum

Steam Centre — **Northants**

Member: HRA

The aims of the controlling trust are to acquire and preserve narrow gauge railway locomotives, rolling stock and exhibits associated with Northamptonshire and the East Midlands, to display the collection for the benefit of the public and to restore exhibits to working order so they may be demonstrated in a proper manner

Location: Within Irchester Country Park, 2 miles south of Wellingborough

Operating society/organisation: The Irchester Narrow Gauge Railway Trust, 3 The Ashes, Wootton, Northampton NN4 6AQ

Internet addresses:
E-mail: irchester@btinternet.com
Web site: www.irchester.btinternet.co.uk
SatNav postcode: NN29 7DL
On site facilities: Shop, museum, demonstration line, picnic area

Industrial locomotives — 3ft and metre gauge

Name	No	Builder	Type	Built
—	85*	Peckett (1870	0-6-0ST	1934
—	86*	Peckett (1871	0-6-0ST	1934
—	87*	Peckett (2029)	0-6-0ST	1942
Cambrai	—*	Corpet (493)	0-6-0T	1888
—	ND3645*	R/Hornsby (211679)	4wDM	1941
—	—†	R/Hornsby (281290)	0-6-0DM	1949
—	ED10*	R/Hornsby (411322	4wDM	1958
—	—†	M/Rail (1363)	4wPM	1918
The Rock	—*	Hunslet (2419)	0-4-0DM	1941

*metre gauge
†3ft gauge

Access by public transport: Main line Wellingborough (Midland Road) station, buses to Irchester and Little Irchester
Car Parks: Main park car parks
Toilets: Main park complex
Public opening: Every Sunday (summer 10.00-17.00, winter 10.00-16.00), at other times by arrangement
Facilities for disabled: Museum and site on level, staff available if required
Membership details: Membership Secretary, 1 Wilby Street, Northampton NN1 5JX

Ironbridge Gorge Museums

Museum — **Shropshire**

The railway items form only a small part of the displays on one of the museum's main sites: Blists Hill Victorian Town. The Blists Hill site offers an opportunity to see a number of industrial and other activities being operated in meticulously reconstructed period buildings. A working foundry is just one of the exciting exhibits. A full size working replica of Richard Trevithick's 1802 steam locomotive built by the Coalbrookdale Company can also be seen operating at certain times during the summer season at the Blists Hill site. The Ironbridge Gorge was designated a World Heritage Site in 1987

Industrial locomotives

Name	No	Builder	Type	Built
—	—	Sentinel/Coalbrookdale (6185)	0-4-0VBT	1925
—	—	Sentinel/M/Wardle (6155)	0-4-0VBT	1925
—	5	Coalbrookdale	0-4-0ST	1865
—	—	A/Barclay	0-6-0ST	1896

Location: Ironbridge, Shropshire
OS reference: SJ 694033
Operating society/organisation: Ironbridge Gorge Museum Trust, Coach Road, Coalbrookdale, Telford, Shropshire TF8 7DQ
SatNav postcode: TF7 5DU
Telephone: Telford (01952) 433424
Fax: (01952) 435999
Internet address: *Web site:* www.ironbridge.org.uk
Car park: At the sites — fee charged
Access by public transport: Various operators. Please telephone Telford Travel Link 01952 200005 for further details
Catering facilities: Licensed Victorian pub, sweet shop and tea rooms at the Blists Hill site, serving drinks and mainly cold snacks. Tea,

England

coffee and light refreshments at the Museum of Iron, Coalbrookdale and Jackfield Tile Museum
Public opening: Main sites, including Museum of Iron and Blists Hill, daily (except Christmas Eve, Christmas Day and New Year's Day)
Special notes: Tickets for all the sites or just for single sites available. Special access details are available online or by calling 01952 433424

Isle of Wight Steam Railway

Timetable Service | **Isle of Wight**

Member: HRA, TT

Separated from the mainland by the Solent, the line's isolation encouraged the maintenance and retention of Victorian locomotives and coaching stock which still operate on the line today. Its rural charm enhances its attraction for the island's holidaymakers during the summer season

Commercial Manager: Jim Loe
General Manager: Peter Vail
Headquarters: Isle of Wight Steam Railway, Haven Street Station, Ryde, Isle of Wight PO33 4DS
Telephone: (01983) 882204
Internet addresses: *E-mail:* havenstreet@iwsteamrailway.co.uk
Web site: www.iwsteamrailway.co.uk
Main station: Haven Street
OS reference: SZ 556898
Other public stations: Wootton, Ashey and Smallbrook Junction
Car park: Haven Street
Access by public transport: 'Island Line' service from Ryde or Shanklin to Smallbrook Jct
Refreshment facilities: Light refreshments available (licensed)
Souvenir shop: Haven Street
Museum: Small exhibits museum at Haven Street.
   Carriage & Wagon workshop open for viewing most days
Depot: Haven Street
Length of line: 5 miles

Locomotives

Name	No	Origin	Class	Type	Built
Freshwater	W8 (32646)	LBSCR	A1X	0-6-0T	1876
Newport	W11 (32640)	LBSCR	A1X	0-6-0T	1878
Calbourne	W24	LSWR	O2	0-4-4T	1891
—	41296	LMS	2MT	2-6-2T	1952
—	41313	LMS	2MT	2-6-2T	1952
—	46447	LMS	2MT	2-6-0	1952
—	D2059	BR	03	0-6-0DM	1959
—	D2554	BR	05	0-6-0DM	1956

Industrial and Army locomotives

Name	No	Builder	Type	Built
Invincible	37	H/Leslie (3135)	0-4-0ST	1915
Ajax	38	Barclay (1605)	0-6-0T	1918
Waggoner	192	Hunslet (3792)	0-6-0ST	1953
Royal Engineer	198	Hunslet (3798)	0-6-0ST	1953

Stock

1 IWR coach; 4 LBSCR coaches; 3 SECR coaches; 2 LCDR coaches; 5 IWR coaches (bodies only); 5 LCDR coaches (bodies only); 1 LBSCR coach (body only); 1 crane; 1 Wickham trolley; 30 wagons; 6 parcels vans; 2 ex-LT hoppers; 1 ex-BR Lowmac; 1 LSWR Road van; 1 cattle van (on loan from the National Railway Museum).
Non-passenger vehicles are not normally accessible for public viewing

Passenger trains: Wootton-Smallbrook Jct
Period of public operation: Daily — June to mid-September. Selected days — March to May, October and November
Special events: The railway hosts a large number of special events throughout the season. Please contact for details

Facilities for disabled: Limited facilities, but can be catered for individually, or in groups (by prior arrangement), toilets available
Membership details: Membership Secretary at above address
Membership journal: *Island Rail News* — quarterly

Keighley & Worth Valley Railway

Timetable Service | **West Yorkshire**

Member: HRA

1968 saw the re-opening of the Worth Valley branch following the first sale of a standard gauge railway to a preservation society. Qualified volunteers have now managed and operated the KWVR every weekend, summer and winter for over four decades. The KWVR is justifiably proud of having led the British independent railway movement in establishing the now ubiquitous late 1950s/early 1960s house style. Many have copied, but few succeed so well as the Worth Valley with totems, A5 handbills, period posters, red uniform ties, hanging baskets, gas lights and coal fires. One of the most community-orientated independent railways, being the first to create a 'Resident's Railcard' discount fares scheme

Chairman: Mathew Stroh

England

Headquarters: Haworth Station, Keighley, West Yorkshire BD22 8NJ

Telephone: Haworth (01535) 645214

Internet address: *Web site:* www.kwvr.co.uk

Main stations: Keighley, Ingrow West, Haworth, Oxenhope

Other public stations: Damems, Oakworth

OS reference: SE 034371

Car parks: Keighley (small charge), free at Ingrow West, Oakworth and Oxenhope. Parking at Haworth (small charge, part refundable if travelling). Coaches at Ingrow West and Oxenhope only

Access by public transport: Fast and frequent electric Metro trains from Leeds, Bradford and Skipton to Keighley (joint station with KWVR). Grand Central run direct services from London to Bradford. East Coast direct services to Leeds and Keighley. Northern Trains through services from Carlisle, Morecambe, Heysham Port, Lancaster to Keighley station. Northern Train services from Blackpool, Preston, Blackburn, Accrington, Burnley, Manchester to Hebden Bridge for connection via bus service 500 to Oxenhope (tel 01535 603284 for days of operation and timings)

Refreshment facilities: Buffet facilities at Oxenhope and Keighley (open when train service in operation). The only CAMRA-approved 'Real Ale' bar operates on most steam trains. Wine and Dine services by prior booking only — the 'White Rose Pullman' and 'West Riding Ltd'

Picnic areas: Keighley Station, Haworth Locomotive Depot, Oxenhope Station

Viewing areas: Keighley (ex-Garsdale) turntable, Haworth Locomotive Depot

Souvenir shops: Keighley, Haworth and Oxenhope stations; Ingrow Vintage Carriages Museum

Museums: Vintage Carriages Trust's carriage and locomotive museum at Ingrow Railway Centre. Open daily (except Christmas Day) 11.00-16.30

Depots: Carriage and wagon — Oxenhope; Motive power/loco works — Haworth, 'Bahamas Locomotive Society' workshops and museum at Ingrow Railway Centre

Length of line: 4.75 miles

Locomotives and multiple-units

Name	No	Origin	Class	Type	Built
—	41241	LMS	2MT	2-6-2T	1949
—	43924	MR	4F	0-6-0	1920
—	45212	LMS	5MT	4-6-0	1935
Bahamas	45596	LMS	'Jubilee'	4-6-0	1935
—	48431	LMS	8F	2-8-0	1944
—	47279	LMS	3F	0-6-0T	1925
—	1054	LNWR	—	0-6-2T	1888
City of Wells	34092	SR	WC	4-6-2	1949
—	80002	BR	4MT	2-6-4T	1952
—	75078	BR	4MT	4-6-0	1956
—	78022	BR	2MT	2-6-0	1953
—	30072	SR	USA	0-6-0T	1943
—	5775	GWR	5700	0-6-0PT	1929
—	957	L&Y	2F	0-6-0	1887
—	19*	L&Y	Pug	0-4-0ST	1910
—	51218	L&Y	Pug	0-4-0ST	1901
—	752	L&Y	—	0-6-0ST	1881
—	85	TVR	02	0-6-2T	1899
—	5820	USATC	S160	2-8-0	1945
—	90733	MoS	WD	2-8-0	1945
—	D226	BR	—	0-6-0DE	1956
—	D2511	BR	—	0-6-0DM	1961
—	D3336	BR	08	0-6-0DE	1954
—	D8031	BR	20	Bo-Bo	1960
—	D5209	BR	25/1	Bo-Bo	1963
—	50928	BR	108	DMBS	1959
—	51189	BR	101	DMBS	1958
—	51565	BR	108	DMC	1959
—	51803	BR	101	DMCL	1959
—	79962	W&M	—	Railbus	1958
—	79964	W&M	—	Railbus	1958

Industrial locomotives

Name	No	Builder	Type	Built
Hamburg	31	H/Clarke (679)	0-6-0T	1903
Nunlow	—	H/Clarke (1704)	0-6-0T	1938
Brussels	118	H/Clarke (1782)	0-6-0ST	1945
Tiny	—	Barclay (2258)	0-4-0ST	1949
Merlin	231	H/Clarke (D761)	0-6-0DM	1951
—	MDHB No 32	Hunslet (2699)	0-6-0DM	1944

Stock

30 coaches including examples of pre-Grouping types; BR Mk 1 stock including the oldest vehicle in existence, part of the prototype batch; 2 Pullman cars, NER and L&Y observation cars

Owners

19, 752 and 51218 the L&YRPS Trust
75078 and 78022 the Standard 4 Preservation Society
Bahamas, Nunlow, Tiny the Bahamas Locomotive Society
1054 the National Trust
957 the Bowers 957 Trust
34092 the *City of Wells* Syndicate

Passenger trains: Early morning local shoppers' services worked by diesel railbus/diesel multiple-unit, otherwise all steam-hauled.

Frequent bus service between Haworth station and Haworth village top on Sundays (May-September) and Bank Holidays

Period of public operation: Steam-hauled passenger services every weekend and Bank Holiday throughout the year (in December diesel-hauled). Daily during July and August

Special events: Railway Children Weekend — 5-7 May; Haworth Village 1940s Weekend — 19/20 May; Heritage Diesel Weekend — 25-27 May; Keighley Festival of Transport — 8 July; Steam Gala — 12-14 October; Beer & Music Festival — 25-28 October; Santa Specials — pre-Christmas weekends and Christmas Eve; Mince Pie Specials — daily 26 December-2 January 2013. Plus: Vintage Trains — 24 June, 1, 8, 15, 22, 29 July, Fish & Chip Specials (evenings) — 7 April, 12 May, 16 June, 14 July, 4 and 25 August, 20 October; Luxury Summer `Saloons — 6-9 April, 5, 12, 26/27 August. Dining and Luncheon Trains — ring for details

Facilities for disabled: Level access to all stations.Wheelchair ramps available at all stations (except Damems). Full disabled toilet facilities at Haworth station. Newly restored coach with disabled area conveyed on most trains, or if not available non-folding wheelchairs can be accommodated in guard's compartments. Staff available to offer assistance and advice at all stations. Museum of Rail Travel at Ingrow offers easy access to wheelchair users (inc toilet facilities). Audio loop and Braille facilities available and attention given to those with special needs

Special notes: Accompanied children under 5 years of age free. Children 5-15 and senior citizens at discount rate. Family ticket available (2 adults + 3 children/senior citizen). Free entry to VCT Museum with rover tickets

Membership details: Membership Secretary c/o above address

Membership journal: *Push & Pull* — quarterly

Kent & East Sussex Railway

Timetable Service

Kent

Member: HRA, TT

The Kent & East Sussex Railway owes much of its charm to its origin as the world's first light railway. The tightly curved line with steep gradients is typical of those country railways that were developed on shoestring budgets to bring the 'iron horse' to sparsely populated areas. Services operate over 10.5 miles of line from the picturesque town of Tenterden to Bodiam.

Pride of the line's coach fleet is the magnificently restored train of vintage carriages built between 1860 and 1901

Company Secretary: Nick Pallant

Headquarters: Kent & East Sussex Railway Co Ltd, Tenterden Town Station, Tenterden, Kent TN30 6HE

Telephone: Tenterden (01580) 762943 (24 hour talking timetable); Tenterden 01580 765155 (office)

Internet address: *Web site:* www.kesr.org.uk

Main station: Tenterden Town

Other public stations: Rolvenden, Wittersham Road, Northiam, Bodiam

Car parks: Tenterden, Northiam

OS reference: Tenterden TQ 882336, Northiam TQ 834266

Access by public transport: Stagecoach No 400 from Ashford (Kent) main line station. Arriva

Locomotives and multiple-units

Name	No	Origin	Class	Type	Built
Bodiam	3	LBSCR	A1X	0-6-0T	1872*
Knowle	2678	LBSCR	A1X	0-6-0T	1880*
—	753	SECR	P	0-6-0T	1909*
Wainwright	DS238	SR	USA	0-6-0T	1943
Maunsell	65	SR	USA	0-6-0T	1943*
—	1638	GWR	1600	0-6-0PT	1951*
—	4253	GWR	4200	2-8-0T	1917
—	20	GWR	AEC	diesel railcar	1940
Norwegian	376	NSB	21c	2-6-0	1919
—	D2023	BR	03	0-6-0DM	1958◊
—	D2024	BR	03	0-6-0DM	1958*
Dover Castle	D3174	BR	08	0-6-0DE	1955
—	D9504	BR	14	0-6-0DH	1964
Ashford	D6570	BR	33	Bo-Bo	1961*
—	51571	BR	108	DMC	1959*
—	53971	BR	108	DMBS	1959*

Industrial locomotives

Name	No	Builder	Type	Built
Marcia	12	Peckett (1631)	0-4-0T	1923
Charwelton	14	M/Wardle (1955)	0-6-0ST	1917*
Holman F. Stephens	23	Hunslet (3791)	0-6-0ST	1952*
Rolvenden	24	Hunslet (3800)	0-6-0ST	1953*
Northiam	25	Hunslet (3797)	0-6-0ST	1953*
—	40	BTH	Bo-Bo	1932*

*in passenger traffic

Passenger stock in service

SECR family saloon; SECR 'Birdcage' brake; SECR 4-wheel full third; SECR 4-wheel third brake ; SR Maunsell CK; GER 6-wheel composite; District Railway 4-wheel third; 2 SR Maunsell nondescript brake-opens; BR Mk 1 RU and 6 other BR Mk 1 coaches; 1926 Pullman Parlour Cars *Barbara* and *Theodora*

Stock

1 ex-SECR 'Birdcage' coaches; 2 ex-LSWR coaches; 2 Pullman cars;

No 12 Maidstone-Headcorn station-Tenterden & Rye.
St Michael's Car Hire: 01580 762277

Refreshment facilities: Tenterden Town. Also on many trains. Lunch and afternoon teas on many trains (advance booking essential). Picnic areas at Tenterden, Wittersham Road; seasonally at Northiam and Bodiam

Souvenir shop: Tenterden Town Station; seasonally at Northiam and Bodiam

Museum: Colonel Stephens Railway Museum at Tenterden Town

Locomotive depot: Rolvenden

Carriage & Wagon depot: Tenterden

Length of line: 10.5 miles

Passenger trains: Tenterden-Bodiam. Weekends mid-March to end October. All Bank Holidays and school holidays. Daily end July to early September. Most days ring for details, full steam service in August

Special events: Day out with Thomas — 11/12, 18/19 February; Mother's Day — 18 March; Grandparents' Weekend — 14/15

1 ex-SR Maunsell coach; 2 steam cranes; large interesting collection of freight vehicles, totalling 51 vehicles.

Owner
Charwelton the Rother Valley Railway

April; Spring Walks — 28/29 April; Gala — 5-6 May; 1940s weekend — 19/20 May; Jubilee Celebration — 5 June; CAMRA Beer Festival — 16 June; Father's Day — 17 June; Summer Walks — 7/8 July; 1960s Weekend — 4/5 August; Hoppickers" Weekend — 8/9 September; Pensioners' Treat — 18-20 September; Day out with Thomas — 22/23, 29/30; Austin Counties Car Rally — 13/14 October; Autumn Walks — 20/21 October; Halloween Week — 22-27 October; Santa Specials — 1/2, 8/9, 15/16, 22-24 December; Post Christmas Blues 28-31 December

Facilities for disabled: All facilities are carefully designed with disabled and elderly passengers in mind. 'Petros', a specially designed coach for wheelchair users, is due to return to traffic early 2012. Car

parking for the disabled is available at Tenterden and Northiam. Toilets with disabled access at Tenterden, Northiam and Bodiam, also in 'Petros'. Plus induction loop at Tenterden. A multi-media guide will be available from March 2012

Special notes: The Wealden Pullman luxury dining car service operates on most Saturday evenings April to October. Roast lunch served most Sundays. Advance booking is essential for these trains. Santa Special services operate on each weekend in December and days immediately prior to Christmas Day. Advance booking recommended

Membership details: Membership Secretary, c/o above address

Membership journal: *The Tenterden Terrier* — 3 times/year

Steam Centre — Kew Bridge Steam Museum — London

The museum is housed in a magnificent 19th century Pumping Station and centres around the station's five world famous Cornish Beam Engines, three of which can be seen in steam on selected 'Giants of Steam' weekends. Originally used to pump West London's water supply for more than a century, one of them, the 'Grand Junction 90', is the world's largest working beam engine. In surrounding buildings other large engines work at weekends, demonstrating more modern steam and diesel pumping machinery.

The Water For Life Gallery reveals the fascinating history of London's water supply from Roman toilet spoons to the massive 'high-tec' London ring main.

Many Victorian waterworks had their own railway. At Kew Bridge this is demonstrated by a short line, operated by the museum.

Ticket prices: adults £10.00/

Industrial locomotives — 2ft gauge

Name	No	Builder	Type	Built
Thomas Wicksteed	—	Hunslet (3906)	0-4-0ST	2009
Alister	2	Lister (44052)	4wDM	1958

Stock
1 Manrider, 2 skips

concessions £9.00, children (5-15 years £4.00) Tickets are valid for 12 months from date of issue, to be used for return visits as frequently as you wish. All children must be accompanied by an adult

Location: 100yd from the north side of Kew Bridge, next to the tall Victorian tower

Operating group: Kew Bridge Engines Trust, Green Dragon Lane, Brentford, Middx TW8 0EN

Telephone: 020 8568 4757 (information line)

Internet addresses: *E-mail:* info@kbsm.org
Web site: www.kbsm.org

Car park: Free on site

Access by public transport:
Rail: South West Trains, Kew Bridge (from Waterloo via Clapham Junction) and North London Line to Gunnersbury;
Bus: Nos 65, 237, 267, 391, alight at Kew Bridge station;
Tube: Gunnersbury (District Line, then 237 or 267 bus), or Kew Gardens (District Line, then 391 bus). Look for the tall Victorian tower

Length of line/gauge: About 140yd, 2ft gauge

Public opening:
Museum open, Tuesday to Sunday

and Bank Holiday Mondays 10.00-16.00,
Closed other Mondays, Friday 6 April, 27/28 September and weekdays from 10-28 December December 2011 inclusive
Special events: Mad Science — 10/11 March; Stirling Air Engine Rally — 25 March; Magic of Meccano — 21/22 April; Museums at Night — 19 May; Historic Fire Engine Rally — 20 May; Grand Summer Steam Up — 2-5 June; Made@Kew 21-24 June; Infernal Combustion — 1/2 September; Waterworks at War — 29/30 September; Halloween Howlers — 27-31 October; Modelling Mayhem — 3/4 November; Santa Specials

— 8/9, 15/16, 22/23 December; Grand New Year Steam-up — 29-31 December, 1 January 2013 The railway is scheduled to operate on 18/25 March; 1, 8/9, 21/22, 28 April; 6/7, 13, 19/20, 27 May; 2-5, 10, 17, 24 June; 1, 8, 15, 22, 29 July; 5, 12, 18/19, 26/27 August; 1/2, 9, 16, 23, 29/30 September; 7, 14, 21, 28 October; 3/4 November; 8/9, 15/16, 22/23, 29-31 December; 1 January 2013
On site facilities:
Bookshop/toilets/car park. Refreshments available at weekends only, 11.00-15.30 (with hot meals available 12.30-14.30)
Facilities for disabled: Wheelchair access to 90% of ground floor areas

via ramp and lift. Large print guide available and guide dogs welcome. Wheelchair loan service and wheelchair accessible toilet
Special note: The museum offers a range of special admission rates and packages for group visits, please contact for information brochure
Special facilities: The museum can be hired for corporate or private events. Special steamings can be arranged. Please contact for brochure
Museum contact: Kew Bridge Steam Museum, c/o above address
Other attractions: Museum displays a selection of stationary steam engines and associated water supply displays

---

Kidderminster Railway Museum

Museum | Worcestershire

Established in an 1878 GWR warehouse, the museum houses an enormous collection of railway relics, photographs and documents, with a number of 'hands-on' exhibits.
Contact address: Station Approach, Comberton Hill, Kidderminster, Worcestershire DY10 1QX
General Manager: David Postle
Telephone: Kidderminster (01562) 825316

Internet addresses:
E-mail: krm@krm.org.uk
Web site: www.krm.org.uk
OS reference: SO 837763
Location: Adjacent to SVR station
Car park: SVR car park
Access by public transport: Kidderminster main line station, Midland Red bus service X92 to Kidderminster
Facilities for disabled: Ramp access for wheelchairs to ground level

Special events: Practical signalling courses using museum and SVR resources. Filmshows, model railway exhibitions, railway art exhibitions, postcard/photograph fairs,
On site facilities: Souvenirs, refreshments
Public opening: Open on SVR operating days

Kirklees Light Railway

Timetable Service | West Yorkshire

Member: HRA
Location/headquarters: Clayton West, A636 Wakefield-Denby Dale road
General Manager: Stuart Ross
Operating society/organisation:
Kirklees Light Railway,
Park Mill Way, Clayton West,
Nr Huddersfield, West Yorkshire HD8 9XJ
Telephone: 01484 865727
Fax: 01484 866333
Internet address: *Web site:*
www.kirkleeslightrailway.com
Facebook fan pages:
http://www.facebook.com/

Locomotives — 15in gauge

Name	No	Builder	Type	Built
Fox	—	Taylor	2-6-2T	1987
Badger	—	Taylor	0-6-4T	1991
Tram †	7	Taylor	2-2PH (S/O)	1990
				rebuit 1995
Jay	—	Taylor	4wDH	1992
Hawk*	—	Taylor	0-4-4-0	1998
Owl*	—	Taylor	4w-4wTG	2000

†used only during Days out with Thomas events
*articulated locomotives

Rolling stock
2 x 16-seat guard's vans (heated in winter), 10 x 20-seat enclosed coaches (heated in winter), 2 x 20-seat semi-open coaches, 1 x 4-wheel flat wagon, 1 x 4-wheel mine car, 2 x bogie well wagons, 1 x 4-wheel tool van

England

kirkleeslightrly
Location: Clayton West, the terminus and headquarters of the railway, is situated midway between Wakefield, Barnsley, Holmfirth and Huddersfield, on the A636 Wakefield-Denby Dale road. It is close to junctions 28 and 39 on the M1 motorway
Main station: Clayton West
Other station: Cuckoo's Nest, Skelmanthorpe, Shelley
SatNav postcode:
Park Mill Way — HD8 9XJ
Length of line: 4 miles, 15in gauge
Car park: Clayton West only — free
Access by public transport:
By bus: from Huddersfield Nos 80, 81 and 82; from Wakefield No 435 and No 436. Ask driver for Park

Mill Way, Clayton West
By train: to Huddersfield, Wakefield and Denby Dale stations
Refreshment facilities: Café at Clayton West, tea room at Shelley
Souvenir shop: Clayton West
On site facilities: Toilets, picnic area, indoor and outdoor play areas at Clayton West and Shelley. The headquarters of Barnsley Society of Model Engineers is located at Clayton West
Facilities for disabled: Clayton West station is fully accessible. Disabled visitors or carers should contact the railway before their visit to discuss requirements
Period of public operation: Winter — weekends and local school holidays.
Summer — weekends and local

school holidays and daily from 26 May until 2 September
Special events: Day out with Thomas — 17/18 March; Easter Eggspress —6-9 April; Day out with Thomas — 19/20 May; Olly Owl's Family Fun Day — 16/17 June; Day out with Thomas — 14/15 July; Day out with Thomas — 17-20 August, Friends of Kirklees Light Railway 7th Annual Steam and Diesel Gala — 8/9 September; 21st Anniversary Weekend — 20/21 October; Halloween Ghost Trains — 27/28, 31 October; Day out with Thomas — 10/11 November; Santa Specials — 1-24 December
Special facilities: Full programme of driver experience courses throughout the year

---

Timetable Service	Lakeside & Haverthwaite Railway	Cumbria

Member: HRA, TT
Originally this Furness Railway branch line carried passengers and freight from Ulverston to Lakeside but now the only part remaining is the 3.5-mile section from Haverthwaite to the terminus at Lakeside where connections are made with the steamers which ply the 10-mile length of Windermere
General Manager: M. A. Maher
Headquarters: Lakeside & Haverthwaite Railway Co Ltd, Haverthwaite Station, Nr Ulverston, Cumbria LA12 8AL
Telephone: Newby Bridge (015395) 31594
Internet address: *Web site:* www.lakesiderailway.co.uk
Main station: Haverthwaite
Other public stations: Intermediate station at Newby Bridge. Terminus at Lakeside
OS reference: SD 349843
Car parks: Haverthwaite, Lakeside, charges payable at both
Access by public transport: Lakeside steamers on Windermere call at Lakeside. CMS bus to Haverthwaite
Refreshment facilities: Haverthwaite
Souvenir shop: Haverthwaite
On site facilities: Picnic area at Haverthwaite. Disabled toilets

Locomotives and multiple-units

Name	No	Origin	Class	Type	Built
—	42073	LMS	4MT	2-6-4T	1950
—	42085	LMS	4MT	2-6-4T	1951
—	17(AD601)	LMS	—	0-6-0DE	1945
—	8(D2117)	BR	03	0-6-0DM	1959
—	D2072	BR	03	0-6-0DM	1959
—	20214	BR	20	Bo-Bo	1967
—	D5301	BR	26	Bo-Bo	1958
—	52071	BRCW	110	DMBC	1961
—	52077	BRCW	110	DMBC	1961

Industrial locomotives

Name	No	Builder	Type	Built
Rachel	9	M/Rail (2098)	4wDM	1924
Repulse	11	Hunslet (3698)	0-6-0ST	1950
Princess	14	Bagnall (2682)	0-6-0ST	1942
—	—	Bagnall (2996)	0-6-0ST	1951
—	10	Barclay (1245)	0-6-0T	1911
David	13	Barclay (2333)	0-4-0ST	1953
—	20	Jones crane	0-4-0DM	1952
Sir James	21	Barclay (1550)	0-6-0F	1917

Stock
10 ex-BR Mk 1 coaches; selection of freight vehicles

Depot: All rolling stock at Haverthwaite
Length of line: 3.5 miles
Passenger trains: Steam-hauled Haverthwaite-Lakeside
Period of public operation: 31 March to4 November 2010 (inclusive)
Special events: Santa Specials, Day

out with Thomas, Halloween (advance booking essential), please contact for details
Facilities for disabled: Access to trains, shop and restaurant
Special notes: Combined railway/lake steamer tickets available from the station at Haverthwaite and lake steamer piers

at Bowness and Ambleside. Lake steamers are operated by Windermere Lake Cruises Ltd

Membership journal: *The Iron Horse* — quarterly

Miniature Railway — Lakeside Miniature Railway — Lancashire

The longest continuously running 15in gauge railway in Great Britain, running during both world wars. The first train ran at 3pm on 25 May 1911. The line was extended in 1948, now running between two stations, Pleasureland and Marine Parade-Ocean Plaza.
Location: Marine Lake, Southport
Headquarters: 1 Wingates, Penwortham, Preston, Lancs PR1 9YN
Contact: Mr D. Clark
Telephone: 01772 745511
Internet addresses: *E-mail:* jenc47@hotmail.co.uk
Web site: www.lakesideminiaturerailway.co.uk
Car parking: In Ocean Plaza car parks, opposite

Locomotives — 1ft 3in gauge

Name	No	Builder	Type	Built
Duke of Edinburgh	—	Barlow	4-6-2+4-4DE	1947
Prince Charles	—	Barlow	4-6-2+4-4DE	1954
Golden Jubilee	—	Barlow	4-6w+4-4DE	1963
Princess Anne	—	S/Lamb	6w-6DH	1971
Jenny	—	A. Moss	2-6-2DH	2006

Rolling stock
3 sets of carriages each seating 72 passengers

SatNav postcodes:
Marine Parade station PR8 1SQ
Pleasureland station PR8 1RX
On site facilities: Shop (selling ice cream, soft drinks, and Thomas the Tank Engine)
Length of line: 800yd, 15in gauge
Period of public operation:

Easter to end of October, and during school holidays (weather permitting), 12.00-16.30. Journey time 5min (single) 14min (return)
Facilities for disabled: Wheelchair access
Fare: £2.00 (single), £2.50 (return)

Miniature Railway — Lappa Valley Railway — Cornwall

Member: TT
Location/headquarters:
Benny Halt, St Newlyn East, Nr Newquay, Cornwall TR8 5LX
Telephone: 01872 510317
Internet address: *Web site:* www.lappavalley.co.uk
General Manager: David Milne
Main station: Benny Halt
Other station: East Wheal Rose, Newlyn Downs Halt
Car park: Benny Halt
Access by public transport: Bus service, Newquay to Truro and return. Western Greyhound coaches to St Newlyn East. Signposted, half-mile walk from bus stop to railway. No direct bus service
Refreshment facilities: Café at East Wheal Rose serving hot and cold food, snacks, hot and cold drinks; licensed
Souvenir shop: East Wheal Rose and Benny Halt
On site facilities: 15in, 10.25in and 7.25in gauge railways. Canoes, crazy golf, pedal cars, electric

Locomotives — 10.25in and 15in gauge
(15in gauge)

Name	No	Builder	Type	Built
Muffin	2	Berwyn	0-6-0	1967
		rebuilt Tambling		1991
Zebedee	1	S/Lamb	0-6-4T	1974
		rebuilt Tambling		1990
Gladiator	3	Minirail	4w-4wDH	c1960
Arthur	4	Lister (20698)	4wDM	1942

(10.25in gauge)

Name	No	Builder	Type	Built
Duke of Cornwall	—	S/Lamb	4w-4wDH	c1980
Eric	—	Keef	0-6-0DH	2008

Rolling stock
15in gauge — 10 passenger coaches
10.25in gauge — 4 passenger coaches
7.25in gauge — 1 Mardyke APT set

motorbikes, children's play area, brick path maze, listed engine house and walks
Depot: Benny Halt
Facilities for disabled: Limited number of reserved parking bays. Toilets at East Wheal Rose and

Benny Halt. All buildings are single storey with no steps. Level or gently sloping paths with even surfaces. Main steam train has compartments with doors that will accommodate wheelchairs (only the largest motorised wheelchairs are excluded), ramps and staff available to assist. The smaller train at East Wheal Rose cannot take wheelchairs. Some other attractions are not suitable for wheelchair users

(eg canoes, mine building, maze and country walks)
Public opening: Easter to end of October, usually daily but ring for early and late season opening days

Launceston Steam Railway

Member: HRA, TT
The railway runs through the beautiful Kensey Valley on a track gauge of 1ft 11.5in, following the trackbed of the old North Cornwall Railway. The locomotives formerly worked on the Dinorwic and Penrhyn railways in North Wales. Launceston station contains a museum of vintage cars and motorcycles and a collection of fascinating and intriguing items. There are catering, gift shop and bookshop facilities. At the far end of the line there are pleasant riverside walks and a shaded picnic area, adjacent to Newmills Farm Park (a popular separate attraction). The covered rolling stock ensures an enjoyable visit whatever the weather. The station area was once the site of an Augustinian Priory some of which can be seen by visitors to the railway. Ticket valid for unlimited travel on day of issue
Location: Newport Industrial Estate, Launceston, Cornwall
OS reference: SX 328850
Operating society/organisation: Launceston Steam Railway, Newport, Launceston PL15 8DA
Telephone: (01566) 775665
Internet address: *Web site:* www.launcestonsr.co.uk
Stations: Launceston-Hunts Crossing-New Mills
Car park: Newport Industrial Estate, Launceston
SatNav postcode: PL15 8EX
Access by public transport:

Industrial locomotives — 1ft 11.5in gauge

Name	No	Builder	Type	Built
Lilian	—	Hunslet (317)	0-4-0ST	1883
Velinheli	—	Hunslet (409)	0-4-0ST	1886
Covertcoat	—	Hunslet (679)	0-4-0ST	1898
Dorothea	—	Hunslet (763)	0-4-0ST	1901
—	—	M/Rail (5646)*	4wDM	1933
—	—	M/Rail (9546)	4wDM	1950

Locomotive notes: All passenger trains are steam-hauled.
Dorothea under restoration
*not in use, disamantled for future restoration

Stock
1 electric inspection trolley; 1 diesel-electric railcar for maintenance staff; 1 experimental diesel-electric railcar under construction; 4 bogie carriages (2 open, 2 closed), 1 Post Office underground railway unit

By rail: Plymouth or Bodmin 25 miles then bus
By bus: Plymouth, No 76; Liskeard No 236. Buses also from Bude and Tavistock
Access by road: Just north of Launceston town centre off the A388
Length of line: 2.5 miles
Gauge: 1ft 11.5in
On site facilities: Buffet, transport museum, workshop tours, gift and bookshop, all situated at Launceston
Period of public operation:
6-13 April; 27 May to 1 June; Sundays, Mondays and Tuesdays in June; daily (EXCEPT Saturdays) 1 July until 21 September; 28 October to 2 November
Public opening: Open from 10.30, trains run at 11.00, 12.00, 13.00,

14.00, 15.00, 16.00. Day Rover Tickets, unlimited rides on day of issue of ticket
Family ticket: Available, 2 adults and up to 4 children, £26.50.
Adults £9.00, children £6.00
Free travel: Children under three years old
Senior citizens: Discounted tickets £8.00
Groups: Discounted tickets (advance booking)
Journey time: Return 35min
Facilities for disabled: Easy access to all areas except bookshop and motorcycle museum. No toilet facilities for disabled. However, public toilets are reasonably accessible
Special events: Occasional visiting locomotives — see web site/press for details

Lavender Line

Member: HRA
The Lavender Line is centred around a typical country station, which, somewhat untypically, is in

the village it was built to serve. The image portrayed is of the transition steam-diesel era of the 1950s/1960s on the Southern Region of British

Railways
Location: Isfield Station, Isfield, Nr Uckfield, East Sussex TN22 5XB. Isfield village is off the A26

between Lewes and Uckfield
OS reference: TQ 452171
Operating society/organisation:
The Lavender Line Preservation
Society
Telephone/Fax:
Information line: 0891 800645
Business/fax: 01825 750515 (24hr
answerphone when not manned)
Internet address: *Web site:*
www.lavender-line.co.uk
Car park: On site, free to patrons
Access by car: The village of
Isfield lies just off the A26 between
Lewes and Uckfield and is clearly
signposted. From the Little
Horstead roundabout on the A22
just outside Uckfield, take the A26
south towards Lewes and after
about 1-mile take the small right-
hand turn marked Isfield. Follow
the road until you see the railway
on your right. From the A272
running between Uckfield and
Haywards Heath, take the turn at
Piltdown and follow the signs to the
Lavender Line and Isfield. From
Lewes take the A26 northwards
towards Uckfield. After about 5
miles look for a turning on the left
to Isfield, follow the road until you
see the railway on your right
Access by public transport:
By bus: Service 29 run by Brighton
& Hove Buses calls at Isfield and
runs between Brighton and
Tunbridge Wells. Tel: 01273
886200 or visit
http://www.buses.co.uk
By rail: Main line stations at
Lewes and Uckfield. On Sundays
trains to Uckfield only operate on a
much reduced frequency. Tel:
08457 484950
On site facilities: 'Cinders' buffet,
family garden, signalbox, gift shop,
Display coach (not open during

Multiple-unit

Name	No	Origin	Class	Type	Built
—	03020	BR	03	0-6-0DM	1958
—	03197	BR	03	0-6-0DM	1961
—	69333	BR	422 / 4BIG	TRBS	1965
—*	60151	BR	205	DTC	1962
—*	60678	BR	205	DMBS	1962
—	60822	BR	205	DTC	1957
—*	60832	BR	205	DTC	1962
—	54279	BR	108	DTC	1960
—	999507	BR	Wickham	Railbus	1960

*unit 205033

Industrial locomotives

Name	No	Builder	Type	Built
—	—	H/Leslie (3837)	0-6-0ST	1934
Austin 1	5459	Kitson (5459)	0-6-0ST	1932
Birkenhead	—	RSH (7386)	0-4-0ST	1948
—	—	Barclay	0-4-0DM	1945
—	—	Vulcan	0-4-0DM	1945
—	15	Planet (3865)	4wDM	1965
Valient	01583	R/Hornsby (459517)	0-6-0DH	1961

Stock
A selection of BR Mk 1 vehicles including BCK and BG, as well as a selection of wagons

Owners
H/Leslie the Hawthorn Leslie 3837 Locomotive Society
Austin 1 on loan from Llangollen Railway

Santa Specials), model railway in
the goods shed. Miniature 5in
gauge railway (open some
Sundays). Baby changing facilities
and disabled toilet. Children's
parties on operating days. Private
parties and functions catered for
(tel: 01903 761455).
Length of line: 1 mile each out and
back trip, takes 15min
Public opening: Open Sundays all
year, Bank Holidays, half term,
Wednesdays and Thursdays in
August. On some Saturdays when
Footplate Days are held the site is

open, but public rides are not
available. Entry to the station is free
on these days
Facilities for disabled: Access to
most facilities on site, buffet,
platforms, shop, except signalbox,
display coach and trains. A ramp is
available for partially disabled
access to the trains. Disabled toilets
Special events: These will be
posted on the web site
Special facilities: Occasional wine
and dine services. Please contact for
details

Museum	Leeds Industrial Museum	Leeds

Location: The Leeds Industrial
Museum, Armley Mills, Canal
Road, Leeds LS12 2QF
OS reference: SE 275342
Operating society/organisation:
Leeds City Council, Department of
Learning & Leisure, The Town
Hall, Headrow, Leeds LS1 2QF
Curator of Engineering:

Industrial locomotives

Name	No	Builder	Type	Built
1ft 6in gauge				
Jack	—	Hunslet 684)	0-4-0WT	1898
Coffin	—*	G/Bat (1326)	0-4-0BE	1933
2ft gauge				
Barber	—	T/Green (441)	0-6-2ST	1908
Cheetal	—	Fowler (15991)	0-6-0WT	1923

England

N. Dowlan
Telephone: (0113) 263 7861
Internet address:
www.leeds.gov.uk/armleymills
Car park: Cark park adjacent to
the museum
Access by public transport:
Nos 5, 14 and 67 from City Square,
Leeds (outside the railway station).
Services 15, 33, 33A, 670 and 760
go to the Vue Cinema complex on
Kirkstall Road from Leeds city bus
station
Public opening:
Tuesdays to Saturdays 10.00-17.00,
Sundays 13.00-17.00. Closed
Sundays and Mondays (except
Bank Holidays).
Last admission 16.00 on all days
On site facilities: Museum shop,
refreshments (vending machines),
picnic area
Special notes: Facilities for the
disabled (toilets etc), lifts. Museum
can be viewed by visitors in
wheelchairs (most areas are
accessible)
**Details of locomotive and rolling
stock:** Locomotive collection
includes steam, diesel, mines
locomotives and a narrow gauge
railway and engines

Name	No	Builder	Type	Built
Simplex	—	M/Rail (1369	4wPM	1918
Hudson Fordson	—	Hudson (36863)	4wDM	1928
Layer	—*	Fowler (21294)	4wDM	1936
Hudson Hunslet	—	Hunslet (2959)	4wDM	1944
Resin	—	Hunslet (2008)	0-4-0DM	1939
Nacob	—*	Hunslet (5340)	0-4-0DM	1957
Sharlston	—†	H/Clarke (1164)	0-4-0DM	1959
Demtox	—†*	Hunslet (6048)	0-4-0DM	1961

2ft 1in gauge

Name	No	Builder	Type	Built
Fricl	—*	Hunslet (4019)	0-4-0DM	1948
Pitpo	—*	Hunslet	0-4-0	1955
Calverton	—*	H/Clarke (1368)	0-4-0DM	1965

2ft 6in gauge

Name	No	Builder	Type	Built
Junin	—	H/Clarke (D557)	2-6-2DM	1930
Fimyn	—†	Hunslet (3411)	0-4-0DM	1947

2ft 8in gauge

Name	No	Builder	Type	Built
Ficol	—*	Hunslet (3200)	0-4-0DM	1945

2ft 11in gauge

Name	No	Builder	Type	Built
Lurch	—	H/Clarke (D571)	4wDM	1932

3ft gauge

Name	No	Builder	Type	Built
Lord Granby	—*	H/Clarke (633)	0-4-0ST	1902
Cement	—*	Fowler (20685)	2-4-0DM	1935
Lofti	—*	Hunslet (4057)	0-6-0DM	1953

3ft 6in gauge

Name	No	Builder	Type	Built
Pioneer	—	H/Clarke (D634)	0-6-0DM	1946
Festival of Britain	—*	H/Clarke (D733)	0-6-0DM	1951

Standard gauge

Name	No	Builder	Type	Built
Hodbarrow	—*	Hunslet (299)	0-4-0ST	1882
Aldwyth	—	M/Wardle (865)	0-6-0ST	1882
Capper	—	Fowler (22060)	0-4-0DM	1938
Fort William	—*	Fowler (22893)	0-4-0DM	1940
Trecwn	—	Hunslet (2390)	0-4-0DM	1941
Elizabeth	—	H/Clarke (1888)	0-4-0ST	1958
Southam No 2	—*	H/Clarke (D625)	0-4-0DM	1942
Luton	—	G/Bat (1210)	0-4-0BE	1930
Smithy Wood	—*	G/Bat (2543)	0-4-0WE	1955

Notes
*not currently on public display
†on loan to Red Rose Steam Society/Astley Green Colliery Museum
Simplex is on loan to Moseley Industrial Railway Museum
Barber is on loan to the South Tynedale Railway Trust from February 2004

Timetable Service	**Leighton Buzzard Railway**	Bedfordshire

Member: HRA, TT, AIM
The LBR enables visitors to take a
70min journey into the vanished
world of the English light railway.
Sharp curves and steep gradients
make the locomotives work hard
and it is unique with its roadside

running. The LBR possesses one of
the largest collection of narrow
gauge locomotives in Britain
together with a varied selection of
coaches and wagons — an
important part of the national
railway heritage

General Manager: J. Horsley
Headquarters: Leighton Buzzard
Railway, Page's Park Station,
Billington Road, Leighton Buzzard,
Bedfordshire LU7 4TN
OS reference: Page's Park SP
928242

Telephone: (01525) 373888
Internet addresses: *E-mail:* station@lbngrs.org.uk
Web site: www.buzzrail.co.uk
Main station: Page's Park. The station is on the south side of Leighton Buzzard, near the A505/A4146 roundabout
Other public stations: Stonehenge Works
Car park: Page's Park, free. Prior notification for coaches is advisable
SatNav postcode: LU7 4TN. Note that the station is on the eastern side of Billingon Road
Access by public transport:
By rail: Leighton Buzzard station, London Midland services from London (Euston) to Birmingham and Crewe; Southern services from East Croydon and Clapham Junction; (Tel: 08457 484950).
By bus: No D1 runs from Leighton Buzzard main line station and town centre to and from Page's Park except Sundays and Bank Holidays (Tel: 0871 200 2233 for details)
Refreshment facilities: Buffet at Page's Park for hot & cold snacks, drinks and ice creams.
Refreshments also at Stonehenge Works
Souvenir shop: Page's Park and Stonehenge Works
Depots: Page's Park and Stonehenge Works
Length of line: 2.85 miles, 2ft gauge
Journey time: Single 25min, return 70min
Passenger trains: Page's Park-Stonehenge Works.
 Group discounts for pre-booked parties of 10 or more people. Packages such as Birthday Breaks, Schools trains and Sunset Specials available, plus train hire
Period of public operation:
Sundays 18 March-28 October;
Mondays 9 April, 7 May, 4 June, 28 August;
Tuesdays 5 June, 24 July-21 August;
Wednesdays 4, 11 April, 25 July-29 August, 31 October;
Thursdays 26 July-23 August
Friday 6 April
Saturdays 7 April, 5 May, 2 June, 2-23 August, 15 September
Special events: Little Chuffer's Bank Holiday — 3/4 June; Father's Day — 17 June; Dunstable Dasher

Locomotives — 2ft gauge

Name	No	Builder	Type	Built
—	—	O&K (2544)	0-4-0WT	1907
Pedemoura	—	O&K (10808)	0-6-0WT	1924
—	778	Baldwin (44656)	4-6-0T	1917
Penlee	—	Freudenstein (73)	0-4-0WT	1901
Sezela No 4	—	Avonside (1738)	0-4-0T	1915
Elidir	—	Avonside (2071)	0-4-0T	1933
Peter Pan	114	K/Stuart (4256)	0-4-0ST	1922
Chaloner	1	de Winton	0-4-0VBT	1877
Bluebell	1	Hibberd (2631)	4wDM	1938
Pixie	—	K/Stuart (4260)	0-4-0ST	1922
Rishra	3	Baguley (2007)	0-4-0T	1921
Doll	4	Barclay (1641)	0-6-0T	1919
Elf	5	O&K (12740)	0-6-0WT	1936
Falcon	7	O&K (8986)	4wDM	1938
—	8	Ruston (217999)	4wDM	1943
Madge	9	O&K (7600)	4wDM	1934
Haydn Taylor	10	M/Rail (7956)	4wDM	1945
P. C. Allen	11	O&K (5834)	0-4-0WT	1912
—	12	M/Rail (6012)	4wPM	1930
Arkle	13	M/Rail (7108)	4wDM	1937
—	14	Hunslet (3646)	4wDM	1946
—	15	Hibberd (2514)	4wDM	1941
—	16	Lister (11221)	4wDM	1939
Damredub	17	M/Rail (7036)	4wDM	1936
Feanor	18	M/Rail (11003)	4wDM	1956
—	19	M/Rail (11298)	4wDM	1965
—	20	M/Rail (60s317)	4wDM	1966
Festoon	21	M/Rail (4570)	4wPM	1929
—	22	under construction	4wDM	—
—	23	Ruston (164346)	4wDM	1932
—	25	M/Rail (7214)	4wDM	1938
—	24	M/Rail (11297)	4wDM	1965
Yimkin	26	Ruston (203026)	4wDM	1941
—	26	M/Rail (8720)	4wDM	1941
—	27	Ruston (408430)	4wDM	1957
RAF Stanbridge	28	Ruston (200516)	4wDM	1940
Creepy	29	Hunslet (6008)	4wDM	1963
—	30	M/Rail (8695)	4wDM	1941
—	31	Lister (4228)	4wPM	1931
—	32	Ruston (172892)	4wDM	1934
—	33	Hibberd (3582)	4wDM	1954
Red Rum	34	M/Rail (7105)	4wDM	1936
—	35	Hunslet (6619)	0-4-0DM	1966
Caravan	36	M/Rail (7129)	4wDM	1938
—	37	Ruston (172901)	4wDM	1934
Harry Barnett	38	Lister (37170)	4wDM	1951
T. W. Lewis	39	Ruston (375316)	4wDM	1954
Trent	40	Ruston (283507)	4wDM	1949
Somme	41	Hunslet (2536)	4wDM	1941
Sarah	42	Ruston (223692)	4wDM	1944
—	43	M/Rail (10409)	4wDM	1954
—	44	M/Rail (7933)	4wDM	1941
—	45	M/Rail (21615)	4wDM	1957
—	46	Ruston (209430)	4wDM	1942
—	47	Hudson (38384)	4wDM	1930
MacNamara	48	Hunslet (4351)	4wDM	1952
—	49	Hibberd (2586)	4wDM	1941
—	50	Hibberd (1568)	4wPM	1927
—	52	Ruston (187105)	4wDM	1937
Beaudesert	80	A/Keef (59R)	4wDH	1999
Peter Wood	81	Hunslet (9347)	4wDH	1994
—	3098	M/Rail (1377)	4wPM	1918

England

50 — 1 July; Teddy Bears' Outing — 15 July; Welsh Steam Up — 15/16 September; Motorcycle Rally — 30 September; Halloween Haunting — 28 October; Christmas Trains — dates in December to be confirmed

Facilities for disabled: Priority parking at Page's Park. Ramp access to all facilities including dedicated toilet at Page's Park. Wheelchairs are conveyed in specially adapted coaches. Advance notice appreciated. Web site pages and leaflets available in large print on request

Membership details: The line is operated by unpaid volunteers. Membership secretary, c/o above address

Name	No	Builder	Type	Built
—	2182	M/Rail (461)	4wPM	1917
LOD 758009	—	M/Rail (8641)	4wDM	1941
LOD 758220	—	M/Rail (8745)	4wDM	1942
RTT/767182	—	Wickham (2522)	4wPMR	1938
WD 767139	—	Wickham (3282)	4wPMR	1943
AMW No 165	—	Ruston (194784)	4wDM	1939
—	NG23	B/Drewry (3702)	4wBE	1973
—	NG46	B/Drewry (3698)	4wDH	1974

Stock
10 coaches and a wide selection of wagons

A selection of locomotives and rolling stock is on public display at any one time. Viewing of other stock is by prior arrangement. Some items stored off-site

Membership journal: *Chaloner* — quarterly
Marketing name: The Leighton Buzzard Slow Train, England's Friendly Little Line

---

Miniature Railway	**Lightwater Valley Theme Park**	North Yorkshire

Location: Lightwater Valley Theme Park
Headquarters: North Stainley, Ripon, North Yorkshire HG4 3HT
Contact: Paul Walker (Operations manager), Tony Bolsover (Maintenance Manager)
Telephone: 0871 720 0011
Fax: 0871 721 001
Internet addresses: *E-mail:* leisure@lightwatervalley.co.uk
Web site: www.lightwatervalley.co.uk
Car parking: On site, free
Access by public transport:

Locomotives — 15in gauge

Name	No	Builder	Type	Built
Rio Grande	278	S/Lamb	2-8-0	1984

Rolling stock
6 Severn Lamb-built carriages, including one wheelchair carriage — converted by LVR — to carry two wheelchairs

By rail: Harrogate (12 miles) and Thirsk (9 miles)
On site facilities: Home to three great attractions, all set in 175 acres of gorgeous North Yorkshire parkland (theme park, shopping village and birds of prey centre)

Length of line: 15in gauge; 1-mile, long loop circuit including four stations
Period of public operation: Easter-October. Telephone for details

---

Railway Centre	**Lincolnshire Coast Light Railway**	Lincolnshire

Member: HRA
The Lincolnshire Coast Light Railway is at an early stage of re-opening after an absence of 25 years. The LCLR runs within part of a caravan park that covers 250 acres.
Location/headquarters: Lincolnshire Coast Light Railway, Skegness Water Leisure Park, Walls Lane, Ingoldmells, Lincolnshire PE25 1JF
Postal address: Lincolnshire Coast Light Railway, 55 Burgh Road, Skegness, Lincolnshire PE25 2RJ

Industrial ocomotives — 2ft gauge

Name	No	Builder	Type	Built
Paul	1	M/Rail (3995)	4wDM	1927
Jurassic	2	Peckett (1008)	0-6-0ST	1903
Wilton	4	M/Rail (7481)	4wDM	1940
—	5	M/Rail (8622)	4wDM	1941
—	6	M/Rail (8874)	4wDM	1944
Nocton	7	M/Rail (1935)	4wDM	1920

Rolling stock
Stock includes 2 carriages built for the Ashover Light Railway, Nocton Estates Light Railway carriage, a unique Sand Hutton Light Railway carriage. Also within the collection is the only surviving ambulance van built for the World War 1 trench railways along with a Class P 4-wheel ration wagon

SatNav postcode: PE25 1JF
Contact: John Chappell
Internet addresses:
Web site: www.lincolnshire-coast-light-railway.co.uk
Access by public transport:
By rail: Skegness 3.5 miles
By bus: Main bus routes along the A52 (5-10min frequency), then approx 15min walk
Access by car: Ample parking within the park
On site facilities: Within the park

there is a café, restaurant, fully licensed bar, with adjacent children's play area (see www.skegnesswaterleisurepark.co.uk for full details). Heated toilets
Length of line: 0.7 mile
Period of public operation:
Usually Bank Holiday weekends and weekends in July and August. Opening dates are posted via the web site, comfimed 2012 dates are 2/3 June, 28 July, 4, 11, 18, 25/26 August. Opening times are 10.30-

16.00 (last departure 15.40) when open
Facilities for disabled: All on the level, including RADAR toilets within 50m of 'Lakeview' station
Special events: Gala weekend in September
Special notes: When open the locomotive shed is normally available for tours subject to staff availability

---

Lincolnshire Wolds Railway

Members: HRA
The only standard gauge steam railway in Lincolnshire open to the public. The location is part of the original Great Northern Railway, which opened in 1848 and closed to passengers in 1970, with the section between Grimsby and Louth retained for freight services until 1980
Headquarters: The Railway Station, Ludborough, Grimsby, NE Lincs DN36 5SQ
Telephone: 01507 363881
Internet address: *Web site:* www.lincolnshirewoldsrailway.co.uk
Contact: Frank Street
Main station: Ludborough
OS reference: TF 302986
SatNav postcode: DN36 5SH
Car park: Opposite station site.
Note: Take turning to Fulstow, *not* Ludborough village when travelling via the A16.
Access by public transport:
No access by rail, very limited Grimsby-Louth bus service
Refreshment facilities: Light refreshments available in buffet car in bay platform on diesel and steam days. Open from 10.30 on running days
Souvenir shop: On site
Museum: On site
Depot: On site,
Length of line: 1.5 miles
Period of public operation: Site open for static viewing all weekends except Christmas. April to September 09.00-16.00, October to March 09.00-15.00. Trains depart Ludborough at 10.45, 11.45, 12.45, 13.45, 14.45 and

Locomotives and multiple-units

Name	No	Origin	Class	Type	Built
—	D3167	BR	08	0-6-0DE	1955
—	97650	BR	—	0-6-0DE	1953
—	62887*	BR	4CIG/ 421	MBS	1970
—	1313	SJ	B	4-6-0	1917

*non-runner in use as disabled buffet coach

Industrial locomotives

Name	No	Builder	Type	Built
Spitfire	—	Barclay (1964)	0-4-0ST	1929
Lion	—	Peckett (1351)	0-4-0ST	1914
Fulstow	2	Peckett (1749)	0-4-0ST	1928
M. F. P. No 1	—	Fowler (4210131)	0-4-0DM	1957
M. O. P. No 8	—	Fowler (4210145)	0-4-0DM	1958
Tioxide No 4	—	R/Hornsby (375713)	0-4-0DM	1954
Tioxide No 6	—	R/Hornsby (414303)	0-4-0DM	1957
Tioxide No 7	7	R/Hornsby (421418)	0-4-0DM	1958
—	—	R/Hornsby (423657)	0-4-0DM	
—	—	Sentinel (10166)	0-6-0DH	1963
Colonel B	—	Hunslet (5308)	4wDH	1963

Stock
6 ex-BR Mk 2 coaches, various wagons

Owners
D3167 and 97650 on loan from Lincoln City Council
Lion and *Fulstow* the Great Northern Locomotives Ltd

15.45, returning from North Thoresby 25min later.
Trains operate on the following dates: 18, 25 March; 7-9, 15, 19 April; 6/7, 20 May; 3-5, 17 June; 1, 8, 22 July; 1, 5, 8, 12, 15, 19, 22, 26/27, 29 August; 8/9, 30 September; 14, 24, 28 October; 3, 25 November; 8/9, 15/16 December (Santa Specials pre-booked only)
Ticket allows unlimited travel on day of purchase EXCEPT Easter Gala, 1940s Weekend and Santa Special

Special events: Mother's Day Special — 18 March; British Summertime Special — 25 March; Easter Steam Gala — 7-9 April; May Day Celebration — 6/7 May; Teddy Bears' Weekend — 3/4 June; Lincolnshire Louth Motor Club, Classic Car Day — 17 June; Jubilee Special — 5 June; Strawberries and Cream — 1, 8 July; Schools Out For Summer — 22 July; Scarecrow Festival — 26/27 July; 1940s Weekend — 8/9 September; Mixed Traction and Lincolnshire Day —

England

30 September; Ploughman's Lunch Day — 14 October; Ghost Train, Witches and Wizards — 28 October; Bonfire Night — 3 November; Santa Arrives at Ludborough — 25 November; Santa Special (pre-booking essential) — 8/9, 15/16 December

Facilities for disabled: Disabled persons can ride on the train, have access to the buffet car and disabled toilets
Special notes: Toilet facilities include baby changing area. School groups and coach parties by arrangement. Discounts for parties

over 20. Please contact for details
Membership journal: *On the Line* is the society magazine produced by the supporting association, 3 times/year
Special note: Unlimited travel on the day EXCEPT Easter Gala, 1940s Weekend and Santa Special

Museum
Locomotion — The NRM at Shildon
County Durham

Member: HRA
Locomotion is an £11 million project, a joint venture between the local authority and the National Railway Museum at York, the first branch of a national museum in the region. The development includes interactive displays within buildings which are of historical importance in terms of the town's railway heritage and a high quality 6,000sq ft centre, which houses up to 60 vehicles from the national collection.
Museum Manager: Dr George Muirhead
Location/address: Locomotion, Shildon, Co Durham DL4 1PQ
Telephone: (01388) 777999 / 772000
Telephone/Fax: (01388) 771448
Internet addresses: *E-mail:* locomotion@nrm.org.uk
Web site: www.nrm.org.uk
Car parking: Available on site, also disabled and coach parking
Access by public transport: Rail – 3min walk from Shildon station. Bus – local bus services (call Traveline on 0870 608 2608).
Access by car: From the south, junction 60 A1M, take A689 and A6072 to Coundon roundabout then turn left by a minor road to Shildon
On site facilities: Café, children's playground, picnic area, public art sculpture, shop
Length of line: 1 kilometre
Public opening: 10.00-17.00 every day from Easter to early October. 10.00-16.00 Wednesday to Sunday from early October to Easter. Closed over Christmas and New Year. Limited opening on Mondays and Tuesdays — please call for information
Special events: A full and exciting events programme, contact

Locomotives and multiple-units

Name	No	Origin	Class	Type	Built
Sans Pareil	—	L&MR		0-4-0	1829
Cornwall	3020	LNWR	—	2-2-2	1847
	1	GNR	—	4-2-2	1870
	563	LSWR	T3	4-4-0	1893
	1247	GNR	J52	0-6-0ST	1899
	65033	NER	J21	0-6-0	1899
	1	NER	BTH	Bo electric	1904
	2	NSR	New L	0-6-2T	1923
	13000	LMS	5P4F	2-6-0	1934
Mallard	4468	LNER	A4	4-6-2	1938
	10656	SR	2BIL	DMBSK	1937
	12123	SR	2BIL	DTCK	1937
Green Arrow	4771	LNER	V2	2-6-2	1937
Deltic	—	E/Electric	-	Co-Co	1955
	E5001	BR	71	Bo-Bo	1959
	03090	BR	03	0-6-0DM	1960
Sans Pareil	—*	L&MR		0-4-0	1980

*replica of original Liverpool & Manchester Railway built for the 150th anniversary

Industrial and Army locomotives

Name	No	Builder	Type	Built
Hetton Loco	—	G. Stephenson	0-4-0	1851
	755	Siemens	4wRE	1898
	—	Simplex (4217)	4wPM	1925
Merlin	—	Peckett	0-4-0ST	
Eustace Forth	15	RSH (7063)	0-4-0ST	1942
King Fisal of Iraq	—	Hunslet (3183)	0-6-0ST	1944
Juno	—	Hunslet (3850)	0-6-0ST	1958
	1	Barclay (2373)	0-4-0F	1956
Rowntrees No 3	—	R/Hornsby (441934)	4wDM	1960
	14†	H/Clarke (D1274)	0-6-0DM	1961
	H001	Sentinel (100003)	4wDH	1959

†3ft gauge

Rolling stock powered units – gas turbine
1972   BR Advanced Passenger Train

Rolling stock powered units – electric
1983   BR APT prototype train

Rolling stock powered units — diesel
1937   SR Driving Motor Brake Third No S10656S
1937   SR Driving Trailer Composite No S12123S

Locomotion for full details
Access for disabled: All buildings fully accessible. Call Locomotion in advance to book a wheelchair. Bio-bus accommodates disabled visitors to transport from one end of the site to the other
Special facilities: There are three conference rooms, each holding from 10 to 65 people, catering and presentation equipment available. Space for 200 people for a sit-down meal in the Collection building
Special note: Steam train rides on some school holidays and event days

Rolling stock – departmental
1850	GNR 4-wheel hand crane No 112
1891	NER snow plough No DE900566
1904	MR Officers' Saloon No 2234
1949	BR Matisa tamping machine No 74007
1957	BR Track recording trolley No DX 50002 Neptune

Rolling stock — passenger
1845	S&DR 1st/3rd Composite No 59
1872	NLR Directors' Saloon No 1032
1887	GWR 6-wheel tricomposite No 820
1905	LNWR Corridor 1st Brake 5154 (Royal Train)
1905	LNWR Corridor 1st Brake 5154 (support vehicle)
1908	ECJS Passenger Brake Van No 109
1928	LMS 3rd Sleeping Car No 14241
1962	BR Mk I 1st corridor No 21274

Rolling stock – freight and non-passenger-carrying
1826	Cramlington Colliery Chaldron Wagon
1870	S&DR Chaldron Wagon (replica)
1870	Seaham Harbour Colliery Chaldron Wagon
1889	Shell-Mex oil tank wagon No 512
1901	Shell/BP Tank Wagon No 3171
1907	NER 16-ton bogie stores van No 041273
1912	NER Sand wagon No DE14974
1920	GCR single bolster wagon
1920	GNR double bolster wagon
1926	GWR Fitted open wagon No 108246
1935	GWR Motor car van No 126438
1936	LMS Tube wagon No 499254
1940	WD Warflat No 161042
1940	LNER Tunnel Van No DE471818
1946	SNCF 16-ton mineral wagon No ADB192437
1946	LNER 20-ton hopper wagon No E270919
1950	BR 24-ton iron ore hopper wagon No B436275
1951	BR(SR) Show cattle wagon No S3733S
1952	BR 30-ton bogie bolster wagon No B943139
1953	Buxton Lime Quarries 23-ton bogie hopper wagon No 19154
1954	National Benzole oil tank wagon No 2022
1955	BR china clay tip wagon No B743141
1957	BR Horse box No S96369
1959	BR Conflat No B737725
1960	BR Banana Van No B882593
1961	BR Presflo cement wagon No B873368
1964	Prototype HAA coal hopper wagon, No 350000
1965	BR Boiler Wagon Nos DB902805, DB902806, DB902807, DB902808
1970	Phillips Petroleum 100-ton GLW tank wagon No PP85209
1970	S&D Chaldron Wagon (replica), Shildon
1982	BR MGR wagon No HDA368459

Locomotive tender
SDR 'collier' class *Etherley*

Powered units
SR   2BIL unit, No 2090

Passenger stock
1850	SDR 3rd No 179
1908	ECJS Passenger brake van LNER No 396 S&D Chaldron wagon

Owners
R/Hornsby (441934) on loan from North Yorkshire Moors Railway
65033 the Locomotive Conservation & Learning Trust
Juno on loan from the Isle of Wight Steam Railway

London Transport Museum

Museum — London

Member: HRA, TT
Lively galleries tell the story of London's transport system and how it shaped the lives of people living and working in London, including current and future transport developments. The Design for Travel gallery showcases original artworks and advertising posters
Location: Covent Garden Piazza, London WC2E 7BB
OS reference: TQ 303809

Locomotives
Name	No	Origin	Class	Type	Built
—	23	Met Rly	A	4-4-0T	1866
John Hampden	5	Met Rly		Bo-Bo	1922

Electric stock
4248 District Rly Q23 stock driving motor coach 1923
11182 LPTB 1938 stock driving motor coach
400 Met Rly bogie stock coach 1899
30 City & South London Rly 'Padded Cell' coach 1890

Stock
1 electric tram; 2 horse buses; 4 motorbuses; 1 trolleybus; 1 horse tram

England

Operating society/organisation: Transport for London
Telephone:
020 7565 7299 (24hr recorded)
020 7565 7298 (Administration, education service, group bookings, events and activities, corporate hospitality, mail order enquiries)
Fax: 020 7565 7250
Internet addresses:
E-mail: enquiry@ltmuseum.co.uk
Web site: www.ltmuseum.co.uk
Access by public transport: Tube stations: Covent Garden, Holborn, Leicester Square
Main line station: Charing Cross.
Buses to Strand or Aldwych
On site facilities: Photo and research library (by appointment only), resource centre, lecture theatre, shop, café, lift, toilets (inc disabled) and baby changing facilities
Public opening (museum):
Saturday to Thursday: 10.00-18.00 (last admission 17.15).
Friday: 11.00-18.00 (last admission 17.15).
Closed 24-26 December
Public opening (shop):
Sunday to Tuesday: 10.00-18.30.
Wednesday, Thursday and Saturday: 10.00-19.00.
Friday: 11.00-29.00.
Closed 24-26 December
Public opening (Upper Deck Café Bar):
Monday to Thursday: 10.00-19.00.
Friday: 11.00-19.00.
Saturday: 10.00-21.30.
Sunday: 10.00-19.00.
Closed 25/26 December.

For group bookings please contact the museum in advance, group rates are available for pre-booked parties
Facilities for disabled: A lift and ramps give access throughout the museum. Facilities include a disabled toilet. Reduced admission for registered disabled visitors and person accompanying them. Due to the historic nature of the collection not all the vehicles are accessible
Membership details: Benefits of membership include discount on purchases made at museum shops at Covent Garden and Acton, discounted rate on talks and events. These are just some of the benefits available. Details from the Friends of London Transport Museum on 020 7565 7298

Museum — London Transport Museum Depot — London

Member: HRA, TT
The Depot is a working museum store and treasure trove of over 370,000 objects. Attractions include rare road and rail vehicles, station models, signs, ticket machines, posters and original artwork
Contact: London Transport Museum, 39 Wellington Street, London WC2E 7BB
Depot location:
2 Museum Way, 118-120 Gunnersbury Lane, Acton, London W3 8BQ
Operating society/organisation: Transport for London
Telephone:
020 7565 7299 (24hr recorded information)
020 7565 7298 (Administration, education service, group bookings, events and archives, corporate hospitality, mail order enquiries)
Fax: 020 7565 7250
Internet addresses:
E-mail: enquiry@ltmuseum.co.uk
Web site: www.ltmuseum.co.uk
Access by public transport: Bus (E3) or Underground to Acton Town station
Access by car: Parking on site is reserved for blue badge holders and must be requested in advance. Limited parking available in local

Locomotives and multiple-units

Name	No	Origin	Class	Type	Built
—	13	C&SLR	—		1890
—	ESL107	LT	—	Bo-Bo	1940
—	L35	LT	—	Bo-BoBE	1938
—	10012	LT	1938	DM	1938
—	012256	LT	1938	T	1939
—	12048	LT	1938	M	1939
—	11012	LT	1938	DM	1938
—	320	LT	Standard		1925-34
—	846	LT	Standard		1925-34
—	1789	LT	Standard		1925-34
—	3693	LT	Standard		1925-34
—	3327	LT	Standard		1925-34
—	4184	LT	Q	DM	1923
—	08063	LT	Q35	T	1935
—	4416	LT	Q38	DM	1938
—	4417	LT	Q38	DM	1938
—	22679	LT	R49	DM	1952
—	16	LT	Prototype	DM	1986
—	3530	LT	1972	DM	1972
—	3763	LT	1983	DM	1983
—	—	MR*	—	TC	1887
—	3052	LT	1967	DM	1967

*Metropolitan railway Jubilee coach body

Industrial locomotives

	Origin	Builder	Type	Built
	Wotton Tramway†	A/Porter (807)	0-4-0TG	1872

Rolling stock: freight

City & South London Railway ballast wagon, No 63 of 1921
Metropolitan Railway milk van of 1890

†on loan to Buckinghamshire Railway Museum

area. Parking available for groups booking a private view
On site facilities: Museum shop (Depot open weekends only), lecture theatre, toilets
Public opening:
Pre-booked guided tours on the last Friday and Saturday of the month. Private views can be arranged for groups.
For group bookings, please contact the museum in advance on

020 7565 7298. Group rates available for pre-booked parties of 10 or more
Facilities for disabled: Disabled toilet, on the ground floor, ramps and wheelchair platforms to some areas and a lift to the first floor. Parking on site for blue badge holders must be booked in advance. For further information, contact the Booking Office on 020 7565 7298 or e-mail

enquiry@ltmuseum.co.uk
Membership details: Details from the Friends of London Transport Museum on 020 7565 7296. Benefits include discount on purchases made at London Transport Museum shops in Covent Garden and Acton, discounted rate on talks and events. These are just some of the benefits available

---

Attraction — Longleat Railway — Wiltshire

Contact: Tim Bentley
Headquarters: Longleat Railway, Warminster, Wilts BA12 7NW
Telephone: 01985 845408
Internet address: *Web site:* www.longleat.co.uk
Car parking: On site
Access by public transport: Main line stations at Frome or Warminster
On site facilities: Too numerous to list, but include: Longleat House, safari park, mazes, safari boats, adventure castle, etc
Souvenir shops: Throughout the attraction
Length of line: 1.25 miles, 15in gauge

Locomotives — 15in gauge

Name	No	Builder	Type	Built
Lenka	4	Longleat	4-4DHR	1984
Ceawlin	5	Longleat*	2-8-2DH	1989
John Hayton	6	Exmoor Steam Railway	0-6-2	2004
Flynn	7	Keef (79)	0-6-0DH	2007

*rebuilt from Severn-Lamb 2-8-0DH dating from 1975

Rolling stock
11 passenger coaches and 3 works wagons

Opening times: Longleat House open all year (except Christmas Day). All attractions open daily in February half term, weekends only until end of March then open daily to end of October. 10.00-17.30 (earlier in off-peak season). First train from 10.30 in peak season and 11.30 in off-peak
Special events: Santa trains — end November and December (weekends)
Facilities for disabled: On each train

Timetable Service — Lynton & Barnstaple Railway — Devon

Member: HRA
The Lynton & Barnstaple Railway in North Devon is one of the world's most famous and picturesque narrow gauge lines. Passengers can now travel along part of the original route within the Exmoor National Park above the Heddon Valley near Parracombe. Awarded the HRA Annual Award for Small Groups 'for successfully re-creating the ambience of the legendary L&BR and for successfully running trains on the original trackbed at Woody Bay 69 years after the railway closed'
General Manager: Martyn Budd
Location/headquarters: Lynton & Barnstaple Railway, Woody Bay

Locomotives — 1ft 11.5in gauge

Name	No	Builder	Type	Built
Axe	—	K/Stuart (2451)	0-6-0T	1915
Sid	—	Maffei (4127)	0-4-0WT	1925
Pilton	—*	Drewry (2393)	0-6-0DM	1952
—	—	Hunslet (6652)	4wDH	1965
Heddon Hall	—	Hunslet (6660)	4wDH	1965

*under restoration off-site

Rolling stock
Original L&BR van No 23 (built 1908) is on display at Woody Bay station, and coaches Nos 7 and 17 (built 1897 and 1911 respectively) are being rebuilt off-site

Station, Martinhoe Cross, Parracombe, Devon EX31 4RA
Telephone: 01598 763487
Internet address: *Web site:*

www.lynton-rail.co.uk
Contact: Tony Nicholson, 10 Castle Heights, Lynton, Devon EX35 6JD

England

Steam Centre — Mangapps Railway Museum — Essex

Mangapps re-creates the
atmosphere of a rural light railway,
featuring a large museum
collection, strong in items of East
Anglian interest, railway signalling
and goods rolling stock. Other
features include original station
buildings from Mid-Suffolk Light,
Great Eastern and Midland & Great
Northern Railways
Superintendent of the Line:
John Jolly
Commercial Manager: June Jolly
Location: Mangapps Railway

Locomotives and multiple-units

Name	No	Origin	Class	Type	Built
—	2018	BR	03	0-6-0DM	1958
—	03089	BR	03	0-6-0DM	1960
Lucie	03081	BR	03	0-6-0DM	1960
—	03399	BR	03	0-6-0DM	1961
—	D2325	BR	04	0-6-0DM	1961
	33202	BR	33	Bo-Bo	1962
—	47793	BR	47	Co-Co	1964
—	51381	BR	117	DTS	1961
—	75033	BR	302	DTS	1958
—	75250	BR	302	DTS	1959
—	22624	LT	R38	DMS	1938
—	1030	LT	—	DM	1959

Museum, Southminster Road, Burnham-on-Crouch, Essex CM0 8QG. (Entrance on B1021, 1 mile north of Burnham)
Telephone: (01621) 784898
Fax: (01621) 783833
Internet address: *Web site:* www.mangapps.co.uk
Access by public transport: Burnham station approx 1 mile
On site facilities: Station, car park, souvenir shop, toilets, amenity and picnic areas
Refreshment facilities: Teas and light refreshments
Length of line: Three-quarter-mile
Public opening: Weekends and Bank Holidays all year (except closed November and Christmas/New Year period) and daily during summer school holidays.
Steam trains operate Bank Holiday Sundays and Mondays and special event days. Diesel trains run on all other days
Opening times: Weekends

Name	No	Origin	Class	Type	Built
—	2044	LT	–	T	1959
—	67218*	GER	F5	2-4-2T	—

*new-build under construction

Industrial locomotives

Name	No	Builder	Type	Built
Minnie	—	F/Walker (358)	0-6-0ST	1878
Brookfield	—	Bagnall (2613)	0-6-0PT	1940
Empress	—	Bagnall (3061)	0-6-0ST	1954
Toto	—	Barclay (1619)	0-4-0ST	1919
Hastings	—	Hunslet (469)	0-6-0ST	1888
Elland	No 1	H/Clarke (D1153)	0-4-0DM	1959
—	11104	Drewry (2252)	0-6-0DM	1948

Rolling stock
Large collection of over 80 passenger and goods rolling stock including LNER Gresley and BR Mk 1 coaching stock, with extensive stock of goods wagons, Canadian Pacific Railway brake/conductor's van No 434577

(however, closed 26 December to 31 January), Bank Holidays (except Christmas). Please phone before visiting in July and August.

11.30-17.00
Special events: Santa Specials — pre-Christmas weekends in December

---

Timetable Service — Mid-Hants Railway 'Watercress Line' — Hampshire

Member: HRA
Originally built as the Winchester to Alton link, the Mid-Hants Railway became known as the Watercress Line through regularly carrying this local produce to London markets. Now restored, the line runs from its main line connection at Alton through rolling countryside to its terminus at Alresford. Large and powerful locomotives work impressively over the steeply inclined route, known to railwaymen as 'the Alps'.
Headquarters: Mid-Hants Railway Ltd, Alresford Station, Alresford, Hants SO24 9JG
Telephone: 01962 733810
Fax: 01962 735448
Talking timetable: 01962 734866
Internet addresses: *E-mail:* info@watercressline.co.uk
Web site: www.watercressline.co.uk
Main station: Alresford
Other public stations: Ropley, Medstead & Four Marks, Alton
OS reference: Alresford SU 588325, Ropley SU 629324
SatNav postcodes:

Locomotives

Name	No	Origin	Class	Type	Built
—	30499	LSWR	S15	4-6-0	1920
—	30506	LSWR	S15	4-6-0	1920
Harry A. Frith	E828	SR	S15	4-6-0	1923
—	31625	SR	U	2-6-0	1929
—	31806	SR	U	2-6-0	1926
—	31874	SR	N	2-6-0	1925
Wadebridge	34007	SR	WC	4-6-2	1945
Bodmin	34016	SR	WC	4-6-2	1945
Swanage	34105	SR	WC	4-6-2	1950
Sir Frederick Pile	34058	SR	BB	4-6-2	1947
Canadian Pacific	35005	SR	MN	4-6-2	1945
—	41312	LMS	2MT	2-6-2T	1952
—	45379	LMS	5MT	4-6-0	1937
—	73096	BR	5MT	4-6-0	1956
—	75079	BR	4MT	4-6-0	1956
—	76017	BR	4MT	2-6-0	1954
—	80150	BR	4MT	2-6-4T	1956
—	92212	BR	9F	2-10-0	1959
—	08032	BR	08	0-6-0DE	1954
—	D3358	BR	08	0-6-0DE	1957
—	12049	BR	11	0-6-0DE	1948
—	D5353	BR	27	Bo-Bo	1961
—	33053	BR	33	Bo-Bo	1961
—	D6593	BR	33	Bo-Bo	1962
—	37905	BR	37	Co-Co	1960
—	45132	BR	45	1Co-Co1	1961
—	51592	BR	127	DMBS	1959
—	51604	BR	127	DMBS	1959

Alresford SO24 9JG,
Alton GU34 2PZ
Car park: Alresford, pay & display (free Sundays & Bank Holidays). Alton station pay & display
Access by public transport:
South West Train services — just over 1hr direct from London Waterloo to Alton. Alternatively, travel to Winchester station and catch a bus from nearby City Road.
Bus services – operated by Stagecoach (National Travel line 0871 200 2233 or www.traveline.org.uk)
Refreshment facilities: Buffet service on most trains; 'West Country' buffet, picnic area at Alresford; T. Junction picnic area at Ropley; tea/coffee available at Alton when information office open
Catering facilities: The 'Countryman Pullman' pre-booked Sunday lunch trains, Christmas specials, and some evening trains. The 'Watercress Belle' operates on certain Saturday evenings March-December. Early booking is essential, please telephone to confirm seat availability for both trains. Real Ale trains run selected Saturday evenings featuring beers from local breweries and light snacks to purchase
Souvenir shops: Alresford, Alton and Ropley
On site facilities: Picnic area, children's play area and viewing facilities at Ropley. Interpretative display in Alresford shop. Picnic area at Alresford
Depot: Ropley. Locomotive yard open on operating days 10.30-16.30
Length of line: 10 miles
Passenger trains: Phone Talking Timetable (01962 734866), or visit web site to confirm details. Bank Holidays and weekends January to October; Tuesdays to Thursdays May to September (inc), daily from 24 July to 31 August, school half term in February, October half term 'Wizard Week', Steam Galas, Day out with Thomas at Easter and

Name	No	Origin	Class	Type	Built
—	59719	BR	115	TCL	1960
—†	60124	BR	205	DMBS	1957
—†	60824	BR	205	DTCL	1957

†unit No 205025

Industrial locomotives

Name	No	Builder	Type	Built
Thomas	1	Hunslet (3781)	0-6-0T	1954
Douglas	10	Hunslet (2890)	0-6-0	1943
—	62-521*	Djuro Djakovic	0-6-0T	1954
—	30075*	Djuro Djakovic	0-6-0T	1950s

*based on the USATC 'USA' tank design

Stock
30 ex-BR Mk 1 coaches; 2 ex-BR Mk 2 coaches used for accommodation; 3 ex-BR Mk 1 Pullman Cars; 3 ex-SR coaches; 3 steam cranes; numerous goods vehicles

Owners
62-521 and 30075 Project 62 Group
30499 and 30506 the Urie Locomotive Society
E828 the Eastleigh Railway Preservation Society
34105 the 34105 Light Pacific Group
35005, 45379, 75079, D3358 and Class 205 the Mid-Hants Railway
76017 the Standard 4 Locomotive Group
08032 on loan from Aggregate Industries
34007 the Wadebridge (34007) Ltd/MHRPS Controlling Shareholders
D6539 is privately owned

August. Santa Specials in December (bookings commence October).

Dining and real ale trains operate regularly during the year.

Online booking at: www.watercressline.co.uk
Journey time: Round trip 1hr 40min max
Special events: Mother's Day — 18 March; Great Spring Steam Gala — 23-25 March; Day out with Thomas — 6-15 April; Alresford Watercress Festival — 13 May; War on the Line —9/10 June; Father's Day — 17 June; Alton Bus Rally and running day — 15 July; Day out with Thomas — 18-27 August; Autumn Steam Gala — 7-9 September; Open Day (Members and Shareholders) — 22 September; Peppa Pig — 29 October-2 November; Walk the Line — 10 November; Santa Specials — 1/2, 8/9, 15/16, 21-24 December; Christmas Leave — 26/27 December.
Freight Train running days — 26 May, 29 July, 16, 22 September. Hampshire Unit running days — 28 April, 26 May, 2 June, 15, 21 July, 22, 29 September, 27 October
Facilities for disabled: Toilets at Ropley, the old good shed at Alresford station and Alton. Passengers in fixed wheelchairs can be carried in the brake compartment on most trains. Ramps are provided to ease entry to trains. Ask South West Trains staff at Alton to cross foot crossing
Membership details: Membership Secretary, c/o above address.
E-mail: mhr.membership@btconnect.com

Timetable Service	**Mid-Norfolk Railway**	Norfolk

Member: HRA
The MNR's founding principle is to return a Community Rail Service from a yet to be built interchange platform adjacent to Wymondham main line railway station to Fakenham. The section from Wymondham Abbey station to Dereham has been purchased and

opened for passenger and freight traffic since May 1999. Clearance work is now completed between Dereham and Hoe, where re-sleepering continues; opening within 12 months is possible if donations for sleepers continue. County School tea room is currently open only on summer Sundays. The MNR's new pasing loop at Thuxton has enabled the staging of several two-train events including the Class 37s 50th Anniversary and the MNR's first steam gala. Work continues on the new signalbox

Headquarters: The Railway Station, Station Road, Dereham, Norfolk NR19 1DF

Main station: Dereham

Other principle station: Wymondham Abbey (note: this is not the main line station)

Other public stations: Yaxham, Thuxton, Kimberley Park

County School station: Currently road access only, tel: 01632 668181

SatNav postcodes:
Dereham — NR19 1DF
Wymondham Abbey — NR18 9PH

Telephone: (01362) 690633

Talking timetable: (01362) 851723 (answerphone)

Fax: (01362) 698487

Internet addresses:
E-mail: info@mnr.org.uk
Web site: www.mnr.org.uk

Car parks: Dereham and County School

Museum: Small relics museum at Dereham

Souvenir shop: Dereham

Refreshment facilities: Railway Buffet at Dereham (March-December) and tea room at County School station (summer Sundays only)

Access by public transport:
By rail: Abellio (National Express East Anglia) and East Midland Trains to Wymondham from Norwich and Ely
By bus: From Norwich and King's Lynn

Period of public operation:
Weekends and Bank Holidays 31 March to 4 November. Wednesdays 2 May to 31 October. Thursdays 16 July to 29 August. Steam services commence 2 June until end of August

Special events: Spring Diesel Gala — 30 March-1 April; Easter school

Locomotives and multiple-units

Name	No	Origin	Class	Type	Built
Eagle	08631	BR	08	0-6-0DE	1959
—	D8069	BR	20	Bo-Bo	1961
—	31235	BR	31	A1A-A1A	1960
Sister Dora	31530	BR	31	A1A-A1A	1961
—	37003	BR	37	Co-Co	1960
Aldeburgh Festival	47596	BR	47	Co-Co	1966
Ramillies	50019	BR	50	Co-Co	1968
—	73210	BR	73	Bo-Bo	1966
—	51226	M/Cam	101	DMBS	1958
Matthew Smith	51434	M/Cam	101	MBS	1958
—	51499	M/Cam	101	DMBS	1959
—	51503	M/Cam	101	DMC	1959
—	55009	Gloucester	122	DMBS	1958
—	59117	M/Cam	101	TC	1958
—	56301*	Gloucester	100	DTC	1957
—	68004	BR	MLV/419	DMLV	1959
—	62402†	BR	3CIG	MBSO	1971
—	69318	BR	4BIG	TRSB	1963
—	76764†	BR	3CIG	DTC	1971
—	76835†	BR	3CIG	DTC	1971

*in use as static shop and tea room at County School station
†unit No 1497 and named *Freshwater*

Locomotive notes: 08631, D8069, 31235, 31538, 37003, 47596, 50019 and 73210, also various DMUs are in service. Two Class B17 tenders arrived in December

Rolling stock: 6 BR Mk 1 coaches, 16 BR Mk 2 coaches (including the prototype vehicle), 1 BR Mk 3, 10-ton rail-mounted crane, selection of freight wagons

Owners
50019 and 68004 the Class 50 Locomotive Association
47596 the Stratford 47 Group — www.stratford47group.co.uk
31235 the Colne Valley Enterprises Ltd
D8069 the Type One Association
37003 the Class 37 Locomotive Group — www.c37lg.co.uk

holidays — 2-13 April; Easter Bunnies — 6-9 April; Stratford Depot Weekend — 5-7 May; Southern Gala Weekend — 19/20 May; Railway Children theatrical on site — 2-10 June; Kids for a Quid — 2-5 June; Steam and Diesel Together — 23/24 June; Steam in Action — 23 June-27 August (see web site or phone for further details); Steam Gala — 13/15 July; Railway at War Weekend — 4/5 August; Steam and Diesel Mixed Traffic Event/Beer Festival — 25-27 August — Class 47 50th Anniversary — 21-23 September; Multiple Matters Weekend — 20/21 October; Halloween Train — 27 October; Carol Train — 8 December; Santa

Specials — 1/2, 8/9, 12, 15/16, 21-24 December; Mince Pie Specials — 29 December and 1 January 2013.

A series of four Jazz Trains and six Fish & Chip trains will run during the season — see web site or telephone for further details.

All subject to availablilty, please check web site for latest information

Special facilities: Operational main line connection for charter, freight trains, etc. Line used for training purposes eg: low adhesion driving techniques. Film location

Membership details: Membership Secretary c/o Dereham Station

Membership journal: *The Blastpipe* (four times a year)

An item of GWR motive power in the eastern counties as recently restored No 6023 *King Edward II* visited the Mid-Norfolk Railway for running in during the summer of 2011. *ACB*

Small standard gauge to large narrow gauge. The contrast between Amberley Museum's Simplex 4wDM and Natal Government Railway's North British-built 2-8-4T could not be more marked, yet there is only 14in difference in the track gauge. *Phil Barnes / Mizens Farm (Ken Livermoor)*

England

Great Western away days. The Spa Valley Railway paid host to 2-6-2T No 5521, which is seen here at Eridge station on 24 April 2011. The Mid-Hants Railway saw the visit of both preserved GWR 4-4-0s No 3717 *City of Truro* double-heads with No 9017 *Earl of Berkley* at Medstead & Four Marks station during the MHR's Great Spring Gala on 25 March 2011. *Both Phil Barnes*

England

To visitor to the Chinnor & Princes Risborough Railway during 2011 was No 69621. It is seen here at Wainhill. *C&PRR (Phil Marsh)*

Most heritage railways are more than happy to hire out special trains, No D821 *Greyhound*, departs Bridgnorth on the Severn Valley Railway with an observation coach in tow. *Phil Barnes*

England

Member: HRA

The Mid-Suffolk Light Railway, known affectionately as 'The Middy', was a classic case of a railway built late on in the great railway age that never paid its way. It effectively went broke before it opened but still managed to struggle on for 50 years. This example of quirky English history is remembered in Suffolk's only railway museum

Location: Wetheringsett, Nr Stowmarket, Suffolk IP14 5PW

OS reference: TM 129659

Operating organisation: Mid-Suffolk Light Railway Company

Telephone: 01449 766899

Internet address: *Web site:* www.mslr.org.uk

Car park: On site

Access by public transport:
Buses: Some local buses from Ipswich to Diss set down and pick up on the A140 Ipswich-Norwich road near to the museum. Details of services can be obtained from Traveline — www.traveline.org.uk
Rail: Nearest station is Stowmarket

On site facilities: Souvenir shop, refreshments, railway walk (not when trains are running), railwayana and photographic exhibition, toilets (including disabled), visits to restoration works, real ale bar in summer when steam train running and picnic area

Period of public opening: Usually

Industrial locomotives

Name	No	Builder	Type	Built
Falmouth No 3	—	H/Leslie	0-4-0ST	1926
—	1604*	H/Clarke (1604)	0-6-0ST	1928
—	304470	R/Hornsby (304470)	0-4-0DM	1956

*under restoration

Rolling stock

GER 2-compartment brake third, GER 6-compartment third (under restoration for use as a real ale bar), GER 3-compartment first, 1 GER non-ventilated van, 1 GER 5-plank wagon,1 LMS van, 1 GWR van, private owner coal wagon (rebuilt from BR open wagon), LNER brake van, NER milk van body, 1 GER 5 compartment third body, 1 GER 5 compartment third (restored as 3 compartment third with first class saloon), LNER van, underframe to be used to construct replica MSLR open wagon. GER locomotive coal wagon. GER ventilated van body. GER steel outside frame ventilated van, GER horsebox body, conflat (to provide underframe for horsebox), replica contractor open wagon. Wickham Type 17 engineer's rail motor and trailer

open on Sundays and Bank Holidays from May to end of September (11.00-17.00)

Special events: Steam days: 8/9 April, 6/7 May, 3-5 June, 8, 27-29 July, 5, 10, 12, 19, 24, 26/27 August, 30 September, 28 October, 4 November. Santa Specials selected dates in December (must be pre-booked). Please refer to web site

Special notes: Museum dedicated to Mid-Suffolk Light Railway. MSLR buildings and artefacts. Reproduction MSLR ticket on entry. *Railway World* award winner in 1994 and HRA award winner in 2002 and 2007. Driver experience

details shown on web site. Train is available for photographic charters etc. Site venue for wedding receptions and parties

Facilities for disabled: Most of the site is accessible for disabled users. A wheelchair is available on request and there is wheelchair access to the demonstration passenger train. Toilets are accessible to wheelchair users

Membership details: Membership Secretary, Brockford Station, Wetheringsett, Nr Stowmarket, Suffolk IP14 5PW

Society journal: *Making Tracks —* quarterly newsletter

Member: HRA, MLA Accredited Museum, Registered Charity, Duke of York Community Initiative Award 2011

Please note that we are in Hunslet, NOT Middleton, Leeds

This is the world's oldest working railway, authorised by the first railway Act of Parliament in 1758, first railway in the world to use revenue earning steam locomotives

in 1812, and also the first standard gauge railway to be taken over by volunteers in 1960

Headquarters: Middleton Railway Trust Ltd, Moor Road, Hunslet, Leeds LS10 2JQ

Telephone: 0113 271 0320

Visitors telephone: 0845 680 1758 (09.00-20.00 please)

Internet addresses: *E-mail:* info@middletonrailway.org.uk

Web site: www.middletonrailway.org.uk

SatNav postcode: LS10 2JQ or Beza Street. If using satellite navigation please be aware there are two Moor Roads in LS10

Main station: Moor Road, Hunslet

OS reference: SE 302309

Car park: Moor Road (free)

Access by public transport: Nearest main line station, Leeds

City. Bus services from Aire Street (next to Leeds City station) to Tunstall Road (then 150yd walk)
Directions by car: Next to M621, junction 5. There have been major road alterations around the Middleton Railway.
From the south: M621 northbound and exit at Jct 5. Turn right at the top of the slip road and take the marked exit at the roundabout. The railway is 50yd on the right
From the west: M621 southbound and exit at Jct 6. Turn left at the end of the slip road, and left at the next set of traffic lights into Moor Road. Bear right at the mini roundabout and railway is 250yd on the left
Café, souvenir shop: Moor Road
Engine House: Open weekends and Bank Holiday Mondays Easter to the end of November
Length of line: 1.25 miles
Period of public operation: Weekends and Bank Holiday Mondays only. Easter to end of November, plus Santa trains in December.
Trains run at 40min intervals.
Heritage diesels: Saturdays 13.00-16.20.
August Wednesdays 11.00-15.00.
Heritage steam: Sundays and Bank Holiday Mondays 11.00-16.20 except special events which may have their own timetable.
2012 prices: adult £4.50; child £2.50; family tickets are available. Special events may attract different prices
Special events: Bluebell Walks — 6/7 May; Family Weekend — 2-4 June; 200th Anniversary of Steam at Middleton — 23/24 June; Model Railway Exhibition — 30 June, 1 July; Open Wednesdays in August 11.00-15.00; Autumn Gala — 15/16 September; Ghost Trains — 27/28 October.
Santa steam trains run weekends in December, plus Christmas Eve
Facilities for disabled: Ramped access to building, lift to first floor, access to platform and trains, toilets and parking
Special notes: Operating continually since 1758 on a variety of different routes. The first railway to successfully use 'revenue-earning' steam locomotives in 1812. Part of South Leeds Heritage Trail, highlighting former locomotive works in the area, and other historic places

Locomotives

Name	No	Origin	Class	Type	Built
—	1310	NER	Y7	0-4-0T	1891
—	68153	LNER	Y1	0-4-0VB	1933
—	385	DSB	HsII	0-4-0WT	1893±
John Alcock	7051	LMS	—	0-6-0DM	1932*
(Olive)	RDB998901	BR	—	4wDM	1950*

Industrial locomotives

Name	No	Builder	Type	Built
John Blenkinsop	—	Peckett (2003)	0-4-0ST	1941
—	—	Peckett (2103)	0-4-0ST	1948±
—	—	Bagnall (2702)	0-4-0ST	1943
Henry de Lacy II	—	H/Clarke (1309)	0-4-0ST	1917±
Mirvale	—	H/Clarke (1882)	0-4-0ST	1955±
Manchester Ship Canal No 67	—	H/Clarke (1329)	0-6-0T	1921±
—	11	Hunslet (1453)	0-4-0ST	1925
Picton	—	Hunslet (1540)	2-6-2T	1927±
—	1684	Hunslet (1684)	0-4-0T	1931
—	—	Hunslet (2387)	0-6-0T	1941±
Brookes No 1	—	M/Wardle (1601)	0-6-0ST	1903*
Matthew Murray	—	Cockerill	0-4-0VBT	1890±
Lucy	—	M/Wardle (1210)	0-6-0ST	1891*
Sir Berkeley†	—	M/Wardle (1795)	0-4-0ST	1912±
—	6	H/Leslie (3860)	0-4-0ST	1935
Carroll	—	H/Clarke (D631)	0-4-0DM	1946±*
Mary	—	H/Clarke (D577)	0-4-0DM	1932±*
Grace	—	H/Clarke (D1345)	0-6-0DM	1967
Courage	—	Hunslet (1786)	0-4-0DM	1935±*
—§	—	Hunslet (6273)	4wDH	1965±
Flying Scotsman§§	—	Hunslet (8505)	4wDH	1981±
—	—	Fowler (3900002)	0-4-0DM	1945±
—	—	Fowler (4220033)	0-4-0DM	1966
Conway	—	Kitson (5469)	0-6-0ST	1933
Austin No 1	—	Peckett (5003)	0-4-0DM	1961*
—	—	Thomas Hill (138C)	0-4-0DH	1963*
—	—	Beyer Peacock (7856)	0-4-0DE	1958±*
—	—	G/Batley (420452)	4wDE	1979±

*locomotives in service
†on 10 year loan from Vintage Carriages Trust, but may be away on hire at times
±on display in the Engine House
§3ft gauge
§§2ft 2in gauge

Note: Not all the stock is accessible by the public

Stock
2 CCTs converted for passenger use Nos 1867 and 2048; CCT as stores van No 2073. Various goods vehicles; 5-ton Booth rail crane; 1 3-ton Smith steam crane; 1 3-ton Isles steam crane; 7.5-ton steam crane

Special facilities: Charter trains, birthday party trains, training/conference room; school education facilities aligned to the National Curriculum. Children's University Centre

England

Midland Railway — Butterley

Member: HRA, TT

The Midland Railway — Butterley is a rapidly developing Preservation Scheme with a difference. The massive 57 acre Museum site and 35 acre Country Park enabled it to become 'More Than Just a Railway' as its publicity says. The seven-road Matthew Kirtley Museum allows much of the historic collection to be on display and most of the locomotives to be stored and displayed under cover. A miniature railway (3.5 and 5in gauge) and a 1-mile narrow gauge line (2ft gauge) carry passengers through the Country Park, and of course there is a 3.5-mile standard gauge line complete with Midland signals, three restored signalboxes, Butterley station, the scenic delights of Butterley Reservoir and Golden Valley!

The Victorian Railwaymen's Church, the demonstration signalbox, and all the other many attractions that make up the Midland Railway — Butterley will be open throughout the year

Location: Midland Railway, Butterley Station, Nr Ripley, Derbyshire DE5 3QZ

OS reference: SK 403520

General Manager: Alan Calladine

Operating society/organisation: Midland Railway Trust Ltd

Telephone: Ripley (01773) 747674, Visitor Information Line (01773) 570140.

Fax: (01773) 570271

Internet addresses: *E-mail:* midland.railway@btconnect.com *Web site:* www.midlandrailwaycentre.co.uk

Car park: Butterley station on B6179 1 mile north of Ripley

On site facilities: Museum, country park, souvenir shops, miniature railway, narrow gauge railway, garden railway, model railways

Refreshment facilities: Butterley station buffet, Johnson Buffet (Swanwick), on-train bars and extensive 'Wine and Dine' trains, 'The Midlander' (details from

Locomotives and multiple-units

Name	No	Origin	Class	Type	Built
—	158A	MR	—	2-4-0	1866
Princess Margaret Rose	46203	LMS	8P	4-6-2	1935
Duchess of Sutherland	46233	LMS	8P	4-6-2	1938
—	47564	LMS	3F	0-6-0T	1928
—	47327	LMS	3F	0-6-0T	1926
—	47357	LMS	3F	0-6-0T	1926
—	47445	LMS	3F	0-6-0T	1927
—	53809	SDJR	7F	2-8-0	1925
—	73129	BR	5MT	4-6-0	1956
—	80080	BR	4MT	2-6-4T	1954
—	80098	BR	4MT	2-6-4T	1955
—	92219	BR	9F	2-10-0	1959
—	D2858	BR	02	0-4-0DM	1959
—	D2138	BR	03	0-6-0DM	1960
Red Lion	08590	BR	08	0-6-0DE	1959
—	12077	BR	11	0-6-0DE	1950
—	20048	BR	20	Bo-Bo	1968
—	20205	BR	20	Bo-Bo	1967
—	20227	BR	20	Bo-Bo	1968
—	D7671	BR	25	Bo-Bo	1967
—	31271	BR	31	A1A-A1A	1961
Boadicea	31418	BR	31	A1A-A1A	1959
—	33046	BR	33	Bo-Bo	1960
—	33201	BR	33	Bo-Bo	1962
—	37190	BR	37	Co-Co	1964
Aureol	40012	BR	40	1Co-Co1	1959
Great Gable	D4	BR	44	1Co-Co1	1959
Royal Tank Regiment	45041	BR	45/1	1Co-Co1	1962
—	45108	BR	45/1	1Co-Co1	1961
—	45133	BR	45/1	1Co-Co1	1961
—	46045	BR	46	1Co-Co1	1963
—	47401	BR	47	Co-Co	1963
—	D1516	BR	47	Co-Co	1963
Sir Edward Elgar	50007	BR	50	Co-Co	1967
Western Lady	D1048	BR	52	C-C	1962
Electra	27000	BR	EM2	Co+Co	1953
—	50015	BR	114	DMBS	1956
—	50019	BR	114	DMBS	1956
—	50160	BR	101	DMC(L)	1957
—	50164	Met-Cam	101	DMBS	1957
—	50253	Met-Cam	101	DMBS	1957
—	51118	GC&W	100	DMBS	1957
—	51341	P/Steel	117	DMBS	1959
—	51353	P/Steel	117	DMBS	1959
—	51395	P/Steel	117	DMS	1959
—	51398	P/Steel	117	DMS	1959
—	51567	BR	108	DMCL	1959
—	51937	BR	108	DMBS	1958
—	51591	BR	127	DMBS	1959
—	51625	BR	127	DMBS	1959
—	55513	BR	141	DMS	1983
—	55533	BR	141	DMS(L)	1983
—	55967	BR	127	DPU	1959
—	56006	BR	114	DMC(L)	1956
—	56015	BR	114	DMC(L)	1956

above address).

'Mid-day Midlander' Sunday lunch trains will run on selected Sundays — these need to be booked in advance

Length of line: Standard gauge 3.5 miles, narrow gauge 0.8-mile

Public opening: In 2012 trains run every Saturday, Sunday and Bank Holiday Monday EXCEPT 10 November.

Trains will also run every day 11-19 February, 1-15 April, 2-10 June, 21 July to 2 September, 27 October to 4 November, 20-24 December.

Golden Valley Light Railway: Trains will run every weekend and Bank Holiday Monday April to October, and every day 2-10 June, 21 July to 2 September. Special steam days — check for details.

Butterley Park Miniature Railway: Trains will run Sundays and Bank Holidays Easter to September.

Journey time: Approximately 1hr

Special events: Day out with Thomas — 10/11 March; Mother's Day Lunch Train — 18 March; Easter Trains — 1-15 April; Sunday Lunch — 17 April; Vintage Train Weekend— 5-7 May; Sunday Lunch — 20 May; Day out with Thomas — 7-10 June; Father's Day Sunday Lunch — 17 June; Narrow Gauge Railway Gala, Garden Railway, Modellers' Weekend and Garden Railway Event — 14/15 July; Road Rally — 15 July; Indietracks — 6-8 July; Day out with Thomas — 4-7 August; Vintage Train Weekend — 25-27 August; Sunday Lunch — 16 September; Sunday Lunch — 21 October; Fireworks Night — 3 November; Santa Specials — 17/18, 24/25 November, 1/2, 8/9, 15/16, 20-21 December; Day out with Thomas — 27-31 December.

Note: Day out with Thomas dates subject to confirmation.

All Day out with Thomas events are © Gullane (Thomas) Ltd 2012 and are licensed by Gullane (Thomas) Ltd a HIT Entertainment Company.

'Mid-day Midlander' lunch trains run on selected dates – these need to be booked in advance

Facilities for disabled: Toilets, special coach, access to shop and cafeteria

Special facilities: The railway is licensed for weddings, civil

Name	No	Origin	Class	Type	Built
—	56097	GC&W	100	DTCL)	1957
—	56342	Met-Cam	101	DTCL	1957
—	56484	BR	108	DTCL	1960
—	59521	P/Steel	117	TCL	1959
—	59609	BR	127	TSL	1959
—	59659	BR	115	TS	1960
—	70824	BR	438	TBSM	1966
—	70854	BR	438	TFK	1966
—	76298	BR	438	DTS	1966
—	76322	BR	438	DTS	1966
—	79018	BR	—	DMBS	1954
—	79612	BR	—	DTCL	1954
—	29666	M/Cam	505	TC	1931
—	29670	M/Cam	505	TC	1931

Locomotive notes: In service 47327 (as *Thomas*), 73129, 80080, 6233, 46045, 08590, Class 114 and 127 DMU, D4, 33201, 37190, 45041, 47401, 50007, 40012, 12077, 45133 and D7671. Under restoration: 6233, 47357 47445. Awaiting repairs or stored: 46203, D1516, 92219. Boiler and frames only 47564. Static display: 158A, 27000.

Industrial locomotives

Name	No	Builder	Type	Built
Gladys	—	Markham (109)	0-4-0ST	1894
Stanton	24	Barclay (1875)	0-4-0CT	1925
Whitehead	—	Peckett (1163)	0-4-0ST	1908
Victory	—	Peckett (1547)	0-4-0ST	1919
Lytham St Annes	—	Peckett (2111)	0-4-0ST	1949
Brown Bailey	4	N/Wilson (454)	0-4-0ST	1894
Castle Donington	1	RSH (7817)	0-4-0ST	1954
George	—	RSH	0-4-0ST	19??
Andy	2	Fowler (16038)	0-4-0DM	1923
—	RS9	M/Rail (2024)	0-4-0DM	1921
—	RS12	M/Rail (460)	0-4-0DM	1912
Boots	2	Barclay (2008)	0-4-0F	1935
Castle Donington	2	Barclay (416)	0-4-0DM	1957
High Marnham	—	Barclay (441)	0-4-0DM	1949
Boots	—	R/Hornsby (384139)	0-4-0DE	1955
—	—	H/Clarke (D1152)	0-6-0DM	1959
Albert Fields	—	H/Clarke (D1114)	0-6-0DM	1958
Princess Elizabeth*	6201	H/Clarke (D611)	4-6-2DM	1938
Princess Margaret Rose*	6203	H/Clarke (D612)	4-6-2DM	1938

*21in gauge

Golden Valley Light Railway
2ft gauge unless otherwise shown

Name	No	Builder	Type	Built
—	—	Deutz (10249)	4wDM	1932
Tubby	—	M/Rail (8667)	4wDM	1941
Pioneer	—	M/Rail (8739)	4wDM	1942
—	—	M/Rail (8756)	4wDM	1942
Campbell Brick Works	—	M/Rail (60S364)	4wDM	1968
—	—	Lister (3742)	4wPM	1931
—	—	Lister (10994)	4wDM	1939
—	—	M/Rail (11246)	4wDM	1963
—	2	O&K (7529)	0-4-0WT	1914
Wheal Jayne	19	BEV	4wBE	1985
—	—	Ruston (7002/0567/6)	4wDM	1966
Lyddia	—	Ruston (191646)	4wDM	1938
Berryhill	—	Ruston (222068)	4wDM	1943
—	AD34	Hunslet (7009)	4wDM	1971
—	—	Hunslet (7178)	4wDH	1971
Calverton Colliery	22†	H/Clarke (1117)	0-6-0DM	1958

England

partnership ceremonies, and baby naming ceremonies. There is a woodland burial ground in the country park adjacent to the railway. Trains can be chartered for special meals, educational visits or almost anything else. Footplate Experience and Railway Experience Courses are run. The large museum site is also used for exhibitions and displays. The railway also has an impressive track record in the restoration of diesel multiple-units and coaches for other lines

Membership details: Ian Sharpe, at above address

Membership journal: *The Wyvern* — quarterly

Marketing names: 'More Than Just a Railway'; Golden Valley Light Railway (narrow gauge); Butterley Park Miniature Railway (miniature line)

Name	No	Builder	Type	Built
—	—	Lister (53726)	4wDM	1963
—	—	SMH (40SD529)	4wDM	1983
—	NG24	B/Drewry (3703)	4wBE	1974
Ellison	—	SMH (102T20)	4wDH	1979
Joan	—	T. D. A. Civil (1)	0-4-2T	1997
Darcy	—	B/Drewry (3753)	4wDM	1980
Howell Castle	—	M/Rail (11177)	4wDM	1961

Locomotive notes: In service: *Whitehead, Boots, Castle Donington No 1, Castle Donington No 2,* NG24, Ruston 222068, SMH 40SD529 and 102T20, Lister, Deutz 10249, *Albert Fields,* M/Rail 60S364, *Princess Margaret Rose.* Under restoration: O&K 7529, *Lytham St Annes.* Awaiting repairs or stored on display: RS9, Hunslet 7178, M/Rails 5906/11246. Static display: *Gladys,* 4, *Boots No 2, Victory,* RS12, *Stanton* No 24, *Brown Bailey* (as Oswald the talking engine)

Stock
Numerous carriages, wagons and cranes. Museum display includes MR Royal saloon, MR 4-wheeled coach, MR brake third, LD&ECR all third, BR horsebox, LMS travelling Post Office, L&YR family saloon, MR motor car van, MR bogie brake third, restored freight vehicles, LMS 50-ton steam crane, and much more

Owners
47357, 47327, 47445, 47564, 73129 Derby City Council
46203, 6233, 46203, 80080, 80098 the Princess Royal Class Locomotive Trust
D4, 45041 and 46045 the Peak Locomotive Preservation Co Ltd
92219 the 9F Locomotive Charitable Trust
D7671 Derby Industrial Museum
33201 the Birmingham Railwaymen's Crompton Workgroup
45108 the Peak Locomotive Group
51118 the Llangollen Railcar Group
53809 the 13809 Locomotive Preservation Society

Miniature Railway	Mizens Railway	Surrey

Member: HRA

The Mizens Railway is primarily a 1.25 mile-long, 7.25in gauge miniature railway; however, the range of full size exhibits is being expanded. In adition there is a collection of railwayana on display in the main station area, an engine shed and turntable and 10 acres of woodland for visitors to enjoy

Location/headquarters: The Mizens Railway, Barrs Lane, Knaphill, Woking, Surrey GU21 2JW

SatNav postcode: GU21 2JW
Tel: 01483 720801

Locomotives

Name	No	Origin	Class	Type	Built
—	76887	BR	4VEP / 423	DTC	1972
—	133*	NGR	A	4-8-2	1899

*built by Dübs, Glasgow, for Natal Government Railways, later South African Railways

Locomotives (7.25in gauge)

Name	No	Builder	Type	Built
Marquis	—	L. Chandler	0-6-0T	1984
Richard Bonsey	—	A. Chandler	0-4-0ST+T	c1984
Hazel	—	J. Rowland	0-4-0ST	1985
Koala	5	M. Rickers	2-6-2T	1990
Isabel	—	Page Engineering	0-4-0ST+T	1990
Little John	—	P. Beale	2-4-2T	1990
Earl of Maybury	7	A. Chandler	0-6-0ST	1991

England

NBL Preservation Group - we'll take you there !

Personally escorted trips by private car to see and photograph Britain's preserved railways and main line steam specials.

Let us collect you from your home or hotel and take you to the stations, sheds or line side locations of your choice.

Our days out feature individual itineraries tailored to your own personal requirements - at prices from just £100 for a full day out for up to 4 people.

This is a service run by enthusiasts for enthusiasts and all proceeds go directly towards steam locomotive preservation. Why not treat yourself to a great day out with us, secure in the knowledge that you will be helping us to preserve NBL steam locomotives for future operation.

For further information visit our websites :

www.steam-mastershot.co.uk and www.nbloco.net - or write to :

NBL Preservation Group, 4 Porchfield Close, Earley, Reading, Berks, RG6 5YZ

Contact: Mike Smith (Chairman)
Internet addresses:
Web site: www.mizensrailway.co.uk
Access by public transport:
By rail: Woking (South West Trains), approx 4 miles
By bus: Regular service from Woking station to Knaphill
On site facilities: Free parking, souvenir shops, museum and refreshments.
Length of line: 1.25 miles, 7.25in gauge
Period of public operation: Sundays May to September, 14.00-17.00; also Thursdays in August, 14.00-17.00
Facilities for disabled: Good wheelchair access on site, limited access available on trains
Special events: Please see web site for up-to-date details
Special facilities: Available for birthday parties and other events. Tel: Mrs Betty Sizmur 01932 517941
Membership details: Membership Secretary c/o above address
Membership journal: Quarterly

Name	No	Builder	Type	Built
Alice	—	D. Bradbury	0-4-0ST+T	1996
Dickwillydan	8	Mallerby	0-4-0ST	1996
Sir Thomas	11	M. Smith	0-4-0ST+T	1996
Sophie	6	M. Rickers	2-6-0PH SO	1995
Busy Bee	—	M. Rickers	4wBER	c1986
Sonya	—	J. Rough	0-4-0PH	1996
Ronny Rascal	—	L. & R. Knightley	6wPH	1998
Goliath	912	D. Bradbury	B0-B0 BE	2001
Lemon	—	Roakoke	4wPH	2004
—	18	G. Dare	Railcar	2008
Chestnut	—	R. Scrivner	4wPH	2008
Georgia May	2006	Maxitrak	4wBE	c2009
Bourne Again	—	D. Bradbury / G. Dare	4wPH	1996
—	—	R. Dewar	0-6-0BE	1997
Hogwarts School	—	Compass House	0-6-0BE	1997
Brooklands	—	Cromer White	4+4wBE	1978
Mayflower	—	Maxitrak	4wBE	1985
Yeo	—	D. Bradbury	2-6-2T	2009
Phil Chambers	—	J. Cornell / P. Willis	B0-B0 DH	2009
Paddington	1504	S. Conway	0-6-0PT	u/c
—	D5572	Compass House	A1A-A1A	2011

Near St Peter's Metro station the museum is housed in an original 1840s Victorian station building that was commissioned by the famous railway entrepreneur George Hudson and designed by Thomas Moore, Sunderland's first notable architect.

With a preserved 1860s ticket office, seven interactive galleries and the new Sidings development; the Sidings includes a new Wagon Shed with two significant railway wagons, a 1916 Goods Brake Van and a 1939 Covered Carriage Truck — with a Rover P4 classic car inside. With Victorian cottage gardens in the grounds of the museum, visitors can learn about the history of travel and transport in Tyne and Wear as well as learning about the stories of people who lived and worked in the station
Location: North Bridge Street, Sunderland SR5 1AP

Rolling stock
NER brake van 1915, LNER CCT van 1939

Telephone: (0191) 567 7075
Textphone: 18001 0191 567 7075
Internet addessses: E-mail: info@monkwearmouthstationmuseum.org.uk
Web site: www.monkwearmouthstationmuseum.org.uk
OS reference: NZ 396576
Access by public transport:
By Metro: St Peter's 100m walk
By bus: Wheatsheaf, 200m walk; Fawcett Street, 600m walk
By train: 10min walk from Sunderland Central station
Car parking: Shepfolds (limited spaces) — 100m walk; Stadium of Light Metro car park — 500m walk; St Mary's Way, 400m walk across Wearmouth bridge
Public opening: Free admission.

Daily 1 January-31 December (except New Year's Day, Christmas Day, Boxing Day [please check for Good Friday and Easter Sunday opening times]). Monday to Saturday 10.00-17.00. Sunday 14.00-17.00.
On site facilities: Limited car parking on museum forecourt, shop. Self-service refreshment dispenser, shop.
Access for disabled: Induction loops in shop, learning rooms, booking office and Journeys Gallery. Talking audio guides and listening point. Ramped access, suitable for wheelchair users. Water available on request for guide dogs. Manual wheelchair available which can be pre-booked

Location: Moors Valley Country Park, Horton Road, Ashley Heath, Nr Ringwood, Dorset BH24 2ET
General Manager:
Mr J. A. W. Haylock
Telephone: (01425) 471415
Internet addresses: E-mail: shop@moorsvalleyrailway.co.uk
Web site: www.moorsvalleyrailway.co.uk
Car parking: On site
Access by public transport: Wilts & Dorset bus X34, from Bournemouth/Ringwood to Ashley Heath
On site facilities: Picnic areas, lakeside walks, adventure playground, railway shop and refreshments all set in the beautiful Moors Valley Country Park. Car park and toilets (including disabled)
Depots: Adjacent to main station
Length of line: 7.25in gauge; 1 mile long

Locomotives — 7.25in gauge

Name	No	Builder	Type	Built
Horace	2	Haylock	0-4-2DH	1999
Talos	3	Marsh	0-4-2T	1978
Tinkerbell	4	Marsh	0-4-2T	1968
Sapper	5	Marsh/Haylock	4-6-0	1982
Medea	6	Narogauge Ltd	2-6-2T	1981
Aelfred	7	Narogauge Ltd	2-6-4T	1985
Jason	9	Narogauge Ltd	2-4-4T	1989
Offa	10	Narogauge Ltd	2-6-2	1991
Zeus	11	Narogauge Ltd	2-6-2	1991
Pioneer	12	Narogauge Ltd	4-6-2	1992
Horton	14	Narogauge Ltd	2-4-0	1991
William Rufus	15	Narogauge Ltd	2-4-0+0-4-2	1997
Robert Snooks	16	Manktelow	0-4-4T	1999
Hartfield	17	Colbourn	2-4-4T	1999
Thor	18	Jefford	4-6-2	2005
Athelstan	19	Couling	2-8-0	2006
Vixen	22	Narogauge Ltd	0-4-0+0-4-0DH	2005
Perseus	24	Ash	0-4-2T	2006
Emmet*	20	Haylock	0-4-0T	2003

*2ft gauge

Rolling stock
36 passenger vehicles, selection of wagons

Period of public operation: Weekends all year; daily all school holidays and Spring Bank Holiday to mid-September. Santa Specials in December
Special events: Tank Engine Day — 4 March; Railway Open Day — 25 March; Tinkerbell Rally — 5/6 May; Grand Summer Gala — 9/10 June; Model Railway Weekend — 21/22 July; Tank Engine Day — 11 November; Santa Specials — 9, 16 December (bookable in advance)
Fare: Single and return journey; day rovers; Midday Specials (Sundays only). Party rates available

Member: HRA
Based in the buildings of the world's oldest surviving passenger railway station (dating from 1830), the museum has colourful 'hands-on' galleries that amuse, amaze and entertain. Visitors can find out about our industrial past, and walk through a Victorian sewer complete with sounds and smells
Location: Liverpool Road, Castlefield, Manchester (off Deansgate near Granada TV)
OS reference: SJ 831987
Operating society/organisation: The Museum of Science and Industry in Manchester, Liverpool Road, Castlefield, Manchester M3 4FP
Telephone: (0161) 832 2244
Internet addresses: *E-mail:* info@mosi.org.uk
Web site: http://www.mosi.org.uk
Car parks: On site, plus parking in the area (Museum car park £5, subject to change)
Access by public transport: Manchester Victoria, Piccadilly, Oxford Road and Deansgate main line stations. GM bus 33. Deansgate-Castlefield Metrolink station
On site facilities: Oldest passenger railway station, listed buildings containing exhibitions about science, industry, aviation, space, water supply and sewage disposal, gas and electricity. Experiment, the 'hands-on' science centre. World's largest collection of working steam mill engines in the Power Hall, demonstrated every weekend and at various times during the week (check web site or call for details). The Collections Centre has research facilities and access to reserve collections. Museum shop, restaurant, Learning, Conference Centres and coffee bar
Public opening: Daily, except 24-26 December and 1 January, including Saturdays and Sundays, 10.00-17.00. Entrance in Lower Byrom Street. Admission free to permanent galleries, although prices

Locomotives

Name	No	Origin	Class	Type	Built
—	D2868	BR	02	0-4-0DH	1961
—	06003	BR	06	0-6-0DM	1959
Ariadne	1505 (27001)	BR	EM2 (77)	Co-Co	1954
Hector	26048 cab only	BR	EM1 (76)	Bo-Bo	1952
Pender	3††	IoMR	—	2-4-0T	1873
Novelty	Replica of 1829 locomotive using some original parts				1986
—	3157†	PR	—	4-4-0	1911
—	2352§	SAR	GL	4-8-2+2-8-4	1929
Planet*	—	Replica	—	2-2-0	1992

Industrial locomotives

Name	No	Builder	Type	Built
—	258	E/Electric (1378)	4wBE	1944

*full scale model of 1830-built locomotive
††ex-Isle of Man Railways, 3ft gauge, sectioned (B/Peacock 1255)
†ex-Pakistan Railways, 5ft 6in gauge (V/Foundry 3064)
§ex-South African Railways, 3ft 6in gauge (B/Peacock 6693)

Rolling stock

Reproduction M&BR 1st class carriage c1840 using original fragments
2 full scale working models L&MR 2nd class carriages c1835
1914 L&YR ambulance carriage rebuilt 1923 as Medical Examination Car, LMS No 10825 (under restoration, assembled in 1917 from 1916-made modules)
B782903 4-wheeled covered goods van, BR (Wolverton), 1961
B783709 4-wheeled covered goods van, BR (Wolverton), 1962
3-plank loose coupled goods wagon, GCR (Chatham), c1890
Wickham Type 27 trolley (ex-MoD No 9037) on loan from Marsh Trackworks

Owner

Novelty on loan from the National Railway Museum, York

Note:

Full scale (working) model — reproduction made to other than original specification
Replica — reproduction made by original company in original way
Reproduction — item made in original way by other than original company

still apply for special exhibitions. Please ring for details. Groups can book a visit by calling (0161) 833 0027

Special notes: Good wheelchair access, toilets for the disabled, lecture and conference facilities

Museum — National Coal Mining Museum for England — West Yorkshire

Member: Registered Museum
Museum Director: Dr M. L. Faull
Address: National Coal Mining Museum for England, Caphouse Colliery, New Road, Overton, Wakefield, West Yorkshire WF4 4RH
Operating society/organisation: National Coal Mining Museum for England Trust Ltd
Charity number: 517325
Telephone: 01924 848806
Fax: 01924 840694
Internet addresses:
E-mail: info@ncm.org.uk
Web site: www.ncm.org.uk
OS reference: SE 253164
Car park: Free — on site
Access by public transport:
Bus: Service 128 between Wakefield and Dewsbury serves the museum entrance. No 232 from Huddersfield or Wakefield stops adjacent and is slightly less convenient
Refreshment facilities: Licensed café providing hot and cold food
On site facilities: Souvenir shop
Running lines:
2ft 6in gauge operated locomotive line providing a transport link between Caphouse Colliery and Hope Pit
2ft 3in gauge rope-hauled demonstration 'paddy' line (not expected to be in operation during 2012)
Period of public operation: The museum is open daily 10.00-17.00 (except closed 24-26 December
Special facilities: Underground tours, conference centre, education facilities 'The Learning Curve'
Facilities for disabled: Toilets, full access to all galleries, audio loop, wheelchairs can be accommodated underground with prior booking

Locomotives

Name	No	Origin	Class	Type	Built
—	D2284*	BR	04	0-6-0DM	1960

*currently on loan to Heritage Shunters Trust, Peak Rail

Standard gauge industrial locomotives

Name	No	Builder	Type	Built
Acton Hall No 3	—	Peckett (1567)	0-6-0ST	1920*
—	47	T/Hill (249V)	0-6-0DH	1978*
—	44	Hunslet (6684)	0-6-0DH	1968*
—	40	Hunslet (7307)	0-6-0DH	1973

Narrow gauge and underground locomotives

3ft gauge

Name	No	Builder	Type	Built
—	BEM403	Hunslet (3614)	0-4-0DMF	1948*

2ft 6in gauge

Name	No	Builder	Type	Built
Alicia	—	H/Clarke (DM746)	0-4-0DMF	1951*
—	—	R/Hornsby (480679)	4wDMF	1961*
Deborah	2	H/Clarke (DM1356)	0-4-0DMF	1965+
—	—	H/Clarke (DM1433)	0-6-0DMF	1955+
Kirsten	0592	GMT (0592)	4w-4wDMF	1981
Stephanie	0593	GMT (0593)	4w-4wDMF	1981*
Anna	—	GMT	4w-4wDMF	1984*
—	1	Clayton (3538)	4w-4wBEF	1989+

2ft 4in gauge

Name	No	Builder	Type	Built
—	—	Atlas (2463)	4wBEF	1945
—	—	R/Hornsby (375347)	4wDM	1954

2ft 3in gauge

Name	No	Builder	Type	Built
Caphouse Flyer	—	Hunslet (8832)	4wDEF	1978

2ft 2in gauge

Name	No	Builder	Type	Built
—	—	Hunslet (7530)	4wDF	1977*

2ft 1.5in gauge

Name	No	Builder	Type	Built
—	—	R/Hornsby (379659)	4wDM	1955*

2ft gauge

Name	No	Builder	Type	Built
Fryston No 2	—	H/Clarke (DM655)	0-4-0DMF	1949

*not currently on public display
+in use on Caphouse-Hope railway

Locomotives on loan to other railways
Standard gauge

Name	No	Builder	Type	Built
The Welshman	—	M/Wardle (1207)	0-6-0ST	1890
Airedale	—	Hunslet (1440)	0-6-0ST	1923
Antwerp	—	Hunslet (3180)	0-6-0ST	1944
Progress	—	RSH (7298)	0-6-0ST	1946

Name	No	Builder	Type	Built
—	9	YEC (2521)	0-6-0ST	1952
Monkton No 1	—	Hunslet (3788)	0-6-0ST	1953
—	20	H/Clarke (D1152)	0-6-0DM	1958

3ft gauge

—	BEM402	Hunslet (8505)	0-4-0DMF	1981

2ft 3in gauge
Houghton Main

Flyer	—	Hunslet (7274)	4wDM	1973

2ft 2in gauge

Flying Scotsman	—	Hunslet (6273)	4wDM	1965

2ft gauge

—	—	R/Hornsby (441424)	4wDMF	1961

Carriages and wagons
The museum's collection contains several varieties of standard gauge coal trucks, various narrow gauge manriding cars, coal-carrying cars and coal tubs. There are also two steam cranes

Locomotives on loan
The Welshman (to return during 2012) and 9 the Chesterfield Locomotive Action Group, Barrow Hill Roundhouse
Airedale, Monkton No 1 the Embsay & Bolton Abbey Steam Railway
Antwerp the Kent Coast Locomotive Group (private site)
Progress the Tanfield Railway (to return during 2012)
20 the Midland Railway Centre, Butterley
BEM402 and *Flying Scotsman* the Middleton Railway
Houghton Main Flyer the Corris Railway
R/Hornsby (441424) the Chasewater Railway

National Railway Museum

Museum — North Yorkshire

Member: HRA, TT, MLSOG
Location: National Railway Museum, Leeman Road, York YO26 4XJ
OS reference: SE 594519
Operating society/organisation: Part of the National Museum of Science and Industry
Telephone: 08448 153 139
Internet addresses: *E-mail:* nrm@nmsi.ac.uk
Web site: www.nrm.org.uk
Car park: Available on site, charge applies. Coach parking is available — pre-booking required
Access by public transport: The museum is within a few minutes' walking distance of the railway station and city centre. No 2 Green Line park & ride bus operates to the door. A road-train operates between the museum and the city centre (seasonal)

On site facilities: Museum shops, restaurant, café and toilets (all with baby changing facilities). Miniature railway rides (subject to availability), outdoor play areas, Learning Platform, conference and reference centres. Search Engine Library and archive facility
Public opening: Daily 10.00-18.00. Closed 24-26 December. Admission is free for all. The museum reserves the right to charge for special events
Facilities for disabled: Most areas of the museum are accessible. Wheelchairs may be borrowed from the entrances. Disabled parking is available at the museum's City entrance
Special notes: The museum opened in 1975 and has welcomed over 20 million visitors. It has received numerous awards including two

White Rose Awards 2009: Best Visitor Attraction over 50,000 Visitors and Best Visitor Experience for the production of the Railway Children in conjunction with York Theatre Royal.
As the world's largest railway museum, it offers the visitor three extensive exhibition halls which house a magnificent collection of locomotives, carriages and wagons and thousands of related exhibits.
In the Great Hall there is an impressive array of locomotives around the turntable (demonstrated daily). Icons such as the *Duchess of Hamilton,* a replica of Stephenson's *Rocket* and the Japanese Bullet Train (the only one on display outside Japan) can also be found in the hall, along with a display dedicated to the movement of Mail by Rail.

England

The Warehouse tells the story of the most famous locomotive in the world, *Flying Scotsman*, which was saved for the nation in 2004. Once the current major overhaul of this celebrated locomotive is complete it will spend time both on main line operations as part of the museum's working fleet and, from time to time, in the exhibition. Work in the museum's workshop on *Flying Scotsman* and other rolling stock can be viewed from the balcony galleries as can a live link to York's IECC signalbox. There is an external viewing area overlooking the mouth of York station.

The Warehouse is an Aladdin's cave of railway treasures. Thousands of objects are on open display for visitors to wander among. Regular tours from the Museum's Explainers reveal the stories behind many of these items.

Station Hall illustrates the concept of travel by train — for passengers and freight. Several trains are drawn up at platforms and range from superb Royal carriages to a humble freight train. Queen Victoria's favourite carriage is a particular highlight, capturing the opulence of a bygone era. Access is possible to some footplates, and selected carriages can be opened on request by the Explainers. A range of talks and tours is also on offer.

The Learning Platform, accessible via the South Yard, is an area dedicated to younger visitors and hosts lively, interactive science shows. There is an outdoor play area here and a miniature railway too. Steam rides are usually available during school holidays.

The museum launched a new art gallery space in 2011 and showcases an exiting programme of temporary exhibitions from our unseen art collection and artworks from across the world, inspired by railways. Visit www.nrm.org.uk for a list of upcoming exhibitions.

The Museum offers a continually changing programme of events and exhibitions. More information can be found on the What's On pages of the web site: www.nrm.org.uk

Locomotives — Steam

Name	No	Origin	Builder	Class	Type	Built
Agenoria	—	Shutt End Colliery	Foster/Raistrick	—	0-4-0	1829
Coppernob	3	FR	Bury, Curtis & Kennedy	—	0-4-0	1846
Pet	—	LNWR	Crewe	—	0-4-0ST	1865
Aerolite	66	NER	Gateshead	X1(LNER)	2-2-4T	1869
Bauxite	2	Hebburn Works	B/Hawthorn	—	0-4-0ST	1874
—	1275	NER	Gateshead	—	0-6-0	1874
Boxhill	82	LBSCR	Brighton	A1	0-6-0T	1880
Gladstone	—	LBSCR	Brighton	—	0-4-2	1882
Wren	—	LYR	B/Peacock	—	0-4-0ST	1887
—	1008	LYR	Horwich	—	2-4-2T	1889
Hardwicke	790	LNWR	Crewe	—	2-4-0	1892
—	1621	NER	Gateshead	M	4-4-0	1893
—	245	LSWR	Nine Elms	M7	0-4-4T	1897
—	673	MR	Derby	—	4-2-2	1899
Handyman	—*	—	H/Clarke (573)	—	0-4-0ST	1900
—	737	SECR	Ashford	D	4-4-0	1901
—	2818	GWR	Swindon	2800	2-8-0	1905
Flying Scotsman	4472	LNER	Doncaster	A3	4-6-2	1923
King George V	6000	GWR	Swindon	'King'	4-6-0	1927
Rocket (replica)	—		R. Stephenson	—	0-2-2	1934
—	5000	LMS	Crewe	5MT	4-6-0	1935
—	607	Chinese Govt Rlys	Vulcan	KF7	4-8-4	1935
Green Arrow	4771	LNER	Doncaster	V2	2-6-2	1937
—	C1	SR	Brighton	Q1	0-6-0	1942
Winston Churchill	34051	SR	Brighton	BB	4-6-2	1946
Ellerman Lines	35029	BR(SR)	Sectioned	MN	4-6-2	1949
Evening Star	92220	BR	Swindon	9F	2-10-0	1960
Rocket (replica)	—		Locomotion Enterprises	—	0-4-0	1979

*3ft gauge

Locomotives — Electric

Name	No	Origin	Builder	Class	Type	Built
—	1	NSR	Bolton & Sons	—	0-4-0WE	1917
—	809	GPO	Green Bat	—	2w-2E	1931

Name	No	Origin	Builder	Class	Type	Built
—	26020	BR	Gorton/Metrovick	76	Bo-Bo Electric	1951
—	RA.36	TML	Hunslet	—	4wBE/WE	1990
Royal Scot	87001	BR	Crewe	87	Bo-Bo	1973

Locomotives — Diesel

Name	No	Origin	Builder	Class	Type	Built
—	—	WD	Drewry	_	0-4-0DM	1934
—	08911	BR	Horwich	08	0-6-0 DE	1962
—	D8000	BR	E/Electric	20	Bo-Bo	1957
—	5500	BR	Brush	31	A1A-A1A	1957
—	D200	BR	E/Electric	40	1Co-Co1	1958
—	03090	BR	—	03	0-6-0DM	1960
—	D2860	BR	YEC	02	0-4-0 DH	1960
—	D6700	BR	E/Electric	37	Co-Co	1960
—	09015	BR	Horwich	09	0-6-0DE	1961
King's Own Yorkshire Light Infantry	55022	BR	E/Electric	55	Co-Co	1961
Western Fusilier	D1023	BR	Swindon	52	C-C	1963
—	41001	BR	Crewe	41	Bo-Bo	1972

Locomotives on loan

No 673 _Maude_ (NBR) from the Scottish Railway Preservation Society, Bo'ness
No 65033 (NER) on loan from the TLCCT, and on display at Locomotion
Juno (Hunslet [3853]) on loan from Isle of Wight Steam Railway, and on display at Locomotion
Livingstone Thompson (1ft 11.5in gauge) from the Ffestiniog Railway, curently not on display

Rolling Stock Powered Units — Electric
1916	LNWR Motor Open Third Brake No 28249
1925	SR Motor Third Brake No S8143S
1937	SR Motor Third Open Brake No S11179S
1975	Birmingham Airport Maglev passenger car
1976	Series 'O' Shinkasen No 2214
1958	BR Class 414/2HAP MBS No 61275
1958	BR Class 414/2HAP DTC No 75395
1971	BR Class 423/4VEP DT No 76875

Rolling Stock — Departmental
1890	GNR Locomotive Tender No 1002
1906	NER Dynamometer Car No 902502
1907	NER Steam Breakdown Crane No CME 13
1907	Match Truck No DE942114
1926	LNER Match Truck No DE320952
1931/2	LNER Petrol-driven platelayers' trolley No 960209
1955	GEC 12.5-ton Coles Crane
1969	BR Plasser Tamping & Liner No 73010
1989	Molhouser side-discharge muck car ASDR 3105 (Channel Tunnel)

Rolling Stock — Passenger
1834	B&WR 1st & 2nd composite
1834	B&WR 2nd class
1834	B&WR 3rd class
1842	L&BR Queen Adelaide's Saloon
1850	NER Brake End (body only)
1851	ECR 1st class No 1
1860	Cornwall Rly broad gauge coach (body only)
1861	NBR Port Carlisle branch 'dandy car'
1869	LNWR Queen Victoria's Saloon
1885	MR 6-wheel composite brake No 901
1885	WCJS 8-wheel TPO No 186
1887	GNR Brake Van No 848
1897	Lynton & Barnstaple Rly brake composite No 6992
1898	ECJS 3rd class No 12
1900	LNWR (ex-WCJS) Dining Car LMS 76
1902	LNWR King Edward's Saloon No 800
1902	LNWR Queen Alexandra's Saloon No 801
1903	LSWR Tricomposite brake No 3598
1908	ECJS Royal Saloon No 395
1913	Pullman Car Co 1st class parlour car *Topaz*

1914	MR Dining car No 3463
1930	L&MR 1st *Huskinson* (replica)
1930	L&MR 1st *Traveller* (replica)
1930	L&MR 2nd (replica)
1930	L&MR 2nd (replica)
1936	CIWL Night Ferry sleeping car No 3792
1937	LNER Buffet Car No 9135
1937	LMS corridor 3rd class brake No 5987
1938	GJR TPO (replica)
1941	LMS Royal Saloon 799 (armoured car)
1955	BR Lavatory composite No E43046
1962	BR Mk II 2nd brake corridor No 35468
1969	BR Mk IIb 2nd open No 5455

Rolling Stock — Freight & Non Passenger Carrying
1815	Little Eaton (Derby Canal) Gangroad Wagon
1815	Peak Forest Canal Tramway Wagon No 174
1816	Grantham Canal Tramway Truck
1828	Dandy Cart
1840	Stratford & Moreton Tramway Wagon
1894	LSWR Brake van No 99
1908	LNWR Open carriage truck No 11275
1912	GNR 8-ton van No E432764
1917	GCR Box Van
1917	LNWR Box Van
1920	LSWR Lowmac, No DE563024, NYMR
1924	LMSR Van
1931	GWR Fruit Van No 112884
1931	Stanton Iron Works 12-ton wagon
1933	LMSR 20-ton Goods Brake Van No 295987
1935	SR Bogie goods brake van No 56297
1935	PLM Train Ferry Van No 475014
1936	LMSR 3 plank open wagon No 472867
1937	GWR Siphon bogie milk van No 2775
1937	LMSR Milk Tank Wagon No 44057
1944	LMS Lowmac No M700728
1944	GWR 13-ton open wagon No DW143698
1949	BR Bogie bolster D No B941000
1950	BR 20-ton Weltrol No B900805
1951	ICI Liquid chlorine tank wagon No 47484
1951	BR 8-ton cattle wagon No B893343
1959	BR Fish van No B87905
1962	BR Speedfreight container No BA 4324B
1966	Milk Marketing Board 6-wheel tank No 42801
1989	TML side-tipping muck cart No R T239

Items away from the NRM
Locomotives

Original type/No/Name	Location	Builder	Built
Wylam Colliery	Science Mus	—	1813
Hetton Colliery 0-4-0	Beamish	G. Stephenson	1822
SDR 0-4-0 *Locomotion*	Darlington	R. Stephenson & Co	1825
L&MR 0-2-2 *Rocket*	Science Mus	R. Stephenson & Co	1829
L&MR 0-2-2 *Novelty*	Museum of Science & Technology (Manchester)	Braithwaite & Ericsson	1829
SDR 0-6-0 No 24 *Derwent*	Darlington Nth Rd Mus	A. Kitching	1845
GJR 2-2-2 *Columbine*	Science Mus	Crewe	1845
Wantage Tramway 0-4-0WT No 5 *Shannon*	Didcot Rly Ctr	G. England	1857
LNWR 0-4-0ST 1439	Ribble Valley	Crewe	1865
MR 2-4-0 No 158A	Midland Railway	Derby	1866
South Devon Rly 0-4-0WT *Tiny*	South Devon Rly	Sara	1868
GNR 4-2-2 No 1	Locomotion	Doncaster	1870
LSWR 2-4-0WT No 30587	Bodmin	B/Peacock	1874

England

Original type/No/Name	Location	Builder	Built
NER 2-4-0 No 910	Locomotion	Gateshead	1875
NER 2-4-0 No 1463	Darlington Nth Rd Mus	Gateshead	1885
C&SL No 1	LT Museum	B/Peacock	1890
S&MR 0-4-2WT *Gazelle*	Col Stephens Rly Mus	Dodman	1893
GER 2-4-0 No 490	Bressingham	Stratford	1894
Rhodesia Railways 4-8-0 No 993	Tyseley	Sharp Stewart	1896
GWR 0-6-0 No 2516	Steam	Swindon	1897
TVR 0-6-2T No 28	Llangollen	TVR	1897
GNR No 990 *Henry Oakley*	Bressingham	Doncaster	1899
LSWR 4-4-0 No 120	Bodmin	Nine Elms	1899
MR 4-4-0 No 1000	Bo'ness	Derby	1902
GER 0-6-0 No 1217	Barrow Hill	Stratford	1905
GWR 4-6-0 No 4003 *Lode Star*	Steam	Swindon	1907
LT&SR 4-4-2T No 80 *Thundersley*	Bressingham	R. Stephenson	1909
GCR 2-8-0 No 102	Great Central	Gorton	1911
WD No 1377 (2ft Gauge)	LBR	Simplex	1918
GCR 506 *Butler Henderson*	Barrow Hill	Gorton	1920
LNWR 0-8-0 No 485	North Yorkshire	Crewe	1921
NSR No 2	Locomotion	Stoke	1922
GWR 4-6-0 No 4073 *Caerphilly Castle*	Steam	Swindon	1923
LMS 0-6-0 No 4027	Gloucs & Warwickshire	Derby	1924
GWR 2-2-2 *North Star* (replica)	Steam	R. Stephenson	1925
SR 4-6-0 No 777 *Sir Lamiel*	GCR	N/British	1925
SR 4-6-0 No 850 *Lord Nelson*	Mid-Hants Railway	Eastleigh	1926
SR 4-4-0 No 925 *Cheltenham*	Mid-Hants Railway	Eastleigh	1934
R/Hornsby (187105)	Leighton Buzzard	R/Hornsby	1937
RSH (7063) 0-4-0ST	Locomotion	RSH	1942
GWR 0-6-0PT No 9400	Steam	Swindon	1947
BR 4-6-2 No 70013 *Oliver Cromwell*	Great Central/main line	Crewe	1951
BR 2-10-0 No 92220 *Evening Star*	Steam	Swindon	1960
BR Bo-Bo No E3036	Barrow Hill	N/British	1960
GWR 4-2-2 *Iron Duke*	Gloucs & Warwickshire	RESCO	1985

Powered Units

NER	electric parcels van No 3267, G. Stephenson Museum	
GWR	diesel railcar No 4, STEAM	
BR	Class 101 vehicle Nos 51192/54352 East Lancs	

†private site

Departmental Stock

1932	LMS Ballast plough brake van No 197266, Embsay
1949	BR(LMS) Dynamometer car No 3, No 45049, Midland Railway Centre

Passenger Stock

1846	SDR 1st & 2nd composite No 31, Beamish
1850	NER 4-wheel coach body, Darlington 1899 Privately owned Duke of Sutherland's Saloon No 57A, Bo'ness
1910	GCR Open 3rd class No 666, Nottingham
1925	GWR 3rd class dining car No 9653, Severn Valley Rly
1925	LMS 3rd class vestibule No 7828 *(on loan to LMS Carriage Association)*
1934	GWR Buffet Car No 9631, Steam
1936	LNER 3rd Open, No 13254, NYMR
1945	GWR Royal Saloon No 9007, Gloucestershire & Warwickshire Railway
1960	Pullman Car Co 1st class Kitchen car No 311
	Eagle, Mid-Hants
1985	GWR 3rd (broad gauge replica), Didcot

Freight & Non Passenger Carrying Stock

1850	South Hetton Colliery Chaldron Wagon No 1155, D Bahn Museum, Nuremberg
1898	CR well trolley bogie crocodile, Bo'ness
1899	GWR Hand Crane No 537, Didcot
1902	NER 20-ton wooden hopper wagon No 4551, Tyne & Wear
1909	GWR Girder Wagon Set (Pollen E) Nos DW84997, 84998, 84999, 85000, Didcot
1912	LBSCR Open wagon No 27884, Yeovil
1912	LSWR Gunpowder van No KDS61209, Yeovil
1914	GWR Shunters' truck No W94988, Steam
1922	LBSCR cattle truck No 7116, Isle of Wight Steam Rly
1928	ICI Nitric acid tank wagon No 14, Yeovil
1936	GWR Ballast Wagon No 80659, Didcot
1937	2 x Yorkshire Water Authority side-tipper wagons 1941, Leighton Buzzard Railway
1941	LNER 20-ton brake van, No 246710, NYMR
1948	BR(SR) 12-ton shock absorbing wagon No 14036, NYMR
1950	BR 12-wheel well wagon, No KDB901601, East Lancs

England

| 1954 | Iron ore tippler, Rutland Railway Museum |
| 1955 | BR 16-ton mineral wagon No B227009, Middleton |

Timetable Service — Nene Valley Railway — Cambs

Member: HRA, TT

This international railway's collection includes locomotives and coaches from 9 countries. It is a regular location for TV and film makers — from *Octopussy* with Roger Moore and *Goldeneye* with Pierce Brosnan and including TV series *Silent Witness*, *London's Burning*, *Casualty*, *The Bill* and *Dalziel & Pascoe*. The railway and the pleasant Cambridgeshire countryside have doubled for locations as diverse as Russia, Spain and inner London

Chairman: Brian Claydon

Headquarters: Nene Valley Railway, Wansford Station, Stibbington, Peterborough, Cambs PE8 6LR

Locomotives

Name	No	Origin	Class	Type	Built
92 Squadron	34081	SR	BB	4-6-2	1948
City of Peterborough	73050	BR	5MT	4-6-0	1954
—	44422	LMS	4F	0-6-0	1926
—	9520	BR	14	0-6-0DH	1964
—	14029	BR	14	0-6-0DH	1964
—†	31271	BR	31	A1A-A1A	1961
—	64.305	DB	64	2-6-2T	1936
—	656	DSB	F	0-6-0T	1949
—	101	SJ	B	4-6-0	1944
—	1178	SJ	S	2-6-2T	1914
—	1212	SJ	Y7	railbus	
—	5485	PKP	Typ	0-8-0T	1959

†on loan from Midland Railway

Industrial locomotives

Name	No	Builder	Type	Built
Toby	—	Cockerill (1626)	0-4-0VBT	1890
Muriel	—	E/Electric (1123)	0-4-0DH	1966

Telephone: Stamford (01780) 784444; Talking Timetable (01780) 784404

Internet addresses: *E-mail:* nvorg@nvr.org.uk
Web site: www.nvr.org.uk

Main station: Wansford

Other public stations: Yarwell, Orton Mere, Ferry Meadows, Peterborough NVR

OS reference: TL 903979

Car park: Wansford, Orton Mere (free parking), Ferry Meadows, Peterborough NVR

Access by public transport: *By bus:* from Peterborough to Orton Mere and Ferry Meadows, Peterborough NVR (15min walk from city centre)

Refreshment facilities: Wansford, bar coach on most trains

Souvenir shops: Wansford

Exhibition: Wansford

Depot: Wansford

Length of line: 7.5 miles

Passenger trains: Yarwell Junction-Wansford-Ferry Meadows-Orton Mere-Peterborough NV

Period of public operation: Some

Name	No	Builder	Type	Built
Derek Crouch	—	H/Clarke (1539)	0-6-0ST	1924
Thomas	—	H/Clarke (1800)	0-6-0T	1947
Jacks Green	—	Hunslet (1953)	0-6-0ST	1939
—	75006	Hunslet (2855)	0-6-0ST	1943
—	22	Hunslet (3844)	0-6-0ST	1956
Doncaster	—	YEC (2654)	0-4-0DE	1957
Stanton No 50	—	YEC (2670)	0-6-0DE	1958
Barabel	—	R/Royce (10202)	0-4-0DH	1967
—	DL83	R/Royce (10271)	0-6-0DH	1967
Frank	—	Hibberd (2896)	4wD	1944
—	—	R/Hornsby (294268)	4wDM	1951

Stock

14 BR Mk 1 coaches; Wagons Lits sleeping car, Italian-built; Wagons Lits dining car, Belgian-built; 5 coaches from Denmark; 1 coach from France; 4 coaches from Belgium; 1 steam rail crane; SR Travelling Post Office; TPO coach M30272M; 5 BR Mk 1 TPOs; 1 GNR TPO body; 20 12-ton Vanfits plus items of freight stock

Owner

34081 the Battle of Britain Locomotive Preservation Society
73050 Peterborough City Council
44422 the 4F Locomotive Co Ltd
31271 the A1A Locomotive Society
22 C. Theaker & R. Robinson
14029 Stratrail Ltd
9520, *Stanton No 50*, *Barabel* and R/Royce (10271) the Iron & Steel Traction Group

Sundays in January and November; Sundays February and March; weekends and Bank Holidays April to end October; daily at Easter; Wednesdays from May, plus other midweek services in summer. Please telephone for details or visit web site

Special events: Mum Drives Thomas — 18 March; Visit by *Tornado* — 7-9 April; Diesel Gala — 19/20 May; Murder Mystery Special — 26 May; Dad Drives Thomas — 17 June; Murder Mystery Special — 7 July;

Vintage and Rail Mail Weekend — 14/15 July; Autumn Steam Gala — 8/9 September; Diesel Gala — 28-30 September; 1940s Weekend — 6/7 October (inc Fish & Chip train Saturday evening); Santa Specials — 25 November-24 December (please contact for details)

Thomas Special events: Thomas' Birthday Party — 23/24 June; Thomas' Big Adventure — 22 July, 4/5 August; Thomas and the Travelling Post Office — 18/19 August; Halloween with Thomas — 27/28, 31 October; Bank Holidays

and Half Term Holidays with Thomas

Facilities for disabled: Ramp access to all stations and shops. Toilets at Wansford station. Disabled persons and helpers are eligible for concessionary fares. Passengers can be assisted on and off trains

Membership details: Bill Forman, c/o above address

Membership journal: *Nene Steam* — 4 times/year

Marketing name: Britain's International Steam Railway

Timetable Service — North Bay Railway — North Yorkshire

Member: HRA

This 20in-gauge railway opened in 1931 and is almost a mile long, with all the features of a main line railway including a tunnel, bridges, signals, stations and gradient boards reproduced to scale. The steam outline locomotives are based on Sir Nigel Gresley's Class A1 design for the LNER

Location: Northstead Manor Gardens, Scarborough

Headquarters: Peasholm Park Station, Northstead Manor Gardens, Scarborough YO12 6PF

Telephone: General enquiries: 01723 368791

Internet addresses:
E-mail: info@nbr.org.uk
Web site: www.nbr.org.uk

Main public station: Peasholm Park

Other public stations:

Locomotives — 1ft 8in gauge

Name	No	Builder	Type	Built
Neptune	1931	H/Clarke (D565)	4-6-2DH S/O	1931
Robin Hood	570	H/Clarke (D570)	4-6-4DH S/O	1932
Triton	1932	H/Clarke (D573)	4-6-2DH S/O	1932
Poseidon	1933	H/Clarke (D582)	4-6-2DH S/O	1933

Stock
12 bogie coaches

Scalby Mills
SatNav postcode: Peasholm Park — YO12 6PF
Car parks: Nearby pay & display at both stations
Access by public transport: The railway is within walking distance of the main line stations and local bus services
Refreshment facilities: At both stations, full meals, licensed at Peasholm Park

Journey time: 8 minutes
Length of line: 0.875 mile, 1ft 8in gauge
Period of public operation: Daily, April until end October, then weekends and school holidays at other times
Facilities for disabled: Full
Special events: Santa Specials in December

Railway Centre — North Ings Farm Museum — Lincolnshire

The museum contains agricultural equipment, tractors and railway items

Contact: Mr Hall or Malcolm Phillips (joint owners)

Headquarters: North Ings Farm Museum, Fen Road, Dorrington, Lincoln LN4 3QB

Telephone: 01526 833100

Industrial locomotives — 2ft gauge

Name	No	Builder	Type	Built
Swift	—	Marshall	0-4-0VBT	1970
Indian Runner	—	R/Hornsby (200744)	4wDM	1940
—	—	R/Hornsby (371937)	4wDM	1956
—	—	R/Hornsby (375701)†	4wDM	1954
—	—	R/Hornsby (421433)	4wDM	1959
Penelope	—	M/Rail (7403)	4wDM	1939
—	—	M/Rail (7493)	4wDM	1940

Internet addresses: *E-mail:*
info@northingsfarmmuseum.co.uk
Web site:
www.northingsfarmmuseum.co.uk
Car parks: At the museum
entrance
Access by public transport:
Nearest main line station
Ruskington, 3 miles
Refreshment facilities: Only
available by prior arrangement
Length of line:
600yd, 2ft gauge
Period of public operation: Open
first Sunday, April to October.

Name	No	Builder	Type	Built
—	—	O&K	4wDM	1932
—	—	Lister Railtrack*	4wDM	—
Bullfinch	—	H/Hunslet (7120)	4wDM	1969

†dismantled
*constructed from spare parts

Owner
M/Rail (7403) and R/Hornsby (200744) on loan from Narrow Gauge
Railway Museum Trust

10.00-17.00
Facilities for disabled: Toilet,
wheelchairs can be accommodated

on the train. Part of the museum is
not easily accessible for
wheelchairs

Timetable Service — North Norfolk Railway (The Poppy Line) — Norfolk

Member: HRA, TT
Part of the former Midland & Great
Northern Joint Railway, other
elements of the LNER have crept
in in the guise of the 'B12' and the
newly restored Quad Art set. Guest
locomotives can be viewed at
various times throughout the year.
The line runs through beautiful
coast, wood and heathland scenery
with a nature trail running along its
side between Weybourne and
Kelling Heath
Managing Director: Hugh Harkett
Headquarters: North Norfolk
Railway plc, Sheringham Station,
Sheringham, Norfolk NR26 8RA
Telephone: Sheringham (01263)
820800
Fax: (01263) 820801
Internet addresses: *E-mail:*
enquiries@nnrailway.co.uk
Web site:
www.nnrailway.co.uk
Main station: Sheringham
Other public stations:
Weybourne, Kelling Halt, Holt
OS reference: Sheringham TG
156430, Weybourne TG 118419
Car parks: Sheringham (public),
Weybourne, Holt
SatNav postcodes:
Sheringham — NR26 8RA
Weybourne — NR26 7HN
Holt — NR25 6AJ
Access by public transport:
National rail to Sheringham
(Abellio Greater Anglia). By bus to
Sheringham and Holt stations
Refreshment facilities:
Sheringham, Weybourne, Holt

Locomotives and multiple-units

Name	No	Origin	Class	Type	Built
—	65462	GER	J15	0-6-0	1912
—	1572†	LNER	B12	4-6-0	1928
—	90775*	MoS	WD	2-10-0	1943
Black Prince	92203	BR	9F	2-10-0	1959
—	D2280	BR	04	0-6-0DM	1960
Camulodunum	D3940	BR	08	0-6-0DE	1960
—	D3935	BR	08	0-6-0DE	1961
—	12131	BR	11	0-6-0DE	1952
—	D5207	BR	25	Bo-Bo	1962
—	5580	BR	31	A1A-A1A	1960
—	D5631	BR	31	A1A-A1A	1960
Mirage	D6732	BR	37	Co-Co	1962
—	47367	BR	47	Co-Co	1965
—	51228	M/Cam	101	DTSL	1958
—	56062	M/Cam	101	DMBS	1957
—	79960	W&M	—	Railbus	1958
—	79963	W&M	—	Railbus	1958
—	LEV1	BR/Leyland	—	Railbus	1978

*under restoration
†expected to return to service spring 2012

Industrial locomotives

Name	No	Builder	Type	Built
Ring Haw	—	Hunslet (1982)	0-6-0ST	1940
Wissington*	—	H/Clarke (1700)	0-6-0ST	1938
—	—	Bagnall (2370)	0-6-0F	1929

*under restoration

Stock
3 ex-LNER coaches, GNR Quad Art set (in service, but not on a daily
basis), 7 ex-BR coaches, 3-coach King's Cross suburban set; Gresley
buffet, Wisbech & Upwell Tramway coach, M&GN coach, 2 CCT wagons,
small number of wagons, Southern Railway PMV, LNER BYP, Colman's
Mustard Van

Owners
Wissington, 65462, 1572, D5631 and 90775 the Midland & Great Northern
Railway Society — www.mandgn.co.uk
92203 owned by David Shepherd
5580 A1A Locomotives

STEAMING 'TWIXT SEA AND PINE

TICKETS VALID ALL DAY on any train

Step into the past on North Norfolk's Poppy Line from Sheringham to Holt.
So much more than just a train trip!

Make a day of it!

- **Explore!** Make a day of it. Hop-on, hop off Rover tickets give unlimited travel all day.
- **Enjoy** spectacular views of coast and country
- **Experience** the sights, sounds and smells of big steam engines
- **Enthuse** over three superbly restored stations and the magnificent William Marriott Museum at Holt station
- **Embrace** the pleasures of the past

ALL DAY TRAVEL AT 2009 PRICES

Adult Rover £10.50	Under 5s FREE
Senior citizen £9.50	Cycles & dogs
Child 5 – 15 £7.00	£1 each

£35 family ticket (2 adults + 2 children or 3 adults + 1 child) comes with a £5 voucher to spend on the refreshments and souvenirs available at every station

STEAM TRAINS MOST DAYS APRIL-OCT

Visit www.nnrailway.co.uk or call 01263 820 800

POPPY LINE

NORTH NORFOLK RAILWAY
Sheringham Station NR26 8RA   Holt Station NR25 6AJ

SHERINGHAM 'TWIXT SEA AND PINE

LIVE STEAM – LIVING HISTORY

Souvenir shops: Sheringham, Weybourne, Holt
Depot: Weybourne
Length of line: 5.25 miles
Passenger trains: Steeply graded (1 in 80), Sheringham-Weybourne-Holt
Period of public operation: Daily from 1 April to 31 October. February half-term week plus weekends in March (steam) and November (diesel). Santa specials weekends in December plus 21-24
Special events: Great Spring Steam Gala — 9-10 March; Vintage Bus Running Days and Rally — 14/15 April; Puffing Billy at the Children's Weekend — 5-7 May; History Day — 9 May; Diesel Gala — 8-10 June; 125th Anniversary of the Poppy Line — 16 June; David Shepherd's Wildlife Weekend — 16/17 June; Titfield Thunderbolt Live — 22-24 June; Vintage Transport Festival — 1 July; Quad-Arts Week — 1-8 July; 11th North Norfolk Railway Beer Festival —

47367 The Stratford Class 47 Group — www.stratford47group.co.uk
LEV1 on loan from National Railway Museum

13-15 July; Grand Steam Gala — 31 August, 1/2 September; The Famous '40s Weekend — 15/16 September; Shuddering Spiders, it's Haloween — 27-31 October, 1-4 November; Santa Specials (advance booking only) — 1/2, 8/9, 15/16, 21-24 December; Mince Pie Specials — 26-31 December-1 January 2013. *'North Norfolkman' dining train:* Lunch — 18 March; 15, 22 April; 13, 27 May; 10, 17 June; 22, 29 July; 12, 19 August; 30 September; 14 October; 11 November. Dinner — 4, 19 May; 2, 30 June; 4, 24 August; 27 October. Murder Mystery — 23 June, 22 September; 6 October, 3 November
Special facilities: Weybourne station is licensed for weddings. Special dining trains can be booked for corporate and party entertaining. Online booking available on

www.nnrailway.co.uk
William Mariott Museum: This museum is in a replica M&GN goods shed at Holt station. Artefacts and ephemera commemorating the man who built the railway and ran it for almost 40 years. Open on steam operating days
Facilities for disabled: All stations have level access. Wheelchair access to most trains, and disabled parking at Holt station. There is full wheelchair access to the gift shops and catering facilities at all stations
Membership details: Midland & Great Northern Joint Railway Society, Membership Secretary, c/o Sheringham Station, Sheringham, Norfolk NR26 8RA
E-mail: member@mandgn.co.uk
Web site: www.mandgn.co.uk
Membership journal: *Joint Line* — quarterly

North Yorkshire Moors Railway

| Timetable Service | | North Yorkshire |

Member: HRA, TT
This 18-mile line runs through the picturesque North York Moors National Park and is host to an extensive collection of main line locomotives
General Manager: Philip Benham
Headquarters: Pickering Station, Pickering, North Yorkshire YO18 7AJ
Telephone: Pickering (01751) 472508 for passenger enquiries, charter and diner bookings
Internet addresses:
E-mail: info@nymr.co.uk
Web site: www.nymr.co.uk
Main station: Pickering
Other public stations: Whitby, Grosmont, Goathland, Levisham, Pickering
OS reference: Pickering NZ 797842, Levisham NZ 818909, Goathland NZ 836013, Grosmont NZ 828053
Car parks: Grosmont, Goathland, Levisham, Pickering
Access by public transport: Northern Rail services linking Middlesbrough with Grosmont and

Locomotives and multiple-units

Name	No	Origin	Class	Type	Built
George Stephenson	44767	LMS	5MT	4-6-0	1947
Eric Treacy	45428*	LMS	5MT	4-6-0	1937
—	49395	LNWR	7F	0-8-0	1918
—	2392††	NER	P3	0-6-0	1923
—	63395	NER	T2	0-8-0	1918
Sir Nigel Gresley	60007	LNER	A4	4-6-2	1937
Lord of the Isles	62005	LNER	K1	2-6-0	1949
—	69023§	LNER	J72	0-6-0T	1951
—	3814**	GWR	2884	2-8-0	1940
—	825	SR	S15	4-6-0	1927
—	30830††	SR	S15	4-6-0	1927
Repton	30926	SR	V	4-4-0	1934
Hartland	34101**	SR	WC	4-6-2	1950
—	75029	BR	4MT	4-6-0	1954
—	76079	BR	4MT	2-6-0	1957
—	80135††	BR	4MT	2-6-4T	1956
Cock o' the North	92214	BR	9F	2-10-0	1959
Dame Vera Lynn	3672††	MoS	WD	2-10-0	1943
—	2253††	USATC	S160	2-8-0	1943
—	D2207	BR	04	0-6-0DM	1953
—	08556	BR	08	0-6-0DE	1959
—	08850	BR	08	0-6-0DE	1961
Helen Turner	D5032††	BR	24	Bo-Bo	1959
—	D5061	BR	24	Bo-Bo	1960
Sybilla	D7628	BR	25	Bo-Bo	1965
—	31128	BR	31	A1A-A1A	1959

England

Whitby

Bus services include Leeds-York-Malton-Pickering-Goathland-Whitby; Helmsley-Pickering-Scarborough

Refreshment facilities: Available on most trains and at Grosmont, Goathland and Pickering. Tea bar at Levisham most weekends

Souvenir shops: Pickering, Goathland, Grosmont, Grosmont MPD and Whitby.

Artist in Residence: Chris Ware is based at Levisham station, whose studio is open when trains are running

Locomotive Depot: Grosmont

Length of line: 18 miles (Pickering-Grosmont), 24 miles (Pickering-Whitby)

Passenger trains: Steam-hauled services Grosmont-Pickering. Pullman evening dining service and 'Moorlander' Sunday lunch service run regularly. Saloons are also available for special occasions (eg wedding parties, conferences, etc)

Note: NYMR trains operate to/from Whitby throughout the season. Ring for details

Period of public operation: Weekends in March, daily 1 April-4 November, Santa Specials and other Xmas services in December/January and New Year

Special events: Spring Steam Gala — 4-7, 11-13 May; '60s Weekend — 9/10 June; Vintage Vehicle Weekend — 14/15 July; Heritage Diesel Gala — 14-16 September; Autumn Steam Gala — 28-30 September, 1/2 October; Railway in Wartime — 12-14 October; Santa Specials — 1/2, 8/9, 15/16, 22-24 December

Facilities for disabled: The NYMR welcomes disabled visitors and special attention will gladly be provided if advance notice is given

Name	No	Origin	Class	Type	Built
—	37264	BR	37	Co-Co	1965
Lion	50027	BR	50	Co-Co	1968
—	51511	BR	101	DMC	1959
—	53204	BR	101	DMBS	1957
—	59559	BR	101	TSL	1958

*undergoing major overhaul at Grosmont, due to traffic 2012
§undergoing major overhaul off-site
**undergoing major overhaul at Grosmont, not in traffic
††awaiting overhaul

Industrial locomotives

Name	No	Builder	Type	Built
—	29**	Kitson (4263)	0-6-2T	1904
—	5††	R/Stephenson (3377)	0-6-2T	1909
Neil D. Barker	12139*	E/Electric (1553)	0-6-0DE	1948
—	16	Drewry	0-4-0DM	1941
—	2††	R/Hornsby (421419)	4wDM	1958
—	3*	R/Hornsby (441934)	4wDM	1960
Ron Rothwell	1	Vanguard (129V)	0-4-0DM	1963
—	2††	Vanguard (131V)	0-4-0DM	1963

*on loan to Middleton Railway
**undergoing major overhaul at Grosmont, not in traffic
††awaiting overhaul

Stock

5 pre-Grouping, 12 pre-Nationalisation, 32 x BR Mk 1, 4 x Pullman, 5 other BR coaches, 2 x Camping Coach, 1 x BR Mk 3 sleeper, 11 x brake vans, 4 x diesel cranes, 2 x 45-ton steam cranes, 88 other vehicles

Owners

825 and 30830 the Essex Locomotive Society
62005, 63395 and 69023 the North Eastern Locomotive Preservation Group
60007 Sir Nigel Gresley Locomotive Preservation Trust
5 and 29 Lambton Locomotives Trust
D5032 T. J. Thomson & Co
D5061 the Class 24 Society
50027 the Class 50 Support Group
3814, 34101 and 44767 private
30926, 75029, 76079 and D7628 the North Yorkshire Moors Historical Railway Trust
49395 on loan from National Railway Museum
45212 on loan from the Keighley & Worth Valley Railway
92214 PV Premier Ltd

Special notes: Operates through North York Moors National Park and to Whitby

---

Steam Centre	**Northampton & Lamport Railway**	Northants

Member: HRA

Part of the Northampton to Market Harborough branch originally opened in 1859 and finally closing in 1981. That year a group was formed with the intention of re-opening the branch. Trains restarted in 1995 with 0.75 mile of running line and sidings. When completed to Lamport the line will be 6 miles long

Headquarters: Pitsford & Brampton Station, Pitsford Road, Chapel Brampton, Northampton NN6 8BA

Location: About 5 miles north of Northampton, Pitsford Road off A5199 (formerly A50) or A508

Chairman: Gordon Titmuss

Operating company: Northampton Steam Railway Ltd

Telephone: 01604 820327. Sundays and weekday afternoons, recorded announcements other times

Internet address: *Web site:*
www.nlr.org.uk
Access by public transport: None
On site facilities: NLR souvenir
shop, buffet coach, toilets, second-
hand bookshop
Length of line: 1.3 miles, extension
to bridge 14 now open
Public opening:
Every Sunday and Bank Holiday
Monday from 18 March to
28 October.
Santa Specials, in December (see
below).
Plus some Saturdays during special
events
Special events: Mother's Day —
18 March; Easter Egg Specials —
7-9 April; Members Day —
29 April; Teddy Bears — 5-7 May;
Branch Line Experience —
2-4 June; Father's Day — 17 June;
Vintage Vehicles — 28/29 July;
Seaside Specials — 25-27 August;
Railway at War — 22/23
September; Halloween —
28 October; Santa Specials —
2, 8/9, 15/16, 22/23 December (pre-
booking essential); Mince Pies —
30 December and 1 January 2013
Facilities for disabled: Limited
access
Special notes: All stock is visible
along the side of the line.
Carriages are available for birthday

parties etc on operating dates except
certain special events, and complete
trains are also available for hire
during weekdays for school or
special events. Please contact the
railway for details

Locomotives

Name	No	Origin	Class	Type	Built
Bickmarsh Hall	5967	GWR	'Hall'	4-6-0	1937
—	3862	GWR	2884	2-8-0	1942
—	31289	BR	31	A1A-A1A	1961
—	47205	BR	47	Co-Co	1965

Industrial locomotives

Name	No	Builder	Type	Built
Colwyn	45	Kitson (5470)	0-6-0ST	1933
Westminster	1378	Peckett (1378)	0-6-0ST	1914
—	2104	Peckett (2104)	0-4-0ST	1948
Vanguard	5374	Chrzanow (5374)	0-6-0T	1959
Bunty	146C	Fowler (4210018)/ rebuilt T/Hill	0-4-0DH	1950 1964
—	21	Fowler (4210094)	0-4-0DH	1955
—	1	R/Hornsby (275886)	4wDM	1949
Sir Gyles Isham	764	R/Hornsby (319286)	0-4-0DM	1953
Sir Alfred Wood	11	R/Hornsby (319294)	0-4-0DM	1953

Stock
Coaches: 1 x BR Mk 1 TSO; 1 x BR Mk 1 RBR;1 x BR Mk2 BSO,
2 x Mk 2 TSO; 1 x BR Mk 1 NAV; 2 x BR Mk 1 NVJ, 1 x LMS CCT;
1 x BR 20-ton brake

Owner
Colwyn the Colwyn Preservation Society

Membership details: Membership
Secretary, Pitsford & Brampton
Station, Pitsford Road, Chapel
Brampton, Northampton NN6 8BA
Membership journal: *Premier
Line* — 4 times a year

Steam Centre	Northamptonshire Ironstone Railway Trust	Northants

The museum is a working display
as well as a collection of historic
memorabilia. Many of the items
that are currently being renovated
are housed in a shed that
accommodates the museum display.
  The NIRT completed major
trackwork in 2005 with a further
extension completed. Open the first
Sunday of every month along with
Bank Holiday weekends, NIRT
alsohold special events, which
include Halloween in October,
along with Santa Specials in
December. Please see railway press
or for weekly updated information
go to the web site
Location: Hunsbury Hill Industrial
Museum, Hunsbury Hill Country
Park, Hunsbury Hill Road, Camp
Hill, Northampton NN4 9UW

Multiple-units

Name	No	Origin	Class	Type	Built
—	13004	SR	4DD	DMBS	1949
—	70284	BR	4CEP / 411	TS	1956
—	70296	BR	4CEP / 411	TS	1956
—	70510	BR	4CEP / 411	TS	1956
—	69304	BR	4BIG / 422	TSRB	1965
—	14352†	BR	415 / 4EPB	DMS	1954
—	15396†	BR	415 / 4EPB	TS	1954
—	14351†	BR	415 / 4EPB	DMS	1954

†unit No 415176

Industrial locomotives

Name	No	Builder	Type	Built
Vigilant†	—	Hunslet (287)	0-4-0ST	1882
Belvedere◊	—	Sentinel (9365)	0-4-0TG	1946
Musketeer◊	—	Sentinel (9369)	0-4-0TG	1946
Hylton	—	Planet (3967)	0-4-0DH	1961
Charles Wake	—	Fowler (422001)	0-4-0DH	1965
—	16	Hunslet (2087)	0-4-0DM	1940
Muffin	46	R/Hornsby (242868)	4wDM	1946

England

OS reference: SP 735584
Operating organisation:
Northamptonshire Ironstone
Railway Trust Ltd
Telephone: 01604 702031 or event
hotline 07799 163114
Contact: Mr Bill Nile
Internet addresses: *E-mail:*
nirt@btinternet.com
Web Site: www.nirt.co.uk
Access by public transport:
By bus: First Group bus No 12 to
Camp Hill from Greyfriars bus
station. Bus No 10 from railway
station.
By rail: London Midland runs
regular train services from London
Euston or from Birmingham New
Street. See London Midland web
site for times etc
On site facilities: Café serving
light refreshments, shop, toilets.
Staffed children's play areas and
games room and NIRT garden with
picnic areas and seating
Length of line: 2.25km with yard,
engine shed and workshops, one
station open and one to be rebuilt
and level crossing
Public opening: Museum during
published operating days or by prior

Name	No	Builder	Type	Built
—*	87	Peckett (1871)	0-6-0ST	1934
—	D697	H/Clarke (D697)	0-4-0DM	1950
Cherwell**	—	Bagnall (2654)	0-6-0ST	1942

* metre gauge on loan to Irchester Country Park
◊ static display
† being rebuilt
**3ft gauge

Owner
13004, unit No 415176, 70284/70296 the Northampton Ironstone Railway
Trust Ltd

arrangement only. Train service
from Easter to National Heritage
Weekend in September on first
Sunday of every month plus two
night runs at Halloween in October
and December for Santa specials.
Parties can be catered for on
weekdays or weekends strictly by
appointment
Times of opening: 11.00 to 16.30
for viewing, with train service from
11.00 to 17.00 on Sundays and
Bank Holidays
Facilities for the disabled:
Passenger coach can accommodate
wheelchairs

Special notes: Museum to the
Ironstone Industry of
Northamptonshire, the museum
houses photographs, documents and
other items connected with the
ironstone industry. The railway is
laid on the old trackbed of the
quarry system and partly on a new
formation with remains of the
quarry face and cuttings available
for exploration
Membership details: Mr Ian Cave,
c/o above e-mail or postal address

Steam Centre / Nottingham Transport Heritage Centre / Notts

Member: HRA
Along with access to nearly 10
miles of the ex-Great Central
Railway main line in
Nottinghamshire, the centre is host
to a road and rail transport heritage
vehicle collection. The railway has
a main line connection just south of
Loughborough (Midland) station
and regular freight trains use the
line as far as the British Gypsum
works at East Leake.

Plans are in place to reconnect
this section with the Great Central
Railway at Loughborough. See:
www.bridgingthegap.org.uk
Location: Signposted on the A60
Loughborough road just south of
Ruddington traffic lights, 5 miles
south of Nottingham and 7 miles
north of Loughborough
Operating society/organisation:
Great Central (Nottingham) Ltd,
Mere Way, Ruddington,
Nottingham NG11 6NX

Locomotives and multiple-units

Name	No	Origin	Class	Type	Built
—	2364	USATC	S160	2-8-0	
—	1631	USATC	S160	2-8-0	1942
—	08114	BR	08	Bo-Bo	1955
—	08220	BR	08	Bo-Bo	1956
—	D8007	BR	20	Bo-Bo	1957
—	D7629	BR	25	Bo-Bo	1965
—	D8154	BR	20	Bo-Bo	1966
—	37009	BR	37	Co-Co	1961
—	46010	BR	46	1Co-Co1	1961
—	47292	BR	47	Co-Co	1966
—	47765	BR	47	Co-Co	1964
—	56097	BR	56	Co-Co	1981
—	73110 (E6016)	BR	73	Bo-Bo	1962
—	51138	BR	116	DMBS	1958
—	51151	BR	116	DMS	1958
—	53645	BR	108	DMBS	1958
—	53926	BR	108	DMBS	1959
—	59389	BR	108	TS	1958

Industrial locomotives

Name	No	Builder	Type	Built
Julia	54	H/Clarke (1682)	0-6-0ST	1937

Telephone: (0115) 940 5705
Fax: (0115) 940 5905
Internet addresses:
E-mail: info@gcrn.co.uk
Web site: www.gcrn.co.uk
SatNav postcode: NN11 6JS
Access by public transport: Buses from Nottingham city centre and Broad Marsh via Nottingham railway station. Nottingham City Transport (0115) 950 6070, Trent Barton (01773) 712265
On site facilities: Car park, shop and cafeteria, picnic areas and country park walks. 700m-long triple-gauge passenger-carrying miniature railway. Model railway layouts
Length of line: 8-mile round trip to Rushcliffe Halt by steam train. 18 mile round trip to Loughborough junction by steam and diesel (monthly and galas)
Facilities for disabled: Access to most areas, accessible toilets
Public opening: Various openings

Name	No	Builder	Type	Built
Corby	56	RSH (7667)	0-6-0ST	1950
Ruddington	63	RSH (7761)	0-6-0ST	1954
Dolobran	—	M/Wardle (1762)	0-6-0ST	1910
Rhyl	—	M/Wardle (2009)	0-6-0ST	1921
Arthur	—	M/Wardle (2015)	0-6-0ST	1921
Marblaegis	—	R/Hornsby	0-4-0DM	1947
Quag	1	R/Hornsby (371971)	0-4-0DM	1954
Staythorpe	D2959	R/Hornsby (449754)	0-4-0DE	1961
Morris	15099	M/Rail (2028)	0-4-0DM	1932

Rolling stock: 6 BR Mk 1s, 6 BR Mk 2s, GCR coach (body) CBL No 1663 (oldest surviving GCR coach, built 1903), 4 Barnum coaches, 2 MS&LR 6-wheel coaches, 1 LNER 45-ton steam breakdown crane, various goods wagons

Owner
46010 the 46010 Group

from February through to October 2012. Check web site or phone for exact days. Santa Steam Special weekends in December.
Open 10.30-17.00
(first train from 10.30)

Special events: See web site or phone for details
Membership details: LNER/GC Heritage Trust, c/o above address
Society journal: 3 times per year

Attraction — Old Kiln Light Railway — Surrey

The Old Kiln Light Railway is located in the grounds of the Rural Life Museum which houses the largest countryside collection in the south of England
Location: Rural Life Centre, Reeds Road, Tilford, Farnham, Surrey GU10 2DL
Telephone: (01252) 795571 (museum)
Internet address: *Web site:* www.rural-life.org.uk
On site facilities: Free parking, picnic areas, shop, café
Access by road:
The museum is 3 miles south of Farnham, just off the A287 and midway between Frensham and Tilford villages
Length of line: Half mile, under extension, 2ft gauge
Public opening:
Summer: 7 March to 4 November, 10.00-17.00, Wednesday to Sunday and Bank Holiday Mondays. Winter opening: Wednesdays and Sundays only, 11.00-16.00. Last admission 1hr before closing time.
Please note the railway operates on Sundays.

Industrial locomotives — 2ft gauge

Name	No	Builder	Type	Built
Pamela	—	Hunslet (920)	0-4-0ST	1906
Elouise	—	O&K (9998)	0-4-0ST	1922
Eagle	—	M/Rail (5713)	4wDM	1936
Phoebe	—	M/Rail (8887)	4wDM	1944
—	—	M/Rail (8981)	4wDM	1946
—	—	M/Rail (5297)	4wPM	1931
Norden	—	Ruston (392117)	4wDM	
Emily	—	Hibberd (2528	4wDM	
Sam	—	Hunslet	4wDM	1944
Red Dwarf	—	Ruston (181820)	4wDM	1936
Sand Rock	—	Ruston (177639)	4wDM	
—	—	Hunslet (7010)	4wDM	1971
—	—	Hunslet (7011)	4wDM	1971
—	—	Hunslet (7012)	4wDM	1971
—	—	Hunslet (7012)	4wDM	1971
Sue	—	Wickham (3031)	2w-2PMR	1941
Liz	—	Wickham (3287)	2w-2PMR	1943

Stock
Glyn Valley replica coach, Baguley open coach, RNAD van, brake van

Special events (transport related):
Steam Toy Rally — 7 April; Model Railway Exhibition — 5 May; Village at War — 12/13 May; Days Gone By — 26/27 May; Rustic Sunday — 29 July; Ford Mk II Car Rally — 5 August; Classic Vehicle Gathering — 16 September; Classic Vehicle Gathering — 16 September; Land Rover Day — 14 October; Santa Specials —8/9, 15/16 December

Oswestry Railway Centre
(Cambrian Railways Society)

Member: HRA

Leases have been agreed for the Cambrian Railways Trust to lease the former main line (Oswestry to Llynclys) and the Cambrian Railways Society to lease the branch (Llynclys to Llanddu), from SCC. Under this arrangement the CRT will restore and run the main line, the CRS will be the museum body for the project, will be responsible for the Oswestry station area and will restore and run the branch.

The CRS is currently operating on three sites:

• The Oswestry Railway Centre, located in the former goods yard adjacent to the station. This is home to the Cambrian Railways Museum which has been awarded Phase II status by the Museums & Galleries Commission as being a museum of national importance. Also on site is the CRS engine shed and workshop, the fully restored Oswestry South Signalbox and a 400yd long running line, on which trains can be run for party bookings.

• Weston Wharf. This is a society-owned goods shed sited on the outskirts of Oswestry.

• The Nantmawr branch. This 1.5-mile long line starts at the end of the Network Rail line at Llanddu and was purchased in 2004

Location: Oswestry station yard, Oswald Road, Oswestry, Shropshire SY11 1RE

Industrial locomotives

	Name	No	Builder	Type	Built
—	1	H/Clarke (D843)		0-4-0DM	1954
Adam	1	Peckett (1430)		0-4-0ST	1916
—	3	Hunslet (D3526)		0-6-0DM	1947
Oliver Velton	6	Peckett (2131)		0-4-0ST	1951
—	8	Barclay (885)		0-6-0ST	1900
Alpha	—	Planet (3593)		0-4-0DH	1962
Scottie	—	R/Hornsby (412427)		0-4-0DM	1957
Norma	3770	Hunslet (3770)		0-6-0ST	1952
Telemon	—	Drewry/Vulcan (2568)		0-4-0DM	1955

Stock

1 GWR auto-trailer, 1 BR RBR, 1 GWR brake van; 1 LMS brake van, 1 BR brake van, 4 tank wagons, 3 open wagons, 2 tank wagon 4-wheel chassis (tanks removed, ex-Machynlleth fuel point), 2 box vans, 2 flat wagons, also ex-BR on track plant 98306 (GP TRAMM)

Owners

Telemon and *Scottie* the Cambrian Diesel Group
322 private

OS reference: SJ 294297
Operating society/organisation: Cambrian Railways Society Ltd, Oswald Road, Oswestry, Shropshire SY11 1RE
Telephone: (01691) 671749
Internet address: *Web site:* www.cambrianrailwayssociety.co.uk
Car park: In Society's depot
Access by public transport:
By rail — Gobowen station is 2.5 miles north.
By bus — 2min walk from Oswestry bus station.
Please note that there is no Gobowen-Oswestry bus service on Sundays

Length of line: 400yd, opened 7 December 1996, the Light Railway Order having been granted
Public opening: Cambrian Railways Museum is open: Monday-Saturday 09.00-16.00; Sunday 11.00-16.00.
Trains will normally only run for group bookings or special events, please contact to confirm
On site facilities: Refreshment room — the 'Whistle Stop' (open on special days in former Llansantffraid signalbox) and picnic area

Peak Rail plc

Member: HRA

In 1968 the railway between Matlock and Buxton, through the Peak National Park, was closed and lifted. This was once part of the Midland Railway's route between Manchester Central and London.

Locomotives and multiple-units

Name	No	Origin	Class	Type	Built
—	D2953	BR	01	0-4-0DM	1956
—	D2854	BR	02	0-4-0DH	1960
—	D2868	BR	02	0-4-0DH	1961
—	03027	BR	03	0-6-0DM	1958
—	03099	BR	03	0-6-0DM	1960

In 1975 efforts were started to re-open the line. Services between Matlock and Darley Dale commenced in 1991

Location: *Registered Office:* Matlock Station, Matlock, Derbyshire DE4 3NA

OS reference: Matlock SK 060738

Operating society/organisation: Peak Rail plc, Matlock Station, Matlock, Derbyshire DE4 3NA

Telephone: (01629) 580381

Internet address: *Web site:* www.peakrail.co.uk

Car parks: Matlock station, Darley Dale, Rowsley South station

Length of line: 4.5 miles — Matlock-Rowsley South.
A 2ft gauge railway is now operational at Rowsley

On site facilities: Shop at Matlock. Shop and buffet at Rowsley South. Picnic area and riverside walk

Public opening: Sundays throughout the year, Saturdays April to October. Midweek during summer. Timetable varies

Facilities for disabled: Darley Dale, Rowsley and Matlock. Specially adapted carriage is fully accessible to wheelchair users

Period of public operation: Not advised, see timetable supplement

Special events: Please contact for details

Name	No	Origin	Class	Type	Built
—	03113	BR	03	0-6-0DM	1960
—	03180	BR	03	0-6-0DM	1962
—	D2139	BR	03	0-6-0DM	1960
—	D2199	BR	03	0-6-0DM	1961
—	D2229	BR	04	0-6-0DM	1955
Alfie	D2272	BR	04	0-6-0DM	1960
—	D2284	BR	04	0-6-0DM	1960
—	D2324	BR	04	0-6-0DM	1959
Dorothy	D2337	BR	04	0-6-0DM	1961
—	13000	BR	08	0-6-0DE	1952
Geoff L. Wright	D3023	BR	08	0-6-0DE	1953
—	09001	BR	09	0-6-0DE	1959
—	12061	BR	11	0-6-0DE	1949
—	D9500	BR	14	0-6-0DH	1964
—	D9502	BR	14	0-6-0DH	1964
—	D9525	BR	14	0-6-0DH	1965
—	31270	BR	31	A1A-A1A	1961
—	37152	BR	37	Co-Co	1963
—	37188	BR	37	Co-Co	1964
Penyghent	D8	BR	44	1Co-Co1	1959
Renown	50029	BR	50	Co-Co	1968
Repulse	50030	BR	50	Co-Co	1968
—	97654	BR	—	0-6-0DM	1959

Industrial locomotives

Name	No	Builder	Type	Built
—	68006	Hunslet (3192)	0-6-0ST	1944
Lord Phil	—	Hunslet (3883)	0-6-0ST	1962
—	680	RSH (7136)	0-6-0ST	1944
Zebedee	—	RSH (7597)	0-6-0ST	1949
—	64	Brush (803)	0-6-0DE	1978
—	—	Drewry (2552)	0-6-0DM	1953
Bigga	—	Fowler (4200019)	0-4-0DM	1947
Castlefield	—	H/Clarke (D1388)	0-6-0DH	1970
—	—	NBL (27932)	0-6-0DM	1959
—	—	R/Hornsby (DS88)	0-4-0DM	1957
—	6	Vanguard (265V)	0-4-0DH	1976
Rotherham	—	YEC (2480)	0-4-0DM	
—	—	YEC (2940)	0-4-0DM	1966

Rolling stock — coaches: 1 BR Mk 1 RMB, 1 BR Mk 1 RBR, 1 BR Mk 1 SLF, 1 BR Mk 1 FO, 2 BR Mk 1 TSO, 1 BR Mk 1 BSK, 1 BR Mk 1 CK1 BR Mk 1 SK, 1 BR Mk 1 SO , 5 BR Mk 1 BG, 5 BR Mk 1 GUV, 3 BR Mk 1 CCT, 1 BR Mk 1 Bullion van, 1 BR Mk 2 SO, 2 BR Mk 2 BSO, 1 BR Mk 2 BFK, 1 LMS RK, 2 LMS TK, 5 LMS TO, 2 LMS BCK, 1 LMS BG, 1 LMS CK

Rolling stock — wagons and on-track plant: 1 Mess & Tool Van, 1 diesel crane, 1 steam crane, 1 sleeper-changing machine, 1 Tamper, 1 track aligner, 1 track inspection trolley, 1 crane runner, 2 BR LMS-design brake vans, 1 BR standard brake van, 1 BR ballast plough brake van, 1 LMS MR-design brake van, 1 BR rail carrying wagon, 1 LNER low machine wagon, 2 BR low machine wagons, 2 BR bogie bolsters, 2 BR ballast hoppers, 1 LMS fish van, 2 Austrian ferry wagons, 1 SR parcels van, 1 ex-Army wooden u/f box van, 1 MR box van, 1 BR pallet vans, 2 BR van wide vans, 1 LMS box van, 1 wooden underframe BR body, 4 tank wagons, 1 bolster flat wagon, 2 BR pipe wagons, 1 plank wagon (crane runner),3 MR mineral wagons, 1 BR Medfit open wagon, 1 BR bolster wagon, 3 match wagons, SR 'Queen Mary' brake van, 1 MR 3-plank wagon, 1 flat wagon, 1 BR box van, 1 BR bolster wagon, 1 BR long wheel base stores van

Owners
50029 and 50030 the Renown Repulse Restoration Group

England

D8 the North Notts Loco Group
RSH 7597 Peak Rail and Peak Railway Association
12061 on loan to the Heritage Shunters Trust

Derbyshire Dales Narrow Gauge Railway
Industrial narrow gauge locomotives (2ft gauge)

Name	No	Builder	Type	Built
—	—	M/Rail (5853)	4wDM	1934
—	—	M/Rail (22070)	4wDM	1960
—	—	R/Hornsby (264252)	4wDM	1952
—	85049*	R/Hornsby (393325)	4wDM	1956
—	85051*	R/Hornsby (404976)	4wDM	1956
—	—	R/Hornsby (487963)	4wDM	1963

*plant numbers carried by former British Railways locomotives

---

Miniature Railway	Perrygrove Railway	Glos

Member: HRA, Britain's Great Little Railways
Headquarters: Perrygrove Railway, Coleford, Gloucestershire GL16 8QB
Contact: Michael Crofts
Telephone/Fax: 01594 834991
Internet address:
Web site: www.perrygrove.co.uk
OS reference: SO 579094
Main station: Perrygrove (GL16 8QB)
Other public stations: Rookwood, Heywood, Oakiron
Car park: Parking at Perrygrove for 60 cars plus 2 coach bays
Access by public transport: Network Rail: Lydney (7 miles). Dean Forest Railway: Parkend (3 miles).
Buses (all Stagecoach services) from: Gloucester — 30/31; Lydney — 721; Cinderford — 30/31; Ruardean — 746/747
Refreshment facilities: Light refreshments in Perrygrove station café
Souvenir shops: Small shop at Perrygrove
Museum: Heywood Collection of minimum gauge railways on display at Perrygrove
Depot: All sheds are at Perrygrove. Tours are encouraged under supervision when staff are available
Length of line: 0.75 miles, 15in

Locomotives — 15in gauge

Name	No	Builder	Type	Built
Spirit of Adventure	1	ESR (295)	0-6-0T	1993
Workhorse	2	Simplex (1064)	0-4-0DM	1963
Ursula	3*	J. Waterfield	0-6-0T	1999
Jubilee	4	Hunslet (9337)	0-4-0DH	1994
Tasmania	5	Bush Mills Railway	0-4-0+0-4-0	1990
Lydia	6	Alan Keef (77)	2-6-2T	2008
Ella	7	under construction	0-6-0T	
Lister Autotruck	8	Lister	0-4-0DM	

*based on Heywood locomotive of 1916

Stock
Modern: 6 carriages, 16 goods wagons
Vintage: various carriages and wagons both original and replicas of Duffield Bank and Eaton Hall Railways by Sir Arthur Heywood; Including The Duke of Westminster's Saloon and the Duffield Bank replica Dining Car. New replica vehicles being added regularly

(381mm) gauge
Period of public operation:
Every Saturday and Sunday and Bank Holiday from Easter to end of October.
Daily local school holidays
Special events:
Estate Railway Experience Days — ideal for groups — operate the whole railway and manage traffic demands for the day. Problem solving and shunting puzzles everywhere.
Vintage Trains Day — 24 June
Autumn Gala — 22/23 September, coinciding with Alan Keef open day on 22 September.

See web site for details of special attractions including visiting locomotives and special offers Christmas trains operate in December — advance booking essential: 01594 834991
Facilities for disabled: All disabilities catered for. About 75% of the site is accessible to wheelchairs, although some of the woodland paths are rough. There is space for 3 wheelchairs on the train
Membership details: Volunteers welcome
Membership journal: Diary pages on web site

Plym Valley Railway

Member: HRA

A scheme dedicated to the restoration of services over the former GWR Marsh Mills-Plym Bridge line, a distance of 1.5 miles

Location: 5 miles from centre of Plymouth, Devon, north of A38. From Marsh Mills roundabout, take B3416 to Plympton, follow signs for Coypool park & ride

Internet address:

Web site: www.plymrail.co.uk

OS reference: SX 517564

Operating society/organisation: Plym Valley Railway Co Ltd, Marsh Mills Station, Coypool Road, Marsh Mills, Plymouth, Devon PL7 4NW

Access by public transport: Buses from Plymouth, Nos 20, 20A, 21, 22A, 51 stop close to site

On site facilities: Shop and refreshments at Marsh Mills, Coypool (Sundays only)

Public opening: Sundays from 11.00, and other selected days. Trains are scheduled to operate: 8, 22 April, 13, 27 May, 10, 17 June, 8, 22 July, 12, 26/27 August, 9, 23 September, 14, 28 October, 2, 9, 16, 23, 30 December. Trains 13.00-16.00 at regular intervals

Length of line: Half-mile currently in use for passenger rides

Special events: Spooky Sunday — 30 October, Christmas Specials —

Locomotives and multiple-units

Name	No	Origin	Class	Type	Built
—	D2046	BR	03	0-6-0DM	1958
—	13002	BR	08	0-6-0DE	1953
William Cookworthy	37207	BR	37	Co-Co	1963
Royal Oak	50017	BR	50	Co-Co	1968
—	51365	BR	117	DMBS	1960
—	51407	BR	117	DMS	1960

Industrial locomotives

Name	No	Builder	Type	Built
—	705	Barclay (2047)	0-4-0ST	1937
Albert	—	Barclay (2248)	0-4-0ST	1948
Byfield No 2	—	Bagnall (2655)	0-6-0ST	1941
—	—	T/Hill (125V)	4wDH	1963
—	—	Hibberd (3281)	4wDM	1948

Rolling stock: 1 x BR Mk 1 coach, 4 x BR Mk 2 coaches, 1 LBSCR compartment coach (body only), 2 x BR GUVs, 3 x brake vans, various wagons. Self-propelled Smith & Rodley diesel crane of 1956

4, 11, 18 December. Please contact for details

Disabled facilities: Ramps available for less able visitors giving access to shop, café and trains

Special notes: Visitors are advised that, at the moment, the railway and two locomotives are still under restoration. Two working locomotives and DMU. The line was extended beyond the first bridge in 2003. Train rides behind *Albert* or No 13002 on some Sundays (normally 2nd in the month) to Lee Moor Crossing

Membership details: Membership Secretary, Plym Valley Railway, Marsh Mills Station, Coypool Road, Marsh Mills, Plymouth, Devon PL7 4NW

Membership journal: *Plym Valley Railway News* — 3/year

Marketing name: The Woodland Line

Railworld

Member: HRA

Railworld promotes 'Sustainable Transport' and the environment with emphasis on the rail industry, with superb model railway, tranquil nature haven and a variety of unique exhibits and 'hands-on' activities to explore

Location: Situated alongside the Town station of the Nene Valley Railway.

Walk — 15min walk from train and bus stations, Stagecoach route 1 (every 10min).

By car — turn off A1139 at jct 5, signs to city centre, follow brown and white 'Little Puffer' signs to Oundle Road into Council's long stay car park, drive under arches to Railworld. The Railworld car park is free to visitors.

By bike — situated on the 'Green Wheel' cycle route.

By boat — alongside river quay

OS reference: TL 189981

Operating society/organisation: Railworld, Oundle Road, Peterborough, Cambridgeshire PE2 9NR

Charity number: 291515

Contact: John Turner

Telephone and Fax: 01733 344240 and 01733 319362

Internet addresses: *E-mail:* info@railword.net

Web site: www.railworld.net

On site facilities: Light regreshmants. Picnic area, toilets

Public opening:

November-Easter — closed unless by appointment.

Easter-October — closed Monday

to Fridays (except except school and Bank Holidays). Weekends open 11.00-16.00
NB: please check web site for details. Closed Good Friday
Special events: Please check web site for details
Access for disabled: Reasonable wheelchair access
Admission charge: Adult £3, Concessions £2, Children free
Membership details: c/o above address
Membership journal: *Friends of Railworld* — biannually
Special notes: Railworld is a no smoking site

Locomotives

Name	No	Origin	Class	Type	Built
—	996	DSB	4MT	4-6-2	1950

Industrial locomotives

Name	No	Builder	Type	Built
—	804	Alco (77778)	Bo-Bo	1949
—†	740	O&K (2343)	0-6-0T	1907

†2ft gauge (off-site at present) remainder standard

Other stock: Britain's RTV 31 Hovertrain vehicle, Presflo 2-axle flyash wagon (No B874076 of 12965) and a 2-axle 8,650gal tank wagon (No 55223 of 1966). Birmingham International Airport Maglev car No 01 of 1984 supplied by Metro-Cammell, operational 1984-1995 — the world's first train without wheels in commercial service

Timetable Service — Ravenglass & Eskdale Railway — Cumbria

Member: HRA
From the coast through two of Lakeland's loveliest valleys to the foot of England's highest mountain, small steam engines haul trains in the heart of the national park
General Manager: Trevor Stockton
Headquarters: Ravenglass & Eskdale Railway, Ravenglass, Cumbria CA18 1SW
Telephone: (01229) 717171
Fax: (01229) 717011
Internet addresses: *E-mail:* steam@ravenglass-railway.co.uk
Web site: www.ravenglass-railway.co.uk
Main station: Ravenglass
Other public stations: Muncaster Mill, Irton Road, The Green, Beckfoot, Eskdale (Dalegarth)
OS reference: SD 086964
Car parks: All stations
Access by public transport: Main line services to Ravenglass; bus service from Whitehaven
Refreshment facilities: Ravenglass, Dalegarth. Bar meals at 'Ratty Arms'
Picnic areas: At both termini
Souvenir shops: Ravenglass, Dalegarth
Museum: Ravenglass
Length of line: 7 miles, 15in gauge
Passenger trains: Steam- or diesel-hauled narrow gauge trains Ravenglass-Dalegarth
Period of public operation: Daily late March-early November. Limited winter service November-March
Family ticket: All day travel at reduced price
Facilities for disabled: Special coaches for wheelchair passengers; advance notice preferred. Wheelchair access to toilets, café and museum at Ravenglass; toilets, shop and café at Eskdale (Dalegarth)
Special notes: At Ravenglass the R&ER has two camping coaches

Locomotives — 15in gauge

Name	No	Builder	Type	Built
River Irt	—	Heywood	0-8-2	1894
River Esk	—	Davey Paxman (21104)	2-8-2	1923
River Mite	—	Clarkson (4669)	2-8-2	1966
Northern Rock	—	R&ER	2-6-2	1976
Bonnie Dundee	—	K/Stuart (720)	0-4-2	1901
Shelagh of Eskdale	—	R&ER / S/Lamb	4-6-4D	1969 rebuilt 1998
Quarryman	—	Muir-Hill (2)	0-4-0P/Paraffin	1928
Perkins	—	Muir Hill (NG39A)	0-4-4DM	1929
Lady Wakefield	—	R&ER	B-B	1980
Synolda	—	Bassett-Lowke	4-4-2	1912
—	—	Greenbat (2782)	0-4-0BE	1957
Cyril	—	Lister	0-4-0DM	1987
Douglas Ferreira	—	TMA Engineering	Bo-Bo	2005

and the company also operates the 'Ratty Arms' public house formed by conversion of the former BR station buildings. During the high summer, mid-July through August, four steam locomotives are normally in use Monday-Thursday
Membership details:
Mr P. Taylor, 12 Wholesale House, Seascale, Cumbria CA20 1QY
Membership journal: *The R&ER Magazine* — quarterly
Marketing names: 'la'al Ratty' — Cumbrian dialect for little narrow track, now a watervole stationmaster!

England

Ribble Steam Railway

Member: HRA

Preston Docks have had a railway infrastructure since 1850, and when the final tar trains ran in 1995, it looked like that tenancy had come to an end. However, Steamport Southport began negotiations with Preston Borough Council, and during 1999, the group formerly based at the old engine shed in Southport moved to their new home on the dockside at Preston.

Heritage passenger and modern freight operations blend together as restored diesel locomotives handle bulk bitumen trains on behalf of Total Bitumen. This traffic has switched from road transport since the railway re-opened

Location: Off Chain Caul Way, Riversway, Preston Docks, Preston, Lancs

SatNav postcode: PR2 2PD

OS reference: SD 504295

Operating society/organisation: Ribble Steam Railway Ltd, 3 Lincoln Drive, Old Roan, Liverpool L10 3LJ

Telephone: 01772 728800

Internet addresses: *E-mail:* enquiries@ribblesteam.org.uk *Web site:* www.ribblesteam.org.uk

Car park: Free, on site

Main station: Chain Caul Road

Access by public transport:

By rail — to Preston (www.nationalrail.co.uk).

By bus — services 88c and 75. Buses stop on Peddars Way between McDonalds and roundabout on Navigation Way.

By road — follow the signs for Riversway Docklands, use the A583

On site facilities: Museum, workshop, tea room and gift shop

Length of lines: 1.75 miles

Public opening: Generally weekends and Bank Holidays from Easter to end of September, plus special events.

1, 7-9, 11, 15, 22, 29 April; 5-7, 12/13, 19/20, 26-31 May; 2-4, 6, 9/10, 16/17, 23/24, 30 June; 1, 7/8, 14/15, 21/22, 28/29 July; 1, 4/5, 8, 11/12, 15, 18/19, 22, 23, 25-27, 29 August; 1/2, 8/9, 15/16, 22/23, 29/30 September; 6/7 October;

Locomotives

Name	No	Origin	Class	Type	Built
—	1439	LNWR	—	0-4-0ST	1865
—	46441	LMS	2MT	2-6-0	1950
—	1097	LYR	—	0-4-0ST	1910
—	1300	L&Y	27	0-6-0	1896
—	D2148	BR	03	0-6-0DM	1960
—	03189	BR	03	0-6-0DM	1961
—	D2595	BR	05	0-6-0DM	1959
—	08628	BR	08	0-6-0DE	1959
—	D9539	BR	14	0-6-0DH	1965
—	601 / 671	NSR	—	0-6-0DE	1956

Industrial locomotives

Name	No	Builder	Type	Built
—	272	G/Ritchie (272)	0-4-0T	1894
Daphne	—	Peckett (737)	0-4-0ST	1899
The King	—	Borrows (48)	0-4-0WT	1906
Lucy	—	Avonside (1568)	0-6-0ST	1909
Windle	—	Borrows (53)	0-4-0WT	1909
Efficient	—	Barclay (1598)	0-4-0ST	1918
MDHB No 26	—	Avonside (1810)	0-6-0ST	1918
—	1883	Avonside (1883)	0-6-0ST	1922
Niddrie	6	Barclay (1833)	0-6-0ST	1924
Alexander	—	Barclay (1865)	0-4-0ST	1926
Heysham No 2	—	Barclay (1950)	0-4-0F	1928
Derbyshire	—	Barclay (1969)	0-4-0ST	1929
Gasbag	—	Sentinel (8024)	4wVBT	1929
Hornet	—	Peckett (1935)	0-4-0ST	1937
Linda	—	H/Leslie (3931)	0-6-0ST	1938
Kinsley	—	Hunslet (1954)	0-6-0ST	1939
North Western Gas Board	—	Peckett (1999)	0-4-0ST	1941
Walkden	—	Hunslet (3155)	0-6-0ST	1944
St Monans	—	Sentinel (9373)	4wVBT	1947
Agecroft No 2	—	RSH (7485)	0-4-0ST	1948
No 6	—	Barclay (2261)	0-4-0ST	1949
Respite	—	Hunslet (3696)	0-6-0ST	1950
Shropshire	—	Hunslet (3793)	0-6-0ST	1953
Glasshoughton No 4	—	Hunslet (3855)	0-6-0ST	1954
Hotto	—	Howard (965)	4wPM	1930
Mighty Atom	—	H/Clarke (D628)	0-4-0DM	1943
Sparky	—	H/Clarke (D629)	0-4-0DM	1945
Persil	—	Fowler (4160001)	0-4-0DM	1950
Margaret	—	H/Clarke (D1031)	0-4-0DM	1956
BICC	—	NBL (27653)	0-4-0DH	1957
D2870	—	YEC (2667)	0-4-0DH	1960
Energy	—	Sentinel (10165)	4wDH	1965
Stanlow	—	T/Hill (160V)	0-4-0DH	1966
Enterprise	—	Sentinel (10282)	4wDH	1968
Progress	—	Sentinel (10283)	4wDH	1968
—	—	Barclay (D615)	0-4-0DH	1977
'Yellowbat'	—	E/Electric (EE788)	4wBE	1930
Greenbat	—	G/Batley (2000)	4wBE	1945

England

1/2, 8/9, 15/16, 22/23 December.
Other special events may be
arranged, see web site for details
Open from 10.30. Trains hourly
11.00-16.00.
Return trip c40min.
Specially adjusted timetable
operates on Wednesdays, Galas and
Santa Specials
Unlimited travel on day of
admission
Special events: Easter Egg Steam
— 7-9 April; Honda Goldwings
Day — 29 April; Friendly Engines
— 5-7 May; Tornado —
26-29 May; Teddy Bear Kids' Party
— 2-4 June; Hands on Gang, kids
for a Quid — 9/10 June; Classic
Cars — 17 June; Friendly Engines
— 14/15 July; Friendly Engines
Riversway Festival — 21/22 July;
Preston Dock Event (tbc) —
4/5 August; Friendly Engines Gala
Party — 25-27 August; Steam Gala
— 15/16 September; Diesel
Weekend — 6/7 October;
Halloween — 27/28 October;
Spooky Trains — 31 October Santa
Specials — 1/2, 89/9, 15/16, 22/23
December (booking essential).
Additional events will be advertised
on the web site
Facilities for disabled: Full access
in museum, onto platform, ramped
to trains and specially adapted

Rolling stock
The railway holds one of the largest collections of industrial standard
gauge locomotives, currently 42 strong. In addition there are over 60 other
items of rolling stock, including BR Mk 1 passenger coaches in regular
service, 305 Engineer's coach built at York in 1902 for the North Eastern
Railway, pre- and ex-BR and private owner tank wagons, covered vans,
16- and 20-ton mineral and coal wagons, brake vans, Dogfish and other
railway maintenance plant including TRAMM DR98404 and rail-mounted
7.5-tonne crane DRT81201. 75% of locomotives and 60% of other rolling
stock are usually in public view. Items move around regularly as
maintenance takes place

Furness Railway Trust
Member: HRA
Internet address: *Web site:* www.furnessrailwaytrust.org.uk

Locomotives and multiple-units

Name	No	Origin	Class	Type	Built
—	20	FR	A5	0-4-0	1863
—	5643	GWR	5600	0-6-2T	1925

Industrial locomotives

Name	No	Builder	Type	Built
Cumbria	10	Hunslet (3794)	0-6-0ST	1953

Note
The FRT locomotives may be out on loan during 2012

coach for wheelchairs and carers
Membership details:
RSR Membership Secretary, c/o 32
Barn Meadow, Clayton Brook,
Preston PR5 8DU
Membership journal: *The Ribble*

Pilot — 3 copies a year
Special note: The railway is not
open or accessible at any other
times than those advertised. Access
will be refused outside these times

Industrial
Heritage
Museum

Rocks by Rail: The Living Ironstone Museum

Rutland

Member: HRA
This museum is dedicated to
portraying the ironstone quarrying
history of the Midlands and has a
wide range of authentic locomotives
and rolling stock. Indeed, its
collection of quarry freight rolling
stock is probably the most
comprehensive in the country and
regular demonstrations are a feature
of the 'open days'.
Location: Cottesmore Iron Ore
Mines Siding, Ashwell Road,
Cottesmore, near Oakham, Rutland
— museum situated midway
between villages of Cottesmore and
Ashwell, approximately 4 miles
north of Oakham (locally
signposted)
OS reference: SK 886137

Industrial locomotives

Name	No	Builder	Type	Built
Stamford	—	Avonside (1972)	0-4-0ST	1927
Cranford No 2	—	Bagnall (2668)	0-6-0ST	1942
Firefly	—	Barclay (776)	0-4-0ST	1896
—	—	Barclay (1931)	0-4-0ST	1927
Sir Thomas Royden	—	Barclay (2088)	0-4-0ST	1940
Uppingham	—	Peckett (1257)	0-4-0ST	1912
Elizabeth	—	Peckett (1759)	0-4-0ST	1928
Holwell No 14	—	H/Leslie (3138)	0-6-0ST	1915
Singapore	—	H/Leslie (3865)	0-4-0ST	1936
Rhos	—	H/Clarke (1308)	0-6-0ST	1918
Vigilant	—	Hunslet (287)	0-4-0ST	1883
—	8	Peckett (2110)	0-4-0ST	1950
—	20-90-01	Barclay (499)	0-4-0DH	1965
Ketton No 1	—	Fowler (4220007)	0-4-0DH	1960
—	3	N/British (27656)	0-4-0DH	1957
Betty	8411/04	R/Royce (10201)	0-4-0DH	1964
Jean	—	R/Royce (10204)	0-4-0DH	1965
Graham	—	R/Royce (10207)	0-4-0DH	1965

Secretary: Simon Layfield
Operating society/organisation:
Rutland Railway Museum,
Cottesmore Iron Ore Mines Siding,
Ashwell Road, Cottesmore, Nr
Oakham, Rutland LE15 7BX
Telephone: Oakham (01572)
813203
Internet addresses: *E-mail:*
curator@rutlandrailwaymuseum.org.
uk
Web site:
www.rutlandrailwaymuseum.org.uk
Car park: Free car park on site
Access by public transport:
Nearest main line station, Oakham.
Bus service, Paul James,
Nottingham-Melton Mowbray-
Ashwell-Oakham,
Corby/Peterborough-Oakham-
Ashwell (service 19)
On site facilities: Train rides, open-
air quarry feature, demonstration
freight trains, toilets, museum,
picnic sites, demonstration line with
lineside walk and viewing areas,
static displays of quarrying
equipment, large operational wagon
collection, steam and diesel
locomotives.
Museum shop and refreshments
available on open days
Length of line: One mile
Passenger trains: Regular service
operates on open days

Name	No	Builder	Type	Built
—	110*	R/Hornsby (411319)	4wDM	1958
Elizabeth	3	R/Hornsby (421436)	0-4-0DE	1958
—	—	R/Hornsby (544997)	0-4-0DE	1969
Mr D	—	T/Hill (9249V)	4wDH	1967
—	DE5	YEC (2791)	0-6-0DE	1962
—	1382	YEC (2872)	0-6-0DE	1962

*not on site

Locomotive notes: In service Barclay (1931)

Stock
4 brake vans; 14 covered goods vans; 57 wagons (includes rakes of wagons as used in local ironstone and industrial railways); 2 rail cranes

Owner
H/Clarke (1308) the 1308 Trust

Public opening: Open Tuesdays, Thursdays and Sundays, Easter to end of September (11.00-17.00.
   (Leaflets available, SAE please.)
   School and private parties by special arrangement
Special events: Relaunch weekend — Rocks & Rail: the living ironstone museum— 8/9 April
Special facilities: Steam, diesel and digger driving experience days (pre-bookings only)
Facilities for disabled: Site relatively flat, but uneven surface. Disabled facilities
Special notes: The open-air museum houses an extensive collection of industrial locomotives and rolling stock typifying past activity in local ironstone quarries. A demonstration line approximately a mile long has been relaid on the former MR Cottesmore mineral branch (originally built to tap local ironstone quarries), on which restored locomotives and stock are run.
   Admission £4 per head. Special charges for Santa Specials
Membership details: Membership Secretary, c/o above address

Romney, Hythe & Dymchurch Railway

Member: HRA
This line was built in 1926/27 as a one-third size miniature main line, and is by far the longest and most fully equipped 15in gauge railway in the world. It carries not only daytrippers and holidaymakers but also children to and from the local school at New Romney.
Headquarters: Romney, Hythe & Dymchurch Railway, New Romney Station, Kent TN28 8PL
Telephone: (01797) 362353/363256
Fax: 01797 363591
Internet addresses: *E-mail:*
info@rhdr.org.uk
Web site: http://www.rhdr.org.uk
OS reference: TR 074249
Main station: New Romney
Other public stations: Hythe, Dymchurch, St Marys Bay, Romney

Sands, Dungeness.
Also Romney Warren Halt, which serves Kent Wildlife Trust's Romney Marsh Visitor Centre, is served by a shuttle service that operates from New Romney station on selected dates (see www.rhdr.org.uk). Other trains will stop specially for pre-booked parties
SatNav postcodes:
Hythe — CT21 6LD
Dymchurch — TN29 0PJ
St Marys Bay — TN29 0SG
Romney Warren Halt — TN28 8AY
New Romney — TN28 8PL
Romney Sands — TN28 8RN
Dungeness — TN28 9NB
Car parks: Hythe, Dymchurch, New Romney, Dungeness
Access by road: Hythe — M20,

Jct 11 then A259; New Romney and Dungeness — M20, Jct 10 then via A2070/A259. Follow the brown signs on most local routes
Access by public transport:
By train: Folkestone Central station (Southeastern Trains) and then bus to Hythe (4 miles) or Rye station (Southern) and then bus to New Romney (8 miles).
National Rail 0845 748 4950
By bus: buses serve the railway from Ashford, Canterbury, Dover, Folkestone, Hastings and Rye. A combined Bus / RH&DR ticket is available on most Stagecoach services in Kent and East Sussex (0845 600 2299)
By coach: National Express, daily between London and Hythe (0871 781 8181)
By boat: On many days a silent

134

England

electric boat will operate between Hythe RH&DR station and Hythe Boat Station/Waitrose supermarket along the Royal Military Canal

Refreshment facilities: Cafeterias at New Romney and Dungeness, picnic areas at Dymchurch, New Romney and Dungeness. Also licensed observation coach on certain trains

Souvenir shops: Hythe, New Romney and Dungeness (plus Dymchurch in main season)

Model Railway Exhibition: New Romney, with displays of old, and not so old, toys; plus two large operating model railways. Open all operating days and selected other days

Depot: New Romney

Length of line: 13.5 miles, 15in gauge

Passenger trains: Train frequency depends on the time of year: maximum frequency is 45 minutes, more frequent on certain special event days

Period of public operation: Trains run daily from 24 March to 4 November. Also weekends and school holidays January to March. Out of season the school train departs New Romney to Hythe with limited public accommodation, please telephone 01797 362353 (Monday-Friday, term times only)

Special events: Kent Great Day Out — 17/18 March; Mother's Day Special — 18 March; Easter Egg Hunt competition — 8 April; Bug Club Day — 21 April; RH&DR Association AGM — 19 May; Queen's Diamond Jubilee — 2-5 June; Father's Day Special — 17 June; Day out with Thomas — 29/30 June, 1 July; Hythe Festival, Morning Safari — Monday 2 July; Hythe Festival, Back Stage with the General manager — Thursday

Locomotives — 1ft 3in gauge

Name	No	Builder	Type	Built
Green Goddess	1	Davey Paxman	4-6-2	1925
Northern Chief	2	Davey Paxman	4-6-2	1925
Southern Maid	3	Davey Paxman	4-6-2	1926
The Bug	4	Krauss (8378)	0-4-0TT	1926
Hercules	5	Davey Paxman	4-8-2	1926
Samson	6	Davey Paxman	4-8-2	1926
Typhoon	7	Davey Paxman	4-6-2	1926
Hurricane	8	Davey Paxman	4-6-2	1926
Winston Churchill	9	YEC (2294)	4-6-2	1931
Doctor Syn	10	YEC (2295)	4-6-2	1931
Black Prince	11	Krupp (1664)	4-6-2	1937
John Southland	12	TMA Birmingham	Bo-Bo	1983
Captain Howey	14	TMA Birmingham	Bo-Bo	1989
—	PW1	M/Rail (7059)	4wDM	1938
—	PW2	RH&DR	4wPM	1965
Redgauntlet	PW3*	Jacot/RH&DR	4wPM	1963
Trembly	—*	Lister (37658)	4wDM	1952

*usually stored out of sight

Stock

40 saloon bogie coaches; 12 open bogie coaches; 4 luggage/brake saloons; 1 parlour car; 4-wheelchair-accessible coaches; 1 mess coach; 40 assorted wagons

5 July; Hythe Festival, Evening Dining Train — 7 July; RH&DR 85th Anniversary — 15 July; Olympic Torch Relay comes to Hythe — Wednesday 18 July; RNLI Dungeness Lifeboat Station Open Day (10.00-16.00) — 5 August; Dymchurch Day of Syn — 25-27 August; Bus Rally — 9 September; Vintage on the Railway — 29/30 September; Halloween — Monday/Tuesday 30/31 October; Fright Night Train — Friday 2 November; Santa Specials —1/2, 8/9, 15/16, 20-24 December (pre-booking essential); New Year's running — 29 December to 1 January 2013.

Special notes: Senior citizen concessions every day. Family tickets available. Parties can be catered for at New Romney and

Dungeness cafés. Evening dining train service on selected summer Saturdays

Special facilities: Special trains can be run at most times by prior arrangement

Facilities for disabled: Ramps and level crossings at all stations for easy access. Special wheelchair coach available on any train by prior arrangement. Stair lift between café and Model Railway Exhibition. Disabled toilets at Hythe, Dymchurch, New Romney and Dungeness

Membership details: RH&DR Association, 26 Norman Close, Battle, East Sussex TN33 0BD

Membership journal: The Marshlander — quarterly

Diesel Centre — Rother Valley Railway — East Sussex

Member: HRA

The original section of what was to become known as the Kent & East Sussex Railway was thought to be lost to preservation for ever following decisions of Transport Minister Barbara Castle in the late

1960s. However, more enlightened attitudes in recent years mean that work is now in hand to reinstate the missing link between Robertsbridge and the K&ESR at Bodiam

Location/headquarters: Robertsbridge Junction Station,

Station Road, Robertsbridge, East Sussex TN32 5DG

Telephone: 01580 881833

Internet address: Web site: www.rvr.org.uk

Operating society/organisation: Rother Valley Railway Ltd,

3-4 Bower Terrace, Maidstone, Kent ME16 8RY, and the Rother Valley Railway Supporters Association
OS reference: TQ 734235
Access by public transport: Southeastern Trains on Charing Cross and Tunbridge Wells to Hastings service call at Robertsbridge station. Arriva bus services 4 and 5 on Maidstone-Hastings service call at High Street, Robertsbridge
Car parks: Robertsbridge station and Station Road, Robertsbridge
On site facilities: Visitor centre housed in former VSOE lounge with souvenir shop and light refreshments. Rolling stock under restoration, picnic area
Facilities for disabled: Access to the visitor centre, buffet, shop and all public areas

Locomotives

Name	No	Origin	Class	Type	Built
—	D2112	BR	03	0-6-0DM	1960

Industrial locomotives

Name	No	Builder	Type	Built
Charwelton	14	M/Wardle (1955)	0-6-0ST	1917*
Titan	43	Vulcan/Drewry	0-4-0DM	1955
Mr Useful	D77	Vulcan/Drewry	0-4-0DM	1947

*on loan to Kent & East Sussex Railway

Rolling stock
Ex-SR brake van, ex-SR Maunsell brake third, ex-SR GBL and BY vans, Trout hopper wagon, 2 tank wagons, open wagon, Lowma, and Permaquip Panex track machine

Length of line: Standard gauge, at present c400yd at Robertsbridge being extended c800yd during 2012. Plus 1,500yd west from end-on connection with KESR at Bodiam. Total length will be 3.5 miles

Public opening: Sundays 09.00-17.00 (dusk if earlier)
Special events: Annual model railway exhibition. KESR trains will run over the extension to Junction Road on special occasions
Journal: *The Phoenix* — quarterly

Miniature Railway	Royal Victoria Railway	Hampshire

Location: Royal Victoria Country Park
Headquarters: Royal Victoria Railway, Royal Victoria Country Park, Netley, Southampton SO31 5GA
Contact: Peter Bowers
Telephone: 023 8045 6246
Internet address: *Web site:* www.royalvictoriarailway.co.uk
SatNav users: Do NOT use the postcode to locate the RVR. Please follow the brown signs marked Royal Victoria Country Park
Main station: Netley
Car parking: On site, daily charge £3.00
Access by public transport:
By rail: South West Trains to Netley, follow signs to Royal Victoria Country Park.
By road: Exit M27 at Jct 8 and follow brown tourist signs to Royal Victoria Country Park, approx 3 miles
On site facilities: Small souvenir shop. Museum on site for Royal Victoria Hospital, historic war grave cemetery (graves date from 1856), playground, tea room with public toilets
Depots: At main station, engine and carriage sheds and turntable,

Locomotives — 10.25in gauge

Name	No	Builder	Type	Built
Maurice the Major	1	P. Bowers	Bo-Bo	1995
Basil the Brigadier*§	2	Kitson	2-6-0-0-6-2	1935
Trevithick	3	R. Marsh	0-6-2	1976
Isambard Kingdom Brunel	4	D. Curwen	2-6-0	1977
Peter the Private	5	Curwe/Bowers	2-6-0	2009
Western Independence	D1000	D. Curwen	Co-Co	1964
Western Explorer§	D1002	Severn Lamb	Co-Co	1968
Western Thunderer	D1011	D. Curwen	Co-Co	1964
Royal Scot*§	6100	B/Lowke	4-6-0	1938
Royal Scot*§	6100	E. Dove	4-6-0	c1950

*historic locomotive
§on site awaiting restoration

Rolling stock
2 Triang Pullman coaches, 4 Triang toastrack coaches, 2 4-car articulated units (2 covered, 2 open carriages), various goods vehicles

Note: If wishing to view the historic locomotives please contact before making journey

possibly largest for 10.25in gauge railway
Length of line: 1 mile, 10.25in gauge
Period of public operation: All local school holidays except 3 days before Xmas and closed Christmas Day. Weekends all year
Special events: Please check web site

Facilities for disabled: Most areas accessible and assistance available (for those wishing to ride the train) to transfer from wheelchairs into the coaches. The park also has a special playground for disabled and several toilets

Rudyard Lake Railway

Member Britain's Great Little Railways

The railway provides a 3-mile scenic return trip alongside the lake that gave Rudyard Kipling his name. Trains are always steam hauled and a two-train service operates on busy days. The fleet of goods wagons is extensive and impressive and so goods trains also often feature. A further one-mile extension is being planned

Contacts: Mike & Eileen Hanson, Directors

Headquarters: Rudyard Station, Rudyard, Nr Leek, Staffordshire ST13 8PF

Telephone: 01538 306704

Fax: 01995 672280

Internet addresses:

E-mail: info@rlsr.org

Web site: www.rlsr.org

Main station: Rudyard

OS reference SJ 955579

Other stations: The Dam (SJ953584), Hunthouse Wood (SJ946598)

Car parking: On site, free at Rudyard

Access by public transport; Nearest mainline rail at Stoke on Trent, Macclesfield, Congleton. Bus services to Leek

On site facility: Short 7.25in gauge railway operates on special events

Souvenir shop: Rudyard station

Refreshment facilities: Platform 2 Café at Rudyard station at weekends March to October

Length of line: 1.5 miles,

Locomotives — 10.25in gauge

Name	No	Builder	Type	Built
Mordred	2	T. Stanhope	4w	1969
Rudyard Lady	5	L. Smith	4-4w	1989
Waverley		D. Curwen	4-4-2	1952
Excalibur	6	Exmoor SR (293)	2-4-2T	1993
Merlin	7	Exmoor SR (296)	2-4-2T	1998
Pendragon	9	Exmoor SR (297)	2-4-2T	1994
King Arthur	8	Exmoor SR (324)	0-6-2T	2005
Sir Ernie	—	RLSR	2-2-2BE	2008
Victoria	—	D. Ware	2-6-2T	1993

Rolling Stock

12 coaches

1 4w van, 3 4w open, 1 4w brake van, 3 bogie ballast

Owners

Waverley — the Waverley Group

Victoria — the Mull & West Highland Railway

Special note

All locomotives should be in operation in 2012

10.25 inch gauge

Operation (2012):

Every Sunday and Bank Holiday: 1 January to 25 November, 11.00-16.00;

Every Saturday: 24 March to 27 October, 11.00-16.00.

Daily: 12-19 February, 31 March-15 April, 18 July to 2 September, 20-28 October

School Holidays — daily

Special Events:

Easter Egg Specials — 6-9 April; Lollipop Specials —5-7 May, 25-27 August; Steam Gala — 22/23 September; Santa Specials —

9, 15/16 December

Special facilities: Driver training courses run throughout the year; children's birthday parties. All trains allow carriage of prams, bikes, wheelchairs, etc

Disabled facilities: Access to all stations although wheelchairs with occupant not allowed on trains, but wheelchairs can be carried. Disabled toilets at the Dam Head

Membership details: Eileen Hanson at above address or via e-mail

---

Ruislip Lido Railway

Member: HRA

One of the few 12in gauge railways in the UK and operates as an attraction within the London Borough of Hillingdon's Ruislip Lido

Location: Ruislip Lido, Reservoir Road, Ruislip, Middlesex

SatNav postcode: HA4 7TY

Operating society/organisation:

Ruislip Lido Railway Society Ltd, Suite 123, Rye House, 113 High Street, Ruislip, Middx HA4 8JN

Telephone: 01895 622595 (whilst railway is open) or 0795 058888

Internet address: *Web site:* http://www.ruisliplidorailway.org

Car park: Free car parking available (overspill car park in Breakspear Road for use on busy

days)

Access by public transport: Ruislip LUL station (Metropolitan and Piccadilly lines) then by H13 or 331 (buses run daily) to Ruislip

Access by road: Follow signs for the A4180 (B469) from the A40

Refreshment facilities: The 'Railway Room' café and shop provide a selection of hot / cold drinks, light refreshments and gifts at Woody Bay station. A short walk from Ruislip Lido station is the 'Waters Edge' pub and carvery open all year round

Length of line: 1.25-miles. The line runs in a horseshoe shape around the Lido. Trains run from the beach area at Woody Bay to Waters Edge adjacent to pub and car park

Public opening: The railway is open at weekends and during public holidays from Saturday 1 February until 6 January 2013. For more information about times and special events, please contact the railway or visit the web site

Journey time: Single 20min, return 40min

Special events: Please contact or see web site for details

Facilities for disabled: All trains are wheelchair- and pushchair-friendly

Locomotives — 12in gauge

Name	No	Builder	Type	Built
Robert	3	S/Lamb	B-2 DH	1973
Lady of the Lakes	5	Ravenglass & Eskdale Railway	B-B DM	1986
Mad Bess	6	RLRS	2-4-0ST+T	1998
Graham Alexander	7	S/Lamb	B-B DM	1990
Bayhurst	8	S/Lamb	B-B DH	2003
John Rennie	9	S/Lamb	B-B DH	2004

Locomotive notes: All locomotives are normally available for service. Limited steam-hauled service

Stock

8 open coaches; 10 closed coaches; permanent way tool wagon plus miscellaneous service or maintenance stock

Special facilities: Group bookings on steam- and diesel-hauled trains available. Contact Group Bookings co-ordinator on 0845 6430182.

Guided workshop tours are available on request

Membership details: RLR

Membership Secretary, Suite 123, Rye House, 113 High Street, Ruislip, Middx HA4 8JN.
E-mail: membership@ruisliplido.org
Membership journal: Woody Bay News — 4-5 times a year

Railway Centre — Rushden Transport Museum — Northants

Rushden station, built by the Midland Railway in 1894, was the only imtermediate station on the Higham Ferrers branch and closed to passengers on 13 June 1959. When the line finally closed to all traffic in 1969 the building was sold to the local authorities who leased it to local businesses until in 1984 the Rushden Historical Transport Society obtained a lease on the building, eventually purchasing it in 1996. Today the building has been restored, acting as a museum and club house for the society

Location/headquarters: Rushden Transport Museum / Rushden Historical Transport Society, Rushden Station, Station Approach, Rushden, Northants NN10 0AW

SatNav postcode: NN10 0AW

Tel: 01933 318988

Internet addresses:

E-mail: via web site

Web site: www.rhts.co.uk

Access by public transport:

By rail: Wellingborough station, 5 miles

By bus: From Wellingborough town centre, Stagecoach No 46 to Asda

Locomotives and multiple-units

Name	No	Builder	Class	Type	Built
—	31206	BR	31	A1A-A1A	1960
—	55029*	P/Steel	121	DMBS	1960

*preserved in ex-Departmental condition as No DB977968

Industrial locomotives

Name	No	Builder	Type	Built
Edmundsons	—	Barclay (2168)	0-4-0ST	1943
—	—	Barclay (2323)	0-4-0ST	1952
Cherwell	—	Bagnall (2654)	0-6-0ST	1942
—	WD70048	Barclay (363)	0-4-0DM	1942
—	—	Sentinel (10159)	0-4-0DM	1962
—	WD72222	Vulcan (2177)	0-4-0DM	1945

Tram (ex-Blackpool)

No	Trucks	Builder	Date
297 (634)		Brush	1937

Rolling stock

3 BR Mk 1s, 1 x BR Mk 2, 1 LNER buffet coach, 4 Post Office sorting/stowage coaches. Small selection of wagons and a rail-mounted crane store, 50yd

Length of line: 0.25 mile demonstration line

Period of public operation:
The museum is open from Easter to the end of October:

Saturdays — 14.00-16.00
Sundays — 10.00-16.00.
Free entry, visits by schools and other groups can be arranged at other times by appointment

England

Member: HRA

The S&D Mendip Main Line Project has secured a foothold on the northern part of the S&D where previous preservation attempts failed. The Somerset & Dorset Railway Heritage Trust (S&DRHT) has the central object of preserving the route and infrastructure wherever the opportunities arise, whether for heritage or conventional railways or, more simply, for public recreation and conservation. In practice, energies are being concentrated at Midsomer Norton, with the aim of extending the running line southwards up the notorious 1 in 53 grade to Chilcompton, and potentially northwards down to Radstock. The Trust is leasing former trackbed with the aim of securing a total run of one mile within 3-5 years. Midsomer Norton station has become one of the few significant visitor attractions in this former coal-mining community, with the S&D legend attracting national and international attention. The Trust has created an operating and commercial subsidiary, the S&D Joint Railway Co

Main station: Midsomer Norton South

OS Reference: ST 664537

Officers:
S&DRHT — Chairman: John Buck; Vice Chairman: John Baxter; Secretary: Peter Russell; Finance Trustee: Douglas Hill; Membership Secretary: Tim Deacon
S&DJR Co — Chairman & Finance Director: Douglas Hill; Secretary: Steve Ehrlicher; Personnel & Admin Director: Keith Himsworth Civil Engineering Director: John Dora; Mechanical & Electrical Enginering Diredtor: Olly Wise; Operations Director: Alex Seal

Headquarters: Somerset & Dorset Railway Heritage Trust, Midsomer Norton Station, Silver Street, Midsomer Norton, BA3 2EY

Locomotives and multiple-units

Name	No	Builder	Class	Type	Built
—	08881	BR	08	0-6-0DE	1961
—	51909	BR	108	DMBS	1960
—	56271	BR	108	DTC	1958

Industrial locomotives

Name	No	Builder	Type	Built
David James Cook	—	E/Electric (D1120)	0-6-0DE	1966
Joyce	(47192)	Sentinel (7109)	0-4-0VBT	1927

Rolling stock:
Coaches — BR Mk 1s: SK, BSK, BR Mk 3 buffet; MR six-wheeler Wagons — 2 ex-MoD box vans, LSWR box van, 3 brake vans (2 LMS, 1 SR Queen Mary), SR PMV, milk tanker, Dogfish, Dace, Barbel, Sturgeon, Lafarge Cement internal box van, Kilmersdon Colliery coal wagon

Owners
Sentinel — Andy Chapman (e-mail: akchapman@aol.com) and Nigel Dickinson (e-mail: nigel@dickybird.fsnet.co.uk)
DMUs the Long Marston Group

Telephone: 01761 411221
Internet addresses:
E-mail: general@sdjr.co.uk
Web site: www.sdjr.co.uk
Car park: Limited parking on site. 200-place free car parking — 300yd towards town centre (OS ref: ST 666542). Somervale School (300yd west, weekends) and Norton Hill School (100yd east, Saturday and Sunday pm only)
Access by public transport:
Nearest rail stations Bath Spa (13 miles), Frome (13 miles), Trowbridge (15 miles).
Bus (First) 173, 177/778, 179/779 connect with Bath/Bristol with drop offs near station (every day excluding public holidays); 184 connects with Frome (weekdays and Saturdays).
Updates on www.firstgroup.com
On site facilities: Sales/information area in main station building during opening times; toilets. Static buffet coach in sidings (light refreshments and meals). Museum (static exhibits) opened September 2009. Exhibits and displays being added

to. Reconstructed signalbox being re-equipped. Pillbox World War 2 Museum. Guided tours of the museums and the signalbox are scheduled for every Sunday
Length of line: 720yd running line verified by ORR with DMU rides on Sundays and special days (see web site for further details) or telephone the station for a timetable. Additional 350yd expected for 2012. Future planned southward extension for approx 720yd towards Chilcompton Tunnel
Opening times: Sundays and Mondays 10.00-16.00 normally throughout the year, depending on availability of volunteers; plus special events days or weeks. If coming for a special visit, ring the station on 01761 411221, or e-mail, to check opening times
Special events: Easter Egg event in April; Teddy Bears' Picnic event in MayMidsummer weekend in June; Summer steam event; Santa weekend in December.
Please see railway/local press and web site for updates.

Disabled access: Wheelchairs can access station forecourt, down platform, main building (via platform) and up platform via barrow crossing. Parking for disabled in station forecourt; phone to ensure space is reserved. Buffet coach, picnic area and museum accessed by gently ramped path
Membership details: Tim Deacon,

24 Morison Road, Swanage, Dorset BH19 1JL
Rates from 2010: Ordinary Adult (16+) £14, Junior or Senior Citizen £10; Senior Citizen Family £16; Family/Household £18; Corporate £22;
Life membership: (single member) £270; Family/Corporate £375; retired spouses/partners £225;

retired single £150.
Visitor / membership / volunteering leaflets available on request or at station
Membership journal: *The S&D Telegraph* — 2 times/year and Member Newsletter (2 time/year, aqlternating (free to members).

Museum — St Albans South Signalbox — Hertfordshire

Member: HRA
The present St Albans South signalbox was built by the Midland Railway in 1892, replacing a smaller and earlier box built when the 'London Extension' was first opened in 1867. The building was listed Grade 2 by English Heritage in 1979 prior to the box being abandoned by British Railways in 1980; the listing including the 'tumbler locked' 44-lever frame left in the building, although all other equipment was removed by BR on closure. In January 2003, local residents formed the the St Albans South Signal Box Preservation Trust because of concern at the derelict state of the box and obtained a 25-year lease from Network Rail in March 2006.

With financial assistance from various sources the box structure has been professionally repaired and the outside restored to its 1950s external appearance. Inside trust members have restored the lever frame and obtained replacement instrument to show the mid-1970s signalling arrangement as it was shortly before closure. The surrounding derelict ground has been transformed into a pleasant garden area with a number of working semaphore and colour light signals, Midland Railway lamp posts, ground frames and replica lamp hut on display.

The box is the largest preserved Midland signalbox in the country. It is the only such box still in the original location where it worked,

adjacent to a busy railway line and open to the public. It was the winner of the St Albans Civic Society's top award for 2008 and of the national Invensys Signalling Award in 2010 in recognition of the restoration work
Location: Ridgmont Road, off Victoria Street, St Albans, Herts AL1 3AJ
Operating society/organisation: St Albans Signal Box Preservation Trust. Registered Charity 1104535
OS reference: TL 155069
SatNav postcode: AL1 3AJ
Tel: 01723 836131
Contact: Mr Keith Webster (Trust President)
Internet addresses:
E-mail: info@sigbox.co.uk
Web site: www.sigbox.co.uk
Access by public transport:
By rail: St Albans City station, 170yd from platform 4 exit
By bus: Numerous routes calling at St Albans City station, bus stops approx 400yd away
Access by car: Far end of Network Rail car park in Ridgmont Road. There is a charge in this car park but we will direct visitors to nearby free parking
On site facilities: Toilet, light refreshments and small souvenirs for sale. Display of signalling and railway equipment downstairs, together with video of the box when working in 1979 and picture displays of the restoration work. Upstairs the restored lever frame and associated instruments, coupled to a computer simulator,

demonstrate the signalling systems in use at the time the box was closed. In the garden around the box there is seating and visitors can watch the trains go by on the adjacent Midland main line
Period of public operation:
April to October: 2nd and 4th Sunday afternoons, 14.00-17.00.
November to Easter: 2nd Sunday afternoon, 14.00-17.00.
Free entry on all open days, donations are very welcome. Edmondson card ticket for each visitor
Facilities for disabled: Access to garden is on the level. The ground floor of the box is accessed down a long but gentle ramp through the garden; the toilet on the ground floor will take wheelchairs. Access to the first floor is by a narrow, but substantial, staircase. there is no wheelchair access to the first floor of the building due to the nature of this listed building
Special events: Heritage Open Days — 9/10 September: extended opening hours 10.00-16.00, also in January 2013). See web site for details
Special notes: Party visits 'out of hours' can be arranged (see internet contact details above)
Membership details: Membership of the trust is available — see web site for details and downloadable application form
Membership journal: *Outside the Box* — a newsheet, is published quarterly

Saltburn Miniature Railway

Location: Valley Gardens, Saltburn-by-the-Sea
Postal address: Miss N. Robson (Secretary) 55 High Street West, Redcar, Cleveland TS10 1SF
Tel: 01642 502863 or 07813 153975
Fax: 01642 502863
Internet addresses:
E-mail:
saltburn.miniaturerailway@ntlworld.com
Web site: saltburn-miniature-railway.org.uk
Main station: Cat Nab (OS ref: SE 668215
Other public station: Forest Halt (OS ref:SE 667209
Access by public transport:
By rail: Saltburn station (Northern Rail) approx half mile, and 150ft higher, away. Cliff railway operate during the summer
By bus: Arriva X4 Middlesbrough-East Cleveland, bus stops approx

Locomotives — 15in gauge

Name	No	Builder	Type	Built (rebuilt)
George Outhwaite	—	Saltburn MRA	0-4-0DH	1994
Prince Charles	—	Barlow	4-6-2DE	1950
Saltburn	—	ex-Cleethorpes	4-6-2DE	(2010)

Rolling stock
4 canopied coaches (2 with wheelchair bays), 1 bogie truck with hydraulic lift, 1 4-wheel wagon, 1 bogie bowser, 1 4-wheel air compressor truck

200yd away on sea front
Car park: Adjacent to Cat Nab station, council pay & display
Refreshment facilities: Available from local establishments not connected with the railway
Souvenir shop: Souvenirs available from booking office
Length of line: Half mile, 15in gauge
Period of public operation: Weekends and Bank Holidays, Easter Sunday to end of September,

daily during local school holidays. 13.00-17.00. All services weather permitting
Special events: 150th Anniversary of the town to be celebrated early August
Special facilities: Charter bookings via Secretary. Occasional visiting steam locomotives
Membership details: Saltburn Miniature Railway Association, c/o above address

---

Science Museum

Built on land acquired with the profits from the Great Exhibition of 1851, the Science Museum was one of the first to include industrial archaeology. The railway exhibits are drawn from the collection based at the National Railway Museum. They form part of a major gallery, 'Making the Modern World', which opened in June 2000 on the site of the former Land Transport gallery
Location: South Kensington
OS reference: TQ 268793
Operating society/organisation: Science Museum, Exhibition Road, South Kensington, London SW7 2DD
Telephone: 020 7942 4000
Internet address: *Web site:* www.sciencemuseum.org.uk
Access by public transport: South

Locomotive

Name	No	Origin	Class	Type	Built
Rocket	—	Liverpool & Manchester Railway	—	0-2-2	1829
Columbine	—	Grand Junction Railway	—	2-2-2	1845
Puffing Billy	—	Wylam Colliery	—	0-4-0	1814

Locomotive note: Restored to static display condition

Kensington Underground station
Catering facilities: Cafés on ground floor, hot meals, tea, coffee, sandwiches, etc. Picnic area in basement
On site facilities: Bookshop, toilets on most floors
Public opening: Daily 10.00-18.00. Closed 24-26 December
Special events: All organised by

the National Railway Museum, York, which is part of the Science Museum. Telephone (01904) 621261 for details
Facilities for disabled: Toilets on most floors, ramp and lifts to all floors. Parties should contact before arrival if extra assistance is required
Special notes: Static exhibits only in 'Making the Modern World'

Member: HRA; CPT; Devon Association of Tourist Attractions; Green Tourism Business Scheme; British Association of Leisure Parks, Peirs and Attractions; Visit England Quality Assurance Scheme

A unique 2ft 9in gauge electric tramway, operating on the trackbed of the former Southern Railway branch line between Seaton and Seaton Junction in east Devon. Trams operate between Seaton, Colyford and Colyton. Panoramic views of the beautiful Axe Valley and estuary together with a host of wading birds and other wildlife
Location: Harbour Road Car Park, Seaton; Swan Hill Road, Colyford (next to White Hart Inn); Station Road, Kingsdon, Colyton
OS reference: SY 252904
Operating society/organisation: Modern Electric Tramways Ltd t/a Seaton Tramway, Riverside Depot, Harbour Road, Seaton, Devon EX12 2NQ
Telephone: 01297 20375
Internet addresses:
E-mail: info@tram.co.uk
Web site: www.tram.co.uk
SatNav postcodes:
Seaton EX12 2TB
Colyton EX24 6HA
Access by public transport: Nearest railway station: Axminster. Buses: Axe Valley Mini Travel service 885 from Axminster; service 899 from Sidmouth. First Southern National service X53 from Weymouth, Exeter and Lyme Regis; service 20 from Taunton and Honiton. Bus enquiries 0870 608 2608 or www.devon.gov.uk/devonbus
On site facilities: Gift shops at Seaton and Colyton. Restaurant,

Trams — 2ft 9in gauge

No	Prototype based on	Type	Built
2	London Metropolitan Tramways	A	1964
4	Blackpool	'Boat'	1961
6	Bournemouth (later Llandudno & Colwyn Bay)	'open-top'	1954
7	Bournemouth (later Llandudno & Colwyn Bay)	'open-top'	1954
8	†—	—	1968
9	Blackburn/Plymouth	double-deck	2004
10	Blackburn/Plymouth	double-deck	2005
11	Blackburn/Plymouth	double-deck	2006
12	London Metropolitan Tramways	'Feltham'	1966
14*	London Metropolitan Tramways	A	1904
16*	Bournemouth		1921
17	Manx Electric Tramway	'toastrack'	1988
19*	Exeter Corporation	—	1906

†a larger version of the ex-Bournemouth design of cars 6 and 7
*rebuilds of heritage trams
9, 10, 11 are based on elements of designs from Plymouth and Blackburn

café and picnic and play area at Colyton
Length of line: 3 miles, 2ft 9in gauge
Period of public operation and departure times (2012):
Weekends: 3-25 March, 10.30-15.00.
Daily: 11-19 February, 31 March-4 November, 10.00-17.00.
26 December-1 January 2013, 10.30-15.00.
Special events: Halloween Tram of Terror — 29-31 October, 1/2 November; Santa Specials — 2, 9, 16, 23/24 December, enquire for details.
Private hire all year round for groups of 20+
Fares for 2012: Seaton to Colyton return fares — Adult £9.00, OAP £8.30, Child £4.50.
Travel all day for £1.00 supplement.

Dogs welcome £1.00 each way
Discounts for loyalty cardholders, and parties of 12 or more
Facilities for disabled: Tramcar No 17 carries up to 10 wheelchairs. Please note that it has open sides and is therefore exposed to the weather. Trams 9, 10 and 11 accommodate 2 wheelchairs and depart every hour. Groups should book in advance. Please phone for times.
Disabled toilets at Seaton and Colyton
Special notes: Tram driving lessons and children's birthday parties available through the season. Bird watching trips available February to May and September to October. Enquire for details. Service operated by open-top double-deck bogie cars (enclosed saloon cars during inclement weather)

Severn Valley Railway

Member: HRA, TT

The railway hosts more main line engines than any other preserved line in the country, enjoying the back-up of a large volunteer and professional workforce and extensive engineering workshops and equipment. Railway travel like it used to be!

General Manager: Nick Ralls

Headquarters: Severn Valley Railway Co Ltd, Railway Station, Bewdley, Worcs DY12 1BG

Telephone: Bewdley (01299) 403816

Internet address: *Web site:* http://www.svr.co.uk

Main stations: Bridgnorth, Bewdley, Kidderminster Town

Other public stations: Arley, Highley, Hampton Loade, Northwood Halt, Country Park Halt

SatNav postcodes: Bridgnorth — WV16 5DT Bewdley — DY12 1BG

Locomotives and multiple-units

Name	No	Origin	Class	Type	Built
Gordon†	AD600	LMR	WD	2-10-0	1943
—†	1000	MR	4	4-4-0	1902
—	43106	LMS	4MT	2-6-0	1951
—†	46443	LMS	2MT	2-6-0	1950
RAF Biggin Hill*	45110	LMS	5MT	4-6-0	1935
—†	47383	LMS	3F	0-6-0T	1926
—†	48773	LMS	8F	2-8-0	1940
—	42968	LMS	5P4F	2-6-0	1934
—	813	GWR	—	0-6-0ST	1901
—	2857	GWR	2800	2-8-0	1918
—	5164	GWR	5101	2-6-2T	1930
—	4150	GWR	5101	2-6-2T	1947
—	6634	GWR	5600	0-6-2T	1928
—§	5764	GWR	5700	0-6-0PT	1929
—†	7714	GWR	5700	0-6-0PT	1930
—	4566	GWR	4500	2-6-2T	1924
Bradley Manor	7802	GWR	'Manor'	4-6-0	1938
Erlestoke Manor	7812	GWR	'Manor'	4-6-0	1939
Hinton Manor	7819	GWR	'Manor'	4-6-0	1939
Hagley Hall†	4930	GWR	'Hall'	4-6-0	1929
Taw Valley	34027	SR	WC	4-6-2	1946
—†	1501	GWR	1500	0-6-0PT	1949
—†	7325	GWR	4300	2-6-0	1932
—	75069	BR	4MT	4-6-0	1955

SPECIAL EVENTS - 2012

23-25 MARCH
SPONSORED BY
STEAM RAILWAY

SPRING STEAM GALA
Back after a break, our springtime steam enthusiasts' weekend welcomes a big turnout in more ways than one.

21-22 JULY

PEEP BEHIND THE SCENES!
Peep Behind the Scenes provides an insight into all the had work that goes into keeping the SVR and its steam trains running.

21-23 SEPT

AUTUMN STEAM GALA
With a great collection of steam locomotives, a very frequent service of trains and all night operation.

For other special events, please visit our website at:

www.svr.co.uk
Tel: 01299 40381

4-6 OCT

DIESEL GALA
Our three day diesel traction event is back in 2012! Diesel only operation on all three days.

**KIDDERMINSTER
BEWDLEY
BRIDGNORTH**

Kidderminster Town — DY10 1QX

OS reference: Bridgnorth SO 715926, Bewdley SO 793753

Car parks: At all main stations

Access by public transport: First Bus service 192 to Kidderminster and Bewdley and 125 & 297 to Bridgnorth. Rail service to Kidderminster (main line) with immediate connections to SVR station. Through tickets available from all manned main line stations

Refreshment facilities: At most stations, but not on all operating days and on most trains. Fully licensed bars at Bridgnorth and Kidderminster Town. Restaurants at Kidderminster Town and the 'Engine House'

Souvenir shops: Bridgnorth, Kidderminster Town and the 'Engine House'

Depots: Bridgnorth (locomotives), Bewdley and Kidderminster (stock)

Miniature railways: At Kidderminster and Hampton Loade

Length of line: 16.5 miles

Passenger trains: Steam-hauled trains running frequently from Kidderminster Town to Bewdley and Bridgnorth. Diesel-hauled service on limited occasions as advertised

Period of public operation: Trains operate most weekends and daily from May to September. Also operates all local school holidays. Pre-booked services in December prior to Christmas

Special events: Steam Railway Magazine Spring Gala — 23-25 March; SVR Celebrates 125 Years — 19/20 May; Bridgnorth Station Gala — 16/17 June; 1940s Weekend — 23/24, 30 June, 1 July; Peep Behind The Scenes — 21/22 July; Steam and Whistle Activity Club — selected dates in August; Bridgnorth Beer Festival — 6-9 September; On The Buses — 9 September; Autumn Steam Gala — 21-23 September; Diesel Enthusiasts' Gala — 4-6 October; The Jazz Train — 27 October; Halloween Specials — 20-28 October; Remembrance Sunday Service — 11 November. Full details of all special events can be found at www.svr.co.uk or by telephone on 01299 403816

Facilities for disabled: Facilities available, special vehicle available to carry wheelchairs by prior

Name	No	Origin	Class	Type	Built
—†	80079	BR	4MT	2-6-4T	1954
—+	82045	BR	3MT	2-6-2T	—
—	D3022	BR	08	0-6-0DE	1953
—	D3201	BR	08	0-6-0DE	1955
—	D3586	BR	08	0-6-0DE	1958
—	12099	LMS	11	0-6-0DE	1952
—	D8059	BR	20	Bo-Bo	1961
—	D8188	BR	20	Bo-Bo	1967
—	D5410	BR	27	Bo-Bo	1962
—	D7029	BR	35	B-B	1963
—	37906	BR	37	Co-Co	1963
Greyhound	D821	BR	42	B-B	1960
Hood	D431	BR	50	Co-Co	1968
Ark Royal	50035	BR	50	Co-Co	1968
Exeter	D444	BR	50	Co-Co	1968
Defiance	D449	BR	50	Co-Co	1968
Western Ranger	D1013	BR	52	C-C	1962
Western Courier	D1062	BR	52	C-C	1963
—	50933	BR	108	DMS	1960
—	51941	BR	108	DMBS	1960
—	52064	BR	108	DMC	1961
—	56208	BR	108	DTCL	1958
—	59250	BR	108	TBS	1958

†on display in the 'Engine House' at Highley (additional charge payable)
+new-build under construction
*on display at Barrow Hill Roundhouse Railway Centre
§away on loan

Industrial locomotives

Name	No	Builder	Type	Built
Warwickshire	—	M/Wardle (2047)	0-6-0ST	1926
The Lady Armaghdale	—†	Hunslet (686)	0-6-0T	1898
—	—	Ruston (319290)	0-4-0DM	1953
—	—	R/Hornsby	0-4-0DE	1957
Silver Spoon	—	R/Hornsby (408297)	0-4-0DM	1957

†on display in the 'Engine House' at Highley (additional charge payable)

Stock
27 ex-GWR coaches; 13 ex-LMS coaches; 24 ex-BR Mk 1 coaches; 9 ex-LNER coaches; numerous examples of ex-GWR, LMS and other freight vehicles and one 6-ton and one 30-ton steam cranes

Owners
600 the Severn Valley Railway
813 the GWR 813 Fund
1501 the 15xx Trust
2857 the 2857 Society
4150 the 4150 Locomotive Fund
4566 the 4566 Fund
4930 and 45110 the SVR(H) plc
5164 the 51xx Fund
5764 and 7714 the Pannier Tank Fund
6634 the Waterman Railway Heritage Trust
7325 the Great Western (SVR) Association
7802 and 7812 the Erlestoke Manor Fund
7819 the Severn Valley Rolling Stock Trust
34027 is privately owned
42968 the Stanier Mogul Fund
43106 the Ivatt 4 Fund
46443 the SVR 46443 Fund
47383 the Manchester Rail Travel Society
48773 the Stanier 8F Locomotive Society
75069 the 75069 Fund

England

arrangement. Disabled people's toilets and ramp access to refreshment facilities at Bridgnorth, Kidderminster and the 'Engine House'.

Enlarged versions of all leaflets are available for the visually impaired from staffed booking offices

Special notes: A number of special enthusiasts' weekends and special events are held when extra trains are operated. In addition, supplementary trains with diesel haulage are run as advertised. 'Severn Valley Limited' and 'Severn Valley Venturer' Restaurant

80079 the Passenger Tank Fund
D431, 50035, D444 and D449 Class 50 Alliance Ltd
D821 and D7029 the Diesel Traction Group
D1013 and D1062 the Western Locomotive Association
D3022 the Class 08 Society
D5410 Sandwell Metropolitan Council
82045 the 82045 Steam Locomotive Trust (new-build)

Car service operates on Sundays, some Wednesdays and as required on other occasions. Advance booking required. Charter trains with or without dining facilities can be arranged. Large visitor centre with exhibitions, restaurant and gift shop at Highley — fully disabled

compliant
Membership details: Mrs Kate Kirk, c/o above address
Membership journal: *Severn Valley Railway News* — quarterly
Share details: Mrs W. Broadhurst, c/o above address

Railway Centre	**Shillingstone Railway Project**	Dorset

Member: HRA

The station, dating from August 1863, was on the famous Somerset & Dorset Joint Railway. It remained open until closure of the line in 1966, the site being taken over by Dorset County Council and remained in use until December 2002. In November 2003 the North Dorset Railway Trust took over the custody of the station and commenced restoration. The signalbox has now been restored with operating signal. Work will continue through 2012 on re-laying track and erecting a platform shelter and greenhouse. The diesel shunter will be operational on some weekends.
Location: Shillingstone Station, Shillingstone, Blandford Forum, Dorset DT11 0SF
OS reference: ST 825117

Industrial locomotives

Name	No	Builder	Type	Built
—	—	R/Hornsby (466629)	4wDH	1962

Stock

Ex-BR Mk 1 coach, 4-wheel tank wagon, GSWR gunpowder van, LMS brake van

SatNav postcode: DT11 0SF
Operating society/organisation: North Dorset Railway Society
Contact: Tony Ward (e-mail: tonyward50@btinternet.com)
Telephone: (01258) 860078
Internet addresses:
E-mail: shillingstone50@btinternet.com
Web site: www.shillingstone-station-project.co.uk
On site facilities: Car park, light refreshments available, shop and museum

Access by public transport: Bus — Damory Coaches 309 from Blandford and Gillingham, approx four per day, no Sunday service
Length of line: Track laid in up platform area and half a mile of track and associated pointwork has been acquired with tracklaying to continue in 2012
Public opening: Wednesdays, Saturdays and Sundays 10.00-16.00
Membership cost: £12.50/year
Membership journal: Three times per annum

Cable Tramway	**Shipley Glen Tramway**	West Yorkshire

The Shipley Glen cable tramway is the oldest working example of this system in Great Britain (cliff lifts excepted). Dating from 1895, the line was built to serve the local beauty spot of Shipley Glen, near Saltaire in West Yorkshire. At nearly a quarter of a mile long, the

woodland ride provides a pleasant alternative to the steep path
Postal address: Tramway Office, Prod Lane, Baildon, Shipley, Wesy Yorkshire BD17 5BN
OS reference: SE 235338
Tel: 01274 589010
Internet address:

Web site: www.glentramway.co.uk
Access by public transport:
By rail: Local services to Saltaire station
By bus: 624, 625, 626, 627 from Bradford Interchange
Access by car: Take Otley Road, A6038, out of Shipley, follow

brown tourist signs to a large car park (Salt's Grammar School)
On site facilities:
Top station: Souvenir shop also selling sweets

Bottom station: Museum including replica Edwardian shop, access to Roberts Park and Saltaire
Length of line: 0.25 mile, 20in gauge, maximum gradient 1 in 7

Period of public operation: Most Sundays throughout the year
Facilities for disabled: No toilets. Access to top and bottom stations via steep slopes

The Silk Mill — Derby's Museum of Industry and History

Museum

Derbyshire

Member: TT
The museum is currently not open to the public, but appointments can still be made for visitors to the Midland Railway Study Centre through: www.midlandrailwaystudycentre.org.uk
Location: Silk Mill Lane, off Full

Street, Derby DE1 3AF
Operating society/organisation: Derby City Council
Fax: (01332) 255108
Car park: Local car parks around city
Access by public transport:
By train — three-quarters of a mile
By bus — bus station half a mile

On site facilities: Toilets
Opening times: Midland Railway Study Centre by appointment, admission free
Facilities for disabled: Parking by arrangement. Lifts to study centre, toilets

Sittingbourne & Kemsley Light Railway

Timetable Service

Kent

Member: HRA
The Sittingbourne & Kemsley Light Railway is part of the 2ft 6in-gauge railway built to convey paper and other materials between mills at Sittingbourne and Kemsley and the Dock at Ridham on the banks of the Swale. The first section of the line opened in 1877 with horse-drawn haulage, while steam haulage was introduced in 1906. One of the first two locomotives, *Leader*, will return to service this season. Two of the engines then in use remain on the line today. The railway now operates on the old paper mill's trackbed as a tourist attraction. Passenger trains are normally steam-hauled and are formed of a varied selection of open and covered coaches. For the first half mile of the journey the narrow gauge railway twists and turns through Milton Regis on a unique early reinforced concrete viaduct which was one of the first of its kind. The railway was forced to close, by its landlord, in December

Locomotives — 2ft 6in gauge

Name	No	Builder	Type	Built
Alpha	—	Bagnall (2472)	0-6-2T	1932
Triumph	—	Bagnall (2511)	0-6-2T	1934
Superb	—	Bagnall (2624)	0-6-2T	1940
Unique	—	Bagnall (2216)	2-4-0F	1924
Premier	—	K/Stuart (886)	0-4-2ST	1905
Leader	—	K/Stuart (926)	0-4-2ST	1905
Melior	—	K/Stuart (4219)	0-4-2ST	1924
Edward Lloyd	—	R/Hornsby (435403)	4wDM	1961
Victor	—	Hunslet (4182)	4wDM	1953
Barton Hall	—	Hunslet (6651)	4wDM	1965

Industrial standard gauge locomotives

Name	No	Builder	Type	Built
Bear	—	Peckett (614)	0-4-0ST	1896
—	1	Barclay (1876)	0-4-0F	1925

Locomotive notes: In service: *Melior, Leader, Edward Lloyd, Barton Hall, Victor*
Under repair: *Triumph*, (awaiting boiler repairs), *Superb* (boiler retubing in 2012), *Premier* (dismantled for restoration/overhaul)
Static display: *Alpha, Unique* and standard gauge exhibits

Stock
10 bogie coaches (including 4 ex-Chattenden & Upnor Railway); 2 open coaches; 35 various wagons

England

2008 but trains will return to Sittingbourne Viaduct this season

Managing Director: Robert Newcombe

Registered Charity: 1057079

Headquarters: Sittingbourne & Kemsley Light Railway Ltd, PO Box 300, Sittingbourne, Kent ME10 2DZ

Telephone: 01795 424899 (talking timetable)

Internet addresses:
E-mail: info@sklr.net
Web site: www.sklr.net
Facebook: www.facebook.com/groups/SandKLR
Podcast: search iTunes for Sittingbourne and Kemsley or www.youtube.com/user/stopem

Main station: Sittingbourne Viaduct

Other public stations: Milton Regis (Asda) Halt, Kemsley Down

Car park: Sittingbourne Viaduct (opposite McDonalds and Pizza Hut, Milton Regis (Asda) Halt use Asda car park

SatNav postcodes: Sittingbourne Viaduct — ME10 2XD
Milton Regis (Asda) Halt — ME10 2PD

Party, credit card & advance bookings and Footplate Experience Courses: E-mail info@sklr.net or write to S&KLR, PO Box 300, Sittingbourne, Kent ME10 2DZ.
Tel: 01795 424899 and leave a message

Access by public transport: Sittingbourne Viaduct — Sittingbourne (Southeastern) station;
Milton Regis Halt — Mill Way, Sittingbourne (access from Asda car park); (Kemsley Down access by rail or on foot from Saxon Shore Way only)

Access by road: M2, A249 then A2 then follow signs to Sittingbourne Industry. At Mill Way roundabout turn right and follow brown tourist signs to Sittingbourne Viaduct station or turn left and park at Asda

OS reference:
Sittingbourne TQ 905642
Milton Regis (Asda) Halt TQ 909648
Kemsley Down TQ 920661

On site facilities at Kemsley Down: Refreshment facilities; souvenir shop; small exhibits museum; museum walk; wildlife garden; children's play/picnic area; model and miniature railways (expected to re-open this season)

Depot: Kemsley Down (access by rail or on foot from Saxon Shore Way only)

Length of line: 1.75 miles, 2ft 6in gauge

Passenger trains: Hourly from 13.00 to 16.00 (refer to timetable: www.sklr.net or 01795 424899)

Journey time: 15min each way

Period of public operation: Easter to end of September. Sundays and Bank Holidays. Wednesday during most school holidays during season. Special events throughout the season

Special notes: The Trustees are delighted to announce that the S&KLR will fully re-open from Good Friday 6 April 2012. A full programme of events throughout the season is available to download from www.sklr.net or send a stamped address envelope to Timetables at the above address. There is no public access to Kemsley Down other than by the railway or on foot from Saxon Shore Way on operating dates. When the line is closed all stock is stored in security compounds within the paper mill premises.
Normal fares apply except for the Steam & Beer Festival and Santa Specials. Family fares and senior citizens' tickets available. Special rates for parties. Dogs welcome and travel free

Disabled facilities: Limited access by prior arrangement until full facilities become available. E-mail info@sklr.net or call 01795 424899 for details/to arrange

Special facilities: Footplate experience courses, special trains and children's parties available. Movie filming opportunities

Membership details: John Sparrow, 20 Park Road, Sheerness, Kent ME12 1UY

Marketing name: Sittingbourne's Steam Railway

| Museum | Snibston | Leicestershire |

Members: TT

Location: Snibston, Ashby Road, Coalville, Leicestershire LE67 3LN

Telephone: (01530) 278444

Fax: 0116 3054597

Operating group: Leicestershire County Council

Internet address: *e-mail:* snibston@leics.gov.uk
Web site: www.snibston.com

Museum contact: Mr N. Pell, Curator, Transport & Mining (museum collection enquiries). Tel: 0116 3053452 or nick.pell@leics.gov.uk

Public opening: April-October — daily 10.00-17.00. November-

Multiple-unit

Name	No	Origin	Class	Type	Built
—	70576	BR	4CEP/411	TBC	1956

Industrial locomotives (standard gauge)

Name	No	Builder	Type	Built
Mars II†	—	RSH (7493)	0-4-0ST	1948
—	2§	Barclay (1815)	0-4-0F	1924
—*	—§	Brush (314)	0-4-0ST	1906
Cadley Hill No 1†	—	Hunslet (3851)	0-6-0ST	1962
—	16	Hunslet (6289)	0-6-0DM	1966
—	—	R/Hornsby (393304)	4wDM	1955

§on display in museum galleries
†locomotive is stored, but may be brought out for display on special events
*originally Powlesland & Mason No 6 taken over by GWR in 1924 and numbered 921

March — Monday to Friday 10.00-15.00, weekends and school holidays (10.00-17.00)
Car & coach parking: On site, free
Access by public transport: Arriva Fox from Loughborough and Nottingham (route 99); X1 and X2 from Leicester (217 and 218 on Sundays); Hinckley (route 159); routes 118 and 254 also run from Leicester. Connections at Ashby with Burton upon Trent. Further information, tel: 0870 608 2608
On site facilities: Shop, toilets, car park, café. Meeting and training rooms available for hire. Family tickets, picnic areas, science play area
Special events: Transport Festival — 15 May
Disabled facilities: Fully available

Industrial locomotives (2ft 6in gauge)

Name	No	Builder	Type	Built
—	—	E/Electric (2416)	4wBE	1957
—	—	H/Clarke (DM1812)	0-6-0DM	1960
—	63/000/449	Hunslet (8973)	4wDH	1979

Locomotive notes: 2012 locomotive for passenger trains will be Hunslet (6289) No 16
Plus 2ft 6in gauge English Electric battery-operated electric manriding locomotives — ex-NCB

Rolling stock: 1920 Midland Railway brake van, other goods vehicles

on site apart from small section of colliery tour. Access to passenger trains
Railways on site: Approx two-thirds of a mile of standard gauge track with passenger trains on selected days. Please telephone for further information.

Narrow gauge railway about 80yd in length (non operational).
Volunteers to help maintain and run the railway are welcome to join our volunteer support group; please contact sales and enquiries on 01530 278444

Museum	**Somerset & Dorset Railway Trust**	Somerset

Member: HRA, AIM
Situated at Washford on the West Somerset Railway, the Trust museum houses Somerset & Dorset memorabilia and artefacts to stir memories of cross-country travel in the era of steam. The sidings and restoration shed give the visitor a chance to see locomotives, wagons and carriages close up. Midford signalbox display
Headquarters: Washford Station, Minehead Road, Washford, Somerset TA21 0PP
Telephone: 01984 640869
Internet address: *Web site:* http://www.sdrt.org
Car park: Small car park by main road
Access by public transport: West Somerset Railway trains on operating days, March to end October. Nearest main line station:

Locomotive

Name	No	Origin	Class	Type	Built
—	53808	S&DJR	7F	2-8-0	1925

Working on adjacent West Somerset Railway

Industrial locomotives

Name	No	Builder	Type	Built
Kilmersdon	—	Peckett (1788)	0-4-0ST	1929

Stock
3 Somerset & Dorset 6-wheeled coaches undergoing restoration. Large wagon collection. Display of narrow gauge equipment from Sedgemoor peat railways

Taunton. First Bus service 28 (Taunton-Minehead) passes the station
On site facilities: Souvenir counter at the station. No refreshments on station but adjacent inn offers food and children are welcome
Public opening: 10.30-16.30, see web site for up-to-date details of

opening, plus Bank Holiday weekends and Gala Days
Membership details: Terry Dart, Membership Secretary, 17 Earl Edwin Mews, Whitchurch, Shropshire SY13 1DT
Membership journal: *Pines Express* (4 issues/year)

Timetable Service	**South Devon Railway**	Devon

Member: HRA, TT
The quintessential Great Western branch line meandering down the valley of the River Dart from

Buckfastleigh — which is home to the railway's workshops, a butterfly farm and otter sanctuary amongst other attractions — to Totnes where

the station adjoining the rare breeds farm is a 4min walk via a footbridge from the main line station

England

General Manager: R. Wood
Headquarters: South Devon Railway, The Station, Dartbridge Road, Buckfastleigh, Devon TQ11 0DZ
Telephone: 0843 357 1420
Internet addresses: *E-mail:* trains@southdevonrailway.org
Web sites: Commercial — www.southdevonrailway.co.uk
Engineering — wwwsouthdevonrailwayengineering.co.uk
Enthusiast — www.southdevonrailwayassociation.org
Unofficial — www.sdronline.org.uk
Main station: Buckfastleigh (SatNav postcode TQ11 0DZ)
Other public stations: Staverton, Totnes (Littlehempston)
OS reference:
Buckfastleigh SX 747663
Staverton SX 785638
Car park: Buckfastleigh (free), Staverton (50p). Totnes council or main line station pay & display car parks. No road access to Totnes (Littlehempston)
Access by public transport:
By rail: Totnes, then 500yd walk to Totnes Littlehempston
By bus: X38/9 Exeter-Plymouth; 88 Newton Abbot-Buckfastleigh; X80 Plymouth-Torquay.
Access by road: Follow brown signs from A38.
Refreshment facilities: Buckfastleigh, Totnes (café at Totnes Rare Breeds Centre adjacent to and only accessible via SDR station)
Souvenir and model shop: Buckfastleigh. Second-hand books at all stations
Museum: Buckfastleigh
Depot: Buckfastleigh
Vintage bus: Circular service may operate to Buckfast Abbey and Buckfastleigh town centre from Buckfastleigh station 5-7 times daily according to season. Included in train fare
Miniature railway: Operates most Sundays and gala days at Buckfastleigh (7.25in gauge, half mile)
Model railway: Extensive 00 gauge model railway on free display in souvenir and model shop
Length of line: 7 miles
Passenger trains: Buckfastleigh-Totnes alongside the River Dart
Period of public operation: Daily

Locomotives and multiple-units

Name	No	Origin	Class	Type	Built
—	1420	GWR	1400	0-4-2T	1933
—	1369	GWR	1366	0-6-0PT	1934
—	3205	GWR	2251	0-6-0	1946
—	3803	GWR	2884	2-8-0	1939
Dumbleton Hall	4920	GWR	'Hall'	4-6-0	1929
—	5526	GWR	4500	2-6-2T	1929
—	5786	GWR	5700	0-6-0PT	1930
—	6412	GWR	6400	0-6-0PT	1934
—	D2246	BR	04	0-6-0DM	1956
—	D3721	BR	09	0-6-0DE	1959
—	D8110	BR	20	Bo-Bo	1962
—	D7612	BR	25	Bo-Bo	1966
—	D7641	BR	25	Bo-Bo	1965
—	33002	BR	33	Bo-Bo	1960
Loch Treig	D6737	BR	37	Co-Co	1962
Superb	50002	BR	50	Co-Co	1967
Broad gauge — 7ft 0.25in					
Tiny	—	SDR	—	0-4-0VBT	1868

Industrial locomotives

Name	No	Builder	Type	Built
Ashley	1	Peckett (2031)	0-4-0ST	1942
Lady Angela	1690	Peckett (1690)	0-4-0ST	1926
Glendower	—	Hunslet (3810)	0-6-0ST	1954
Carnarvon	47	Kitson (5474)	0-6-0ST	1935
—	—	Fowler (421014)	0-4-0DM	1958
4ft 6in gauge				
Lee Moor No 2	—	Peckett (784)	0-4-0ST	1899

Stock

10 ex-BR Mk 1 coaches; 19 ex-GWR coaches; 3 ex-BR(W) auto trailers; 52 wagons. Lee Moor Tramway china clay wagon (4ft 6in gauge)

Owners

Tiny, 7ft 0.25in gauge, part of the National Collection
Glendower is privately owned
5526 — 5526 Ltd
3205 — 2251 Fund
D2246, D6737 and 50002 the Devon Diesel Society Ltd
D7612, D8110 and 33002 the South Devon Diesel Traction Ltd
5786 the Worcester Locomotive Society
3803, 6412 and 4920 the South Devon Railway Trust
1369 and 1420 the South Devon Railway Association

end of March to early November
Special events: Mothering Sunday — 18 March; Half Price Weekend — 24/25 March, Easter Heritage Gala — 6-9 April; 140th Anniversary of opening of the Buckfastleigh, Totnes & South Devon Railway — 1 May; Day out with Thomas — 5-7 May; 1960s BR Mixed Traffic Weekend — 19/20 May; Diamond Jubilee Weekend — 2-5 June; Father's Day — 17 June; Military Weekend — 7/8 July; August Bank Holiday Rails and Ales — 24-27 August; Heritage Transport Gala and Behind the Scenes — 15/16 September; Halloween Evening Diesel Special — 3/4 November; Half Price Weekend — 3/4 November; Carols Down the Line — 4-6 December; Santa by Steam — 2, 8/9, 15/16, 18-23 December; Mince Pie Specials — 29-31 December to 1 January 2013
Special facilities: Friday evening dining trains, approx three-weekly April to October (not August); steam and diesel experience days; train hire for private parties

Facilities for disabled: Excellent
Volunteers and supporting association Membership: South Devon Railway Association, c/o

above address
Membership journal: *Bulliver* — quarterly

| Miniature Railway | South Downs Light Railway | West Sussex |

Location/headquarters: Stopham Road Station, Pulborough Garden Centre, Stopham Road, Pulborough, West Sussex RH20 1DS
OS reference: TQ 032183
SatNav postcode: RH20 1DS
Tel: 07518 753784
Contact: Alan Jackson
Internet addresses:
E-mail: sdlrs@btconnect.com,
Web site: www.sdlrs.com
Access by public transport:
By rail: Pulborough station is served by Southern Trains from London Victoria and the south coast, approx 1 mile east of the railway.
By bus: Hourly service between Worthing and Midhurst
Access by car: Stopham Road is the A283 through Pulborough
On site facilities: Ample free parking and café at the garden centre, public house opposite. On the banks of the River Arun

Locomotives — 10.25in gauge

Name	No	Builder	Type	Built
Flying Scotsman	4472	—	4-6-2	1934
Sir Sagramore	771	Richards Engineering	4-6-0	1970s
Royal Scot	6100	—	4-6-0	1952
	13245	P. Howard	2-6-0	1987
Pulborough	319	Exmoor	0-6-0	2004
Peggy	334	Exmoor	0-6-0	2009
Alice	D7062	G. & A. Favell	0-4-2ST	2001
Arctic Prince	—	Mardyke	4w+4PH	1982
Merlin	—	Roanoke	4wDH	—

Souvenir shop: On site
Length of line: 7/8ths mile, 10.25in gauge
Period of public operation: Weekends and Bank Holidays from March to September, Wednesdays in school holidays and for 8 days at Christmas
Facilities for disabled: Toilets and access to station — no train rides
Special events: Mothering Sunday

— 18 March; Easter Egg Hunt — 6/7, 9 April; Father's Day — 17 June; Teddy Bears' Olympics — 14/15 July; Gala — 22/23 September
Membership details: Alan Jackson, Tel: 07518 753784
Membership journal: *South Downs Way* — twice yearly

| Timetable Service | South Tynedale Railway | Cumbria |

Member: HRA
A narrow gauge line passing through the attractive scenery of the South Tyne valley, in the North Pennine area of outstanding natural beauty
Location: Less than 5min walk north of Alston town centre, off A686 Hexham road
OS reference: NY 717467
Operating society: South Tynedale Railway Preservation Society, The Railway Station, Alston, Cumbria CA9 3JB
Telephone: Alston (01434) 382828 (timetable information); (01434) 381696 (other enquiries)
Internet address: *Web site:* www.strps.org.uk
Car park: Alston station and

Industrial locomotives — 2ft gauge

Name	No	Builder	Type	Built
Barber*		T/Green (441)	0-6-2ST	1908
Naworth	4	H/Clarke (DM819)	0-6-0DM	1952
Thomas Edmondson	6	Henschel (16047)	0-4-0T	1918
—	9	Hunslet (4109)	0-4-0DM	1952
Naklo	10	Chrzanow (3459)	0-6-0WTT	1957
Cumbria	11	Hunslet (6646)	0-4-0DM	1967
—	13	Hunslet (5222)	0-4-0DM	1958
Helen Kathryn	14	Henschel (28035)	0-4-0T	1948
—	—	Hunslet (4110)	0-4-0DM	1952
—	—	H/Clarke (DM1167)	0-6-0DM	1960
Carlisle	16	Hunslet (1859)	0-4-2T	1937
—	—	EE/Baguley (2519/3500)	4wBE	1958
—	17	B/Drewry (3704)	4wBE	1973
		rebuilt A/Barclay (6526)		1987
—	18	H/Clarke (DM1247)	0-6-0DM	1961
Permanent Way Trolley	DB965062 Wickham (7597)		4wDM	1957

*off site from June 2012 for full overhaul

Linley halt

Access by public transport: Bus services vary seasonally. Routes include Haltwhistle-Alston and Carlisle-Alston. Please check with local Tourist Information Centres or, for public transport information in Cumbria, phone 0871 200 2223

On site facilities: Book and souvenir shop, picnic area, toilets (including disabled persons), parking, lineside footpath

Catering facilities: Alston station café is now run by the society with light meals, snacks and soft drinks. Buffet car on some trains, mainly at weekends and holidays. Confectionery, ice cream and cold drinks in the station shop

Length of line: 3.3 miles Alston (Cumbria) to Linley Haly (Northumberland); newly extended for 2012; further extension to Slaggyford planned. 2ft gauge

Public opening: Trains will run: 1, 6-10, 12, 14/15, 21/22, 28/29 April; 6-8, 10, 12/13, 15, 17, 19/20, 22, 24, 26/27 May; 2-5, 7, 9/10, 12, 14, 16/17, 19, 21, 23/24, 26, 28, 30 June; 1, 3, 5, 7/8, 10, 12, 14/15, 17-31 (except Mondays) July; daily in August; daily in September

Stock
6 bogie coaches, 1 fully disabled accessible; 2 buffet coachs; 2 brake vans; 3 bogie open wagons; 8 4-wheel open wagons; 1 4-wheel box van; 3 4-wheel flat wagons; 1 4-wheel fuel tank wagon; 2 bogie well wagons, 4 4-wheel skip wagons; 5 bogie flat wagons; 6 bogie hopper wagons; 1 4-wheel hopper wagon; 1 4-wheel weedkiller wagon; 1 bogie compressor wagon; 2 4-wheel chassis

Owners
4, 6, 9, 10, 16, 17 and 2519/3500 the South Tynedale Railway Preservation Society
11, 13, 14, 18, DM4110, DM1167, DB965082 and Baguley/Drewry are privately owned

(except Mondays, Wednesdays and Fridays); weekends plus 23, 25 October.
  Steam haulage scheduled for: 1, 6-9 April; 6/7, 12/13 May; weekends in June; weekends plus 17-19, 24-26, 31 July, daily in August (except 3, 6, 10, 13, 17, 24); weekends in September. Steam trains on other dates whenever possible

Special events: 1 April; 12/13 May; 2, 16 June; 20 August; 8 September — details on web site; Santa Specials — special announcement on web site.

Please telephone or check web site for additional information

Facilities for disabled: A carriage with access for wheelchair users is available. Advance booking is recommended: tel: 01434 381696. Wheelchair-accessible toilet at Alston

Special notes: The line has been constructed on the trackbed of the former BR Haltwhistle-Alston branch

Membership details: Membership Secretary, c/o above address

Membership journal: *Tynedalesman* — quarterly

| Steam Centre | Southall Railway Centre | London |

The GWR Preservation Group has relocated to the Three Road Sidings on the south side of the depot. The potential for this area is considerable and the Group's intention is to develop the area into a full supporting attraction being the only location of its kind in London. Substantial work is required prior to opening to the public and enthusiasts. However, group visits can be arranged in the interim period

Operating society/organisation: GWR Preservation Group Ltd, 16 Grange Close, Heston, Middx TW5 0HW

Contact: Bob Gorringe, Chairman

Tel: 020 8574 1529

Fax: 020 8571 6538

Internet address: *Web site:* www.gwrpg.co.uk

Location: Southall, former steam/DMU depot

Car parking: Currently on site

Locomotives

Name	No	Origin	Class	Type	Built
—	2885*	GWR	2885	2-8-0	1938
—	4110†	GWR	4100	2-6-2T	1936
—	9682§	GWR	5700	0-6-0PT	1949

*cosmetically restored and on display at Moor Street station, Birmingham
†under restoration at Tyseley Locomotive Works
§withdrawn for 10-year overhaul, undertaken at Southall

Industrial locomotives

Name	No	Builder	Type	Built
William Murdoch	—	Peckett (2100)	0-4-0ST	1949
Birkenhead	—	RSH (7386)	0-4-0ST	1948
—	1	AEC	0-4-0	1939
—*	AD251	R/Hornsby (390772)	0-4-0DM	1956
—	—	R/Hornsby (418588)	0-4-0DM	1957
—	AD911	B/Drewry	4wDM	—

All operational except * which has been stored since 1963 with initial restoration work in hand

Rolling stock
BR Mk 1 TSO, BR Mk 1 BSK, BR box van, LMS brake van, BP tank wagon, BR generator van, BR stores van, BR parcels van, LNER CCT, GWR Rectank, GWR Gane A, GWR 'Mink' tool van, GWR Toad brake van

Access by public transport:
Southall station, access via Park Avenue or alternatively Armstrong Way
On site facilities:
Light refreshments and shop
Period of public opening:
Please see web site or press for re-opening details

Owner
William Murdoch the GWRPG are custodians for Portsmouth City Museum

Membership details: c/o above address
Membership journal: *Southall Semaphore* — quarterly

Member: HRA

This railway originally formed part of a system of cross-country lines in East Sussex running through the Wealden countryside

Location: The main station at Tunbridge Wells West is located in the western end of the town close to the A26 road and the popular 'Pantiles' area. Eridge station is located close to the A26 four miles south of Tunbridge Wells

OS reference: Tunbridge Wells West station TQ 577384 Eridge TQ 542345

General Manager: Stephen Woolven

Operating society/organisation: Tunbridge Wells & Eridge RPS, Tunbridge Wells West Station, Nevill Terrace, Tunbridge Wells, Kent TN2 5QY

Telephone: 01892 537715

Internet address: *Web site:* www.spavalleyrailway.co.uk

Car parking: Tunbridge Wells West — several car parks nearby in town centre. Note: Sainsbury's car park, adjacent to station, is limited to 2 1/2 hours.
High Rocks — large free car park.
Groombridge — there is *no* parking here.
Eridge — large car park

SatNav postcodes:
Tunbridge Wells West — TN2 5QY
High Rocks — TN3 9JJ
Groombridge — TN3 9RD
Eridge — TN3 9LE

Access by public transport:
Tunbridge Wells West
Main line services to Tunbridge Wells, then 15min walk, or short bus ride. Nearest bus stop served by many local bus services is at Sainsbury's, Tunbridge Wells, then

Locomotives and multiple-units

Name	No	Origin	Class	Type	Built
Sutton	32650*	LBSCR	A1X	0-6-0T	1876
—	47493	LMS	3F	0-6-0T	1927
—	68077*	LNER	J94	0-6-0ST	1947
Colonel Tomline	D3489*	BR	10	0-6-0DE	1958
—	15224	BR	12	0-6-0DE	1949
R J Mitchell	33063	BR	33/0	Bo-Bo	1962
Sealion	33065*	BR	33/0	Bo-Bo	1962
Driver Robin Prince MBE	37254	BR	37	Co-Co	1965
—	E6047	BR	73	Bo-Bo	1966
—	51669	BR	115	DMBS	1960
—	51849	BR	115	DMBS	1960
—	54408	BR	101	DTS(L)	1958
—	60142*	BR	207	DMBS	1962
—	60616*	BR	207	TC	1962
—	60916*	BR	207	DTS	1962

*undergoing overhaul
D3489, 60142 and 60916 expected to enter service during 2012

Industrial locomotives

Name	No	Builder	Type	Built
Samson*	57	RSH (7668)	0-6-0T	1950
Ugly	62	RSH (7673)	0-6-0ST	1950
North Downs*	13	RSH (7846)	0-6-0T	1955
Princess Margaret	—	Barclay (376)	0-4-0DM	1947
Lady Ingrid*	—	Barclay (2315)	0-4-0ST	1951
Southerham	—	Drewry/Vulcan (2591)	0-4-0DM	1959
Topham*	—	Bagnall (2193)	0-6-0ST	1922
Fonmon*	—	Peckett (1636)	0-6-0ST	1924
Spartan	—	Chrzanow (3135)	0-6-0T	1954
Hotspur*	—	Chrzanow (2944)	0-6-0T	1952

*undergoing overhaul

Stock
6 BR Mk 1 coaches; 1 BR Mk 2 coaches; buffet car from Class 420 EMU; 2 ex-London Transport T stock coaches; 3 brake vans; various freight wagons

Owners
Sutton the London Borough of Sutton
33063 and 33065 the South East Locomotive Group (www.selg.co.uk)
68077 the Keighley & Worth Valley Railway (www.kwvr.co.uk)
37254 the 37254 Fund (www.37254.co.uk)

152

England

approx 100yd walk.
Groombridge
Served by service No 291, Crawley-Tunbridge Wells, stops on B2110 approx 400yd from station
Eridge
Interchange with main line services on adjacent platform. Bus service No 29 or 29A Tunbridge Wells-Brighton stops on A26 road approx 100yd walk from station
Refreshment facilities: Static buffet car at Tunbridge Wells West. At Groombridge there is a refreshment kiosk with seating area on the platform for picnics. Also bar car *Kate* on most trains.
Souvenir shop: Tunbridge Wells West (within engine shed)
Depot: Tunbridge Wells West shed is an original LBSCR design dating from 1891 and consists of four

roads which house various items of rolling stock and motive power
Length of line: 5 miles Tunbridge Wells West-Eridge
Passenger trains: Tunbridge Wells West-Eridge
Period of public operation: Weekends and Bank Holidays from 31 March to 4 November plus some weekdays in June, July and August. Santa Specials in December.
Special events: Easter Specials — 8/9 April; Spring Steam Gala — 14/15 April; Day out with Thomas — 12/13, 18/19 May; Steaming Through the '40s — 22-24 June; Diesel Gala — 3-5 August; Teddy's Day Out — 18/19 August; Swinging '60s Weekend — 15/16 September; Day out with Thomas — 6/7, 13/14 October; CAMRA Beer Festival — 20/21 October; Santa Specials —

weekends 3-23 December; Kids for a Quid — 29 December-1 January 2013
Facilities for disabled: Separate disabled persons' toilet at Tunbridge Wells West station. Ramps available for wheelchair access to trains. Tunbridge Wells West and Groombridge have easy step-free access to the platforms. High Rocks station has a sloping access for which wheelchair users will require assistance. Note: at present Eridge has no step-free access for wheelchairs to the platforms
Special facilities: A private train can be hired for the day. Please contact address above for details
Membership details: c/o Tunbridge Wells West Station
Membership journal: *Spa Valley Starter*

Railway Centre | **Stainmore Railway** | **Cumbria**

Member: HRA
Stainmore Railway Co is a volunteer-run organisation established in 2000 to restore the station building and establish a heritage centre and operational railway at Kirkby Stephen East station (KSE). The station formed the junction between the Stainmore and Eden Valley lines on the original South Durham & Lancashire Union Railway which first opened in 1861. The line closed to passenger traffic in 1962 and the site was formally opened to the public at Easter in 2009
Location/headquarters: Kirkby Stephen East Station, South Road, Kirkby Stephen, Cumbria CA17 4LA
Contact: Dr Sue Jones, Secretary, 1 West End, Sedgefield TS21 2BW (e-mail: suelizjones@hotmail.com
SatNav postcode: CA17 4LA
Internet addresses:
Web sites:
www.kirkbystepheneast.co.uk
www.stainmore150.co.uk (events)
Main station: Kirkby Stephen East
Access by public transport:
By rail: Kirkby Stephen station on the Settle-Carlisle line (0.5 miles)

Locomotives

Name	No	Origin	Class	Type	Built
—	D8169	BR	20	Bo-Bo	1966
—	D5669	BR	31	A1A-A1A	1960
—	37146	BR	37	Co-Co	1963
—*	D6869	BR	37	Co-Co	1963
The Statesman	D1909	BR	47	Co-Co	1965
—	51572	BR	108	DMCL	1959
—	53274	BR	108	DTCL	1958

*named *Saint Blaise Church 1445-1995*

Industrial locomotives

Name	No	Builder	Type	Built
F. C. Tingy	—	Pecket (2084)	0-4-0ST	1948
—	68009	Hunslet (3825)	0-6-0ST	1954
—	—	Planet (3598)	0-4-0DM	1962
—	—	YEC (305)	0-4-0DH	—

Rolling stock
5 ex-LNER Gresley coaches (including a buffet car), 1 ex-GNR coach, 1 ex-NER coach, 1 ex-LMS full brake, 1 ex-SR full brake. Selection of goods wagons

On site facilities: Shop and museum within station building, buffet car within station (seasonal for light refreshments), picnic area and wildlife area. Coglin Castle public house and microbrewery nearby

Length of line: 0.5 miles
Period of public operation: Weekends, excluding Christmas and New Year
Facilities for disabled: Station building wheelchair accessible

STEAM — Museum of the Great Western Railway

Member: HRA

STEAM — Museum of the Great Western Railway tells the remarkable story of the men and women who built, operated and travelled on the Great Western Railway. Situated on the old Swindon Railway Works site, the museum is housed in a 72,000sq ft Victorian machine shop. As well as locomotives, carriages and wagons the story is told by imaginative displays and plenty of 'hands-on' exhibits — build a bridge and shunt the wagons! Have a go at putting a locomotive together and take a ride on the train-driving simulator

Keeper: Felicity Jones

Location: Kemble Drive, Swindon, Wiltshire SN2 2TA

OS reference: SU 143849

Operating society/organisation: Swindon Borough Council

Telephone: Swindon (01793) 466646

Internet address: *Web site:* www.swindon.gov.uk/steam

Locomotives

Name	No	Origin	Class	Type	Built
—	2516	GWR	2301	0-6-0	1897
—	2818	GWR	2800	2-8-0	1905
Lode Star	4003	GWR	'Star'	4-6-0	1907
—	4248	GWR	4200	2-8-0T	1916
Caerphilly Castle	4073	GWR	'Castle'	4-6-0	1923
—	9400	GWR	9400	0-6-0PT	1947
North Star*	—	GWR		2-2-2	1837
—	4	GWR	Diesel railcar	Bo-Bo	1934

*broad gauge (7ft 0.25in) replica

Owner

All locomotives are part of the National Railway Museum Collection

Car park: Swindon Designer Outlet

Access by public transport: Swindon main line station 1 mile (20min walk)

On site facilities: Gift/souvenir shop

Facilities for disabled: Fully accessible

Period of public opening: Open daily 1 March-4 December 10.00-17.00. Open daily 5 December-29 February 11.00-16.00. Closed Christmas Day, Boxing Day and New Year's Day.

Membership details: The Friends of Swindon Railway Museum, c/o STEAM

Membership journal: *North Star* — quarterly

Steeple Grange Light Railway

Established in 1985, the Steeple Grange Light Railway is an 18in-gauge line near Wirksworth in Derbyshire. It is built on the trackbed of the old Cromford & High Peak Railway, now the High Peak Trail. Motive power is provided by ex-industrial diesel, battery-electric and petrol locomotives. Pasengers are carried in an old National Coal Board manrider

Tel/Fax: 07769 802587 during running hours

Internet address:

Web site: www.steeplegrange.co.uk

Access by public transport:

By rail: Matlock Bath, then by bus

By bus: On Sundays and Bank Holiday Mondays the 6.1, Belper-

Industrial locomotives — 1ft 6in gauge

Name	No	Builder	Type	Built
Number 5	1	G/Bat (2493)	4wBE	1946
Hudson Trolley	2	Hudson/SGLR	2w-2P	1989
Greenbat	3	G/Bat (6061)	4wDM	1961
Lizzie	4	Lister / Clay Cross Co	4wDM	1973
551 BEV	5	BEV (551)	4wBE	1924
No 1 Spondon	6†	Notts & Derby EPC	4wBE	1935
Hibberd Y Type	7†	Hibberd (1881)	4wPM	1934
Hibberd	8†	Hibberd (3424)	4wDM	1949
Hibberd DY Type	9	Hibberd (4008)	4wDM	1963
Lister	10†	Lister (37736)	4wDM	1951
ZM32 Horwich	11	R/Hornsby (416214)	4wDM	1957
Greenburg Scout	12	Greenburg Scout	4wBE	
Plymouth EB2	13	Plymouth	4wBE	
Lady Margorie	14	Clayton	4wBE	
L10	15	Clayton (5431)	4wBE	1968
L16 Peggt	16	Clayton (B0109B)	4wBE	1973

*worked at British Railways' Horwich Works

†stored off site

Matlock and 17 Chesterfield-Ashbourne stop at Steeple Grange. On Saturdays the 6.3, Derby-Bakewell and 411 Matlock-Ashbourne both stop at Steeple Grange
Gauge: 18in
Period of public operation: Sundays April to end of October. Saturdays in July, August and

Rolling stock
3 four-wheel manriders, various ex-NCB wagons

September with extra days on Bank Holiday weekends.
Opening times 12.00-17.00.
The railway may not operate if the weather is inclement, please contact if in doubt

Stephenson Railway Museum & North Tyneside Railway

Steam Centre

Tyne & Wear

Member: HRA
A display in buildings which began life as the Tyne & Wear Metro Test Centre now features locomotives and exhibitions which illustrate railway development from waggonways to the present day
Location: Middle Engine Lane, West Chirton
OS reference: NZ 396576
Internet address: NTSRA web site: www.ntsra.org.uk
Operating society/organisation: The Stephenson Railway Museum and the North Tyneside Railway are managed as a partnership between North Tyneside Council, Tyne & Wear Museums and the North Tyneside Railway Association (NTSRA). Each can be contacted c/o Stephenson Railway Museum, Middle Engine Lane, West Chirton, North Shields, Tyne & Wear NE29 8DX
Car park: On site, free
Length of line: North Tyneside Railway, 2 miles, Stephenson Railway Museum to Percy Main Village
Access by public transport: Bus services 300 from Newcastle (Haymarket bus station); 337 from Wallsend (Metro station interchange). Ring 0870 608 2608 for times and fares. Tyne & Wear Metro to Percy Main (then short walk to NTR station) when North Tyneside Railway is in operation
Public opening:
Museum — 11.00-16.00, every weekend from April to October,

Locomotive and multiple-unit

Name	No	Origin	Class	Type	Built
—	D2078	BR	03	0-6-0DM	1959
—	3267	NER	—	DMLV	1904

Industrial locomotives

Name	No	Builder	Type	Built
Billy	—	Killingworth or RS & Co (1)	0-4-0	c1826
—	A No 5	Kitson (2509)	0-6-0PT	1883
Ashington No 5 / Jackie Milburn	5	Peckett (1970)	0-6-0ST	1939
Ted Garrett, JP, DL, MP	1	RSH (7683)	0-6-0T	1951
—	E4	Siemens-Schuckert (457)	Bo-BoWE	1909
Thomas Burt MP 1837-1902	401	Bagnall (2994)	0-6-0ST	1950
—	10	Consett Iron Co	0-6-0DM	1958
—	801*	Alco	Bo-Bo	1950

*in store for restoration and future use on Aln Valley Railway

Stock
1 LNER Gresley BFK; 3 BR Mk 1 non-gangwayed coaches, 2 BR Mk 2 coaches, 1 LNER Gresley BGP

Owners
NER van National Railway Museum
801 the UK Alco Group

including all Bank Holidays. Every day during North Tyneside school holidays. Admission free. November to March closed.
Steam train rides — every Sunday and Bank Holiday Mondays, April to October. First train 11.30. Small charge applies, please contact the museum on 0191 200 7146 for details, or visit the web site www.twmuseums.org.uk/stephenson
Special notes: Stephenson Railway

Museum and North Tyneside Railway share facilities in buildings. North Tyneside Steam Railway Association operates and maintains exhibits from the museum collection
Facilities for disabled: Access for wheelchairs to museum building at Middle Engine Lane. Access to stations; also wheelchair ramp onto train

Swanage Railway — 'The Purbeck Line'

Member: HRA

Overlooked by the historic ruins of Corfe Castle, this railway is slowly extending towards Wareham and the connection to the main line network enables occasional stock and locomotive workings

Location: Swanage station

Operations Manager: Mel Cox

Operating society/organisation: Swanage Railway Co Ltd, Station House, Swanage, Dorset BH19 1HB

Telephone: Swanage (01929) 425800. Talking Timetable — (01929) 425800

Fax: (01929) 475208

Internet addresses: *E-mail:* info@swanage-railway.co.uk *Web site:* www.swanagerailway.co.uk

Other public stations: Herston Halt, Harmans Cross, Corfe Castle and Norden

OS reference: SZ 026789

Car park: Norden park & ride (charge payable) signposted off A351 Wareham-Swanage road on the approach to Corfe Castle. Limited parking available in Swanage town centre

Access by public transport: Regular bus services operated by Wilts & Dorset from Bournemouth, Poole and Wareham to Swanage and Norden park & ride

On site facilities: Souvenir shop at Swanage. Exhibition and cinema coach at Corfe. Purbeck Mineral Mining Museum under development at Norden

Catering facilities: Buffets at Swanage and Norden as well as on some trains. Picnic areas at Swanage, Harmans Cross and Norden

Length of line: 6 miles, Swanage-Herston Halt-Harmans Cross-Corfe Castle-Norden

Public opening: Buffet at Swanage station open every day except Christmas Day. Trains operate daily from April to October and most weekends

Special events: Railway at Work Weekend — 24/25 March; Easter Specials — 6-9 April; Diesel Gala — 11-13 May; Grand Steam Gala

Locomotives and multiple-units

Name	No	Origin	Class	Type	Built
—	6695	GWR	5600	0-6-2T	1928
—	53	LSWR	M7	0-4-4T	1905
Sidmouth	34010	SR	WC	4-6-2	1945
Eddystone	34028	SR	WC	4-6-2	1946
Sir Keith Park	34053	SR	BB	4-6-2	1947
Manston	34070	SR	BB	4-6-2	1947
257 Squadron	34072	SR	BB	4-6-2	1948
—	80078	BR	4MT	2-6-4T	1954
—	80104	BR	4MT	2-6-4T	1955
—	08436	BR	08	0-6-0DE	1957
—	D3591	BR	08	0-6-0DE	1958
—	D6515	BR	33	Bo-Bo	1960
—	33111	BR	33	Bo-Bo	1960
—	51346	P/Steel	117	DMBS	1959
—	51388	P/Steel	117	DMS	1959
—	51933	P/Steel	108	DMBS	1960
—	54504	P/Steel	108	DTC	1960
—	59486	P/Steel	117	TCL	1960
—	55028	P/Steel	121	DMBS	1960

Industrial locomotives

Name	No	Builder	Type	Built
May	2	Fowler (4210132)	0-4-0DM	1957
Beryl	—	Planet (2054)	4wPM	1937
Secondus*	—	Bellis & Seekings	0-6-0WT	1874
Snapper†	—	R/Hornsby (283871)	4wDM	1950

*2ft 8in gauge, on display in Corfe Castle goods shed
†2ft gauge, stored nearby for use on Purbeck Mineral & Mining Museum project

Locomotive notes: Steam locomotives may be away periodically on short-term loan

Stock

3 ex-LSWR coach bodies; 4 ex-SR vans; 9 ex-SR coaches; 20 ex-BR Mk 1 coaches; 15 various types of wagons; 1 ex-BR Mk 3 Sleeping coach; 1 ex-SR 15-ton diesel-electric crane; 1 ex-BR Corridor 2nd converted to disabled persons' coach. Brake vans from SR, LMS, LSWR including 3 'Queen Marys', GWR.

Owners

6695 the 6695 Locomotive Group
34010 (stored), 34028, 34053, 34070, 34072 (under overhaul), 80078 (awaiting overhaul) and 80104 — Southern Locomotives Ltd
53 the Drummond Locomotives Ltd
D6515 the 71A Locomotive Group
33111 the Class 33/1 Preservation Co Ltd

& Vintage Transport Rally — 7-9 September; Family Fun Week — 27 October-4 November; Santa Specials — 1/2, 8/9, 15/16, 22-24 December.
On special event days timetables and fares are liable to alteration. See web site for further details of these and other local events involving the Swanage Railway

Facilities for disabled: Access to shop and toilets with level access at

all stations. Special carriage designed for easier access by wheelchair passengers and disabled toilet on some services. Hearing loops at Booking Office, shop and static buffet
Membership details: Liz Sellen, c/o above address

Membership journal: *Swanage Railway News* — 3 times/year
Marketing name: The Purbeck Line

Swindon & Cricklade Railway

Steam Centre   Wiltshire

Member: HRA, TT
This is the only preserved section of the former Midland & South Western Junction Railway, the society having had to re-lay track and associated works. There is the station and the engine shed complex at Hayes Knoll
Location: Tadpole Lane, Blunsdon (approximately midway between Blunsdon St Andrew and Purton)
Chairman: John Ferris
Operating society/organisation: Swindon & Cricklade Railway, Blunsdon Station, Blunsdon, Swindon, Wiltshire SN25 2DA
Telephone: 01793 771615
Internet address: *Web site:* www.swindon-cricklade-railway.org
Station: Blunsdon
OS reference: SU 110897
Length of line: 2.5 miles
Car park: Tadpole Lane, Blunsdon
Access by road: The S&CR is situated to the west of the A419 between Cirencester and Swindon. Follow the signs to Blunsdon Stadium, and continue for 2.5 miles following the brown signs
Refreshment facilities: Blunsdon station in former Norwegian State Railways coach. Buffet car at Hayes Knoll on open days. Picnic area
Toilet: Blunsdon station amenities building, Hayes Knoll
Souvenir shop: Blunsdon station. Various sales stands on Open Days around station area. Museum
Depot: Hayes Knoll
Public opening: Site open: 10.00-16.00 Saturdays, Sundays and Bank Holidays throughout the year and Wednesdays in local school holidays
Passenger trains: A steam train planned to operate from 11.00-16.00 every Sunday from Easter to 23 October and on the dates listed below unless stated otherwise. A train service will also operate on Sundays from 6 February and on Saturdays and Sundays from 5

Locomotives and multiple-units

Name	No	Origin	Class	Type	Built
—	2022	BR	03	0-6-0DM	1958
—	D2152	BR	03	0-6-0DM	1960
—	13261	BR	08	0-6-0DE	1956
—	09004	BR	09	0-6-0DE	1959
Sir Herbert Walker	E6003	BR	73	Bo-Bo	1962
—	51074	GRCW	119	DMBC	1959
—	51104	GRCW	119	DMS	1958
—	59514	P/Steel	117	TCL	1959
—	60127	BR	207	DMBS	1962
—	60901	BR	207	DTS	1962

Industrial locomotives

Name	No	Builder	Type	Built
Swordfish	—	Barclay (2138)	0-6-0ST	1941
Salmon	—	Barclay (2139)	0-6-0ST	1942
—	—	Barclay (2352)	0-4-0ST	1954
Richard Trevithick	—	Barclay (2354)	0-4-0ST	1954
Woodbine	—	Fowler (21442)	0-4-0DM	1936
—	—	Fowler (4210137)	0-4-0DM	1958
Blunsdon	—	Fowler (4220031)	0-4-0DH	1964
—	70	H/Clarke (1464)	0-6-0T	1921
Gunby	—	Hunslet (2413)	0-6-0ST	1941
Phoenix	70	H/Clarke (1464)	0-6-0T	1921

Stock
11 BR Mk 1 coaches; 3 GWR coaches 1 TVR coach; selection of goods rolling stock; Wickham railcar. Self-propelled Plasser & Theurer track machine (98504 of 1985)

Owners
51074, 51104 and 59514 the Gloucester Railcar Trust
E6003 the Electro-Diesel Group

March 11.00-16.00 when special events are not planned and on Wednesdays during local school holidays
Special events: 11.00-16.00 unless otherwise noted.
Mother's Day — 18 March (Wine & Dine on the Moonraker*); Kids Go Free Weekend — 31 March, 1 April; Easter Egg Specials (diesel-hauled) — 6, 9 April; Easter Egg Specials (steam-hauled) — 7/8 April; Kids Go Free Weekend — 5-7 May; Cream Tea in the Moonraker — 13 May; Real Ale and Cider Festival — 2-5 June; Cream Tea in the Moonraker — 10 June; Kids Go Free Weekend — 9/10 June; Father's Day (Wine & Dine on the Moonraker*) — 17 June; Murder Mystery Evening (19.15 start)*— Friday 22 June; Cream Tea in the Moonraker — 1 July; Kids Go Free Weekend — 21/22 July; Murder Mystery Evening (19.15 start)* — Friday 27 July; Cream Tea in the Moonraker — 5 August; Vintage Weekend — 11/12 August (10.30≠17.00); Wine & Dine on the Moonraker* — 19 August; Children's Treasure Hunt — 26/27 August; Cream Tea in the Moonraker — 2 September;

Murder Mystery Evening (19.15 start)* — Friday 7 September; Wartime Weekend (10.00-18.00) — 8/9 September; Kids Go Free Weekend — 15/16 September; Model Rail Day — 6 October; Halloween (18.30-20.45) — 28, 31 (Wednesday) October ; Santa Specials — 1/2, 8 (11.00-18.00), 9, 15/16, 22/23 December; Saturday 8th trains also run 18.00-20.00.
*pre-booking required
Service operates:

School holiday Wednesdays (diesel)-hauled 11.00-16.00:
4, 11 April, 6 June, 25 July, 1, 8, 15, 22, 29 August, 31 October
When special events are not planned the following service will operate:
Sunday service (diesel)
from 5 February to 1 April, 4-25 November (11.00-16.00)
Sunday service (steam),
from 15 April to 21 October (11.00-16.00);
Saturday service (diesel)

From 3 March throughout the year (11.00-16.00);
Facilities for disabled: Access to trains, locomotive shed, shop, toilets and refreshments
Special facilities: Licensed for civil/wedding ceremonies. Suitable for up to 60 guests. Trains can be hired for special events
Membership details: Graham Clark, Membership Secretary, 18 Glevum Road, Swindon SN3 4AF
Membership journal: *Tiddly Dyke*, quarterly

Timetable Service — Tanfield Railway — County Durham

Member: HRA
The oldest railway in the world, featuring 1725 route, 1725 Causey embankment, 1727 Causey arch, 1766 Gibraltar bridge and 1854 Marley Hill engine shed. Also collection of local engines, Victorian carriages and vintage workshop
Location: Off the A6076 Sunniside to Stanley road
OS reference: NZ 207573
Operating society/organisation: The Tanfield Railway, Marley Hill Engine Shed, Sunniside, Gateshead NE16 5ET
Telephone: General enquiries — 0845 463 4938.
Party and Santa bookings — 0845 463 4836
Internet addresses: *E-mail:* info@tanfield-railway.co.uk
Web site: www.tanfield-railway.co.uk
Main stations: Andrews House, Sunniside, Causey, East Tanfield
Car park: Marley Hill, Causey picnic area, East Tanfield
Access by public transport: X30/31 stop outside the railway evtrance on weekdays; 705, 706, 770 Sundays to Sunniside only, near to Sunniside station
Catering facilities: Light refreshments available on operating days
On site facilities: Shop and toilets
Length of line: 3 miles
Public opening: Trains run every Sunday and Bank Holiday Monday from January to November. Also Wednesdays and Thursdays last

Locomotive

Name	No	Origin	Class	Type	Built
—	M2*	TGR	M	4-6-2	1951

*3ft 6in gauge, Tasmanian Government Railways (RSH 7630)

Industrial locomotives

Name	No	Builder	Type	Built
—	9	AEG (1565)	4w-4wE	1913
Gamma	—	Bagnall (2779)	0-6-0ST	1945
—	—	Baguley (3565)	2w-2DHR	1962
Horden	—	Barclay (1015)	0-6-0ST	1904
—	6	Barclay (1193)	0-4-2ST	1910
—	17	Barclay (1338)	0-6-0T	1913
—	32	Barclay (1659)	0-4-0ST	1920
Beryl	—	S/Crossley (7697)	0-6-0DM	1953
—	3	E. Borrows (37)	0-4-0WT	1898
—	6	Fowler (4240010)	0-6-0DH	1960
Enterprise	—	R&W Hawthorn (2009)	0-4-0ST	1884
Cyclops	112	H/Leslie (2711)	0-4-0ST	1907
—	2*	H/Leslie (2859)	0-4-0ST	1911
Stagshaw	—	H/Leslie (3513)	0-6-0ST	1923
—	3	H/Leslie (3575)	0-6-0ST	1923
—	13	H/Leslie (3732)	0-4-0ST	1928
—	3	H/Leslie (3746)	0-6-0F	1929
Renishaw Ironworks No 6	—	H/Clarke (1366)	0-6-0ST	1919
Irwell	—	H/Clarke (1672)	0-4-0ST	1937
—	38	H/Clarke (1823)	0-6-0T	1949
—	501	Hunslet (6612)	0-6-0DH	1965
—	—	Planet (3716)	0-4-0DM	1955
—	4	Sentinel (9559)	0-4-0T	1953
Twizell†	3	Stephenson (2730)	0-6-0T	1891
—	L2	R/Hornsby (312989)	0-4-0DE	1952
—	35	R/Hornsby (418600)	0-4-0DE	1958
—	158	RSH (6980)	0-4-0DM	1940
Hendon	—	RSH (7007)	0-4-0CT	1940
—	62	RSH (7035)	0-6-0ST	1940
—	3	RSH (7078)	4w-4wE	1940
—	49	RSH (7098)	0-6-0ST	1943
Progress	—	RSH (7298)	0-6-0ST	1946
Cochrane	—§	RSH (7409)	0-4-0ST	1948
Bromborough No 2	—	RSH (7746)	0-6-0DM	1954

158

England

week in July and August. Santa trains in December before Christmas. Marley Hill engine shed open daily for viewing

Special events: Mother's Day — 18 March; Easter Eggstravaganza — 6-9 April; Light Railway Weekend — 21/22 April; Jubilee Weekend — 3-5 June; Photographic Evening — Friday 7 September; Legends of Industry Weekend — 8/9 September; North Pole Express — 25 November, 1/2, 8/9, 15/16, 22-24 December (pre-booking essential); Winter Warmers — 26, 30 December

Family tickets: Available

Facilities for disabled: Access to East Tanfield and Andrews House stations and Marley Hill engine shed. Toilets at Causey car park and Andrews House station

Membership details: Miss E. Martin, 33 Stocksfield Avenue, Fenham, Newcastle upon Tyne NE5 2DX

Membership journal: *Tanfield Railway News* — 4 times/year

Special notes: Families can alight at Causey station for 2 miles of walks through the picturesque Causey Woods; picnic facilities and toilet available in car park

Name	No	Builder	Type	Built
—	44	RSH (7760)	0-6-0ST	1953
—	38	RSH (7763)	0-6-0ST	1954
—	21	RSH (7796)	0-4-0ST	1954
—	47	RSH (7800)	0-6-0ST	1954
—	1	RSH (7901)	0-4-0DM	1958
—	16	RSH (7944)	0-6-0ST	1957
—	2	A/Whitworth (D22)	0-4-0DE	1933

*on loan to Locomotion
†on long-term loan from Beamish
§ expected to return to National Coal Mining Museum

2ft gauge

Name	No	Builder	Type	Built
Escucha	11	B/Hawthorn (748)	0-4-0ST	1883
—	—	Clayton (133141)	4wBE	1984
—	—	Hunslet (7332	4wDM	1973
—	—	L/Blackstone (53162)	4wDM	1962
—	—	L/Blackstone (54781)	4wDM	1962
—	—	R/Hornsby (323587)	4wDM	1952
—	—	R/Hornsby (244487)	4wDM	1946
—	25	RSH (8201)	4wBE	1960
—	—	W/Rogers	4wBE	—

Stock

19 4-wheel carriages; 3 6-wheel carriages; 1 6-wheel van; 14 hopper wagons; 9 contractors' bogies; 3 brake vans; 3 steam cranes; 8 covered wagons; 4 open wagons; 4 black wagons; 3 flat wagons

Owner

Progress on loan from the National Coal Mining Museum

Steam Centre	**Telford Horsehay Steam Trust**	Shropshire

Member: HRA

Telford Steam Railway is based at Horsehay & Dawley station and goods yard in Telford on the Great Western branch from Wellington to Craven Arms via Ironbridge. The site at Horsehay has a longer history, being at the site of one of the Coalbrookdale companies' first blast furnaces. The line saw its last passenger train in 1962 but the route from Lightmoor to Horsehay was kept open for freight traffic until 1979. The TSR acquired the former goods yard at Horsehay & Dawley in 1983. The railway is now extending northwards to Lawley Common, and southwards to Doseley. Excavation of Lawley Common cutting was completed in 2008 and most of the trackwork is now in place for the new northern

Locomotives and diesel multiple-units

Name	No	Origin	Class	Type	Built
—	5619*	GWR	5600	0-6-2T	1925
—	D3429	BR	08	0-6-0DE	1958
—	50531	BRCW	104	DMC	1957
—	50479	BRCW	104	DMBS	1957
—	50556	BRCW	104	DMC	1957
—	59228	BRCW	104	TBSL	1958

*expected to be away on loan during 2012

Industrial locomotives

Name	No	Builder	Type	Built
Rocket	—	Peckett (1722)	0-4-0ST	1926
Ironbridge No 3	—	Peckett (1990)	0-4-0ST	1940
Beatty	—	H/Leslie (3240)	0-4-0ST	1917
—	MP1	Barclay (1944)	0-4-0F	1944
Tom	27414	N/British (27414)	0-4-0DH	1954
Folly	—	R/Hornsby (183062)	4wDM	1937
—	—	R/Hornsby (313394)	0-4-0DM	1952
—	D2959	R/Hornsby (382824)	4wDM	1955
—	—	R/Hornsby (525947)	0-4-0DH	1968
Joanna	—	T/Hill (177C)	0-4-0DM	1967

terminus at Lawley station. The opening of this extension is imminent and the web site should be consulted for progress reports
Location: Horsehay, Telford, Shropshire
OS reference: SJ 675073
Operating society/organisation: Telford Horsehay Steam Trust, The Old Loco Shed, Horsehay, Telford, Shropshire TF4 2LT
Sales line: 07816 762790
Internet address: *Web site:* www.telfordsteamrailway.co.uk
On site facilities: Extensive model railway display, tea room, picnic area, children's play equipment, narrow gauge steam tramway, miniature railway operated by Phoenix Model Engineers (separate charge); ticket gives unlimited travel (except miniature railway)
Public opening: Every Sunday and

Name	No	Builder	Type	Built
		rebuild of Sentinel (9401) 0-4-0ST of 1950		
—	—	YEC (2687)	0-4-0DE	1968
Thomas	—*	Kierstead	4wVBT	1979

*2ft gauge

Stock
2 ex-BR Mk 1 coaches; 1 ex-BR Mk 3 sleeper; 1 ex-GWR auto-trailer; 1 ex-GWR Toad brake van; 1 ex-GWR 3-ton hand crane; 1 Wickham trolley; Permaquip p-way transporter vehicle No 68800; various wagons

Bank Holiday from Easter until last Sunday in September 11.00-16.30. Steam-hauled trains on most Sundays, with heritage diesels running for one Sunday in most months
Special events: Easter Bunny — 8/9 April; Father's Day. Drive a steam train — 17 June; Model Gala — 15 July; Bank Holiday Weekend — 26/27 August; Santa Specials —

1/2, 8/9, 15/16/ December
Facilities for disabled: DMU vehicle usually acts as a carriage and has ramped access to brake van. Small chairs can be accommodated in GWR brake van, platforms have easy access and shop, although steep ramp at Horsehay & Dawley. Tea room and model railway have level access

---

Steam Centre — Threlkeld Quarry & Mining Museum — Cumbria

Member: HRA, TT
It is possible to find out about four centuries of mining in Cumbria and take a guided underground tour. Exhibits include the largest collection of working vintage excavators in Europe which now includes the oldest surviving steam navvy in the world, Ruston Proctor No 306 dating from 1909, which runs on rails. The narrow gauge railway has views of Blencathra and the surrounding fells
Contact: W. I. Hartland
Postal address: Threlkeld Quarry Museum, Threlkeld Quarry, Keswick, Cumbria CA12 4TT
OS reference: NY 320245
SatNav postcode: CA12 4TT
Tel: 01768 779747
Internet addresses:
E-mail: info@threlkeldquarrymuseum@btc onnect.com
Web site: www.threlkeldmining.co.uk
Access by public transport:
By rail: Nearest main line station is Penrith
By bus: Local services to Threlkeld
Access by car: In the village of Threlkeld, 3 miles north of Keswick

Locomotives — 2ft gauge

Name	No	Builder	Type	Built
Sir Tom	—	Bagnall (2135)	0-4-0ST	1925
—	—	Hunslet (3595)	4wDM	1948
—	89	M/Rail (4565)	4wPM	1928
—	2	M/Rail (8627)	4wDM	1941
—	—	M/Rail (8860)	4wDM	1944
—	—	M/Rail (8937)	4wDM	1944
—	R6	R/Hornsby (221626)	4wDM	1943
—	—	R/Hornsby (242918)	4wDM	1947
—	—	R/Hornsby (444208)	4wDMF	1961
—	2	W/Rogers		
—	7	W/Rogers		
—	—	W/Rogers		
Bredbury	—	Bredbury	2w-2PM	c1954

Rolling stock
6 passenger coaches

on the A66, follow brown tourist signs
Car parking: On site for patrons only
On site facilities: Tea room, underground mine tours, panning for gold
Length of line: 0.5 mile, 2ft gauge
Period of public operation: Open daily and all Bank Holidays Easter to the end of October, 10.00-17.00. Please contact for details of the railway operating dates and

times
Facilities for disabled: Wheelchair-friendly, requires able-bodied assistance. Access to the railway
Special events: Santa Specials, please contact for dates and times
Special notes: Excavator working days and visiting steam locomotives
Membership details: Vintage Excavator Trust, 362 Halesowen Road, Cradley Heath, Warley, West Midlands B64 7JF

Membership journal: *The Navvy Driver* — published 3 times a year by the Vintage Excavator Trust

Museum — Tiverton Museum of Mid Devon Life — Devon

The museum, dominated by No 1442, affectionately known as the 'Tivvy Bumper', houses a large collection of railway relics. The museum is family-friendly and visitors can enter the cab of the 'Tivvy Bumper'
Location: Tiverton, Devon
OS reference: SS 955124
Operating society/organisation: Tiverton & Mid Devon Museum Trust, Beck's Square, Tiverton, Devon EX16 6PJ
Telephone: (01884) 256295

Locomotives

Name	No	Origin	Class	Type	Built
(Tivvy Bumper)	1442	GWR	1400	0-4-2T	1935

Internet address: *Web site:* www.tivertonmuseum.org.uk
Car park: Short term in Beck's Square, long term in multi-storey
Access by public transport: Rail to Tiverton Parkway, then by bus, or bus from Exeter
On site facilities: Museum, shop and toilets

Public opening:
February to Christmas:
Monday to Friday — 10.30-16.30;
Saturdays — 10.00-13.00;
closed Sundays
Facilities for disabled: Museum totally accessible for wheelchair users, disabled toilet

Steam Centre — Tyseley Locomotive Works — Birmingham

Member: HRA
Location: 670 Warwick Road (A41), Tyseley, Birmingham B11 2HL
OS reference: SP 105841
Operating organisation: Tyseley Locomotive Works Ltd
Supporting society: Vintage Trains Society
Telephone: (0121) 708 4960
Fax: (0121) 708 4963
Internet addresses: *E-mail:* vintagetrains@btconnect.com
Web site: www.vintagetrains.co.uk/brm.htm
Car park: Site
Access by public transport: Travel West Midlands route 37 from city centre. Main line rail service to Tyseley station (Central Trains and Chiltern Connections at Solihull and Moor Street)
On site facilities: The Museum is on the site of a former GWR/BR steam shed and has been equipped with specialised railway engineering machinery. It carries out many contract repairs to steam locomotives and rolling stock. Souvenir shop, passenger

Locomotives

Name	No	Origin	Class	Type	Built
Kinlet Hall	4936	GWR	'Hall'	4-6-0	1929
Rood Ashton Hall	4965	GWR	'Hall'	4-6-0	1929
Nunney Castle	5029	GWR	'Castle	4-6-0	1934
Earl of Mount Edgcumbe	5043	GWR	'Castle	4-6-0	1936
Defiant†	5080	GWR	'Castle'	4-6-0	1939
Clun Castle	7029	GWR	'Castle'	4-6-0	1950
—	4110	GWR	5101	2-6-2T	1937
—	4121	GWR	5101	2-6-2T	1937
—	7752	GWR	5700	0-6-0PT	1930
—	7760	GWR	5700	0-6-0PT	1930
—	9600	GWR	5700	0-6-0PT	1945
Kolhapur§	5593	LMS	'Jubilee'	4-6-0	1934
—	670	LNWR*	Bloomer	2-2-2	1986
—	13029	BR	08	0-6-0DE	1953
The Queen Mother	47773	BR	47	Co-Co	1964
Rodney	50021	BR	50	Co-Co	1968
Glorious	50033	BR	50	Co-Co	1968
Les Ross	86259	BR	86	Bo-Bo	1965

*replica built at Tyseley Locomotive Works
†on loan to Buckinghamshire Railway Centre
§on loan to Barrow Hill Roundhouse

Industrial locomotives

Name	No	Builder	Type	Built
Cadbury No 1	—	Avonside (1977)	0-4-0T	1925
—	1	Peckett (2004)	0-4-0ST	1942
—	—	Baguley (800)	0-4-0PE	1920

England

demonstration line and station
Refreshment facilities: Available in visitor centre
Length of line: Third of a mile
Public opening: Advertised open days normally summer and autumn
Special events: 'Shakespeare Express' runs from July to mid-September 2012. Running from Birmingham Snow Hill to Stratford-upon-Avon twice daily
Special notes: Tyseley is a centre for 'Steam on the Main Line' railtours (operated by Vintage Trains) over a large area of the national rail network
Membership details: Membership

Name	No	Builder	Type	Built
—	—	RSH (7289)	0-6-0ST	1945

Note: Not all locomotives are on site, and some are undergoing restoration. Contract restoration work includes Nos (GWR) 7820 *Dinmore Manor* and industrial RSH 7289/1945; locomotives away on loan *Henry* (Barrow Hill), 5080 (Buckinghamshire)

Stock
22 BR Mk 2 coaches, 6 BR Mk 1 coaches, 3 BR Mk 1 Pullman Cars, goods and departmental vehicles, steam and diesel cranes

is available to the public, providing free entry to site events and four copies of *Steam in Trust* magazine
Facilities for disabled: Disabled access to 'Shakespeare Express'

available, but must be notified in advance
Note: All attractions and facilities are advertised subject to availability

---

Museum	**Vintage Carriages Trust Museum of Rail Travel**	West Yorkshire

Member: HRA, TT, AIM, ABTEM
A fascinating collection of elderly railway carriages and small locomotives, interestingly presented. Sit in a fully restored, prize winning 1876-built Manchester, Sheffield & Lincolnshire Railway carriage or relive the dark days of wartime travel in one of the three Metropolitan Railway carriages. Listen to the 'Travellers' Tales' and view the collection of railway posters and other items. Video presentations. The carriages and locomotives have appeared in over 70 cinema and television productions including *South Riding* (2010), *Timeshift: Between the Lines* (2008), *The Story of BP* (2007), *Brideshead Revisited* (2007), *Housewife, 49* (2006), *Booze Cruise 3* (2005), *North & South* (2004), *The Railway Children* (1970 and 1968 versions)
Location: Museum of Rail Travel, Ingrow Station Yard, Halifax Road, Keighley, West Yorkshire BD21 5EH.
On the A629 road
Operations Manager: David N. Carr, Hon Secretary, VCT
Operating society/organisation: Vintage Carriages Trust (Registered Charity No 510776)
Telephone: Keighley (01535) 680425
Fax: (01535) 610796

Stock

Railway	BR or previous owner Number	Type	Date built	Seats	Weight	Length
MS&LR	176	4-wheel 1st/2nd/3rd/luggage	1876	34	12T	28ft 0in
GNR	589	6-wheel 3rd brake	1888	40	14T	34ft 11in
MR	358	6-wheel 1st/3rd/luggage	1886	32	15T	34ft 0in
Met	427	BS	1910	84	30T	54ft 0in
Met	465	S	1919	108	30T	54ft 0in
Met	509	F	1923	84	30T	54ft 0in
SR (SECR)	S3554S	BSK	1924	42	33T	65ft 3in
BR (SR)	S1469S	TSO	1951	64	32T	67ft 1in
GN	2856	Non vestibule composite, lav brake	1898	34	22T	45ft 0in

Nos 358, 589 and 427 currently in the workshop

Industrial locomotives

Name	No	Builder	Type	Built
*Bellerophon**	—	Haydock Foundry (C)	0-6-0WT	1874
Sir Berkeley†	—	M/Wardle (1210)	0-6-0ST	1891
Lord Mayor	—	H/Clarke (402)	0-4-0ST	1893

*on loan to the Foxfield Railway for 10 years
†on 10 year loan to Middleton Railway

Internet addresses: *E-mail:* admin@vintagecarriagestrust.org
Web site: www.vintagecarriagestrust.org
Web site includes four databases:
over 5,600 preserved carriages, with over 5,100 images;
over 7,500 preserved wagons, with over 4,800 images;
over 60 horse-drawn, with over 20 images;
over 40 turntables, with over 30 images;
over 300 trams, with over 170 images;
Car Park: Yes. Also coach parking

162

at Ingrow station
Access by public transport:
Northern Rail through trains from Carlisle, Settle, Morecambe, Lancaster to Keighley (one mile). Fast and frequent Metro Train services from Bradford Forster Square, Leeds, Shipley, and Skipton to Keighley. Then either KWVR train to Ingrow West (adjacent) or buses 500, 502, 663, 664, 665, 696, 697 and 720 from Keighley bus station.
Buses: Keighley & District 500 from Hebden Bridge (daily). First Calderline 502 from Halifax (Sundays only). Keighley & District buses 696 and 697 from Bradford via Thornton and Denholme.
Tel: (0113) 245 7676 for bus and Metro Train information or log on to VCT web site for internet links to timetables and route map

On site facilities: Transport relics shop specialising in out of print magazines, second-hand railway books and models. Hot and cold drinks, ice cream and chocolate available. Toilets with full disabled access. A determined effort has been made to provide a museum which will interest the casual visitor who is not knowledgeable about railways
Public opening:
Daily from 11.00, last admission 16.00, openings outside these times can be arranged for groups.
Closed 25 December
Facilities for disabled: The museum building is level, with easy access for wheelchair users. A stairlift has been provided to allow wheelchair users to view carriage interiors, and enter guards' brake areas, though naturally wheelchairs are too wide to enter individual

passenger compartments. Toilets with full access for wheelchair users. Braille leaflet, guidebook and audio tape for loan during visit. Wheelchair available for loan.
  Winner of the 1998 Adapt Museum Award for best practice in access for disabled and older people. Runners up for the 1998 Yorkshire Electricity/Yorkshire & Humberside Museums Council Access Awards. Highly commended in the 1999 White Rose Tourism For All Awards
Special notes: Free admission to holders of Worth Valley Railway 'Day Rover' tickets — otherwise small admission charge
Membership details: Membership Secretary, c/o above address
Marketing names: Vintage Carriages Trust or VCT

Timetable Service — Volks Electric Railway — East Sussex

Member: HRA
In 1883 Magnus Volk opened an electric-powered railway along the seafront at Brighton. It was the first 'proper' electric railway in Britain. Today it holds the deserved position of being the oldest remaining operating electric railway in the world
Manager: Stuart Strong
Assistant Manager: Barry Fuller
Headquarters: Quality of Life & Green Spaces, Brighton & Hove City Council, Kings House, Grand Avenue, Hove BN3 2LS
Office/Works: 285 Madeira Drive, Brighton BN2 1EN
Telephone:
01273 292718 (railway)
Internet addresses: *E-mail:* volksrailway@brighton-hove.gov.uk
Web site: www.brighton-hove.gov.uk
Main stations: Aquarium, Black Rock (5min walk from Marina)

Motor cars

Nos	Type	Seats	Body	Built
3, 4	Semi-opens	40	—	1892
5	Winter car		—	1930
6, 7, 8	Semi-opens	40	—	1901
9	Open	40	—	1910
10	Open	40	—	1926

Other public stations: Peter Pan's Playground
Car parks: Along the Promenade and city centre car parks
Access by public transport:
By rail: main line services to Brighton
Bus services: No 7 from station to Marina (every 7min) then short walk to Black Rock station
Depot: Peter Pan's Playground
Length of line: Approx 1 mile, 2ft 8.5in gauge
Period of public operations:
Easter to mid-September
Weekdays (10.00-17.00)
Weekends and Bank Holidays (10.00-18.00)

Note: There are also late running evenings subject to weather; these are advertised locally. All days subject to weather conditions
Facilities for disabled: Disabled toilets in Black Rock station building and 50yd from Aquarium. Disabled access to stations and trains

Volks Electric Railway Association
Hon Chairman: Ian Gledhill
Editor — *Volks News*: Derek Smith
Internet address: *Web site:* www.volkselectricrailway.co.uk

Waltham Abbey Royal Gunpowder Mills

Member: HRA, TT, ERIH

The Royal Gunpowder Mills at Waltham Abbey are set in 175 acres of natural and peaceful parkland with 21 buildings of major historical importance.

Recipient of Transport Trust 'Red Wheel' in 2009

Location: Royal Gunpowder Mills, Beaulieu Drive, Waltham Abbey, Essex EN9 1JY

Telephone: 01992 707370

Fax: 01992 707372

Internet addresses: *E-mail:* info@royalgunpowdermills.com

Web site: www.royalgunpowdermills.com

OS reference: TL 387011

Car parking: Free on site

Cycle parking: Cycle shed is available to secure bicycles

Access by car: Just off Jct 26 on M25, follow A121 towards Waltham Abbey, cross traffic lights into Beaulieu Drive

Access by public transport: *By rail:* trains from London Liverpool Street and Tottenham Hale Underground station to Waltham Cross, then 25min walk or short bus ride. Served by local buses (5min walk)

On site facilities: Toilets, café, baby changing. Bench-style seats and picnic tables around the site

Depots: On western boundary

Length of line: 2ft 6in gauge under construction, 1ft 6in gauge to follow

Industrial locomotives

Name	No	Builder	Type	Built
—	—*	B/Drewry (3755)	4wDH	1981
—	—*	Hunslet (8828)	0-4-0DH	1988
—	—*	Ruhrthaler (3920)	0-4-0DH	1969
—	—†	G/Batley (6099)	2w-2DE	1964
Budleigh	—§	R/Hornsby (235624)	4wDM	1945
Carnegie	—§	Hunslet (4524)	0-4-0+0-4-0DM	1954
Woolwich	—§	Avonside (1748)	0-4-0T	1916

*2ft 6in gauge

†3ft 0in gauge

§1ft 6 in gauge

Woolwich is on loan to the Crossness Engines Trust

Rolling stock

Selection of wagons of the above gauges

Other exhibits

Boiler from *Mars* (Vulcan 1160 of 1885, 1ft 6in gauge) from Museum of Army Transport.

Cast iron tramway plates, c1880, from Woolwich Arsenal (1ft 6in gauge)

Period of public operation: Weekends and Bank Holidays 31 March to 5 November; daily throughout local school holidays. 11.00-17.00, last entry 15.30. It is suggested that 3-4 hours are allowed for the visit. Comfortable walking shoes recommended

Special events: Demonstration freight trains run most weekends in season

Special facilities: Guided group visits available on Tuesdays and Wednesdays by appointment, minimum group size applies (not January and February). Lecture Theatre and Saltpetre House available for meetings

Facilities for disabled: A Land Train can accommodate wheelchairs (please check availability on arrival). Only guide and assistant dogs will be allowed on site, and must remain harnessed during visit

Membership details: Volunteers very welcome, please ring Volunteer Manager on 01992 707340

Weardale Railway

Member: HRA

The line was originally built by the Stockton & Darlington Railway in 1847 to transport limestone to the ironworks of Teesside, and by 1895 had been extended to its final terminus of Wearhead. Although the passenger service was withdrawn in 1953, the line was retained for freight use transporting bulk cement from the Blue Circle works at Eastgate. This use also ceased in 1993, so the line was mothballed and threatened with lifting. 1993 saw the formation of the Weardale Railway with services re-commencing in 2004. Today the railway is owned by an American railway company, Iowa Pacific, using a newly formed company — British American Railway Services (BARS). The Weardale Railway company is made up of BARS 75% holding, Weardale Railway Trust 12.5% and Durham County Council 12.5%

General Manager: David Million

Headquarters: Weardale Railways CIC, Stanhope Station, Station Road, Stanhope, Bishop Auckland, Co Durham DL13 2YS

Telephone: 01388 526203

Internet addresses: *E-mail:* info@weardale-railway.org.uk

Web site: www.weardale-railway.org.uk

Main stations: Wolsingham, Stanhope and Bishop Auckland West

Other public stations: Frosterley

Car park: Limited parking at each station

Access by public transport: Buses from Crook daily. Main line station at Bishop Auckland, a short walk from Bishop Auckland West

Refreshment facilities: Stanhope (the Whistle Stop Buffet) in station building with light refreshments

Souvenir shop: Stanhope (in station building)

Depot: Wolsingham (no public access)

Length of line: Present length is 16 miles Bishop Auckland West to Stanhope. 18.5 miles when fully opened, Bishop Auckland to Eastgate.

Period of public operation: Heritage service on special event days and selected weekdays / weekends. For full details telephone

Locomotives and multiple-units

Name	No	Origin	Class	Type	Built
—	08870	BR	08	0-6-0DE	1960
—	08588	BR	08	0-6-0DE	1959
Hydra	31468	BR	31	A1A-A1A	1962
—	55503	BR	141	DMS	1984
—	55510	BR	141	DMS	1984
—	55523	BR	141	DMSL	1984

Industrial locomotives

Name	No	Builder	Type	Built
(40)	7765	RSH (7765)	0-6-0T	1954
Herman	653*	E/Electric	6wDE	1956

*former Netherlands Railway Class 600 locomotive

Owner
55503, 55513 on loan from Llangollen Railway

or visit web site as above

Special events: Mother's Day, Father's Day, Commercial Vehicle Rallies, Classic Car Rallies, War theme weekend, Halloween Specials, Santa Specials and Mince Pie specials. See timetable/leaflet

for full details

Membership details: Mr Frank Holmes, Membership Secretary, Weardale Railway Trust, at above address. Tel: 01388 526203

Membership journal: *Between the Lines* — quarterly

Timetable Service	**Wells & Walsingham Light Railway**	Norfolk

Member: HRA, TT

One man's railway, the life and love of retired naval commander Roy Francis, this delightful line which is totally uncommercialised runs along the old Wells branch to Walsingham where the old station has been transformed into a Russian Orthodox Church by the addition of an onion-shaped dome to its roof. A must if you find yourself nearby

Location: On A149, Stiffkey Road, Wells next the Sea, Norfolk

General Manager: Lt-Cdr R. W. Francis

Operating organisation: Wells & Walsingham Light Railway, Wells next the Sea, Norfolk NR23 1GB

SatNav postcode: NR23 1GB

Enquiries: 01328 711630

Internet address: *Web site:* www.wellswalsinghamrailway.co.uk

Car park: Yes

Access by public transport: Eastern Counties and Coast Hopper buses

Locomotive — 10.25in gauge

Name	No	Builder	Type	Built
Norfolk Heroine		R. Soleby/J. Wicket	2-6-0+0-6-2	2010
Norfolk Hero	3	N. Simkins	2-6-0+0-6-2	1986
Weasel	2	A. Keef	6wDH S/O	1986
Norfolk Harvester	—	A. Mills	4w-4wDH	1993

On site facilities: Souvenir shop, toilets and tea shop

Length of line: 4 miles, 10.25in gauge

Public opening: Daily Good Friday to the end of October

Special notes: Journey may be commenced at either end. Believed to be the world's longest 10.25in gauge line. Built on the old Wells & Fakenham Railway trackbed. Old Swainsthorpe signalbox on site at Wells. Motive power is provided by a Garratt and a tram locomotive. A second Garratt will be in service for the 2011 season.

Life passes in the form of a gilt-edged enamel medallion now

available, please enquire for details

Facilities for disabled: Disabled can be seated in normal carriages and wheelchairs carried in luggage van. Occupied wheelchairs cannot be carried due to limitations of track gauge

Membership details: Membership Secretary, Wells & Walsingham Light Railway Support Group, c/o above address

Membership journal: Newsletter — quarterly

Wensleydale Railway

Member: HRA

The Wensleydale Railway Association was formed in 1990 with a view to restoring the route from Northallerton to Garsdale. In 2000 agreement was reached to transfer the remaining 22 miles of line from Northallerton to Redmire to Wensleydale Railway plc. In 2003 services started between Leeming Bar and Redmire. Medium-term plans are to extend eastwards to Northallerton and in the west from Redmire and then on towards Aysgarth. The ultimate aim is to restore the entire route from Northallerton to Garsdale

Membership: HRA

Contact address:
Wensleydale Railway plc, Leeming Bar Station, Leases Road, Leeming Bar, Northallerton DL7 9AR

Ticketline: 08454 505474

Fax: 01677 427029

Internet addresses: *E-mail:* admin@wensleydalerailway.com *Web site:* www.wensleydalerailway.com

Main stations: Leeming Bar and Leyburn

Other stations: Bedale, Finghall and Redmire

Car Parking: On site

SatNav postcode: DL7 9AR

Access by public transport: Yes

Refreshment facilities: Leeming Bar and Leyburn

Souvenir shops: Leeming Bar and Leyburn

Depots: Leeming Bar

Length of line: 22 miles (18 additional miles to rebuild)

Passenger trains: Normally DMU or diesel locomotive hauled. Steam (provisional) in August and/or September

Locomotives and multiple-units

Name	No	Origin	Class	Type	Built
Western Waggoner	D2114	BR	03	0-6-0DM	1961
—	D9516	BR	14	0-6-0DH	1964
—	20020	BR	20	Bo-Bo	1959
—	20166	BR	20	Bo-Bo	1960
—	25313	BR	25	Bo-Bo	1966
—	47540	BR	47	Co-Co	1964
—	47703	BR	47	Co-Co	1966
Poseidon	47715	BR	47	Co-Co	1966
—	51210	BR	101	DMBS	1958
—	51247	BR	101	DMBS	1958
—	53746	BR	101	DMC	1957
—	59500	BR	117	TSL	1959
—	59509	BR	117	TSL	1959
—	51813	BRCW	110	DMBC	1961
—	51842	BRCW	110	DMCL	1961
—	59701	BRCW	110	TSL	1961

Industrial locomotives

Name	No	Builder	Type	Built
Wensley	—	R/Hornsby (476141)	4wDM	1963

Owners

Class 101 and 117 Wensleydale Railway plc
Class 110 Allan Schofield
R/Hornsby the Wensleydale Railway Association
D2144 the UK Government
20166, 47703 the Harry Needle Railroad Co
47715 and 25313 Wensleydale Railway Association volunteers
20020 on loan from Bo'ness & Kinneil Railway

Period of public operation: Weekends and Bank Holidays after 1 March; daily June to September. Also Santa Specials. See web site or phone 08454 505474 for more information

Special events: Forties weekend and diesel gala. See web site for details

Facilities for disabled: Ramp to facilitate access to trains. All platforms are wheelchair-friendly. Disabled toilets at Leeming and Leyburn

Membership details: Wensleydale Railway Association, c/o above address

Membership journal: *Relay* – 3 per year.

Special notes: Very helpful tourist information centre at Leyburn – tel 01969 623069 – will deal with a wide range of enquiries including Wensleydale Railway matters

West Lancashire Light Railway

Member: HRA

The WLLR is located in the village of Hesketh Bank, midway between Preston and Southport. Built by enthusiasts in 1967 in an endeavour to conserve some of the mainly industrial equipment that was fast disappearing. The railway serves as a working museum for a variety of historic locomotives and other railway equipment from industrial sites from Britain and overseas

Location: Alty's Brickworks, Station Road, Hesketh Bank, Nr Preston, Lancashire PR4 6SP

166

England

OS reference: SD 448229
Operating society/organisation:
The West Lancashire Light Railway
Trust, Secretary, 8 Croft Avenue,
Orrell, Wigan, Lancs WN5 8TW
Telephone: (01772) 815881
Railway (24hr) or (01695) 622654
Secretary (evenings)
Internet addresses:
E-mail: secretary@westlancs.org
Web site: www.westlancs.org
Car parks: On site
Access by public transport: Main
line rail to Preston or Southport.
Bus route — service 2, between
Preston and Southport
On site facilities: Gift shop, light
refreshments, picnic tables, 2ft-
gauge line
Public opening: Steam trains
operate Sundays 1 April to last
Sunday in October inclusive.
Also: 6, 9 April, 7 May, 4/5 June,
27 August.
Opening times 11.30-16.30
Special events: Friendly Engines
Day — 1 April; Teddy Bears'
Outing — 6 May; Summer Gala
Weekend — 11/12 August; Autumn
Steam Gala — 7 October;
Halloween Specials — 27 October;
BBC Children-in-Need —
11 November; Santa Specials —
15/16, 22/23 December
Membership details: The Hon
Secretary, WLLR, Station Road,
Hesketh Bank, Nr Preston,
Lancashire PR4 6SP

Industrial locomotives — 2ft gauge

Name	No	Builder	Type	Built
Clwyd	1	R/Hornsby (264251)	4wDM	1951
Tawd	2	R/Hornsby (222074)	4wDM	1943
Irish Mail	3	Hunslet (823)	0-4-0ST	1903
Bradfield	4	Hibberd (1777)	4wPM	1931
—	5	R/Hornsby (200478)	4wDM	1940
—	7	M/Rail (8992)	4wDM	1946
Pathfinder	8	H/Hunslet (4480)	4wDM	1953
Joffre	9	K/Stuart (2405)	0-6-0T	1915
—	10	Hibberd (2555)	4wDM	1946
—	11	M/Rail (5906)	4wDM	1934
—	16	R/Hornsby (202036)	4wDM	1941
—	19	Lister (10805)	4wPM	1939
—	20	Baguley (3002)	4wPM	1937
—	21	H/Hunslet (1963)	4wDM	1939
—	25	R/Hornsby (297054)	4wDM	1950
Mill Reef	27	M/Rail (7371)	4wDM	1939
—	30	M/Rail (11258)	4wDM	1964
—	32	M/Rail (11246)	4wDM	1963
Montalban	34	O&K (6641)	0-4-0WT	1913
Utrillas	35	O&K (2378)	0-4-0WT	1907
—	36	R/Hornsby (339105)	4wDM	1953
—	38	Hudswell (D750)	0-4-0DM	1949
—	39	Hibberd (3916)	4wDM	1959
—	40	R/Hornsby (381705)	4wDM	1959
—	41	Lister (29890)	4wPM	1946
—	43	Greenbat (1840)	4wBE	1942
Welsh Pony	44	Wingrove (640)	4wWE	1926
—	45	Chrzanow (3506)	0-6-0T+WT	1957
—	47	Henschel (14676)	0-8-0T	1917
—	48	Fowler (15513)	0-4-2T	1920
Samson	49	Hibberd (1887)	4wDM	1934

Stock
Toastrack coach built 1986 by WLLR
Semi-open coach built 1993 by WLLR
Brake van built 1987 by WLLR
Large collection of goods rolling stock

Timetable Service — West Somerset Railway — Somerset

Member: HRA, TT
2012 will see the 150th Anniversary
of the opening of the original West
Somerset Railway between Norton
Fitzwarren Junction and Watchet.
Today's normal service trains run
for 20 miles between Bishops
Lydeard and Minehead, making it
Britain's longest standard gauge
heritage railway, superbly capturing
the secondary main line atmosphere
from the steam era. At Williton the
original Bristol & Exeter Railway
signalbox is still controlling trains
whilst at Blue Anchor the
signalman still controls the level
crossing gates in the traditional
manner with a large wheel in his
box. Places of interest along the
line include the ancient harbour
town of Watchet where the town
museum has displays relating to the
former West Somerset Mineral
Railway, Cleeve Abbey and Torre
Cider Farm at Washford and the
medieval village of Dunster with its
castle
General Manager: Paul Conibeare
Headquarters: West Somerset
Railway, The Railway Station,
Minehead, Somerset TA24 5BG
Telephone:
Minehead (01643) 704996
Internet addresses: *E-mail:*
info@west-somerset-railway.co.uk
Web sites:
www.west-somerset-railway.co.uk
**Main station with SatNav
postcode:**
Minehead — TA24 5BG
**Other public stations with SatNav
postcodes:**
Dunster — TA24 6PJ
Blue Anchor — TA24 6LB
Washford — TA23 0PP
Watchet — TA23 0BA
Doniford Halt — no parking
Williton — TA24 4RQ
Stogumber — TA4 3TR
Crowcombe Heathfield — TA4 4PA
Bishops Lydeard — TA4 3BX

OS reference:
Minehead SS 975463
Williton ST 085416
Bishops Lydeard ST 164290
Car parks: Free parking at
Bishops Lydeard, Crowcombe
Heathfield, Stogumber, Williton and
Dunster. Pay & display at Minehead
and Watchet. No parking at
Doniford Halt
Access by public transport: First
service 28 runs from Taunton bus
station and Taunton railway station
to Bishops Lydeard station on
operating days. Timetable booklets
are available from Somerset County
Council 0845 345 9155
Refreshment facilities: Minehead,
Bishops Lydeard (limited opening).
Dining Trains from Bishops
Lydeard (01823 433856). Please
contact for dates, reservations
essential.
Buffet car on most steam trains
Souvenir shops: Large shops at
Bishops Lydeard (01823 432125)
and Minehead (01643 700387).
Sales counters at other stations
except Doniford Halt. 'Readers
Halt' second-hand stall at Minehead
Museum: Somerset & Dorset
Railway Museum Trust, Washford
(contact 01984 640869 for opening
times). GWR Museum at Blue
Anchor (open Sundays and Bank
Holidays during main WSR
operating season plus gala events).
Gauge Museum at Bishops Lydeard
(open daily). Diesel Heritage
Visitor Centre open Saturdays May-
September, plus during gala events
Depots: Bishops Lydeard, Williton
(Diesel & Electric Preservation
Group and West Somerset
Restoration), Washford (Somerset
& Dorset Railway Trust), Minehead
Length of line: 20 miles
Passenger trains: Steam and diesel
trains to Bishops Lydeard
Period of public operation: 3/4,
10/11, 16-18, 21-25, 27-29, 31
March; daily in April EXCEPT 16,
20, 23, 27; daily in May EXCEPT
11, 14; daily 1 June to 31 October
EXCEPT 12, 15, 19, 22, 26
October; 1-4 November; 1/2, 7/8,
10-12, 15/16, 22-24, 27-31
December; 1/2 January 2013
Main special events: Spring Steam
Gala — 17/18, 22-25 March
(advance booking strongly
recommended); Mixed Traffic
Weekend — 15-17 June (advance
booking recommended); Day out

Locomotives and multiple-units

Name	No	Origin	Class	Type	Built
—	53808	S&DJR	7F	2-8-0	1925
—	2874*	GWR	2800	2-8-0	1918
—	3845*	GWR	2884	2-8-0	1942
—	3850	GWR	2884	2-8-0	1942
—	4160	GWR	5101	2-6-2T	1948
—	4561†	GWR	4500	2-6-2T	1924
—	5542†	GWR	4575	2-6-2T	1928
Raveningham Hall	6960±	GWR	6959	4-6-0	1944
Dinmore Manor	7820	GWR	'Manor'	4-6-0	1950
Ditcheat Manor	7821	GWR	'Manor'	4-6-0	1950
Odney Manor§	7828	GWR	'Manor'	4-6-0	1950
—	9351	GWR	9351	2-6-0	2004
Braunton	34046	SR	WC	4-6-2	1946
—	D2133	BR	03	0-6-0DM	1959
—	D2271	BR	04	0-6-0DM	1952
—	D9518	BR	14	0-6-0DH	1964
—	D9526	BR	14	0-6-0DH	1964
—	D6566	BR	33	Bo-Bo	1961
—	33057	BR	33	Bo-Bo	1961
—	D7017	BR	35	B-B	1962
—	D7018	BR	35	B-B	1962
North Star	D1661	BR	47	Co-Co	1965
Western Campaigner	D1010	BR	52	C-C	1962
—	51663	BR	115	DMBS	1960
—	51859	BR	115	DMBS	1960
—	51880	BR	115	DMBS	1960
—	51887	BR	115	DMBS	1960
—	59506	BR	117	TC	1960
—	59678	BR	115	TC	1960

Note: 9351 rebuilt from '5151' class 2-6-2T No 5193
*stored off-site until restoration commences
†undergoing overhaul, 4561 at Williton, 5542 at South Devon Railway
§currently carries the name *Norton Manor 40 Commando*
±on loan for the 2012 season
No 7821 is on display at STEAM in Swindon

Industrial locomotives

Name	No	Builder	Type	Built
Kilmersdon	—	Peckett (1788)	0-4-0ST	1929
—	24	Ruston (210479)	4wDM	1941
—	—	Ruston (183062)	4wDM	1937
—	16	Sentinel (10175)	0-6-0DH	1964

Stock

23 ex-BR Mk 1 coaches; 2 ex-BR Restaurant cars; 1 ex-BR Sleeping car;
3 ex-S&DJR 6-wheel coaches, 7 ex-GWR camping coaches*; 1 ex-GWR
Sleeping coach; 1 ex-GWR 5-ton hand crane; more than 40 freight vehicles.
*The first coach restored as part of the West Somerset Steam Railway
Trust's Heritage Carriages Project, Hawksworth 6705 should enter service
in 2012. Details from Williton Station, Somerset TA4 4RQ

Owners

53808, *Kilmersdon* the Somerset & Dorset Museum Trust
D1010, D7017, D7018 and D9526 the Diesel and Electric Preservation
Group
5542 the 5542 Ltd
2874, 3845, 3850 and 7820 the Dinmore Manor Locomotive Ltd
4160 the 4160 Ltd
7828, 9351 and D2271 the WSR plc

with Thomas — 7/8 July; Toy and Collectors' Fair at Minehead station — 29 July; Steam Fayre & Vintage Rally at Bishops Lydeard — 4/5 August; Late Summer Weekend — 1/2 September; CAMRA Real Ale Festival at Minehead station — 8/9 September; Autumn Steam Gala — 4-7 October (advance booking strongly recommended); Dunster by Candlelight — 7/8 December (advance booking essential); Carol Trains — 10-12 December (advance booking essential); Santa Specials — 8/9, 15/16, 22-24 December (advance booking essential); Winter Steam Festival — 28/29 December
Other special events: Details on application
Facilities for disabled: Trains have limited accommodation for passengers in wheelchairs. There is level or ramped access to all stations except Doniford, and RADAR key access toilets at Bishops Lydeard and Minehead. Advance booking essential for groups
Special facilities: Conference room in Gauge Museum at Bishops Lydeard (contact 01823 433856); Steam and diesel footplate experience courses (01643 700398). Yarn Market Hotel in Dunster will open its restaurant especially for pre-booked WSR groups at lunchtime (01643 821425)
Membership details: West Somerset Railway Association, The Railway Station, Bishops Lydeard, Taunton TA4 3BX.
Tel: 01823 433856

Membership journal: *WSR Journal* — quarterly
Other information: Vintage bus links run between Dunster station and Dunster village on Bank Holiday Sundays and Mondays and also for Dunster Country Fair and Dunster Show. WSR ticket holders can obtain discounted admission to Dunster Castle. 'Dunster Castle Express' and 'Hestercombe Gardens Express' packages operate on Wednesdays mid-April to end of October. 'Exmoor Mystery Trips', 'Mineral Line Explorer', 'Murder Mystery', Fish and Chip and Cream Tea and other special trains operate on selected dates. Details and online bookings at www.west-somerset-railway.co.uk or ring 01643 704996

Whitwell & Reepham Station

Steam Centre | Norfolk

The station was opened at the end of February 2009, the 50th anniversary of the closure of the line to passenger services on the former Midland & Great Northern Joint Railway. Open mostly at weekends and 'In Steam' on the first Sunday of every month; other events please see web site
Location: Whitwell Road, Reepham, Norfolk NR10 4GA
SatNav postcode: NR10 4GA
Operating society/organisation: The Whitwell & Reepham Railway Preservation Society Ltd
Contact: Mike Urry
Telephone: (01603) 871694
Fax: (01603) 875101
Internet addresses:
E-mail: mike@whitwellstation.com
Web site: www.whitwellstation.com

Multiple-units

Name	No	Origin	Class	Type	Built
—	70527	BR	4CEP	TS	1960

Industrial locomotives

Name	No	Builder	Type	Built
Georgie	7	B/Drewry (3733)	4wDH	1977
Annie	—	Barclay (945)	0-4-0ST	1904

Stock
2 BR Mk 1 coaches, bogie brake and BR box van, brake van, London Underground tube car

On site facilities: Car park, shop, museum and café
Access by public transport: There is no access to the site by public transport
Length of line: 1,800ft
Public opening: Mostly at weekends and 'In Steam' on the first Sunday of every month
Membership details: Membership Secretary, c/o above address
Membership journal: Quarterly

Winchcombe Railway Museum

Museum | Glos

One mile from Winchcombe station on the Gloucestershire Warwickshire railway, the diverse collection includes signalling equipment, lineside fixtures, horse-drawn road vehicles, tickets, lamps, etc. Indoor and outdoor displays set in half an acre of traditional Victorian Cotswold garden. Visitors are encouraged to touch and operate exhibits
Location: 23 Gloucester Street, Winchcombe, Gloucestershire
OS reference: SP 023283
Operating society/organisation: Winchcombe Railway Museum Association, 23 Gloucester Street, Winchcombe, Gloucestershire

Telephone: Winchcombe (01242) 609305
Internet address: *E-mail:* timpetchey@btconnect.com
Car park: On street at entrance
Access by public transport: Bus service from Cheltenham operated by Castleways Ltd
On site facilities: Relics and souvenir shop
Public opening: Easter to end September 2012. Wednesdays, Thursdays, Fridays, weekends and Bank Holiday Mondays — 13.30-17.00; daily throughout school holiday periods, 13.30-17.00
Facilities for disabled: Access to most parts except toilets
Special notes: Many visitor-operated exhibits, picnic area

Attraction	Windmill Farm Railway	Lancashire

The line was set up in 1997 by Austin Moss as a place to store and operate the historic engines and rolling stock he had collected. Of particular interest is the collection of ex-Fairbourne Railway locomotives and rolling stock; these include *Katie* and *Whippet Quick*.
Location: Situated within the grounds of Windmill Animal Farm
Headquarters: Windmill Animal Farm, Red Cat Lane, Burscough, L40 1UQ
Contact: Austin Moss
Telephone: Farm 01704 892282; Austin Moss 07971 221343;
Internet address: *Web site:* www.windmillfarmrailway.co.uk
Main station: At farm
Other station: Lakeview, 1/2 mile away
Car parking: On site
Access by public transport: None
On site facilities: Farm café, shop
Depots: At farm site
Length of line: 1/2 mile each way (1 mile return) 15in gauge
Period of public operation: Weekends from February half term

Locomotives — 15in gauge

Name	No	Builder	Type	Built
Red Dragon	—	B/Lowke	4-4-2	1909
Prince Charles	—	Barlow	4-6-2	1950
Katie	—	Guest	2-4-2	1953
Siân	—	Guest	2-4-2	1963
Blue Pacific	4	Guinness	4-6-0VB s/o	1935
Whippet Quick	–	Lister	4w-4DM	1935
Gwril	–	Lister	4wDM	1943
Princess Anne	—	Barlow	4-6w-2DE s/o	1948
Duke of Edinburgh	—	Barlow	4-6-2DH s/o	1950
Black Smoke	—	Smith	2-4-2PM	c1956
Konigswinter	—	Severn-Lamb	2-8-0DH	1972
Goram	—	Hayne/Minirail	2-2w-4BE	1977
—	362	Severn-Lamb	2-8-0DH s/o	1978
—	14	Walker	2w-2PM	1985
City Of London	2870	Volante	4-6-0DH s/o	1987
'The Bar Stool'	—	Moss	2w-2PM	1989
—	5407	Moss	4-6-0BE	2001

until Christmas. Daily during school holidays and the summer. Trains every 30min from 11.00 until 16.30
Special events: None planned but see web site
Facilities for disabled: Accessibility for wheelchairs around farm facilities etc, prior warning on railway
Membership details: No membership as such, just volunteer. Contact Austin Moss for details
Fares: In addition to farm entry fee.

Timetable Service	Wirral Transport Museum	Merseyside

The museum and tramway are currently owned by Wirral Borough Council and run by employees assisted by volunteers. The tramway licence is also held by the council as are two Hong Kong-built 4-wheel trams. The museum houses several locally rebuilt trams owned by the Merseyside Tramway Preservation Society which are used in turn with the Hong Kong trams. The museum also contains numerous local buses, cars, lorries, motorbikes, etc and a 1930s garage scene
Location/Headquarters: Wirral Transport Museum, 1 Taylor Street, Birkenhead, Wirral CH41 1BG
Telephone: 0151 647 2128
Fax: As above, but must ring first
Car parking: Pay & display at Woodside Ferry, Canning Road, Taylor Street and George Street, limited free parking in local roads
Access by public transport:
By rail —Merseyrail stations at Hamilton Square (0.25 miles from Woodside Ferry) and Conway Park (0.5 miles from museum) with services from Liverpool Lime Street and Chester.
By bus — bus stations at Woodside Ferry (25 metres) and Birkenhead town centre (half mile)
On site facilities: Merseyside Tramway Preservation Society stall

England

(open certain days when trams are operating). Woodside Ferry Terminal has a gift shop, café and toilets

Depots: Wirral Transport Museum/depot across Old Colonial office block car park

Length of line: 0.7 mile (c1km) of standard gauge. Woodside Ferry Terminal via Pacific Road to Old Colonial tramstop

Refreshments: None on site, but several pubs and cafés around Chester Street and Hamilton Square

Period of public operation: Most weekends, Wednesday to Sunday during school holidays, all Bank Holidays. Half-hour service operates from both ends — 13.00 then every half-hour, last return trip from Woodside 16.00

Special events: Annual Bus & Tram Show — 1st Sunday in October; Merseyside Model

Trams

No	Trucks	Builder (notes)	Date
69		Hong Kong	1992
70		Hong Kong	1992
605*	E/Electric ±	E/Electric	1934
626*	EMB	Brush (on loan)	1937
20†	4-wheel	—	1901
2+	4-wheel	—	1903
78§	4-wheel	—	1920
762±	E/Electric	—	1931
73±	4-wheel	horse tram	
7±	4-wheel	horse tram (in store)	1875

*ex-Blackpool & Fleetwood Tramway
†ex-Birkenhead
§ex-Wallasey
±ex-Liverpool Corporation
+ex-Warrington

Owner
605 the Lancastrian Transport Trust

Railway Show — last weekend in October

Facilities for disabled: Access to both levels in museum. Audio visual display for those unable to travel on the trams. No toilet facilities in museum, but places with toilets close to tramway

---

Railway Centre — Yeovil Railway Centre — Somerset

Member: HRA

The Yeovil Railway Centre is operated by the South West Main Line Steam Co and is adjacent to the former London & South Western Railway main line at Yeovil Junction. It features the original British Railways turntable

Location: Adjacent to the main line at Yeovil Junction on the London (Waterloo)-Salisbury-Exeter line

Chaiman: Paul Gould

Contact address: South West Main Line Steam Co (Yeovil Railway Centre), Yeovil Junction Station, Stoford, Nr Yeovil, Somerset BA22 9UU

Telephone: 01935 410420

Fax: 01935 478373

Internet address: *Web site:* www.yeovilrailway.free servers.com

Car park: On site. Follow signs to Yeovil Junction from Yeovil town centre or from A35 Dorchester-Yeovil road

Access by public transport: South West Trains to Yeovil Junction or bus from Yeovil bus station (Monday-Saturday)

Locomotive

Name	No	Origin	Class	Type	Built
Fearless	50050	BR	50	Co-Co	1967

Industrial locomotive

Name	No	Builder	Type	Built
Lord Fisher*	1398	Barclay (1398)	0-4-0ST	1915
Pectin	—	Peckett (1579)	0-4-0ST	1921
—	—	Fowler (22900)	0-4-0DM	1941
Cockney Rebel	—	Fowler (4000007)	0-4-0DM	1947
Yeo	DS1174	R/Hornsby (458959)	4wDM	1961

*expected to enter service during 2012

Locomotive notes: Main line locomotives occasionally present for servicing or stabling between railtours

Rolling stock: Selection of freight wagons

Owner
50050 the D400 Fund (www.d400fund.org.uk)

On site facilities: Exhibition of relics and photographs in the historic transfer shed (dating from 1864) and shop. Light refreshments when brake van rides are operating

Length of line: 500 metres

Opening times: Shop open Sunday mornings throughout the year (except Christmas/New Year). Train Days run from March to October (see web site or telephone for dates and times). Brake van rides and turntable demonstrations feature. Also open on days when main line steam is being serviced (telephone or see web site for details) for Santa

England

Specials in December and special events

Special facilities: Transfer shed available for wedding receptions, parties, shows, etc (train hire can be arranged)

Disabled access: To site, but no wheelchair access (at present) to brake van rides

Membership details: Membership

Secretary, Yeovil Railway Centre, Yeovil Junction, Stoford, Somerset BA22 9UU

Membership journal: *The Turntable*, three times a year

Mardy Monster, on loan from Elsecar, propels a single DMU driving coach in use as passenger accommodation on the Pontypool& Blaenarvon Railway. *Alistair Grieve*

All heritage railways require some sort of covered accommodation, be it for restoration or storage. This was the scene at the Nene Valley Railway's Wansford depot on 16 April 2011 with LMS No 44422 in view. *Phil Barnes*

The Sittingbourne & Kemsley Light Railway, built to carry paper and associated materials, will once again operate over the unique reinforced concrete viaduct at Milton Regis for the first time since the line's forced closure in 2008. *S&KLR*

From paper to sand as the Leighton Buzzard Railway was used to extract the material from the pits around the town. The LBR was host to a 'coffee pot festival' during 2011. *Taffy*, a privately-owned vertical-boilered locomotive is seen here with a couple of hopper wagons alongside a working excavator. *Phil Barnes*

Built by Alan Keef in 2008 *Lydia* is one of the younger steam locomotives to feature in *Railways Restored*, it is seen in action on the 15in gauge Perrygrove Railway in Gloucestershire. Although not shown here the line's rolling stock includes a carriage built by Sir Arthur Heywood for the Duke of Westminster's private Eaton Hall Railway in 1904. *PR*

Again of 15in gauge, though this time dating from 1933, this is No 1 *Sutton Belle*. Built for the Sutton Park Miniature Railway it was stored for several decades following closure of the line until acquisition by the Cleethorpes Coast Light Railway saw its return to service. *Phil Barnes*

The best way to see a steel works in action would be to take trip courtesy of the Appleby Frodingham RPS around the Tata steelworks at Scunthorpe. Here the AFPRS's 1916-built Peckett is at the head of a tour train at Frodingham station

A busy time at Yeovil Railway Centre on 16 July 2011 as resident Peckett *Pectin* takes on coal, 'Merchant Navy' No 35028 *Clan Line* is being attached to the 'Blackmoor Vale Express' and 'Battle of Britain' class No 34067 *Tangmere* is stabled between excursions. *YRC*

Whilst to the unwary the above image might look like a normal passenger carriage, it is actually a steam railmotor. The boiler and engine parts were built new and installed in an original body that had been converted to locomotive haulage by the Great Western Railway many decades ago. Having proved the concept that a 'stand alone' item of rolling stock could provide an economical service on lightly used lines the GWR then built some diesel-mechanical railcars. Both these views were taken at the Didcot Railway Centre during the Steam Railmotor's launch event on 28 May 2011. *Both Phil Barnes*

With British Railway's need to reduce operating costs in the 1950s the diesel-mechanical muiltiple-unit (DMU) became a familiar sight over most of the country apart from the Southern Region where electric multiple-units held the fort. One of the Midland Railway's first generation DMUs is seen here in the company of a second generation prototype, RB004, and a visiting 'Hastings' line diesel-electric multiple-unit from Brighton. Several second generation vehicles are now in preservation with the Weardale Railway's Class 141 multiple-unit seen here. *Phil Barnes / WR*

Alford Valley Railway

The Alford Valley Railway operates from the restored station yard which once marked the terminus of the branch line linking the villages of upper Donside with Kintore Junction, thence to Aberdeen
Location: On A944, 25 miles west of Aberdeen, adjacent to Grampian Transport Museum
Headquarters: Alford Valley Railway Co Ltd, Alford Station, Alford, Aberdeenshire
Internet address: *Web site:* www.alfordvalleyrailway.org.uk
Main station: Alford
Car park: On site
Length of line: 3km, 2ft gauge
Museum: Grampian Transport Museum adjacent,
Curator: Mr M. Ward
Depot: Alford station
Period of public operation:

Industrial locomotives — 2ft gauge

Name	No	Builder	Type	Built
Hamewith	—	Lister (3198)	4wDM	c1930
—	—	A/Keef (63)	4wDM	2001
—	—	M/Rail (22129)	4wDM	1962
—	—	M/Rail (2221)	4wDM	1964
James Gordon	—	Keef (63)	0-4-0T (SO)	2001
Aberdeen Corporation Gas Works	3*	A/Barclay (1889)	0-4-0ST	1926

*standard gauge

Rolling stock

Two 24-seat coaches, 50-seat coach, 24-seat ex-Aberdeen tramcar, various wagons

Seasonal, please refer to web site. Season tickets and Weekly Family tickets available. Alford Heritage Centre is open daily (10.00-17.00)

Special events: As per web site. Santa Specials — 1/2, 8/9 December (weather permitting) please contact for details

---

Almond Valley Heritage Trust

Member: HRA
Part of a wide-ranging heritage centre containing a museum of Scotland's shale oil industry with award-winning children's exhibits, working watermill, farmsteading with traditional livestock, indoor play areas, countryside walks and farmhouse kitchen tea room.
Operating society/organisation: Almond Valley Heritage Centre, Millfield, Livingston Village, West Lothian EH54 7AR
OS reference: NT 034667
Telephone: 01506 414957
Fax: 01506 497771
Internet addresses: *E-mail:* info@almondvalley.co.uk
Web site: www.almondvalley.co.uk
Access by public transport: Main line trains to Livingston North (1 mile)
On site facilities: Children's exhibits, indoor play areas, tea room

Industrial locomotives – 2ft 6in gauge

Name	No	Builder	Type	Built
05/576	—	Barclay (557)	4wDH	1970
Oil Company No 2	—	Baldwin (20587)	4wWE	1902
—	20	Brook Victor (612)	4wBE	1972
—	38	Brook Victor (698)	4wBE	1972
—	42	Brook Victor (700)	4wBE	1972
—	—	Brook Victor (1143)	4wBE	1972
3585	13	Greenwood (1698)	4wBE	1940
ND3059	Yard No B10	Hunslet (2270)	0-4-0DM	1940
—	7330	Hunslet (7330)	4wDM	1973
—	—	Simplex (40SPF522)	4wDM	1981
—	—	B/Drewry (3752)	4wDM	1980

Note

Barclay 557 and Hunslet 2270 operate passenger services

Public opening: Daily (except 25/26 December, 1/2 January) 10.00-17.00.
Trains operate weekends from March-September, daily July and August and certain public holidays
Length of line: 500m 2ft 6in gauge

line from Livingston Mill to Almondhaugh stations, with plans to extend
Facilities for disabled: Full disabled access to site, but not to coaches

Bo'ness & Kinneil Railway

Member: HRA, TT, Registered Museum

Historic railway buildings, including the station and train shed, have been relocated from sites all over Scotland. In two purpose-built exhibition halls, the Scottish Railway Exhibition tells the story of the development of the railways in Scotland, and their impact on the people. The rich geology of the area, with its 300 million year old fossils, is explained during a conducted tour of the caverns of the former Birkhill Fireclay Mine.

Operating society/location: Scottish Railway Preservation Society, Bo'ness Station, Union Street, Bo'ness, West Lothian, EH51 9AQ

Access by public transport: Nearest ScotRail station — Linlithgow. Bus services from Linlithgow, Falkirk, Stirling

OS reference: NT 003817

Telephone: Train services & Events 01506 825855

Talking timetable: 01506 822298

Fax: 01506 828766

Internet addresses: *E-mail:* enquiries@srps.org.uk *Web site:* www.srps.org.uk

Main station: Bo'ness

Other station: Birkhill

Car parks: At Bo'ness and Birkhill (free)

Refreshment facilities: Extensive (unlicensed) buffet at Bo'ness. Picnic tables at both stations

Souvenir shop: Bo'ness

Depot: Bo'ness

Length of line: 3.5 miles

Period of public operation: 31 March to 28 October. For full details of operating dates please refer to the web site

Special events: Easter Egg Specials — 6-9 April; Day out with Thomas — 19/20 May; Father's Day Event — 17 June; Diesel Gala — 28/29 July; Day out with Thomas — 3-5 August; Day out with Thomas — 22/23 September; Steam & Scream Weekend — 27/28 October; Santa Specials — 1/2, 8/9, 15/16, 22/23 December; Hogmanay 'Black Bun' Specials —

Locomotives

Name	No	Origin	Class	Type	Built
	419	CR	439	0-4-4T	1908
Morayshire	246	LNER	D49	4-4-0	1928
Gordon Highlander	49	GNSR	F	4-4-0	1920
—	1000	MR	4	4-4-0	1902
—	42	NBR	Y9	0-4-0ST	1887
Maude	673†	NBR	J36	0-6-0	1891
—	80105	BR	4MT	2-6-4T	1955
—	D2774	BR	—	0-4-0DH	1960
—	08443 (D3558)	BR	08	0-6-0DE	1958
—	20020*	BR	20	Bo-Bo	1959
—	25235 (D7585)	BR	25	Bo-Bo	1965
—	26004 (D5303)	BR	26	B0-Bo	1958
—	26024 (D5323)	BR	26	Bo-Bo	1959
—	27001 (D5347)	BR	27	Bo-Bo	1961
—	27005 (D5351)	BR	27	Bo-Bo	1961
—	37025	BR	37	Co-Co	1961
—	37175	BR	37	Co-Co	1963
—	37403	BR	37	Co-Co	1965
—	47643	BR	47	Co-Co	1968
—	51017	BR	126	DMS	1959
—	51043	BR	126	DMS	1959
—	59404	BR	126	TC	1959
—	79443	BR	126	TRBF	1956
—	61503	BR	303	MBS	1959
—	75597	BR	303	DTSO	1959
—	75632	BR	303	BDTSO	1959

*on loan to Wensleydale Railway
†on loan to National Railway Museum

Industrial locomotives

Name	No	Builder	Type	Built
Clydesmill	3	Barclay (1937)	0-4-0ST	1928
Lord Ashfield	—	Barclay (1964)	0-4-0ST	1929
—	3	Barclay (2046)	0-4-0ST	1937
—	24	Barclay (2335)	0-6-0T	1953
FGF	—	Barclay (D552)	0-4-0DH	1969
Texaco	—†	Fowler (4210140)	0-4-0DM	1958
(Lord King)	—	H/Leslie (3640)	0-4-0ST	1926
—	19	Hunslet (3818)	0-6-0ST	1954
DS3	—	R/Hornsby (275883)	4wDM	1949
DS4	P6687	R/Hornsby (312984)	0-4-0DE	1951
(Ranald)	—	Sentinel (9627)	4wVBT	1957
—	970214	Wickham (6050)	2w-2PMR	c1951
—	—	Matisa (48626)	—	—
—	5	Hunslet (3837)	0-6-0ST	1955
—	(7)	Bagnall (2777)	0-6-0ST	1945
Borrowstounness	—*	Barclay (840)	0-4-0T	1899
—	—*	M/Rail (110U082)	4wDH	1970
—	—	Wickham (10482)	2w-2PMR	1970
—	(17)	Hunslet (2880)	0-6-0ST	1943
—	970213	Wickham (6049)	2w-2PMR	c1951
—	17†	Barclay (2296)	0-4-0ST	1952
Lady Victoria	3	Barclay (1458)	0-6-0ST	1916

30/31 December.
Special facilities: Private trains can be hired. Available for weddings
Facilities for disabled: Disabled access to platform and a specially adapted carriage for wheelchair users. Toilets at Bo'ness station. No facilities for wheelchairs at Birkhill Fireclay Mine
Special notes: Two large museum buildings: Fireclay Mine at Birkhill (both open same days as trains operate, except December); Scottish Railway Exhibition (open daily 2 April to 30 September)

Name	No	Builder	Type	Built
The Wemyss Coal Co Ltd	20	Barclay (2068)	0-6-0T	1939
—	(6)	Barclay (2127)	0-4-0CT	1942
No 1	—	Barclay (343)	0-6-0DM	1941
City of Aberdeen	—**	B/Hawthorn (912)	0-4-0ST	1887
F82 (Fairfield)	—	E/Electric (1131)	4wBE	1940
Kelton Fell	13	Neilson (2203)	0-4-0ST	1876
Lord Roberts	1§	N/Reid (5710)	0-6-0T	1902
(Tiger)	—	N/British (27415)	0-4-0DH	1954
Kilbagie	DS2	R/Hornsby (262998)	4wDM	1949
—	—	R/Hornsby (321733)	4wDM	1952
DS6	(1)	R/Hornsby (421439)	0-4-0DE	1958
St Mirren	(3)	R/Hornsby (423658)	0-4-0DE	1958
—	D88/003	R/Hornsby (506500)	4wDM	1965
John	—	Sentinel (9561)	4wVBT	1958
(Denis)	—	Sentinel (9631)	4wVBT	1958
—	—	Arrols (Glasgow)	2w-2DM	c1966
—	—	Barclay (AB552)	0-4-0DH	1968

*3ft 0in gauge, *Borrowstounness* may move to Ireland
**on loan to Tanfield Railway
†at present off site at Scottish Vintage Bus Museum, Lathalmond, Fife
§official licensed 'Thomas' replica locomotive

Stock
A large selection of coaching stock, many built by Scottish pre-Grouping companies, ex-BR Class 126 DMU, and an appropriate collection of early freight vehicles

Owners
80105 and (*Denis*) the Locomotive Owners Group (Scotland)
246 and 24 the Museum of Scotland
49 the Glasgow Museum of Transport
1000 on loan from National Railway Museum
27001 the Class 27 Preservation Group

26004 and 26024 the 6LDA Group
37025 the Scottish Class 37 Group
37175 and 37403 are privately owned

Caledonian Railway (Brechin)

Member: HRA
This Scottish country steam railway is a classic branch line starting at the Strathmore line junction station of Bridge of Dun, last stomping ground of the Gresley 'A4' Pacific locomotives, and climbs some steep gradients through scenic farmland with assorted wildlife and flora. The summit is reached at the Edzell & Forfar junction just short of Brechin station, itself one of the most impressive of Britain's preserved railways.
  The National Trust for Scotland property House of Dun, built by William Adam in 1730, is approximately 1 mile from Bridge of Dun station, which is also close to the Montrose Basin, a tidal

Locomotives
Name	No	Origin	Class	Type	Built
Brechin City	D3059	BR	08	0-6-0DE	1954
*—	12052	BR	11	0-6-0DE	1949
*—	12093	BR	11	0-6-0DE	1951
—	25072	BR	25	Bo-Bo	1963
—	25083	BR	25	Bo-Bo	1963
—	D5314	BR	26	Bo-Bo	1959
—	26035	BR	26	Bo-Bo	1959
—	27024	BR	27	Bo-Bo	1962
Old Fettercairn	37097	BR	37	Co-Co	1962

*on loan from Scottish Industrial Railway Centre

Industrial locomotives
Name	No	Builder	Type	Built
—†	—	Barclay (1863)	0-4-0ST	1926
Harlaxton	—	Barclay (2107)	0-6-0T	1941
BAC No 1	—	Peckett (1376)	0-4-0ST	1915
Menelaus	—	Peckett (1889)	0-6-0ST	1935
—	5	Peckett (2153)	0-6-0ST	1954

† operational during 2012, others in store/under restoration

wildlife centre. Brechin itself has many attractions including the cathedral and round tower, and the Pictavia centre.

The railway is run entirely by volunteer members of the Brechin Railway Preservation Society
Headquarters: Caledonian Railway (Brechin) Ltd, The Station, 2 Park Road, Brechin, Angus DD9 7AF
Telephone: 01356 622992 / 01561 377760
Internet addresses: *E-mail:* calrail@engineer.com
Web site: www.caledonianrailway.com
Main stations: Brechin and Bridge of Dun
OS reference: NO 603603
Car park: Brechin, Bridge of Dun
SatNav postcodes:
Brechin— DD9 7AF
Bridge of Dun — DD10 9LH
Access by car: Via A90 Dundee/Aberdeen to Brechin bypass. Brown tourist signs to stations. Free parking
Access by public transport: By ScotRail, GNER and Virgin services to Montrose (5 miles). By bus from Montrose, Strathtay Scottish — Dundee (01382) 228054/227201
Refreshment facilities: Light refreshments at Brechin on operating days
Picnic area: Bridge of Dun
Souvenir shop: Brechin
Museum: Brechin
Length of line: 4 miles 22 chains
Depots: Brechin (steam)
Bridge of Dun (diesel)

Coaching Stock
In service: 6 x BR Mk 1, 3 x BR Mk 2s
Stored: 4 x BR Mk 1s, plus 1 x BR Mk 1 in use as volunteer accommodation
BR Mk 3a restaurant car in use as a buffet

Engineer's Stock
c50 wagons including: 1 ex-BR diesel-electric 12-ton crane, 6 Dogfish, 1 Mermaid, 4 warflats, 3 rectanks, 1 Ferry van, 2 Lowmacs, 2 minfit, 1 21-ton minfit, 2 LNER vans, 2 LMS vans, 2 demountable tank wagons, 7 ex-BR vans, 1 ex-BR bolster

Departmental Stock
1 CR origin electrification coach, 1 ex-BR BCK, various vans

Owners
No 1 and *Menelaus* the Angus Railway Steam Engineers
D5314 the Class Twenty Six Preservation Group
D3059, 26035 and 27024 the Caledonian Diesel Group

Passenger trains: Industrial steam and heritage diesel-hauled trains between Brechin and Bridge of Dun
Period of public operation: Steam trains run Sundays from end of May to beginning of September. Diesels Saturdays in August
Bridge of Dun station is open daily for static viewing
Special events: Easter Egg Specials — 8 April; Diesel event — 6 May; Day out with Thomas — 7/8, 14/15 July; Murder on the Brechin Express — 28 July; Diesel Saturdays — 4, 11, 18, 25 August; Murder on the Brechin Express — 11 August; Day out with Thomas — 25/26 August; Santa Specials — selected dates in December
Facilities for disabled: Ramp access to both stations. Vehicular access to Brechin platforms by prior arrangement. Coach converted to take wheelchairs and attendants, prior notice required for access and car parking
Disclaimer: The Caledonian Railway (Brechin) Ltd reserves the right to amend, cancel or add to these events. And whilst every effort will be made to maintain the above services, the company does not guarantee that trains will depart or arrive at the time stated and reserves the right to suspend or alter any train without notice and will not accept any liability for loss, inconvenience or delay thereby caused
Membership details: Pamela Ruddy, c/o above address
Membership journal: Quarterly
Marketing name: The Friendly Line

Keith & Dufftown Railway

Member: HRA
The Keith & Dufftown Railway is an 11 mile line linking the world's malt whisky capital, Dufftown, to the market town of Keith, towns famous round the world for names such as Glenfiddich and Chivas Regal. The line re-opened in 2001, and passes through some of Scotland's most picturesque scenery
Operating society/organisation: Keith & Dufftown Railway

Association, Dufftown Station, Dufftown, Banffshire AB55 4BA
Contact: R. D. Furr (Publicity & Marketing)
Telephone: (01340) 821181 (operating days only)
01343 870429 (Monday to Thursday)
Internet addresses: *E-mail:* info@keith-dufftown-railway.co.uk
Web site: www.keith-dufftown-railway.co.uk

Main station: Dufftown
SatNav postcodes:
Dufftown — AB55 4BA
Keith Town — AB55 3BR
Other public stations: Drummuir (access by rail only), Keith Town (not the ScotRail station)
Length of line: 11 miles, with 42 bridges and the twin span 60ft high Fiddich Viaduct
Car park: Dufftown and Keith Town stations

Keith and Dufftown Railway

Experience Malt Whisky Country by Train

Visit the Keith & Dufftown Railway, the most northely heritage railway in Scotland. Relax in the comfort of our Class 108 DMU's as you spot the wildlife and enjoy the spectacular Scottish scenery

Timetable 2012

Departures from Dufftown at:

11:25 14:00 1550

Departures from Keith Town at:

12:15 14:50
16:40

Open every Saturday and Sunday from Easter to the end of September, and Fridays in June, July & August. A return trip takes 90 mins. Break you journey to visit the "Buffer Stop" restaurant at Dufftown Station.

Group bookings welcome and charter trains available.

Dufftown Station is on the A941, adjacent to the Glenfiddich Distillery. Keith Town Station in on the A96 in the centre of Keith. A 15 min walk from the First Scotrail station.

Telephone: 01340 821181 or 01343 870429
E-mail: info@keith-dufftown-railway.co.uk
Website: www.keith-dufftown-railway.co.uk

Access by public transport:
By rail — ScotRail station at Keith (short walk to Keith Town)
By bus — Stagecoach service 10 (Inverness to Aberdeen) passes Keith Town station, Stagecoach service 336 Elgin to Dufftown stops at Dufftown station
Refreshments: Dufftown
Souvenir shop: Keith Town
On site facilities: Visitor centre and heritage display at Keith Town station. Information on local accommodation providers, visitor attractions and souvenirs. Woodland walks from Drummuir station and access to the Walled Garden at Drummuir Castle
Period of public operation: Weekends — Easter until end of May and throughout September. Fridays, Saturdays and Sundays during June, July and August, and during festivals
Special events: Spring and autumn Whisky Festivals. Summer evening specials. Santa Specials in December. Dates and details on the web site
Facilities for disabled: Access to

Locomotives and multiple-units

Name	No	Origin	Class	Type	Built
—	51568	BR	108	DMC(L)	1959
—	52053	BR	108	DMC(L)	1960
—	53628	BR	108	DMBS	1958
—	56224	BR	108	DTC(L)	1959
—	56491	BR	108	DTC(L)	1959
—	55500*	BR	140	DMS	1981
—	55501*	BR	140	DMS	1981

*unit No 140001, in storage awaiting restoration

Industrial locomotives

Name	No	Builder	Type	Built
Spirit o' Fife	—	E/Electric (D1193)	0-6-0DH	1967
Wee Mac	—	Clayton	4wDH	1979

Rolling stock
1 BR Mk 2F coach, 3 Canadian 2- and 4-seat 'Speeder' vehicles
A selection of freight vehicles for maintenance purposes

all stations, the refreshment coaches and trains. Disabled facilities at Dufftown and Keith Town
Special facilities: Group booking welcome. Trains available for private charter on non-operating days. Keith Town station is licensed for weddings

Special note: The stations and stock are not available for viewing except on operating days
Membership details: Membership Secretary, c/o above address, or via web site
Membership journal: *The Keith & Dufftown Express* — half-yearly

Location: Along the sea front to the west of town
Headquarters: West Links Park, Arbroath, Angus DD11 1QB
Contact: Jill Kerr (Proprietor)
Telephone:
(01241) 874074/879249
Internet addresses:
E-mail:
john@kerrsminiaturerailway.co.uk
Web site:
www.kerrsminiaturerailway.co.uk
Access by public transport:
First ScotRail Arbroath station 1.5 miles; Stagecoach Buses Nos 73 and 39
On site facilities: Small shop. The park has toilets, snack bar, etc
Length of line: 10.25 in gauge; 400yd (alongside main line)
Period of public operation:

Locomotives — 10.25in gauge

Name	No	Builder	Type	Built
Ivor	—	Coleby-Simkins	0-6-0	1972
King George VI	2005	Bullock	4-6-0	1935
Auld Reekie	9872	Jennings	4-4-2	1936
Elliot	25081	Eastwood	Bo-Bo	1981
Angus	D7594	Eastwood	Bo-Bo	1994
Firefly	3007	Bullock	0-6-0	1936

Note: All locomotives can be viewed when the railway is running, please ask for a tour.

Rolling stock
4 open coaches; 1 works wagon; 2 bogie flat wagons

Easter-end of September — weekends (11.00-16.00). All of July and first half of August — daily 11.00-16.00. Occasional Sundays throughout the winter (end September-end March).

All times weather permitting
Facilities for disabled: Level access
Fare: £1.50 adult / £1 child

Member: HRA
Situated in the Lowther Hills between Abington and Sanquhar, the society was formed in 1983 to construct and operate a 2ft gauge tourist railway between the villages of Leadhills and Wanlockhead. The track now extends to the old county boundary between Lanarkshire and Dumfriesshire. The highest adhesion worked railway in Great Britain at 1,498ft above sea level. Signalbox built using terracotta bricks from the demolished viaduct at Risping Cleuch, with a variety of pre-Grouping signalling & telegraph equipment (eg North British Railway lever frame and Caledonian Railway lattice post signal)
Operating society/organisation:
The Secretary, Leadhills & Wanlockhead Railway, The Station, Leadhills, ML12 6XP
Telephone: 01555 662963
Internet addresses: *E-mail:*
info@leadhillsrailway.co.uk
Web site:
www.leadhillsrailway.co.uk

Industrial locomotives

Name	No	Builder	Type	Built
Charlotte	—	O&K	0-4-0T	1913
Elvan	2	M/Rail (9792)	4wDM	1955
Luce	4	R/Hornsby (7002/0467/2)	4wDM	1966
Little Clyde	5	R/Hornsby (7002/0467/6)	4wDM	1966
Clyde	6	Hunslet (6347)	4wDH	1975
Nith	8	H/Clarke (DM1002)	0-4-0DMF	1956
Mennock	10	H/Barclay (LD 9348)	0-4-0DM	1994
—	—	Decauvill (917)	0-4-0T	1917
—	—	Clayton (18190)	4wDM	1978
—	—	Möis	4wDM	1941

Rolling stock
2 air-braked passenger coaches and guard's van built at Leadhills. 1 air-braked coach chassis built by Talyllyn Railway, with the L&WR completing the bodywork. Assorted permanent way wagons and former industrial stock

Main station: Leadhills
Access by public transport:
ScotRail trains stop at Sanquhar on Nith Valley Line (approx 10 miles) every 1hr 30min-2 hours. Bus service (Western Scottish Stagecoach) to Leadhills (please check for times). Nearest motorway

— M74 — J13 from south/J14 from north. From A76 take B797 to Leadhills
Length of line: 1 mile
Journey time: Approx 30min round trip
On site facilities: Shop, ticket office, toilets, small museum and

picnic tables. Extensive country walks. Also on 'Southern Upland Way'. Scottish Lead Mining Museum at Wanlockhead (1 mile). Guided tour of signalbox and engine shed. Disabled access to shop and toilet

Period of public operation: Saturdays and Sundays 11.00-16.20 Easter weekend to September including Bank Holiday Mondays if staff available and special events (please see web site for details).
Special events: Easter; Diesel Gala;

Santa Express — first weekend in December
Membership details: Mrs Mary Drummond, 1 Rogermoor, Moffat DG10 9JZ — membership@leadhills.co.uk
Society journal: Quarterly

Paddle Steamer Preservation Society

Timetable Sailings

Coastal & Inshore Waters

Member: TT, Heritage Afloat
Paddle steamers: *Waverley* & *Kingswear Castle*. Pleasure cruise ship: *Balmoral*
The Paddle Steamer *Waverley*, the last sea-going paddle steamer in the world, was built for the London & North Eastern Railway in 1946, and replaced a vessel of the same name which was sunk off Dunkirk during May 1940. Sold to the PSPS — a Registered Charity — in 1974, *Waverley* sails on day trips and afternoon cruises from ports and piers in most coastal areas and river estuaries of the United Kingdom, from Easter until October each year. Also in the 'fleet' is the traditional motor cruiser *Balmoral*. The river paddle steamer *Kingswear Castle* sails from Chatham Historic

Dockyard on the River Medway
Commercial Director: Kathleen O'Neil
Operations Director: Ian McMillan
Headquarters:
Waverley and *Balmoral:*
Waverley Excursions Ltd, Waverley Terminal, Anderston Quay, Glasgow G3 8HA
Kingswear Castle:
The Historic Dockyard, Chatham, Kent ME4 4TQ
On ship facilities: Self-service restaurants, bars, toilets (disabled toilets on *Waverley* and *Balmoral*), souvenirs
Special facilities: *Waverley* and *Balmoral* are available for private hire and party bookings
Membership details: Paddle

Steamer Preservation Society, PO Box 365, Worcester WR3 7WH
Membership journal:
Paddlewheels — quarterly.
Details of the full programme of cruises operated by *Waverley* and *Balmoral* can be obtained from the National Booking Office, Waverley Excursions Ltd, Waverley Terminal, Anderston Quay, Glasgow G3 8HA
Tel: 0845 130 4647.
Book online at: www.waverleyexcursions.co.uk
Further info for *Kingswear Castle:*
Tel: 01634 827648
E-mail: kc@pskc.freeserve.co.uk
Online booking for *Kingswear Castle:*
www.pskc.freeserve.co.uk

Prestongrange Museum

Museum

East Lothian

Location: On the B1348 between Musselburgh and Prestonpans.
OS reference: NT 734737
Operating society/organisation: East Lothian Museum Service, Library & Museum Headquarters, Dunbar Road, Haddington, East Lothian EH41 3PJ
Telephone: (0131) 653 2904 (Prestongrange Visitor Centre), (01620) 828200 (Museum Service)
Internet addresses:
E-mail: prestongrange@btconnect.com
Web site: www.prestongrange.org
Car park: On site
SatNav postcode: EH32 9RY
On site facilities: Prestongrange tells the stories of the people and

Industrial locomotives

Name	No	Builder	Type	Built
—	6	A/Barclay (2043)	0-4-0ST	1937
—	17	A/Barclay (2219)	0-4-0ST	1946
Prestongrange	7	G/Ritchie (536)	0-4-2ST	1914
Tomatin	1	M/Rail (9925)	4wDM	1963
—	—*	Hunslet (4440)	4wDM	1952
—	32	R/Hornsby (458960)	4wDM	1962
George Edwards	33	R/Hornsby (221647)	4wDM	1943
—	—	E/Electric (D908)	4wDM	1964

*2ft gauge

Rolling stock
Steam crane, Whittaker No 30, c1890, on open display

Special note: The locomotives are stored under cover with no public access at the time of writing

Scotland

industries of East Lothian. It is the site of a harbour, glassworks, potteries, coal mine and brick works
Visitor centre: Changing exhibitions of local industries. Children's activity area. Cornish beam engine, installed 1874 to pump water from mine workings. Changing exhibitions in powerhouse
Toilets: Visitor centre

Refreshment facilities: Available at visitor centre
Public opening: Museum site open daily throughout the year. Visitor centre and exhibitions April to October, 11.30-16.30. Admission free
Length of line: 400m (standard gauge). No public rides
Facilities for disabled: Access and toilet at visitor centre. Access to

powerhouse exhibition, and footpaths along the site
Special events: Events held throughout the season. Please check web site for details
Contact: For Prestongrange Railway Society — Colin Boyd, 3 Stuart Wynd, Craigmount View, Edinburgh EH2 8XU

Museum — Riverside Museum (Glasgow Museum of Transport) — Glasgow

Member: HRA, TT

The Riverside Museum opened in June 2011 as a successor to Glasgow's Museum of Transport. Within the Zaha Hadid-designed building sit displays about the history of transport and travel in Glasgow and Scotland. The Clydeside location makes the direct link to the city's maritime heritage, while the city's fantastic collection of Glasgow trams, steam locomotives, cars, bicycles, motorbikes, prams and ship models forms the centre of the displays.

The railway collection represents one of the best efforts of a municipal authority to preserve a representative collection of railway heritage and is appropriately displayed in the city that once was 'locomotive builder of the Empire'

Access by public transport:
By rail — Strathclyde PTE Underground: Partick.
Scotrail: Partick
By bus — please check Glasgow Museums and SPT web sites as new routes will have been arranged for the new museum
Operating society/organisation: Glasgow Life on behalf of Glasgow City Counci
Location: Riverside Museum, 100 Pointhouse Place, Glasgow G3 8RS

Locomotives

Name	No	Origin	Class	Type	Built
—	123	CR	123	4-2-2	1886
—	9	G&SWR	5	0-6-0T	1917
—	103	HR	—	4-6-0	1894
Glen Douglas	256	NBR	D34	4-4-0	1913
—	3007	SAR	15F	4-8-2	1945

Industrial locomotives*

Name	No	Builder	Type	Built
—	1	Barclay (1571)	0-6-0F	1917
—	—	Chaplin (2368)	0-4-0TG	1888
—	—	BEV (583)	B	1927

*All in store at Glasgow Museums Resources Centre

Stock (on display)
Glasgow District Subway car 39T; Glasgow District Subway car No 4

In store at Glasgow Museums Resources Centre
Glasgow District Subway car No 1

Telephone: 0141 287 2720
Internet address: *Web site:* www.glasgowlife.org.uk/museums
Car park: Opposite Museum entrance
On site facilities: Toilets, cafeteria, shop and public telephone, cloaking facility
Public opening: Open seven days a week. Monday-Thursday and Saturday 10.00-17.00. Fridays and Sundays 11.00-17.00. Closed Christmas Day and Boxing Day,

New Year's Eve afternoon, New Year's Day and 2 January. Please check www.glasgowlife.org.uk/museums for opening dates and times
Facilities for disabled: Both single-sex and uni-sex disabled facilities now available. A passenger lift to allow disabled access at the front entrance is now in operation

Member: HRA

A number of track panels have now been laid to the west of Birkenbaud level crossing but passenger services over the crossing will not commence until the Light Railway Order is finally granted — now expected in early 2012. Further path work has been carried out, along with ground drainage.

Plans are under-way for the construction of a temporary — movable — platform to be situated initially on the east side of the Birkenbaud crossing. As the passenger operational line extends, this platform will be repositioned to suit.

Bon Accord operated on a number of passenger service days during 2011 but was withdrawn from service towards the end of the season due to recurring wheel bearing problems. It is expected to have these problems resolved in time for the 2012 season.

Most of the 2011 diesel-operated services ran with Barclay 415 hauling the BEMU set, and Class 03 No D2094 hauling the Mk2 BSO(T) and TSO coaches. Additional steam services were operated by *Bon Accord* hauling the Mk 2 coaches. The 2012 service will comprise both steam and diesel locomotives, *Bon Accord*, Nos D2094 and D2134 and Barclay 415 hauling Mk 2 coaches and the BEMU.

The transfer of the GNSR Oldmeldrum station to Milton of Crathes is in progress. The building is now stripped to the point where it its weathertight condition has been maintained for the winter with complete dismantling scheduled for spring 2012. Once dismantled, all sections and components will be transferred to Milton of Crathes for refurbishment and re-erection.

The railway is being rebuilt by volunteers of the Royal Deeside RPS with the invaluable assistance of the Leys Estate, and is managed and operated solely by volunteers

Headquarters: The Station, Milton of Crathes

Operating society/organisation:

Locomotives and multiple-units

Name	No	Origin	Class	Type	Built
—	D2094	BR	03	0-6-0DM	1960
—	D2134†	BR	03	0-6-0DH	1960
—	D9551	BR	14	0-6-0DH	1965
—	79998*	BR	—	DMBS	1956
—	79999*	BR	—	DTCL	1956

†rebuilt with hydraulic drive
*battery-powered multiple-unit

Industrial locomotives

Name	No	Builder	Type	Built
Bon Accord	—	Barclay (807)	0-4-0ST	1897
—	1	Barclay (415)	0-4-0DH	1957

Rolling stock

2 BR Mk 2 coaches, GNSR full brake, GNSR 5-comp lav composite (body only), GNSR 5-comp lav Third (body only), GNSR 5-comp Third (body only), GNSR 4-comp First (body only), GNSR former steam railmotor (body only), LNWR Picnic Saloon (body only), LMS CCT, BR 20-ton brake van, BR Dogfish, Lomac wagon and Tube s, ex-LMS wagon underframe, 75-ton rail-mounted crane (on loan from Strathspey Railway, their No 206)

Owner

Bon Accord — the Grampian Transport Museum, on long term loan to Bon Accord Locomotive Society

The Deeside Railway Co Ltd, The Station, Milton of Crathes, Banchory, Aberdeenshire AB31 5QH

Telephone: 01330 844416 (answering machine)
Internet address: *Web site:* www.deeside-railway.co.uk
OS reference: NO 914962
Car Parking: Free, on site
Access by public transport:
By bus — Stagecoach Bluebird from Aberdeen rail/bus interchange (railway adjacent to A93).
Access by car — from south, A90 to Stonehaven, then A957 (historic Slug Road) to A93 at Crathes; from the west, A93 from Ballater, A980 from Donside to Banchory
On site facilities: Shop and buffet with light refreshments available (seasonal weekend opening plus Wednesdays during school holidays)
Length of line: 1 mile, 2.75 miles when complete
Public opening: 11.00-16.30 (half hourly service) on Sundays from

Easter to end September; Saturdays from June to end August and Wednesdays during school holidays.

Santa Specials on 1/2, 8/9, 15/16, 22/23 December. Mince Pie specials on 27 December. These services operate every half hour from 11.00-16.00.

Full 2012 timetable is available on the web site
Private parties: Are welcome throughout the year and can be arranged by contact through the web site
Special events: Annual Deeside Steam & Vintage Club rally held at Milton of Crathes on third weekend in August.
Special facilities: Diesel footplate rides are available on all services — maximum of two visitors per journey with an age limitation of 16 years and over.
Driver experience days can be arranged by contact through the web site
Disabled facilities: Access for wheelchair users on to the platform,

guard's area on train and station shop. Multi-user footpath alongside railway allowing viewing of passing trains

Note: Some locomotives and rolling stock undergoing restoration off-site with no public access, please

contact for details
Membership details:
Mr D. Pearson, Membership Secretary, 5 Highwood, Banchory, Aberdeenshire AB31 5XE
Membership journal: *The Queen's Messenger* (quarterly)

Affiliated society:
The Bon Accord Locomotive Society, c/o Mr Ted Gardner (Chairman), 94 North Deeside Road, Peterculter, Aberdeen AB14 0QB
Web site: www.bon-accord.org.uk

Steam Centre	Scottish Industrial Railway Centre	Ayrshire

Member: HRA, TT, AIM

The Scottish Industrial Railway Centre is based on part of the former Dalmellington Iron Co railway system which was one of the best known industrial railway networks in Britain. Steam worked up until 1978 when the collieries it served in the scenic Doon Valley closed. It is the aim of the centre to preserve part of the railway.

The centre is operated by the Ayrshire Railway Preservation Group, which also owns the former Glasgow & South Western Railway station at Waterside, half a mile from the centre.

During the winter of 2002/3 the ARPG moved its operations from the former colliery at Minnivey to the Dunaskin Ironworks site at Waterside, and is now based in the former NCB locomotive shed and wagon works there. As part of Doon Valley Heritage, an industrial heritage centre has now been established at the old Dunaskin Ironworks, based on the iron, coal and brickmaking industries

Location: 10 miles south east of Ayr on the A713 to Castle Douglas

Contact address: Scottish Industrial Railway Centre, Dunaskin Ironworks, Waterside, Panta, Ayrshire KA6 7JF

OS reference: NS 438085

Operating society/organisation: Ayrshire Railway Preservation Group

Telephone: ARPG information line (01292) 269260. ARPG Secretary (01292) 313579 (evening and weekends)

Internet address: *E-mail:* agcthoms@aol.com

Locomotives

Name	No	Origin	Class	Type	Built
*—	MP228 (12052)	BR	11	0-6-0DE	1949
*—	MP229 (12093)	BR	11	0-6-0DE	1951

*on loan to Caledonian Railway

Industrial locomotives

Name	No	Builder	Type	Built
—	16	Barclay (1116)	0-4-0ST	1910
—	8	Barclay (1296)	0-6-0T	1912
—	19	Barclay (1614)	0-4-0ST	1918
—	8	Barclay (1952)	0-4-0F	1928
—	10	Barclay (2244)	0-4-0ST	1947
NCB No 23	—	Barclay (2260)	0-4-0ST	1949
—	25	Barclay (2358)	0-6-0ST	1954
—	1	Barclay (2368)	0-4-0ST	1955
—	—	Barclay (347)	0-4-0DM	1941
—	118	Barclay (366)	0-4-0DM	1943
—	7	Barclay (399)	0-4-0DM	1956
Lily of the Valley	—	Fowler (22888)	0-4-0DM	1943
—	—	Fowler (4200028)	0-4-0DM	1948
Tees Storage	—	N/British (27644)	0-4-0DH	1959
—	—	R/Hornsby (224352)	4wDM	1943
Blinkin Bess	—	R/Hornsby (284839)	4wDM	1950
Johnnie Walker	—	R/Hornsby (417890)	4wDM	1959
—	—	R/Hornsby (421697)	0-4-0DM	1959
—	107	Hunslet (3132)	0-4-0DM	1944
—	—	Sentinel (10012)	4wDM	1959
—	—	Donnelli (163)	4wDMR	1979

3ft gauge (stored off-site)

—	—	R/Hornsby (256273)	4wDM	1949
—	—	Hunslet (8816)	4wDH	1981

2ft 6in gauge (stored off-site)

—	2	R/Hornsby (183749)	4wDM	1937
—	3	R/Hornsby (210959)	4wDM	1941
—	1	R/Hornsby (211681)	4wDM	1942

Note: Not all standard gauge locomotives are on public display

Stock

1 BR Mk 1 TSO (on loan to Caledonian Railway), 1 BR Mk 1 BSK, ex LMS Inspection Saloon (DM45020). 2 Wickham trolleys; 1 steam crane; various other items

Scotland

Length of line: Approx 0.3 mile
Access by public transport:
By rail: Ayr (10 miles).
By bus: Sundays hourly Stagecoach
bus service from Ayr. Tel: (01292)
613500
On site facilities: Steam-hauled
brake van rides (over third mile).
Small museum of railway relics and
photographs, and souvenir shop
Public opening: Steam days (with
an engine in steam, subject to
availability) will be held on:
Sundays 27 May; 3, 24 June; 1, 8,
15, 22, 29 July; 5, 12, 19, 26
August; 2, 30 September. Opening
times 11.00-16.30.
Membership details: Mrs Catriona
Thom, 38 Ashgrove Street, Ayr
KA7 3BG
Special notes: For further
information and details of special
events, please contact the
information line (01292) 269620, or
the secretary Gordon Thomson
(01292) 313579, or write to
8 Burnside Place, Troon, Ayrshire
KA10 6LZ

Strathspey Railway

Timetable Service · Inverness-shire

Member: HRA, TT
The Strathspey is in the process of
considerable change. New directors
have been appointed and a
Strathspey Railway Charitable
Trust launched to handle the
proposed extension to Grantown-
on-Spey.
   Prospective visitors are advised to
visit the web site for up-to-date
information
Enquiries: Aviemore Station,
Dalfaber Road, Aviemore,
Inverness-shire PH22 1PY (SAE for
copy of timetable brochure)
Telephone: 01479 810725.
Internet address: *E-mail:*
strathtrains@strathspeyrailway.co.uk
Web site:
www.strathspeyrailway.co.uk
Main station: Aviemore. The
railway occupies one platform at the
main line Aviemore station
Other public stations: Boat of
Garten and Broomhill
OS reference: Aviemore NH
898131, Boat of Garten NH 943789
Car parks: Aviemore (Strathspey
Railway side of station, off Dalfaber
Road) for railway customers only,
Boat of Garten (access via A95 and
minor roads 5 miles north of
Aviemore and 10 miles south of
Grantown-on-Spey) and Broomhill
Access by public transport:
ScotRail services and express bus to
Aviemore. Local service to Boat of
Garten
Refreshment facilities: On-train
buffet car or facilities on many
trains. Picnic tables at Boat of
Garten (for use of ticket purchasers)
Souvenir shop: Boat of Garten and
Aviemore

Locomotives and multiple-units

Name	No	Origin	Class	Type	Built
—†	5025	LMS	5MT	4-6-0	1934
E. V. Cooper, Engineer	46512	LMS	2MT	2-6-0	1952
—	828	CR	812	0-6-0	1899
—	D2774	BR	—	0-4-0DH	1960
—	D3605	BR	08	0-6-0DE	1959
—†	D5302	BR	26	Bo-Bo	1958
—†	26025	BR	26	Bo-Bo	1958
—	D5394	BR	27	Bo-Bo	1963
—	D5862	BR	31	A1A-A1A	1962
—	51367	BR	117	DMBS	1959
—	51402	BR	117	DMS	1959
—†	51990	BR	107	DMBS	1961
—	52008	BR	107	DMBS	1960
—	52030	BR	107	DMC	1960
—	54047	BR	114	DTC	1959
—	97651	BR	97	0-6-0DE	1959

Industrial locomotives

Name	No	Builder	Type	Built
—	48†	Hunslet (2864)	0-6-0ST	1943
Cairngorm	9	RSH (7097)	0-6-0ST	1943
Swiftsure	—†	Hunslet (2857)	0-6-0ST	1943
—	60†	Hunslet (3686)	0-6-0ST	1948
Forth	10*	Barclay (1890)	0-4-0ST	1926
Balmenach	2	Barclay (2020)	0-4-0ST	1936
Braeriach	17	Barclay (2017)	0-6-0T	1935
Inveresk	16	R/Hornsby (260756)	0-4-0DM	1950
—	—	T/Hill (277V)	4wDM	1977
—	14	North British (27549)	0-4-0DH	1956
Queen Anne	20†	R/Hornsby (265618)	4wDM	1948

*not on site
†stored and/or not on public display

Locomotive and multiple-unit notes: In service: 17, 51367, 51402,
52008 and 54047. Under restoration: 9, D5394.
No 17 on loan to SRPS as at 30 November 2010

Stock
20 ex-BR coaches; 4 ex-LMS coaches; 2 ex-LMS sleeping cars; 1 ex-
LNER sleeping car; 1 ex-HR coach (stored at Bo'ness); 1 ex-NBR coach;
numerous examples of rolling stock

Depot: Aviemore (open for conducted tours for fare-paying passengers on Saturdays 7 April, 5 May, 2 June, 4 June (Monday), 7 July, 4 August 1 September, 6 October at 14.00, meet in Aviemore booking Hall. Also available on 27/28 October at 11.00 and 14.00. Not open at any other time, sidings at Aviemore and Boat of Garten are not open to the public, those at Broomhill are visible from the road

Length of line: 10 miles

Journey time: Aviemore-Boat of Garten 15min; Aviemore-Broomhill 45min (outward) 35min, (inward). Round trip takes approximately 90min

Passenger trains: Steam-hauled services. Aviemore-Boat of Garten/Broomhill

Period of public operation:

Owners

6, 17 and 46512 the Highland Locomotive Co Ltd
828 the Scottish Locomotive Preservation Trust Fund
5025 the Watkinson Trust
D5302 and 26025 the Highland Diesel Locomotive Co Ltd
51367 and 51402 the Blue Square Heritage Group
51990, 52008, 52030 and 54047 My Little Sprinter Ltd

Weekends and some weekdays in April, May, June, September and October. Every day in July and August

Facilities for disabled: Access for disabled is available at each station. Please contact in advance for directions and if a party involved

Special notes: First and third class travel available on most trains. Family fares available for third class travel. Special rates/arrangements for parties. Groups of cyclists are asked to give prior notice to ensure space is available in the guard's van.

Afternoon tea available on the 14.45 ex-Aviemore service. 1st Class £21.95/adult, Country Class £19.95/adult; price includes train fare (pre-booking essential)

Membership details: Strathspey Railway Association, Spey Lodge, Aviemore Station.

Web site: www.strathspeyrailway association.co.uk

Membership journal: *Strathspey Express* — quarterly

Museum | Summerlee — The Museum of Scottish Industrial Life | Lanarkshire

Summerlee Museum is one of Scotland's leading heritage attractions. With its operational tramway, miners' cottages and mine tours, large external exhibits and dramatic new exhibition hall, Summerlee is an ideal day out, rain or shine

Manager: Tommy Gallagher

Operating society/organisation: Summerlee Heritage Park, Heritage Way, Coatbridge ML5 1QD (operated by North Lanarkshire Council)

Telephone: (01236) 638460

Fax: (01236) 638454

Public opening: Daily except 1/2 January and 25/26 December.
April-November — 10.00-17.00
November-March — 10.00-16.00

Access by public transport:

By rail — ScotRail trians now run from Edinburgh Waverley, as well as Glasgow Queen Street Low Level (Helensburgh to Edinburgh line), alight at Coatbridge Sunnyside

Car park: Opposite site

Locomotives

Name	No	Origin	Class	Type	Built
Springbok	4112	SAR	GMAM	4-8-2+2-8-4	1956
(3ft 6in gauge/built by North British Loco Co)					
Unit 936103	977844	BR	303	DTS	1966
(303103)	977845	BR	303	MBS	1966

Industrial locomotives

Name	No	Builder	Type	Built
—	—	Barclay (472)	0-4-0DH	1966
—	—	H/Clarke (895)	0-6-0T	1909
—	—	G/Hogg	0-4-0T	1898
Robin	—	Sentinel (9628)	4wTG	1957

Stock

2 rail-mounted steam cranes.
Also on site are two former Glasgow trams: one, the Coplawhill Motor School training car, has just entered service at Summerlee; the second, a 'Coronation' class car, will shortly commence a full restoration to operational standards

On site facilities: Tea room, gift shop. Working electric tramway, underground mine tour and miners' cottages. Playpark and picnic areas

Special events: Organised events from April-October, details on request

Facilities for disabled: Toilets, wheelchair available. Blue badge parking to right of main entrance

Bala Lake Railway (Rheilffordd Llyn Tegid)

Member: HRA, TT

This delightful narrow gauge railway follows the route of the former Bala-Dolgellau Railway, along the shore of Wales' largest natural lake. The railway's headquarters are to be found in the fine old station building at Llanuwchllyn at the south-western end of the line. Do not be deterred by the fact that the railway runs down the opposite shore of the lake to the main road — it is well worth the detour

General Manager: Roger Hine
Headquarters: Rheilffordd Llyn Tegid (Bala Lake Railway) Llanuwchllyn, Bala, Gwynedd LL23 7DD
Telephone: Llanuwchllyn (01678) 540666
Internet address: *Web site:* www.bala-lake-railway.co.uk
SatNav postcodes: Llanuwchllyn — LL23 7DD Bala — LL23 7BS
Main station: Llanuwchllyn
Other public stations: Llangower, Bala. Request halt at Pentrepiod
OS reference: Llanuwchllyn SH 880300, Bala SH 929350
Car parks: Llanuwchllyn, Llangower and Bala town centre

Industrial locomotives — 1ft 11.625in gauge

Name	No	Builder	Type	Built
George B	—	Hunslet (680)	0-4-0ST	1898
Holy War	3	Hunslet (779)	0-4-0ST	1902
Alice	—	Hunslet (780)	0-4-0ST	1902
Maid Marian	5	Hunslet (822)	0-4-0ST	1903
Meirionnydd	11	Severn-Lamb (7322)	Bo-Bo	1973
Chilmark	12	R/Hornsby (194771)	4wDM	1939
Bob Davies	—	YEC (L125)	4wDM	1983
Lady Madcap	—	R/Hornsby (283512)	4wDM	1949

Locomotive notes: *Alice*, *Holy War* and *Maid Marian* are in regular use, remainder are on static display
George B is being re-assembled

Access by public transport: Arriva service No 94 to both Bala and Llanuwchllyn (from Wrexham or Barmouth)
Road access: Off the A494 Bala-Dolgellau road
Refreshment facilities: Llanuwchllyn. Large picnic site with toilet facilities by lake at Llangower
Souvenir shop: Llanuwchllyn
Depot: Llanuwchllyn
Length of line: 4.5 miles, 1ft 11.625in gauge
Passenger trains: Llanuwchllyn-Bala. Journey takes 25min in each direction

Period of public operation: Easter-end of September (except some Mondays and Fridays)
Facilities for disabled: Facilities available on most trains
Special notes: Small parties (10/12) may just turn up, but a day's notice required for larger groups
Family tickets: Available for all round-trip journeys
Membership details: Membership Secretary, c/o Llanuwchllyn station
Society web site: www.bala-lake-railway-society.org.uk
Membership journal: *Llanuwchllyn Express*

Barry Tourist Railway

Member: HRA

At the end of 2008 the local council handed over the operation of the Bary Island Railway to a new operating company — Cambrian Transport. At the time of going to press no details were available of the 2012 operating dates. Please contact for details.

Location: Barry Island Station, Barry Island, South Wales
General Manager: —
Operating Society/organisation: The Station Buildings, Barry Island, Vale of Glamorgan

Locomotives and multiple-units

Name	No	Origin	Class	Type	Built
—	6686*	GWR	5600	0-6-2T	1928
—	44901*	LMS	5MT	4-6-0	1945
—	45166†	LMS/WD	8F	2-8-0	1942
—	92245*	BR	9F	2-10-0	1958
—	20228	BR	20	Bo-Bo	1966
—	D1725	BR	47	Co-Co	1964
Julia Pride of Barry	73118	BR	73	Bo-Bo	1966
—	50222	BR	101	DMBS	1959
—	50338	BR	101	DMCL	1959
Unit 488206	72505	BR	488/2	TFH	1984
Unit 488206	79626	BR	488/2	TSH	1984
Unit 488311	72620	BR	488/3	TSH	1984
Unit 488206	72710	BR	488/3	TS	1984

CF62 5TH
Telephone: 01446 748816
(Monday-Friday)
Internet addrersses:
E-mail:
enquiries@barrytouristrailway.com
Web site:
www.valeofglamorgan.gov.uk
Car park: Free parking at the
Waterfront station, Hood Road
OS reference: ST 115667
Access by public transport:
By rail: Frequent train services
from Cardiff to Barry Island for
cross platform interchange (Tel:
08457 484950).
By bus: Travel Line Wales (Tel:
0871 2002233 for local routes).
By road: Jct 33 on M4, onto A4232
and A4050 - follow Barry signs
On site facilities: Museum, shop,
light refreshments
Public opening: Easter to mid-
September (weekends and Bank
Holidays), December (tel: 01466
748816 for more details)
Length of line: 3.5 miles
Facilities for disabled: Barry
Island station is all on the level with
no steps. Ramp access available for
all trains. 100m level walk from

Name	No	Origin	Class	Type	Built
Unit 488206	72621	BR	488/3	TSH	1984
Unit 489110	68509	BR	489	GLV	1959

†ex Turkish State Railways' number
*stored, not on display

Locomotive notes:

Industrial locomotives

Name	No	Builder	Type	Built
Pamela	—	Hunslet (3840)	0-6-0ST	1956
—	7705	RSH (7705)	0-4-0ST	1952
Bill Caddick	—	H/Clarke (1168)	0-6-0DM	1959
—	—	Unilok (2183)		1964
—	—	Hunslet (6688)	0-4-0DH	1968

Stock
BR Mk 1 and Mk 2 coaches, TVR coach No 153, operational steam crane,
various freight vehicles

Owners
D1725 privately owned
20228 Traditional Traction
73118 on loan from Eurostar

ticket office to train. Parking by
special arrangement to private car
park
Further information: The
Chairman, Vale of Glamorgan

Railway Co, Barry Island Station,
South Wales CF62 5TH
Membership details: Membership
Secretary c/o above address

Timetable Service	**Brecon Mountain Railway**	Merthyr Tydfil

A narrow gauge passenger-carrying
railway close to Merthyr Tydfil
built on part of the trackbed of the
former Brecon & Merthyr Railway.
Gradually being extended
northwards, the railway has some
interesting narrow gauge steam
locomotives imported from East
Germany, South Africa, South
America and Russia
General Manager: A. J. Hills
Headquarters: Brecon Mountain
Railway, Pant Station, Dowlais,
Merthyr Tydfil CF48 2UP
Telephone: Merthyr Tydfil (01685)
722988
Fax: (01685) 384854
Internet addresses: *E-mail:*
enquiries@breconmountainrailway.
co.uk
Web site:
www.breconmountainrailway.co.uk
Main station: Pant
Car park: Pant station

Locomotives — 1ft 11.75in gauge

Name	No	Builder	Type	Built
Santa Teresa	1	Baldwin (15511)	2-6-2	1897
—	2	Baldwin (61269)	4-6-2	1930
Sybil	—	Hunslet (827)	0-4-0ST	1903
Graf Schwerin-Löwitz	—	Arn Jung (1261)	0-6-2WT	1908
Pendyffryn	—	de Winton	0-4-0VBT	1894
Redstone	—	Redstone	0-4-0VBT	1905
—	—	Brecon MR (001)	0-6-0DH	1987
—	—	H/Hunslet	0-4-0DM	1960
—	—	Kambarka	Bo-BoDH	1980

Stock
Two balcony end 39-seat coaches; 2 balcony end 40-seat coaches; 1 19-seat
Caboose; 2 coal cars, 8 flat cars, crane and tamper, miscellaneous rail-
carrying and ballast wagons; Wickham petrol trolley

OS reference: SO 063120
Access by public transport: Bus to
Pant Cemetery — half hour
frequency from Merthyr bus station.
Main line rail service to Merthyr
from Cardiff Central

Depot: Pant
Length of line: 5 miles (3.5 miles
open for passenger traffic),
1ft 11.75in gauge
Journey time: Return trip approx
65min

Wales

Period of public operation: Weekends in January; weekends in February, plus local half term week; weekends in January, February and March, plus local half term week. Daily 1 April-4 November 2012. EXCEPT for: 2, 16, 20, 23, 27, 30 April; 4, 11, 14, 18, 21, 25, 28 May; 17, 21, 24, 28 September; 1, 5, 8, 12, 15, 19, 22, 26 October See also web site
Refreshment facilities: Cafés at Pant and Pontsticill
Special events: Santa Specials — December
Facilities for disabled: Facilities for disabled include ramps, toilets and carriage designed to carry wheelchairs
Special notes: There is no road access to Pontsticill

Museum	Conwy Valley Railway Museum	Betws-y-coed (Conwy CB)

Conveniently situated alongside Betws-y-coed railway station, the Museum presents some well-displayed distractions to pass the time including model train layouts to delight both adult and child
Location: Adjacent to Betws-y-coed station
OS reference: SH 796565
General Manager: Mr C. M. Cartwright
Operating society/organisation: Conwy Valley Railway Museum, The Old Goods Yard, Betws-y-coed, Conwy LL24 0AL
Telephone: 01690 710568
Fax: 01690 710132
Internet addresses: *E-mail:* info@conwyrailwaymuseum.co.uk *Web site:* www.conwyrailwaymuseum.co.uk
Car park: On site
Access by public transport: Betws-y-coed main line station
On site facilities: Refreshments in buffet car. Bookshop and model/gift shop in museum foyer, operating train layouts, miniature railway (1.25-miles, 7.25in gauge) steam-hauled. Picnic area.
15in Tramway (operates daily) with 1989-built single-deck bogie tram. A recent addition is a 60ft long 00

Locomotives – 7.25in gauge

Name	No	Builder	Type	Built
Britannia	70000	TMA Engineering	4-6-2	1988
			(1ft 3in gauge)	
Old Rube*	—	Milner Eng	2-8-0	1983
Shoshone*	—	Simkins/Milner	2-8-0	1975
Union Pacific*	—	R. Greatrex	Bo-Bo	1991
Douglas*	—†	P. Frank	2-4-0T	2004
Gwydir Castle*	—§	P. Zwicky-Ross/P. Frank	Bo-Bo	2004
—	—§	—	4-6-2	1935

*7.25in gauge
†based on Isle of Man Railway locomotives
§6in gauge Canadian Pacific locomotive, a prize winner at the Model Engineer Exhibition

Stock
Standard gauge: 1 GWR fitter's van; 1 LMS 6-wheel van; 1 LNER CCT van; 1 BR Mk 1 coach; 2 SR luggage vans; 1 Pullman coach; 15in bogie tramcar.
7.25in gauge: 2 rebuilt triple sets; 5 articulated sit-in coaches; 2 twin-set articulated sit-in covered coaches; 2 sets 3-articulated sit-in open coaches; 1 3-coach articulated covered set; 4 wagons plus 'self-drive' 0-4-0 'Toby Tram' and 2-4-0 *Billy*;1 bogie ballast wagon and 2 three-plank wagons (P. Frank)
15in gauge: 1 wagon

gauge model railway in a bogie coach
Public opening: Daily 10.00-17.00 with trains from 10.30. Last entry 30min before closing

Facilities for disabled: Access to café, museum and toilets from car park. Toilets are adapted for disabled

---

Railway Centre/Museum	Corris Railway and Museum	Gwynedd

Member: HRA
In the heart of Wales' 'narrow gauge country', the Corris Railway provides a 50min round trip on the restored section of Mid Wales' first public narrow gauge railway. The museum, situated in the remaining buildings of Corris station, displays relics, photographs and models of the railway. In October 2010 the CR Society published details for the redevelopment of the Corris station area including an overall roofed station building. These can be viewed on the web site
Location: In Corris village off A487 trunk road. Turn opposite Braichgoch Hotel, five miles north

of Machynlleth and 11 miles south of Dolgellau

OS reference: SH 755078
Operating society: The Corris Railway Society, Corris Station Yard, Gwynedd (postal address: Corris, Machynlleth, Powys SY20 9SH)
Telephone: 01654 761303
Internet addresses:
E-mail: enquiries@corris.co.uk
Web site: www.corris.co.uk
Car park: Adjacent
Access by public transport:
By rail: Arriva Trains services to Machynlleth, then by bus.
By bus: Bus Gwynedd services 2 (Aberystwyth-Dolgellau-Machynlleth), 30 (Machynlleth-Tywyn) and 34 (Machynlleth-Aberllefenni); Dyfi Valley service 530 (Tywyn-Machynlleth-Abergynolwyn).
Traveline Cymru 0871 200 22 33.
On cycle/foot: National Cycle Network No 8 via Machynlleth and Esgairgeiliog (from south), via Aberllefenni and Dolgellau (from north)
By taxi: Machynlleth (01654) 702048
Catering facilities: Snacks, teas and light refreshments
On site facilities: Souvenir shop, toilets and children's playground; close to Corris Craft Centre and King Arthur's Labyrinth; two miles from Centre for Alternative Technology
Passenger trains: Corris to Maespoeth
Length of line: Three-quarter-mile, 2ft 3in gauge track. Planning permission for a further two miles of track has been granted and work

Locomotives — 2ft 3in gauge

Name	No	Builder	Type	Built
Alan Meaden	5	M/Rail (22258)	4wDM	1965
—	6	R/Hornsby (51849)	4wDM	1966
—	7	Winson/Watkins	0-4-2ST	2005
—	8	Hunslet (7274)	4wDM	1973
Aberllefenni	9	Clayton (8045)	4wBE	1974

Locomotive notes: 5, 6 and 7 operational. No 7 is based on Corris No 4 (now Talyllyn No 4 *Edward Thomas*.) No 8 is being restored at Maespoeth Junction, No 9 is stored off-site.

The appeal to build the next steam locomotive, which will take the number 10, will be a recreation of the original CR Nos 1 to 3, a 0-4-2ST design know as 'Falcon' is moving ahead with the boiler completed along with many patterns and some smaller components. Details from CRS 38 Underwood Close, Callow Hill, Redditch B97 5YS or via website.

Stock
3 carriages (3 more under construction) , 4 brake vans, 18 works wagons and 5 historic wagons

Owner
8 on loan from the National Mining Museum
9 donated by Wincilate Ltd

has now started on the extension. See web site for details
Public opening:
Museum and shop 10.30-17.00 on train operating days. (Full details on web site.)
Railway — passenger trains (usually steam-hauled) operate: 6-8, 22 April; 5-7, 13, 20, 27 May; 2-10, 17, 23/24 June;1, 7/8, 14/15, 21-24, 28-31 July; 4-7, 11-14, 18-21, 25-27 August; 1/2, 9, 16, 23, 30 September; 7, 14, 20 (diesel service) October; 10/11 December. Trains leave Corris hourly 11.00-16.00.
Special trains and museum openings by prior arrangement.

Please contact publicity@corris.co.uk
Special events: Father's Day — 17 June; Family Fun Weekend — 28/29 July; Model Railway & Toy Exhibition at Corris School — 25-27 August; Sweet Music — 1/2 September; Diesel Locomotive Day — 20 October; Santa Steam Specials — 15/16 December
Facilities for disabled: Disabled access carriage on all trains. Access to display area of museum and shop
Membership details: CRS, 34 Mayfair Avenue, Normanby, Middlesbrough TS6 0SG or via web site

---

Timetable Service	**Fairbourne Railway**	Gwynedd

Member: Britain's Great Little Railways
Since 1986 this railway has had three different gauges, becoming its current 12.25in in 1986. The locomotives are mostly half size replicas of 2ft gauge prototypes. The journey along the beach and through the sand dunes affords unparalleled views of the Mawddach estuary. During the peak

season a two-train service is in operation. An indoor model railway and small museum are open at Fairbourne terminus
Headquarters: Fairbourne Railway Ltd, Beach Road, Fairbourne, Gwynedd LL38 2EX
Telephone: (01341) 250362
Fax: (01341) 250240
Internet addresses: *E-mail:* fairbourne.rail@btconnect.com

Web site: http://www.fairbournerailway.com
Main station: Fairbourne
Other public stations: Beach Halt, Golf Halt, Loop Halt, Estuary Halt, Barmouth Ferry
OS reference: SH 616128
Car parks: Fairbourne
Access by public transport:
By rail: Fairbourne railway station.
By bus: Arriva service (No 28)

By ferry: From Barmouth Harbour
Access by road: Signposted off the A493 Dolgellau / Tywyn road
Refreshment facilities: Harbour view café, Fairbourne station café
Souvenir shop: Fairbourne
Depot: Fairbourne
Length of line: 2 miles, 12.25in gauge
Passenger trains: A 2-mile journey connecting with ferry at Penrhyn Point to Barmouth. 20min single journey. Through tickets to Barmouth (including ferry) available.
Period of public operation: 1 March until 28 October (closed off peak Mondays and Fridays); open daily 22 October to 4 November
Special events: Little to Large — 3/4 June; Santa Specials — 15/16 December
Facilities for disabled: Wheelchair coach available on request. Disabled toilet at Barmouth Ferry station

Locomotives — 12.25in gauge

Name	No	Builder	Type	Built
Beddgelert§	—	Curwen	0-6-4ST	1979
Yeo	—	Curwen	2-6-2T	1978
Sherpa	—	Milner	0-4-0STT	1978
*Russell**	—	Milner	2-6-4T	1985
Lilian Walter†§	—	FR	A1-1AD	1985
Gwril	—	Hunslet (9354)	4wDM	1994

FR — Fairbourne Railway
*built as replica Leek & Manifold *Elaine*, rebuilt to present form 1985 at FLW
†originally built by G&S Engineering in 1961 as 15in gauge *Sylvia*. Rebuilt at Fairbourne in 1985
§currently out of service

Stock
21 coaches; 14 freight

Special facilities: Evening and full day Driver Experience Courses available (prior booking required)
Membership details: Membership Secretary, Fairbourne Railway Preservation Society, 8 Centre One, Lysander Way, Old Sarum Park, Salisbury SP4 6BU
Special notes: During inclement weather the service may be restricted or cancelled. Extra trains and special parties by arrangement

---

Timetable Service	**Ffestiniog Railway**	Gwynedd

Member: HRA

The world's oldest independent railway, founded in 1832. In many ways, evocative of the early Swiss mountain railways as it climbs from Porthmadog to Blaenau Ffestiniog with some breathtaking views. The railway still operates an interesting variety of locomotives including some unusual Victorian survivors. Passengers have replaced slate as the principal traffic over this former quarry line
General Manager: Paul Lewin
Headquarters: Ffestiniog Railway Co, Harbour Station, Porthmadog, Gwynedd, LL49 9NF
Telephone: Porthmadog (01766) 516000
Fax: 01766 516005
Internet address: *Web site:* http://www.festrail.co.uk
Main stations: Porthmadog Harbour, Tan-y-Bwlch, Blaenau Ffestiniog
Other public stations: Boston Lodge, Minffordd, Penrhyn, Plas Halt, Dduallt, Tanygrisiau
SatNav postcodes:

Locomotives — 1ft 11.5in gauge

Name	No	Builder	Type	Built
Princess+	1	G/England (199/200)	0-4-0STT	1863
Prince	2	G/England	0-4-0STT	1863
Palmerston	4	G/England	0-4-0STT	1863
Welsh Pony+	5	G/England (234)	0-4-0STT	1867
Earl of Merioneth	—	FR	0-4-4-0T	1979
Merddin Emrys	10	FR	0-4-4-0T	1879
David Lloyd George	12	FR	0-4-4-0T	1992
Taliesin	—	FR	0-4-4T	1999
Moelwyn	—	Baldwin (49604)	2-4-0DM	1918
Lilla	—	Hunslet (554)	0-4-0ST	1891
Blanche	—	Hunslet (589)	2-4-0STT	1893
Linda§	—	Hunslet (590)	2-4-0STT	1893
*Britomart**	—	Hunslet (707)	0-4-0ST	1899
Mountaineer§	—	Alco (57156)	2-6-2T	1917
Livingston Thompson†+	3	FR	0-4-4-0T	1886
Lyd	—	FR	2-6-2T	2010
*Hugh Napier**	—	Hunslet (855)	0-4-0ST	1904
Harlech Castle	—	B/Drewry (3767)	0-6-0-DH	1983
Ashover	—	Hibberd (3307)	4wDM	1948
Moel Hebog	—	Hunslet (4113)	0-4-0DM	1955
Mary Ann	—	M/Rail (596)	4wDM	1917
Criccieth Castle	—	FR	0-6-0DH	1995
The Colonel	—	M/Rail (8788)	4wDM	1943
The Lady Diana	—	M/Rail (21579)	4wDM	1957
Stefcomatic	—	Matisa (48589)	2-2-0DH	1956
Vale of Ffestiniog	—	Funkey	Bo-Bo	1968
Moel-y-Gest	—	Hunslet (6659)	0-4-0DM	1965

194

Porthmadog Harbour LL49 9NF
Minffordd LL48 6HF
Tan-y-Bwlch LL41 3AQ
Tanygrisiau LL41 3TW
Blaenau Ffestiniog LL41 3ES
OS reference: SH 571384
Car parks: Porthmadog,
Minffordd, Tan-y-Bwlch,
Tanygrisiau, Blaenau Ffestiniog
Access by public transport:
By rail: Minffordd and Blaenau
Ffestiniog main line stations. *By
bus:* Porthmadog, Minffordd and
Blaenau Ffestiniog served by local
buses
Refreshment facilities: Spooner's
café and bar at Porthmadog, open
all day. Licensed café at
Tan-y-Bwlch, seasonal opening.
Refreshments available on most
trains
Souvenir shops: Porthmadog,
Blaenau Ffestiniog
Museum: Interesting artefacts in
Spooner's Bar, Porthmadog
Depot: Boston Lodge
Length of line: 13.5 miles,
1ft 11.5in gauge
Passenger trains: Porthmadog-
Blaenau Ffestiniog

Name	No	Builder	Type	Built
Harold	—	Hunslet (7195)	0-4-0DM	1974
—**	—	Hunslet (9248)	0-4-0DM	1985
—**	—	Hunslet (9262)	0-4-0DM	1985

*privately owned
†on loan to National Railway Museum
+museum condition, not operational
§out of service in 2012
**2ft 6in gauge, to be regauged to 1ft 11.5in

Stock
37 bogie coaches; 8 4-wheel coaches; 4 brake vans, plus numerous service
vehicles

Period of public operation: Daily
mid-March to end October. Limited
winter service
Special events: Spring Gala —
5-7 May; Autumn Gala —
5-7 October; Halloween Trains —
October; Santa Specials —
December
Facilities for disabled:
Porthmadog and Blaenau Ffestiniog
easily accessible for wheelchairs.
Limited facilities on trains for
disabled in wheelchairs by prior
arrangement. Literature available in
large print and Braille
Special facilities:
Tan-y-Bwlch station is a registered
location for civil/wedding
ceremonies. Special Functions
department handles private train
bookings — phone for details
01766 516024
Membership details: Ffestiniog
Railway Society (see above
address)
Membership journal: *Ffestiniog
Railway Magazine* — quarterly

Railway Centre — Garw Valley Railway — Glamorgan

Member: HRA
Location/headquarters:
Pontycymer Locomotive Shed
Postal address: Bridgend Valleys
Railway Co, t/a Garw Valley
Railway, The Train Shed, Old
Station Yard, Pontycymer, Bridgend
CF32 8AZ
OS reference: SS 893842
Internet addresses:
E-mail: via web site
Web site: www.garw-railway.co.uk
Access by public transport:
By rail: Tondu (5 miles)
By bus: Pontycymmrer is served by
buses from Bridgend
Access by car: M4 Jct 36, follow
signs for
Length of line: 5 miles when
completely reopened
Facilities for disabled: All shed
areas available for disabled visitors
Special events: Seasonal open day
events throughout the year — see
web site for further details
Special facilities: Guided tours of

Locomotives and multiple-units

Name	No	Origin	Class	Type	Built
—	51919	BR	108	DMBS	1956
—	52048	BR	108	DMCL	1962

Locomotives

Name	No	Builder	Type	Built
Pamela	—	Hunslet (3840)	0-6-0ST	1956
—	—	RSH (7705)	0-4-0ST	1952
—	—	Hibberd (3890)	0-4-0DH	1958
—	—	Hibberd (4006)	0-4-0DH	1963

Rolling stock
BR Mk 1 BSO(T), BR Shark brake van, BR standard brake van chassis,
BR departmental flat wagon

Owner
RSH (7705) the 7705 Locomotive Group

the locomotive shed available on
Saturdays, no prior invitation
required. The 10.25in gauge
miniature railway is available for
use all year round (subject to
weather and maintenance
requirements)
Special notes: The railway is
preparing funding applications to
grant funding organisations to
obtain volunteer facilities, track
components and equipment in order

Wales

to re-lay the track and construct stations
Membership details: Membership

Secretary, c/o above address
Membership journal: *On Track* — newsletter, two issues a year

---

| Timetable Service | **Great Orme Tramway** | Conwy |

Member: HRA
A cable-hauled street tramway to the summit of the Great Orme is operated as two sections involving a change halfway. Opened to the public in July 1903, it includes gradients as steep as 1 in 3.9
Location: Great Orme Tramway, Victoria Station, Church Walks, Llandudno LL30 2NB
OS reference: SH 7781
Operating society/organisation: Conwy County Borough Council, Engineering & Design Services, Library Buildings, Mostyn Street, Llandudno LL30 2RP

Telephone: (01492) 879306
Internet addresses: *E-mail*: tramwayenquiries@conwy.gov.uk
Web site: www.greatormetramway.gov.uk
Car park: Approximately 100yd from Lower Terminal or adjacent to Summit Terminal
Access by public transport: Good
On site facilities: Shop
Exhibits for viewing: There are exhibits displayed at the Halfway station and a small exhibition (free)
Period of public operation: March to end of October (daily) 10.00-18.00 (17.00 March and

October). Trams run every 20min. Can be subject to change
Special notes: The only remaining cable-hauled street tramway in Britain. 1 mile long rising to 650ft (3ft 6in gauge)
Stock: 4 tramcars each seating 48, built 1902/3
Facilities for disabled: The tramway has limited disabled access and is unsuitable for the wheelchair-bound, although wheelchairs can be folded away in the tramcars.
Access statement available upon request/on our web site

| Timetable Service | **Gwili Railway (Rheilffordd Gwili)** | Carmarthenshire |

Member: HRA, TT
Runs alongside the River Gwili on part of the Carmarthen-Aberystwyth line. Attractions include a fully restored signalbox, historic station building, museum of signalling and other railway artefacts and a TPO. The line runs from Bronwydd Arms to Danycoed Halt. There is a 7.25in gauge miniature railway, picnic site and TPO at Llwyfan Cerrig
Headquarters: Gwili Railway Co Ltd, Bronwydd Arms Station, Bronwydd Arms, Carmarthen, SA33 6HT
Telephone: 01267 238213
Internet addresses: *E-mail:* company@gwili-railway.co.uk
Web site: www.gwili-railway.co.uk
OS reference:
Bronwydd Arms SN 417239
Llwyfan Cerrig SN 405258
Main station: Bronwydd Arms
Car park: Bronwydd Arms (free)
Access by public transport: Traveline Cymru: 0871 200 2233
Refreshment facilities: Bronwydd

Locomotive and multiple-unit

Name	No	Origin	Class	Type	Built
—*	D2178	BR	03	0-6-0DM	1962
—	14901	BR	14	0-6-0DH	1964
—±	51347	BR	117	DMBS	1960
—±	51401	BR	117	DMS	1960
—±	59508	BR	117	TC	1960

14901 on loan for two years from Peak Rail

Industrial locomotives

Name	No	Builder	Type	Built
Olwen	—	RSH (7058)	0-4-0ST	1942
Haulwen	—	V/Foundry (5272)	0-6-0ST	1945
Welsh Guardsman	71516	RSH (7170)	0-6-0ST	1944
Victory*	—	A/Barclay (2201)	0-4-0ST	1945
Mond Nickle No 1§	—	Peckett (1345)	0-4-0ST	1914
Abigail§	312433	R/Hornsby (312433)	4wDM	1951
—§	12514	N/British (12514)	0-6-0DM	7953

Stock
5 ex-BR Mk 1 coaches; 1 ex-BR GUV; 1 ex-BR BG; 1 ex-BR Mk 3 sleeper; 4 ex-TVR coaches; 1 ex-GWR coach; 1 TPO, 2 ex-GWR 'Toad' brake vans; 2 ex-GWR bogie bolsters; 1 ex-GWR 'Crocodile'; 2 ex-GWR 'Mink' vans; 3 ex-GWR Fruit D; 1 ex-GWR Bloater; 1 ex-SECR parcels van; 1 ex-SR parcels van; 2 ex-Army vans; 3 'Tunney' wagons; 1 'Gane' wagon; 1 'Dogfish' wagons; 4 open wagons; 1 Booth diesel-hydraulic crane; 1 ex-LMS hand crane

Wales

Arms and Llwyfan Cerrig
Souvenir shop: Bronwydd Arms
Depot: Bronwydd Arms, stock also kept at other locations on the line
Length of line: 2.5 miles
Passenger trains: Bronwydd Arms-Llwyfan Cerrig-Danycoed. To Llwyfan Cerrig only during special events
Period of public operation: 6-9, 11/12, 15, 17-19, 24-25, 30 April; 1-3, 6-10, 13, 15-17, 20, 22-24, 27, 29-31 May; 2-8, 10, 12-14, 17, 19-21, 24, 26-28, 30 June; Daily in July EXCEPT 2, 6, 9, 13, 16; daily in August; daily in September EXCEPT 3, 7/8, 10, 14, 17, 21, 24,

Owners
* Caerphilly Railway Society
§ Swansea Vale Railway
± Llanelli & Mynydd Mawr Railway Society

28/29; 3, 7, 10,13, 14,17, 21, 23-25, 28 October; weekends ans 21, 24 December
Public opening: Trains leave Bronwydd Arms at:
Timetable A — 10.30, 11.50, 13.20, 14.50, 16.10;
Timetable B — 11.15, 12.45, 14.15, 15.45;
Timetable C — 11.15, 13.00, 14.45. Some special events may have a

more frequent service
Facilities for disabled: Access to stations, TPO and museum
Special events: Day out with Thomas — 6-9 April; Classic Transport Weekend 21/22 July; 1940s Day — 18 AugustSanta Trains — 1/2, 8/9, 15/16, 22-24 December

---

| Timetable Service | Llanberis Lake Railway (Rheilffordd Llyn Padarn) | Gwynedd |

Member: HRA

A narrow gauge passenger-carrying railway starting next to the historic Dinorwic Quarry workshops (now part of the National Museum of Wales) and running along the shores of Llanberis Lake using the trackbed of the former slate railway line to Port Dinorwic. Excellent views of Snowdonia and good picnic spots along the line. The half mile extension from Gilfach Ddu to Llanberis village is now open

General Manager: David Jones

Headquarters: Llanberis Lake Railway, Gilfach Ddu, Llanberis, Gwynedd LL55 4TY

Telephone: Llanberis (01286) 870549

Internet addresses: *E-mail:* info@lake-railway.co.uk
Web site: www.lake-railway.co.uk

Main station: Padarn Park station/Gilfach Ddu
Other public stations: Cei Llydan and Llanberis (village)
OS reference: SH 586603
Car park: Padarn Park station/Gilfach Ddu
Refreshment facilities: Padarn Park station/Gilfach Ddu
Souvenir shop: Padarn Park station/Gilfach Ddu, Llanberis station
Length of line: 2.5 miles, 1ft 11.5in gauge

Industrial locomotives

Name	No	Builder	Type	Built
Elidir	1	Hunslet (493)	0-4-0ST	1889
Thomas Bach/Wild Aster	2	Hunslet (849)	0-4-0ST	1904
Dolbadarn	3	Hunslet (1430)	0-4-0ST	1922
Topsy	7	R/Hornsby (441427)	4wDM	1961
Twll Coed	8	R/Hornsby (268878)	4wDM	1956
—	—	R/Hornsby (425796)	4wDM	1958
Garrett	11	R/Hornsby (198286)	4wDM	1939
—	18	M/Rail (7927)	4wDM	1941
Llanelli	19	R/Hornsby (451901)	4wDM	1961
Una*	—	Hunslet (873)	0-4-0ST	1905

*not part of the railway's motive power stock. Housed at the adjacent slate museum and can sometimes be seen working demonstration freight trains

Stock
13 bogie coaches; 20 wagons

Journey time: approx 60min
Passenger trains: Gilfach Ddu-Llanberis-Penllyn-Gilfach Ddu
Journey time: Return trip approx 60min
Period of public operation: Tuesdays and Wednesdays from mid-February to mid-March, daily February half-term week (20-27 February). Sundays, Tuesdays/Wednesdays and Thursdays from 14 March until Easter. Sundays to Fridays from Easter to September, daily 22 May to 2 September; Sundays to Thursdays in October; Tuesdays and Wednesdays in November. Family tickets available, under 3s free

Special events: Easter Egg Hunt over Easter weekend; 40th Anniversary Gala — 2/3 July; Teddy Bears' Picnic — August Bank Holiday Weekend; Halloween Hunt — 24-30 October; Santa Trains in December
Facilities for disabled: Level approaches throughout shop, café and to train. Special toilet facilities provided nearby. Specially adapted carriage for wheelchair users
Marketing names: Rheilffordd Llyn Padarn Cyfyngedig (Padarn Lake Railway Ltd); Llanberis Lake Railway

Llanelli & Mynydd Mawr Railway

Member: HRA

The company was formed in 1999. The railway, at present a quarter of a mile long, follows the route of the former Carmarthenshire Tramroad, which was the first public operating company in the country by Act of Parliament in 1802. The headquarters is based at the former Cynheidre Colliery which closed in 1989. The line will be extended to just over 1 mile. A heritage centre will be built. The company own all but 100m of the site at Cynheidre. The overhaul of the Avonside tank engine is close to completion thanks to a grant from the Heritage Lottery Fund

Location/headquarters: Llanelli & Mynydd Mawr Railway, 76 Rehoboth Road, Five Roads SA15 5DZ

OS reference: SN 495075

Contact: 01554 759255 or visit web site

Internet addresses:

E-mail: enquiries@lmmrcoltd.com

Web site: www.lmmrcoltd.com

Access by public transport:

By bus: First Cymru bus route 194/195 from Llanelli town centre

Access by car: Leave the M4 at junction 48 then take the A4138 to Llanelli and B4309 (Carmarthen) to

Locomotives and Multiple-units

Name	No	Origin	Class	Type	Built
—	51354	BR	117	DMBS	1960
—	51396	BR	117	DMS	1960
—	52029	BR	107	DMCL	1961

Industrial locomotives

Name	No	Builder	Type	Built
Desmond	—*	Avonside (1498)	0-4-0ST	1906
Sir John	—	Avonside (1680)	0-6-0ST	1914
—	—	Sentinel (10222)	0-4-0DH	1962

*undergoing restoration at Llangollen Railway

Rolling stock

BR/Leyland Experimental Coach No ADB977091, BR Mk 1 BSK (privately owned), BR Mk 2 RFB as static buffet, 2 GWR 6-wheel carriages (bodies only), small selection of freight stock

Owners

Sir John the Vale of Neath Railway Society

ADB977091 the Burry Port & Gwendraeth Valley Railway

Cynheidre

On site facilities: Car park

Length of line: 0.25 mile, to extend to 1 mile

Period of public operation: Please see web site for opening dates / times

Facilities for disabled: Yes

Special notes: The public can visit the building that houses the DMUs

and shunter and brake van on Saturdays, but to ensure that the site is open please contact 01554 759255 before planning a visit

Membership details: Details from 01269 862962 or visit web site

Membership journal: Newsletter, annually

Llangollen Railway

Member: HRA, TT

The line, which is presently 7.5 miles long, is situated in the picturesque Dee Valley and follows the River Dee for much of its route affording good views of the dramatic Welsh countryside between Llangollen and Carrog. A notable event in 2002 was BBC2's Timewatch re-enactment of the Rainhill Trials using the replica locomotives *Rocket, Sans Pareil* and *Novelty,* on the section of line between Glyndyfrdwy and Carrog. The extensive renovation of Berwyn Viaduct the following year won a national award. In 2006 the

Locomotives and multiple-units

Name	No	Origin	Class	Type	Built
—	2859*	GWR	2800	2-8-0	1918
—	3802	GWR	2800	2-8-0	1938
Cogan Hall	5952*	GWR	Hall	4-6-0	1935
—	5532*	GWR	4575	2-6-2T	1928
—	5539*	GWR	4575	2-6-2T	1928
—	6430	GWR	6400	0-6-0PT	1925
Betton Grange	6880†	GWR	6800	4-6-0	—
—	7754*	GWR	5700	0-6-0PT	1930
Foxcote Manor	7822	GWR	'Manor'	4-6-0	1950
—	47298	LMS	3F	0-6-0T	1924
Kenneth Aldcroft	44806	LMS	5MT	4-6-0	1944
The Unknown Warrior	45551†	LMS	5MT	4-6-0	—
—	80072	BR	4MT	2-6-4T	1954
—	03162	BR	03	0-6-0DM	1960

Wales

Wales

199

renovation of Llangollen station was completed with assistance from the Heritage Lottery Fund, and the renovation of Berwyn Stationmaster's House was completed and is now available as a holiday let (see below). Fortunately the railway took the opportunity to reinstate the platform extension cantilevered to the side of Berwyn Viaduct when the structure was restored, allowing the station to regain its original appearance. The platform extension had been removed by British Railways in 1962. Work is also continuing to extend the line to the town of Corwen, which is 2.5 miles from the current terminus at Carrog. There a new station will be constructed. Clearance of the trackbed has been undertaken. Donations to the Corwen Extension Project can be made to the 'Llangollen Railway Trust'

Location: Llangollen station is situated alongside the River Dee at the junction of Abbey Road (A542) with Castle Street/Mill Street (A539). Traffic from the A5 should turn off at the traffic lights into Castle Street (A539)

Chairman: Jim Ritchie

Operating company: Llangollen Railway plc

Supporting Organisation/ leaseholder: Llangollen Railway Trust Ltd

Headquarters/principal station: The Station, Abbey Road, Llangollen, Denbighshire LL20 8SN (both organisations)

Telephone: General enquiries: 01978 860979 (office hours) also for Santa and Day out with Thomas bookings. Talking Timetable: 01978 860951 (24hr).

Fax: 01978 869247

Internet addresses: E-mail: llangollen.railway@btinternet.com Web site: http://www.llangollen-railway.co.uk

OS reference: SJ 214422

Car park: Llangollen car parks (all pay & display) — Royal International Pavilion (SatNav LL20 8SW), Market Street (SatNav LL20 8PS), East Street (SatNav LL20 8SW), Mill Street (SatNav LL20 8RQ) Carrog — station car park on B5437 off A5 west of Llangollen (SatNav LL21 9BD)

Name	No	Origin	Class	Type	Built
—	13265	BR	08	0-6-0DE	1956
—	D5310	BR	26	Bo-Bo	1959
—	D6940	BR	37	Co-Co	1964
Orion	D1566	BR	47	Co-Co	1962
—	50416	Wickham	109	MBS	1958
—	50447	BRCW	104	DMBS	1957
—	50454	BRCW	104	DMBS	1957
—	50528	BRCW	104	DMC	1957
—	51618	BR	127	DMBS	1959
—	51907	BR	108	DMBS	1960
—	54490	BR	108	DTC	1960
—	56171	Wickham	109	DTC	1958
—	54223	BR	108	DTCL	1959
—	56456	Cravens	105	DMBS	1958

*locomotives either stored, under restoration or major overhaul, currently not on public display. The frames and boiler of new-build 6880 *Betton Grange* are located at Llangollen along with the frames for the new-build LMS 'Patriot' 4-6-0
†new-build under construction

Industrial locomotives

Name	No	Builder	Type	Built
Jennifer	—†	H/Clarke (1731)	0-6-0T	1942
Jessie	—†	Hunslet (1873)	0-6-0ST	1937
—	68030	Hunslet (3777)	0-6-0ST	1952
Austin No 1	—	Kitson (5459)	0-6-0ST	1932
—	68072	Vulcan (5309)	0-6-0ST	1945
Davy	—	E/Electric (1901)	0-6-0DE	1951

†expected to be away on hire for 2012

Stock: *coaches, approx 45 in total including* — Service sets of Mk 1 stock, 4 BR suburban coaches; 1 LNER Thompson lounge car; 1 LNER Thompson brake coach; 3 GWR autocoaches; 1 GN brake, etc, some under restoration

Stock: *wagons, approx 50 including* — 2 Bolster wagons; 3 GWR Toad brake vans; 1 BR(E) brake van; 4 BR ballast wagons; 1 BR Presflow wagon; 1 GWR 'Fruit D'; 2 GWR Tube wagons; 1 Esso tank wagon; 1 Shell tank wagon plus various other items of freight stock

Stock: *maintenance* — Cowans 50-ton breakdown crane ARD96718 ex-Laira; DRG 12-ton diesel-hydraulic crane, Matisa track recording machine; O&K road-railer

Owners
2859 and 5532 the Llangollen Railway GW Locomotive Group
3802 the GW 3802 Ltd
5952 and 6880 the 6880 Betton Grange (Society) Ltd
7754, 13265, *Jennifer* and *Austin No 1* the Llangollen Railway Trust Ltd
7822 the Foxcote Manor Society
80072 the 80072 Steam Locomotive Co Ltd (on loan to NYMR for 2012)
03162 Wirral Borough Council
All Heritage Railcars (DMUs) the Llangollen Railcar group
All main line diesel fleet (except 37901) plus *Davy* the Llangollen Diesel Group
Remainder are privately owned

Access by public transport:
By rail: Ruabon (5 miles) on Shrewsbury-Chester line, then by bus
By bus: Regular service runs Monday-Saturday and less frequently on Sundays.
Enquiries:
Traveline Cymru 08712 002233 (www.traveline.org.uk)
Bus: 08712 002233
National Rail enquiries: 08457

Wales

484950

Station information:

Llangollen — Toilets (inc disabled and baby changing), gift and model shop. Victoria's Tea Room selling light refreshments. Cream teas on board (subject to availability and must be pre-booked).

Berwyn — Tea room open only on summer weekends

Deeside Halt — Trains call by request only, please inform guard or give a clear signal to driver to be picked up (please see timetable for specific services as not all trains stop)

Glyndyfrdwy — Toilets, tea room open on peak weekends

Carrog — Car and coach park (free), toilets with disabled access and tea room open on all operating days

Length of line: 7.5 miles

Passenger trains: Llangollen-Carrog

Period of public operation: Saturdays and Sundays from 5 February to 1 April. Daily from 2 April to 7 October. 13/14 October and from 29 October to 4 November.

A mix of steam, heritage railcar and diesel traction depending on timetable in operation

Special events: Real Ale Train (evening) — 17 March; Diesel Day — 31 March; Steel, Steam & Stars — 21-29 April; Murder Mystery (evening) — 5 May; Real Ale Train (evening) — 19 May; Real Ale Train (evening) — 16 June; Heritage Railcar Gala (DMU) — 23/24 June; Murder Mystery (evening) — 14 July; 1960s Weekend — 28/29 July; Day out with Thomas — 4/5, 9-12 August; Murder Mystery (evening) — 18 August; Classic Transport Weekend — 25/26 August; Autumn Steam Gala — 31 August-2 September; Diesel Day — 22 September; Real Ale Train (evening) — 29 September; Day out with Thomas — 20/21, 25-28 October; Ride the Rocket Fireworks Train (evening) — 3 November; Murder Mystery with Fireworks (evening) — 5 November; Poppy Train — 3/4 November; Santa Specials (pre-booking essential) — 1/2, 8/9, 15/16, 20-24 December; Mince Pie Specials — 26 December-1 January 2013

Driver experiences: The railway offers a varied programme of footplate and railway experience courses from early spring through to late autumn, ranging from the basic Evening Ramble to the more advanced all-day freight railway experience. Courses are available on steam and diesel locomotives as well as heritage railcars for both individual and group bookings. More information on the timetable and web site. Early booking is recommended. Gift vouchers, valid for 13 months, are also available

Special facilities: The Robertson Suite at Llangollen is licensed for civil/wedding ceremonies. Train hire available for receptions.

The Grade II-listed stationmaster's house at Berwyn is available as a holiday let (sleeps 6) — contact Hoseasons on 0844 847 1356 or www.hoseasons.co.uk, property code W7641, brochure page 328

Facilities for disabled: Special passenger coach for wheelchairs, toilet facilities at Llangollen and Carrog

Membership details: The Membership Secretary, Llangollen Railway Trust Ltd, c/o above address

Membership journal: *Steam at Llangollen* (SAL Magazine)

Special note: For safety reasons visitors to the railway are not permitted access to locomotive yard, locomotive shed or workshop unless accompanied by a qualified member of the Llangollen Railway

---

Museum	Penrhyn Castle Industrial Railway Museum	Gwynedd

Member: HRA

A collection of historic industrial steam locomotives, both standard and narrow gauge, displayed in Penrhyn Castle, a well-known National Trust property in the area regularly open to visitors.

Location: Llandegai, near Bangor. One mile east of Bangor on the A5

OS reference: SH 603720

Operating society/organisation: National Trust, Penrhyn Castle, Industrial Railway Museum, Llandegai, Nr Bangor LL57 4HN

Telephone: Bangor (01248) 353084

Internet address: *Web site:* www.nationaltrust.org

Car park: Within castle grounds

Access by public transport: *By rail:* Bangor (3 miles).

Industrial locomotives

Name	No	Builder	Type	Built
Kettering Furnaces No 3	—	B/Hawthorn (859)	0-4-0ST	1885*
Watkin	—	de Winton	0-4-0VBT	1893*
Fire Queen	—	Horlock	0-4-0	1848†
Hawarden	—	H/Clarke (526)	0-4-0ST	1899
Vesta	—	H/Clarke (1223)	0-6-0T	1916
Charles	—	Hunslet (283)	0-4-0ST	1882§
Hugh Napier	—	Hunslet (855)	0-4-0ST	1904§
—	1	Neilson (1561)	0-4-0WT	1870
Haydock	—	Stephenson (2309)	0-6-0T	1879
Acorn	—	R/Hornsby (327904)	0-4-0DM	1948

Note: *Hugh Napier* currently on loan to Ffestiniog Railway

*3ft gauge

†4ft gauge

§1ft 10.75in gauge

Stock

10 narrow gauge rolling stock exhibits from the Padarn/Penrhyn system, most of which have been restored.

The small relics section includes a comprehensive display of railway signs

By bus: Arriva Cymru 5, 6, 7 and 67, 5X. Bus stop 1 mile walk through grounds
On site facilities: The castle is open to the public, and contains a gift shop. Light refreshments are available, hot meals are available between 12.00 and 14.30
Public opening: Daily 12 March-30 October 11.00-17.00.
Grounds and Stable block: 11.00-17.00 all season
House: 11.00-17.00 (last admission 16.30)
July/August: 11.00-17.00 (last admission 16.30)
Facilities for disabled: Access to castle and museum
Special notes: For those interested in stately homes the castle is well

and model locomotives in the upper stable block

The museum also has displays of tools used in the quarries and railway systems

Recent restorations now on display:
One of the three coaches built at the quarry for the conveyance of visitors around the works. This one formed part of the train used by Princess Margaret and Lord Snowdon on their royal visit to Wales in May 1962.
The Dinorwic Quarry Pedal Car is thought to have been built c1860 by the New Howe Co of Glasgow. It was used by the chief engineer of the quarry to inspect the trank

worth a visit. The entrance fee covers both the castle and the railway exhibits housed in the castle courtyard. Ruston Hornsby locomotive *Acorn* can be seen operating on some occasions during opening times. For exhibits not on display please ask a member of museum staff for assistance. Reduced entry fee for grounds and railway museum

---

Timetable Service	Pontypool & Blaenavon Railway	Torfaen

Member: HRA
The historic Blaenavon site, complete with its railway installations and locomotives, can easily be included in a visit to Big Pit Mining Museum. The half mile branch from Furnace Sidings to Big Pit Mining Museum is now open
Location: Just off the B4248 between Blaenavon and Brynmawr. Signposted as you approach Blaenavon
OS reference: SO 237093
Operating society/organisation: Pontypool & Blaenavon Railway Co (1983) Ltd, The Railway Shop, 13A Broad Street, Blaenavon, Torfaen NP4 9ND
Telephone/Fax: (01495) 792263
Internet addresses: *E-mail:* info@pbrly.co.uk
Web site: www.pontypool-and-blaenavon.co.uk
Car parks: Whistle Inn, Furnace Sidings, Big Pit (pay and display)
Main station: Furnace Sidings
Other public stations: Blaenavon High Level, Whistle Inn (no parking available)
SatNav postcode: Furnace Sidings —NP4 9SF
On site facilities: Light refreshments, souvenir shop and toilets available at Furnace Sidings.

Locomotives

Name	No	Origin	Class	Type	Built
—	5668	GWR	5600	0-6-2T	1926
—	9629	GWR	5700	0-6-0PT	1946
—	03141	BR	03	0-6-0DM	1960
Steve Organ GM	D5627	BR	31	A1A-A1A	1960
—	37421	BR	37	Co-Co	1965
O.V.S. Bulleid CBE	73128	BR	73	Bo-Bo	1966
—	51351	P/Steel	117	DMBS	1959
—	51397	P/Steel	117	DMS	1959
—	51942	BR	108	DMCL	1964
—	52044	BR	108	DMCL	1960
—	54270	BR	108	DTCL	1959
—	50632	BR	108	DMCL	1960
—	59520	P/Steel	117	TC	1959
—	60117	BR	205	DMBS	1957
—	60828	BR	205	DTC	1960
unit 1198	60573	BR	3CEP	TS	1960
unit 1198	61736	BR	3CEP	DMS	1960
unit 1198	61737	BR	3CEP	DMS	1960

Industrial locomotives

Name	No	Builder	Type	Built
Harry	—	Barclay (1823)	0-4-0ST	1926
Tom Parry	—	Barclay (2015)	0-4-0ST	1935
—	8	RSH (7139)	0-6-0ST	1944
Mech Navvies Ltd	75169	RSH (7169)	0-6-0ST	1944
Llanwern	104	E/Electric (D1249)	0-6-0DH	1968
—	106	E/Electric (D1226)	0-6-0DH	1971
—	RT1	Fowler (22497)	0-6-0DM	1938
Ebbw	17	Hunslet (7063)	0-8-0DH	1971
—	14	H/Clarke (D615)	0-6-0DH	1938
Bill Caddick	—	H/Clarke (D1186)	0-6-0DH	1959
—	DL16	H/Clarke (D1387)	0-4-0DH	1968
Gower Princess	—	Ruston (200793)	4wDM	1940

Wales

Light refreshments available on majority of services

Public opening:
Weekends and Bank Holidays
6 April to 38 October, plus
Wednesdays 8, 15, 22, 29 August,
Friday 14 September and
Wednesday 31 October
Trains run hourly from Blaenavon High Level station 11.00-17.00.
Santa trains run every half hour 11.00-15.30.
Return journey time about 50min
Note: Services are a mix of steam and diesel traction

Special events: Easter Bunnies — 6-9 April; Spring Diesel Gala — 21/22 April; 50th Anniversary, Last Passenger Train to Blaenavon — 29 April; Teddy Bears' Picnic — 5-7 May; Family Fun Weekend — 2-4 June; QEII Diamond Jubilee — 5 June; World Heritage Day — 23 June; Garn Lakes Day — 24 June; Wartime Weekend — 7/8 July; Ivor the Engine — 13/14 August; Family Fun Weekend — 11/12 August; Tenth Transport Rally — 26/27 August; Annual Steam Gala — 14-16 September; Autumn Diesel Gala — 13/14 October; Ghost Train — 27/28, 31 October; Santa Steam Trains — 312, 8/9, 15/16, 23/24 December. Please visit web site for up-to-date information.

Driver experience: Diesel — 29 September; Steam — 27 April, 27 July, 30 September
Membership details: c/o above address, or call at 'The Railway Shop', Broad Street, Blaenavon

Name	No	Builder	Type	Built
—	—	Ruston (421702)	0-6-0DH	1959
Panteg No 1	—	Sentinel (10083)	0-6-0DH	1961
William Ellis	—	T/Hill (136C)	4wDM	1964
—	19*	Bagnall (2962)	0-4-0ST	1950

*on hire from Bodmin & Wenford Railway during 2012

Stock
10 ex-BR Mk 1 coaches, 4 ex-GWR coaches, 3 ex-LSWR coaches, 1 ex-LMS sleeper, 1 SR Post Office Tender, 1 ex-GER coach (No 3, on loan from Stately Trains for three years), 35 other vans, china clay, coke and tank wagons

Owners
Class 108s the Gwent 108 Group
3CEP unit the EMU Preservation Society

Timetable Service	Rheilffordd Eryri — Welsh Highland Railway	Gwynedd

Member: HRA
Travel on the UK's longest narrow gauge heritage railway from the world-famous Caernarfon Castle through the heart of the Snowdonia National Park to Porthmadog with connections to the Ffestiniog Railway services to Blaenau Ffestiniog

General Manager: Paul Lewin
Headquarters: Ffestiniog Railway Co, Harbour Station, Porthmadog LL49 9NF
Telephone: Porthmadog (01766) 516000
Fax: 01766 516005
Internet addresses: *Web site:* http://www.festrail.co.uk
Facebook: www.facebook.com/festrail
Twitter: http://twitter.com/!/festrail
Main stations: Caernarfon, Beddgelert. Porthmadog
Other public stations:

Locomotives – 1ft 11.5in gauge

Name	No	Builder	Type	Built
—	K1	B/Peacock (5292)	0-4-0+0-4-0	1909
—**†	133	S. F. Belge (2683)	2-8-2	1953
—**†	134	S. F. Belge (2684)	2-8-2	1953
—*†	109	B/Peacock (6919)	2-6-2+2-6-2	1939
—	138	B/Peacock (7863)	2-6-2+2-6-2	1958
—*†	140	B/Peacock (7865)	2-6-2+2-6-2	1958
—*	143	B/Peacock (7868)	2-6-2+2-6-2	1958
—*	87	Cockerill (3267)	2-6-2+2-6-2	1936
Castell Caernarfon	—	Funkey	Bo-Bo	1968
Upnor Castle	—	Hibberd (3687)	4wDM	1954
Conway Castle	—	Hibberd (3831)	4wDM	1958
—†	9	Baguley (2395)	4wDM	1951
Bill∏	—	Hunslet (9248)	4wDHF	1985
Ben†	—	Hunslet (9262)	4wDHF	1985

*former South African Railways NGG16 class locomotives
**former South African Railways NG15 class locomotives awaiting restoration
†undergoing restoration

Stock
20 bogie coaches, 2 brake vans (goods), numerous goods and service vehicles

Wales

Bontnewydd, Dinas, Waunfawr, Plas y Nant, Snowdon Ranger, Rhyd Ddu, Meillionen (Beddgelert Forest Camp Site), Nantmor, Pont Croesor

SatNav postcodes:
Caernarfon LL55 2YD
Dinas LL54 2UP
Waunfawr LL55 4AQ
Rhyd Ddu LL54 6TN
Porthmadog LL54 6TN

Car parks: Caernarfon, Dinas, Waunfawr, Snowdon Ranger, Rhyd Ddu, Pont Croesor, Porthmadog

Access by public transport: Caernarfon is served by local buses. The station at Bangor is served by Virgin and Arriva Trains Wales. There is a regular bus service between Bangor and Caernarfon. Beddgelert station is served by local bus services from Caernarfon,

Porthmadog and Betws-y-coed. Porthmadog is served by bus and main line services

Depot: Dinas

Length of line: 25 miles, 1ft 11.5in gauge

Passenger trains: Caernarfon-Porthmadog

Period of public operation: Easter to end of October. Limited winter service

Facilities for disabled: Caernarfon, Dinas, Waunfawr, Rhyd Ddu, Beddgelert, Pont Croesor and Porthmadog stations accessible by wheelchair.
Facilities on trains for disabled in wheelchairs by prior arrangement. Literature available in large print and Braille

Refreshments: Hot and cold food, beers, wines and spirits and a

refreshment trolley are available on most trains. Snowdonia Parc Hotel is situated at Waunfawr station and Spooner's cafe, restirant and bar at Porthmadog Harbour station serve a large selection of snacks, meals and real ale.
  Toilet facilities are available on most trains

Souvenir shop: Gift shops at Caernarfon and Porthmadog

Special event: Spring Gala — April/May; Beer Festival — May; Autumn Gala — 8/9 September; Halloween Trains — October; Santa Specials — December

Membership details: Welsh Highland Railway Society

Membership journal: *Snowdon Ranger* — quarterly

Steam Centre — Rhyl Miniature Railway — Denbighshire

Member: Britain's Great Little Railways

The miniature railway operating around the Marine Lake at Rhyl is among the oldest 15in gauge railways anywhere in the world. Its origins go back to 1911, and on peak days you can ride on the same train that visitors in 1920 would have found. 'Central Station' opened in 1997 and has its own museum with audio-visual touch screen

Operating society/organisation: Rhyl Steam Preservation Trust

Location: Marine Lake, Wellington Road, Rhyl, Denbighshire

Internet address: *Web site:* www.rhylminiaturerailway.co.uk

Trust secretary: Simon Townsend

Postal address: 10 Cilnant, Mold, Flintshire CH7 1GG

Telephone: 01352 759109

OS reference: SN 072124

SatNav postcode: LL18 1LN

Length: Approx 1 mile (1ft 3in gauge)

On site facilities: Car park

Locomotives – 1ft 3in gauge

Name	No	Builder	Type	Built
Joan	101	Barnes	4-4-2	1920
Railway Queen	102	Barnes	4-4-2	1921
Michael	105	Barnes	4-4-2	c1925
Billy	106	Barnes	4-4-2	1934
—	44	Cagney	4-4-0	c1910
Clara	—	Guest & Saunders LE	0-4-2DM (SO)	1961
—	—	Lister	4wDM	1938
—	—	Hayne/Minirail	2w-2-4BER	1983

Rolling stock: 5 bogie 'cars de luxe' built in the 1910s and a similar vehicle built in 2001, 2 Cagney bogie coaches built c1904. Ballast wagon

Owners
Billy Rhyl Town Council

Access by public transport: Approx 1 mile from Rhyl main line station, buses to Towyn and Abergele pass by

Period of public operation: Operation (steam) Bank Holiday Sundays and Mondays, every Sunday from Easter to September, every Thursday to Sunday during school holidays; from 11.00 or

earlier. Also open with diesel or electric haulage, Saturdays from Easter to September, and all other days during summer school holidays

Membership details: Friends of Rhyl Miniature Railway, details from 01745 339477 Newsletters twice a year

Snowdon Mountain Railway

Member: HRA

The only public rack and pinion railway in the British Isles, opened in 1896, this bustling line climbs the slopes of Snowdon to the café at the top

General Manager: Alan Kendall

Engineering Manager: Mike Robertshaw

Commercial Manager: Vince Hughes

Marketing Manager: Jonathan Tyler

Headquarters: Snowdon Mountain Railway, Llanberis LL55 4TY

Telephone: 0844 493 8120 (advance bookings available via telephone)

Fax: (01286) 872518

Internet addresses: *E-mail:* info@snowdonrailway.co.uk *Web site:* www.snowdonrailway.co.uk

Main station: Llanberis

Other public stations: Summit, also Clogwyn/Rocky Valley when Summit is inaccessible

OS reference: SH 582597

Car park: Llanberis

Access by public transport: Bangor railway station then by bus, either direct or alternatively via Caernarfon. Snowdon Sherpa Services to/from Beddgelert and Betws-y-coed stop outside the station

Refreshment facilities: Llanberis, Summit station

Souvenir shops: Llanberis, Summit station

Depot: Llanberis

Length of line: 7.5km, 800mm gauge

Locomotives – 80cm gauge

Name	No	Builder	Type	Built
Enid	2	SLM (924)	0-4-2T	1895
Wyddfa	3	SLM (925)	0-4-2T	1895
Snowdon	4	SLM (988)	0-4-2T	1896
Moel Siabod	5†	SLM (989)	0-4-2T	1896
Padarn	6	SLM (2838)	0-4-2T	1922
Ralph	7*	SLM (2869)	0-4-2T	1923
Eryri	8*	SLM (2870)	0-4-2T	1923
Ninian	9	Hunslet (9249)	0-4-0DH	1986
Yeti	10	Hunslet (9250)	0-4-0DH	1986
Peris	11	Hunslet (9305)	0-4-0DH	1991
George	12	Hunslet (9312)	0-4-0DH	1992

All steam locomotives were built by Swiss Locomotive Works, Winterthur
All diesel locomotives were built by Hunslet Engine Co, Leeds
†currently out of service
*currently stored out of service (boilerless)

Stock

8 closed bogie coaches; 1 bogie works car; 1 4-wheel open wagon

Passenger trains: *Early season:* Llanberis-Clogwyn. Journey time approx 45min. Round trip approx 2hr including a 30min stop. *High season:* Llanberis-Summit. Journey time approx 1 hour. Round trip approx 2hr 30 min, including 30min stop at the Summit. Departures from Llanberis at 30min intervals subject to passenger demand

Period of public operation: Daily late March to first week of November inclusive subject to winter maintenance. Please visit web site for up-to-date opening times

Group bookings: Bookings for groups of 15 or more can be taken in advance. Please call 0844 493 8120 for special rates

Facilities for disabled: Those requiring wheelchair access should please telephone in advance to discuss their particular requirements. Disabled parking is available and there are suitable toilet facilities in both Llanberis station and the Summit. Only officially registered support dogs can travel on the trains

Special notes: Trains depart subject to weather conditions and passenger demand. If weather conditions become severe on Snowdon trains will terminate at Rocky Valley (5/8 distance up Snowdon). Advance bookings can be made by calling 0844 493 8120 or online

---

Talyllyn Railway

Member: HRA, TT, GLTW

The very first railway in the country to be rescued and operated by enthusiasts, the line climbs from Tywyn through the wooded Welsh hills past Dolgoch Falls to Nant Gwernol. The trains are hauled by a variety of veteran tank engines, all immaculately maintained by the railway's own workshops at Tywyn Pendre

Manager: Dave Scotson

Headquarters: Talyllyn Railway Co, Wharf Station, Tywyn, Gwynedd LL36 9EY

Telephone: Tywyn (01654) 710472

Fax: (01654) 711755

Internet addresses: *Web sites:* www.talyllyn.co.uk www.ngrm.org.uk

Main station: Tywyn Wharf

Other public stations: Tywyn Pendre, Rhydyronen, Brynglas, Dolgoch Falls, Abergynolwyn, Nant Gwernol

OS reference:
Tywyn Wharf SH 586005

SatNav postcodes:
Tywyn Wharf car park LL36 0TF
Abergynolwyn LL36 9UR

Car parks: Tywyn Wharf, Dolgoch, Abergynolwyn

Access by public transport: Tywyn main line station. Bus Gwynedd services to Tywyn

Refreshment facilities: Tywyn Wharf hot meals and Bistro service, Abergynolwyn hot and cold snacks available. Picnic areas at Dolgoch Falls and Abergynolwyn. Railway adventure children's playground at Abergynolwyn station

Souvenir shops: Tywyn Wharf, Abergynolwyn

Museum: Tywyn Wharf

Depot: Tywyn Pendre

Length of line: 7.25 miles, 2ft 3in gauge

Passenger trains: Tywyn-Nant Gwernol

Period of public operation: Sundays in March. Daily 1 April to 4 November, 26 December-1 January 2013

Journey times: Tywyn-Nant Gwernol — single 55min, return 2hr 15min

Special events: Mothering Sunday — 18 March; Locals' Day (all welcome) — Thursday 29 March; Easter Bunny at the Talyllyn — 8 April; The Children's *Duncan* Day — Thursday 7 June; Father's Day — 17 June; Have-a-go and Garden Railway Gala — 30 June, 1 July; Evening Themed Train — Tuesday 31 July; Teddy Bears' Picnic — Thursday 2 August; Tom Rolt Steam Rally — 4/5 August; Evening Themed Train — Tuesday 7 August; Evening Floral Train — Tuesday 14 August; Craft Fair at Abergynolwyn — Tuesday 14, Thursday 16 August; Race the Train (limited service) — 18 August; Evening Themed Train — Tuesday 21 August; The Children's *Duncan* Day — Thursday 23 August; Volunteers' Showcase Gala and

Locomotives – 2ft 3in gauge

Name	No	Builder	Type	Built
Talyllyn	1	F/Jennings (42)	0-4-2ST	1864
Dolgoch	2	F/Jennings (63)	0-4-0WT	1866
Sir Haydn	3	Hughes (323)	0-4-2ST	1878
Edward Thomas	4	K/Stuart (4047)	0-4-2ST	1921
Midlander	5	R/Hornsby (200792)	4wDM	1940
Douglas/Duncan	6	Barclay (1431)	0-4-0WT	1918
Tom Rolt*	7	Barclay (2263)	0-4-2T	1949/1991
Merseysider	8	R/Hornsby (476108)	4wDH	1964
Alf	9	Hunslet (4136)	0-4-0DM	1950
Bryneglwys	10	Simplex (101T023)	0-4-0DM	c1985

*virtually a new locomotive rebuilt from the original at Pendre Works.

Locomotive notes: In service — Nos 1, 2, 3 (until May), 4, 6 and 7 Diesels as available

Stock
13 4-wheel coaches/vans; 10 bogie coaches; 45 wagons

Narrow Gauge Museum, Tywyn

Name	No	Builder	Type	Built
Dot	—	B/Peacock (2817)	0-4-0ST	1887
Rough Pup	—	Hunslet (541)	0-4-0ST	1891
—	2†	K/Stuart (721)	0-4-0WT	1902
Jubilee 1897	—	M/Wardle (1382)	0-4-0ST	1897
George Henry	—	de Winton	0-4-0T	1877
—	13§	Spence	0-4-0T	1895
Nutty*	—	Sentinel (7701)	0-4-0VB	1929

Various wagons and miscellaneous equipment
*not currently on site, † from Dundee Gas Works, § from Guinness

Abergynolwyn Village Show — 25 August; Series One Land Rover Gathering and Tywyn Town Festival — 26 August; Evening Themed Train — Tuesday 28 August; Halloween Specials — Thursday/Friday 25/26 October; The Big Draw — 27 October; Santa Specials — 22-24 December.
Also: Fish & Chip Specials — Fridays 3-31 August

Talyllyn Victorian Train: The TR is probably alone in still being able to run its complete original passenger train dating from the 1860s, and invites you to enjoy this unique experience, travelling in Victorian coaches behind a Victorian locomotive. The train will depart at 11.00 on Thursdays on 14, 21, 28 June, 5, 12, 19 July and 6, 13, 20, 27 September, featuring photographic opportunities and guided tour. Advance booking is advised and special fares apply

Family tickets: Available

Facilities for disabled: No problem for casual visitors, advance notice preferred for groups. Access to shop, museum and refreshments possible at Tywyn and Abergynolwyn. Accessible toilet facilities at Tywyn and Abergynolwyn. Limited capacity for wheelchairs on most trains, please check

Special notes: Parties, private charter trains, Talyllyn Treats and driver experience days by arrangement. Children under 5 years of age free. Great Little Trains of Wales discount card accepted

Membership details:
P. and R. Featherstone, PO Box 5295, Rugby CV21 9JP

Membership journal: *Talyllyn News* — quarterly

Marketing names: One of the Great Little Trains of Wales. The world's first preserved railway

Teifi Valley Railway

Member: HRA

The line at Henllan was part of an extensive network of railways that spread through the valleys of west Wales in the mid-19th century. Originally laid in broad gauge, before being relaid to standard gauge. After the closure of commercial operations, the narrow gauge line was laid by enthusiasts

Operating society/organisation: Teifi Valley Railway, Henllan Station, Nr Newcastle Emlyn SA44 5TD

Telephone: (01559) 371077

Internet address: *Web site:* www.teifivalleyrailway.org

Main station: Henllan

Other public stations: Pontprenshitw, Llandyfriog Riverside

Car park: Henllan (on B4334)

OS reference: SN 358407

Access by public transport: BR station — Carmarthen (14 miles). Bus service 461 to Henllan or 460

Refreshments: Henllan

Souvenirs: Henllan

Length of line: 2 miles (2ft gauge)

On site facilities: Children's play areas, woodland waterfall, nature trails, crazy golf and crazy quoits, picnic area, café and gift shop. Display of narrow gauge freight wagons

Depot: Henllan (not open to public)

Facilities for disabled: All facilities including portable ramps and wide door for wheelchairs in two coaches

Period of public operation: April to September. Closed Fridays and Saturdays except during August

Special events: Halloween Ghost Trains; Santa Specials. Please contact for further details

Special notes: Pay once only and ride all day. Steam-hauled trains every day if possible, other trains may be diesel-hauled

Membership details: Teifi Valley Railway Society, c/o Henllan station

Membership journal: *Right Away* — quarterly

Industrial locomotives – 2ft gauge

Name	No	Builder	Type	Built
Alan George	—	Hunslet (606)	0-4-0ST	1894
Sgt Murphy	—	K/Stuart (3117)	0-6-2T	1918
Sholto	—	Hunslet (2433)	4wDM	1941
Sammy	—	M/Rail (605)	4wDM	1959
Henry	—	Ruston (256314)	4wDMF	1959

Industrial locomotive (standard gauge)

Name	No	Builder	Type	Built
Rosyth	—	Barclay (1385)	0-4-0ST	1914
Swansea Vale No 1	—	Sentinel (9622)	4wVBTG	1958

Owner

Standard gauge locomotives The Railway Club of Wales

Vale of Rheidol Railway

Member: Great Little Train of Wales

This narrow gauge railway offers a 23-mile round trip from Aberystwyth to Devil's Bridge providing spectacular views which cannot be enjoyed by road. At Devil's Bridge there are walks to the Mynach Falls and Devil's Punch Bowl. Many artists have been inspired by the magnificence of Devil's Bridge and the Rheidol Valley

General Manager: N. Thompson

Headquarters: Vale of Rheidol Railway, Park Avenue, Aberystwyth SY23 1PG

Locomotives — 1ft 11.75in gauge

Name	No	Origin	Ex-BR Class	Type	Built
Owain Glyndwr	7	GWR	98	2-6-2T	1923
Llywelyn	8	GWR	98	2-6-2T	1923
Prince of Wales	9	GWR	98	2-6-2T	1924
—	10	Brecon MR (002)	98/1	0-6-0DH	1987

Stock

16 bogie coaches; 1 4-wheel guard's van; 14 wagons for maintenance use; 1 inspection trolley, 1 Permaquip trolley

The following locomotives are stored on the railway pending restoration and future display

Name	No	Builder	Type	Built
Wren	—	K/Stuart (3114)	0-4-0ST	1918
—	4	Decauville (1027)	0-4-0T	1926
Kathleen	—	de Winton	0-4-0VBT	1877

Telephone: (01970) 625819
Fax: (01970) 623769
Internet address: *Web site:*
www.rheidolrailway.co.uk
Main station: Aberystwyth
(adjacent to main line station)
Other public stations: Llanbadarn,
Glanyrafon, Capel Bangor,
Nantyronen, Aberffrwd, Rheidol
Falls, Devil's Bridge
OS reference: SN 587812
Car parks: Aberystwyth, Devil's
Bridge
Access by public transport:
Aberystwyth main line station, and
bus services to Aberystwyth
Refreshment facilities:
Aberystwyth (not railway owned),
Devil's Bridge (not railway
operated)

Name	No	Builder	Type	Built
—	6	Fowler (10249)	0-6-0T+T	1905
—	21	Fowler (11938)	0-4-2T	1909
—	23	Fowler (15515)	0-6-2T	1920
Margaret	—	Hunslet (605)	0-4-0ST	1894
—	31	Mafei (4766)	0-8-0T	1916
—	—	H/Clarke (D564)	4wDM	1930
—	—*	R/Proctor (50823)	4wPM	1918
—	—	K/Stuart (3114)	0-4-0ST	1918

*metre gauge
Also Henschel bogie tender (11854/25 of 1917)

Souvenir shop: Aberystwyth
Depot: Aberystwyth (not open to
the public)
Length of line: 11.75 miles,
1ft 11.75in gauge
Journey time: Single 1hr, return
2.5-3hr

Passenger trains: Aberystwyth-
Devil's Bridge
Period of public operation: Daily
3 April to 27 October, with some
exceptions in April, May, June,
September and October

Timetable Service — Welsh Highland Heritage Railway — Gwynedd

Member: HRA, GLTW,
Attractions of Snowdonia.
The Welsh Highland Railway
combines a short narrow gauge
train ride with a visit to the
locomotive sheds and a 7.25in
gauge miniature line. The
locomotive sheds include a detailed
exhibition about the town of
Porthmadog and its narrow gauge
railways including the FR and
WHR, as well as a chance to view
and inspect many items of stock.
More extensive guided tours are
usually available by asking staff.
Most trains include heritage
vehicles from the old Welsh
Highland Railway. Footplate rides
and Driver experience courses are
available
Location: Tremadog Road,
Porthmadog, immediately adjacent
to main line railway station and
opposite the Queen's Hotel
OS reference: SH 571393
Operating society/organisation:
Welsh Highland Railway Ltd,
Tremadog Road, Porthmadog,
Gwynedd LL49 9DY
Telephone:
Porthmadog: 01766 513402
Out of hours phone: 01766 513402
Internet addresses: *E-mail:*
info@.whr.co.uk
Web site: www.whr.co.uk
Car park: Free — overflow pay &

Locomotives – 60cm gauge

Name	No	Builder	Type	Built
Gertrude	—	Barclay (1578)	0-6-0Y	1918
Gelert	—	Bagnall (3050)	0-4-2T	1953
—	590	Baldwin (44699)	4-6-0T	1917
Russell	—	Hunslet (901)	2-6-2T	1906
Karen	—	Peckett (2024)	0-4-2T	1942
Glaslyn	1	R/Hornsby (297030)	4wDM	1952
Kinnerley	2	R/Hornsby (354068)	4wDM	1953
Cnicht	36	M/Rail (8703)	4wDM	1941
—	9	M/Rail (60s363)	4wDM	1968
—	4	M/Rail (60s333)	4wDM	1963
Badco	—	Hunslet (203031)	4wDM	1942
—	5	Hunslet (6285)	4wDM	1968
—	3L5	R/Hornsby (370555)	4wDM	1953
—	6	M/Rail (11102)	4wDM	1959
—	7	Hunslet (7535)	4wDM	1977
—	10	R/Hornsby (481552)	4wDM	1962
—	11	Hunslet (3510)	4wDM	1947
—†	58	August 23 Works (23387)	0-6-0DH	1977
Eryri†	60	August 23 Works (23389)	0-6-0DM	1977
—†	LP-08	August 23 Works (24051)	0-6-0DH	1980
—	—	Barclay (554)	4wDH	1970
—	—	Barclay (555)	4wDH	1970
—	—	M/Rail (264)	4wPM	1916
Kathy	—	H/Barclay (LD 9350)	0-4-0DM	1994
Emma	—	H/Barclay (LD 9346)	0-4-0DM	1994
The Eclipse	—	Greaves	0-4-0WE	1927
The Coalition	—	Greaves	0-4-0WE	1930

†ex-Polish State Railways class LYd2,
August 23 Works is situated in Romania

Locomotive notes: *Badco* is in the locomotive shed with accessible
footplate. *Russell* is currently viewable in the locomotive shed, though may
move to the erecting shops during 2012. Works shunters and *Russell* can

display car park opposite the railway with space for coaches

Catering facilities: 'Russell Tea Room' supplying a range of adult/children's meals and light refreshments

Access by public transport: Arriva Trains Wales to adjacent Porthmadog station. National Express buses 200yd. Bus Gwynedd services 1, 2, 3, 97, 98, 99, 99a, S96, S97

On site facilities: The WHHR shop has a vast book section and also stocks modelling materials and souvenir gifts. There are toilets at Porthmadog station (including disabled facilities) and the locomotive sheds, and a wheelchair-accessible coach is available on all trains

Length of line: Porthmadog (WHR) station to Pen-y-Mount, 1.5 mile return trip. 60cm gauge

Passenger trains: Porthmadog

usually be viewed on request to staff, *Gelert, Gertrude* and *Emma* will operate the 2012 service. There may be visiting locomotives during the year

Stock
Eisteddfod coach No 7 has been converted for wheelchair and pushchair accessibility, coach No 6 sometimes runs a a back up brake van, but also sees service as a carriage. The original WHR buffet car is on display in the locomotive sheds when not in service

(WHR) station to Pen-y-Mount, return journey approx 50min incorporating guided tours of the locomotive sheds

Family tickets: Available, 2 adults + 2 children can travel all day for £15. Under 5s free

Tickets: All day tickets — adults £6, senior £5, child (over 5) £3. Dogs free

Period of public operation: Daily 31 March to 28 October, EXCEPT 1, 5, 8, 12, 15, 19 October. Trains run 10.30, 11.30, 13.00,

14.00, 15.00, 16.00 (the 16.00 does not run in October)

Facilities for disabled: Toilet, ramp and provision on train, wheelchairs provided. Disabled passengers can be accommodated without prior notice

Membership details: Membership Secretaries, R. & P. Hughes, 2 Clos Sulien, Llanbadarn, Aberystwyth, Ceredigion SY23 3GF. Instant membership available at the shop

Membership journal: *The Journal* — every four months

Timetable Service	Welshpool & Llanfair Light Railway	Mid Wales

Member: HRA

There is a decidedly foreign atmosphere to the trains over this line. The steam locomotive collection embraces examples from three continents, and the coaches are turn-of-the-century balcony saloons from Austria or 1950s bogies from Hungary. The line follows a steeply graded route (maximum 1 in 24) through very attractive rolling countryside, and is rather a gem in an area too often missed by the traveller heading for further shores

General Manager: Terry Turner

Headquarters: Welshpool & Llanfair Light Railway Preservation Co Ltd, The Station, Llanfair Caereinion SY21 0SF

Telephone: Llanfair Caereinion (01938) 810441

Fax: (01938) 810861

Internet address: *Web site:* www.wllr.org.uk

Main station: Welshpool (Raven Square)

Other public stations: Castle

Locomotives – 2ft 6in gauge

Name	No	Builder	Type	Built
The Earl	1	B/Peacock (3496)	0-6-0T	1902
The Countess	2	B/Peacock (3497)	0-6-0T	1902
Monarch	6	Bagnall (3024)	0-4-4-0T	1953
Chattenden	7	Drewry (2263)	0-6-0DM	1949
Dougal	8	Barclay (2207)	0-4-0T	1946
Sir Drefaldwyn	10	S. F. Belge (2855)	0-8-0T	1944
Ferret	11	Hunslet (2251)	0-4-0DM	1940
Joan	12	K/Stuart (4404)	0-6-2T	1927
SLR No 85	14	Hunslet (3815)	2-6-2T	1954
Scooby	16	Hunslet (2400)	0-4-0DM	1941
TSC No 175	17	Diema	0-6-0DM	1978
CFI 764.423	18	Resita (1128)	0-8-0T	1954
CFI 764.425	19	Resita (???)	0-8-0T	1954
—	9150	Baguley (3746)	4wDM	1976

Locomotive notes: Locomotives expected in service 2012 — *The Earl, The Countess,* No 19 and *Joan* . Some locomotives may not be accessible by the public and stored off site

Stock
3 replica of original W&LLR Pickering carriages; 7 ex-Zillertalbahn-style coaches; 2 ex-Sierra Leone coaches, 2 Hungarian State Railway coaches, 6 W&LLR wagons; 8 ex-Admiralty wagons; 2 ex-Bowater wagons; 1 Wickham trolley

Note: Not all of the vehicles are in service and some are stored in areas not accessible by the public

Wales

Caereinion, Sylfaen, Llanfair Caereinion
OS reference: SJ 107069
SatNav postcodes: Welshpool (Raven Square) — SY21 7LT Llanfair Caereinion — SY21 0SF
Car parks: Llanfair Caereinion, Welshpool (both free)
Access by public transport: Main line station at Welshpool, one mile from Raven Square. Arriva buses from Shrewsbury, Oswestry and Newtown to Welshpool
Refreshment facilities: Light refreshments at Llanfair Caereinion. Picnic areas at Welshpool and Llanfair

Souvenir shops: Welshpool, Llanfair Caereinion
Depot: Llanfair Caereinion
Length of line: 8 miles, 2ft 6in gauge
Passenger trains: Welshpool-Llanfair Caereinion
Period of public operation: Weekends Easter to October. Daily in school holidays, plus some other days in June, July and September
Special events: W&L Vintage Train 26/27 May, 23/24 June, 21/22 July, 11/12 August; Steam Gala — 1/2 September; Santa Specials — 15/16, 22/23 December
Facilities for disabled: Specially

adapted coaches for wheelchairs. Please phone in advance. Easy access to shops. Disabled toilet facility at Welshpool and Llanfair
Membership details: David Barker, 458 Oxford Road, Gomersal, Cleckheaton, West Yorks BD19 4LB
Membership journal: *The Journal* — quarterly
Marketing name: Llanfair Railway
Special notes: Open balcony coaches — travel right next to the engine at the front of the train. Or see the line rolling away behind the back end!

Steam Centre | Alderney Railway | Channel Islands

In 1997 the Alderney Railway was 150 years old, having opened on 14 July 1847. Queen Victoria was the only passenger until 1980
Location: Alderney, Channel Islands
Operating society/organisation: Alderney Railway Society, PO Box 75, Alderney, Channel Islands
Telephone: (01481) 822978
Internet address: *Web site:* www.alderneyrailway.com
Car park: Yes
Access by public transport: Aurigny Air Services from Southampton
Location: Station at Braye Road (tickets & souvenirs)
Public opening: Weekends and Bank Holidays, Easter to end of

Industrial locomotives

Name	No	Builder	Type	Built
Elizabeth	—	Vulcan (D2271)	0-4-0DM	1949
Molly 2	—	R/Hornsby	0-4-0DM	1958

Stock
4 Wickham cars
2 ex-London Underground 1959 Stock tube cars (locomotive-hauled)
1 Wickham flat known as *Colossus* (not currently in operation)

September
Special events: Alderney Week August. Easter Egg Specials on Easter Sunday. Santa Specials, Saturday before Christmas
Length of line: 2 miles
Facilities for disabled: No, but train crew will always help wherever possible

President: Mr M. L. Thomas OBE
Chairman: Anthony Le Blanc (tel: 01481 822978)
Notes: Engine shed at Quarry. Wickham 'train' operates in low season; *Elizabeth* and tube cars in high season and at Easter

---

Steam Centre | Great Laxey Mine Railway | Isle of Man

The railway was opened on 25 September 2004 and is a reconstruction of the surface section of the former Great Laxey Mine tramway which was used to haul wagon loads of ore from inside the mine and onto the former ore washing and dressing floors at Laxey. The railway runs beneath the main Laxey to Ramsey road — the longest railway tunnel on the Island

Locomotives – 1ft 7in gauge

Name	No	Builder	Type	Built
Ant	—	GNS	0-4-0WT	2004
Bee	—	GNS	0-4-0WT	2004
Wasp	—	Clayton	0-4-0BE	1973

GNS — Great Northern Steam Ltd, Darlington, based on original 1877 design by Stephen Lewin, Poole

Rolling stock
2004-built passenger vehicle, 2007-built passenger vehicle, both built by Alan Keef. 6 replica ore wagons dating from 2000

Contact: Andrew Scarffe
Operating company: Laxey & Lonan Heritage Trust, West Lynne, Mateland Drive, Laxey, Isle of Man IM4 7N4
Telephone: 01624 861706 (there is no direct telephone on the railway)
Car park: Available in nearby Laxey
Main station: Valley Gardens, Laxey

Access by public transport: A few minutes' walk from Laxey station on the Manx Electric Railway and bus stop of the route 3 Douglas to Ramsey service
On site facilities: No refreshment facilities on site, but café and public house nearby
Length of line: 0.25-mile, 1ft 7in gauge
Public opening: Saturdays and Bank Holidays, Easter until end of September; Sundays during August, 11.00-16.30
Special events: As advertised
Facilities for disabled: Unable to carry wheelchair-bound passengers, though Valley Gardens are accessible
Membership details: From above address

Steam Centre — Groudle Glen Railway — Isle of Man

Following the successful development of the glen in the 1890s, and with the arrival of the Manx Electric Railway in 1893, the line was built using entirely local labour. The railway was an instant success, and dubbed as 'the smallest passenger railway in the world'. The line closed in 1962, with the locomotives and rolling stock being disposed. In 1982 a group of enthusiasts began the ambitious restoration project to re-open the line. *Sea Lion* and several passenger coaches survived to operate on the re-opened line
Location: Groudle Glen Railway, Isle of Man
Operating company: Groudle Glen Railway Ltd, 8A Village Walk, Onchan, Isle of Man IM3 4EA
Telephone: (01624) 670453 (weekends)
Internet addresses:
E-mail: ggr@ggr.org.uk
Web site: www.ggr.org.uk
Car park: Yes

Locomotives – 2ft gauge

Name	No	Builder	Type	Built
Dolphin	1	H/Hunslet (4394)	4wDM	1952
Walrus	2	H/Hunslet (4395)	4wDM	1952
Sea Lion	—	Bagnall (1484)	2-4-0T	1896
Annie	—	Booth/GGR	0-4-2T	1998
Polar Bear	—	BEV (556801)	2-B-2	2004
Parracombe	3232	Baguley (3232)	0-4-0DH SO	1947

Access by public transport: Manx Electric Railway (Groudle Hotel)
On site facilities: Sales shop and tea room, visitor centre
Length of line: 0.75-mile, 2ft gauge
Public opening: Easter Sunday and Monday, Sundays May to September (11.00-16.30); Wednesday evening services July/August (19.00-21.00); Santa Trains — December (11.00-15.30)
Special events: Easter Bunny Trains — 8/9 April; Diesel & Electric Day — 20 May; Big 30th Birthday — 27 May; Dreamcatcher Fundraising Day — 24 June; Vintage Nostalgia — 20, 27 June; Jester Express — 22 July; Cliff Top Concerts — 12 August; Santa Trains — 15, 21/22 December; Mince Pie Trains — 26 December
Facilities for disabled: Due to the line's location, those who are disabled will have some difficulty. It is suggested that they e-mail for advice
Further information and membership details: Friends of Groudle Glen Railway, c/o above address
Membership journal: *Down The Glen Newsletter* — published twice yearly

Timetable Service — Isle of Man Railway — Isle of Man

Member: HRA
The 3ft gauge Isle of Man Railway is a survivor of a system which previously also operated from Douglas to Peel and Ramsey. Almost continuous operation since 1873 makes it one of the oldest operating railways in the British Isles. This narrow gauge railway still runs over the 15 mile line with its original locomotives and carriages, through an ever-changing landscape, to a choice of destinations in the south of the Island, such as the impressive Castle Rushden, the Nautical Museum and the beautiful Silverdale Glen. The railway holds special events all year round, some of which include the Manx Heritage Transport Festival, Teddy Bears' Picnic, Island at War and the Santa trains to Santa's Grotto and Christmas market.

The line is owned and operated by the Isle of Man Government
Head of Railways: Ian Longworth
Headquarters: Department of Tourism & Leisure, Heritage Railways, Public Transport

Directorate, Transport Headquarters, Banks Circus, Douglas, Isle of Man IM1 5PT
Telephone: Douglas (01624) 663366
Fax: (01624) 663637
Internet address: *E-mail:* heritagerailways@gov.im
Main station: Douglas
Other public stations: Port Soderick, Santon, Ballasalla, Castletown, Colby, Port St Mary and Port Erin
Car parks: Douglas, Ballasalla, Castletown, Port St Mary and Port Erin
Access by public transport: Isle of Man Transport bus to main centres
Refreshment facilities: Whistle Stop café is situated in Port Erin station building and is open all year. Inside Douglas station The Tickethall serves a range of meals and refreshments
Souvenir shops: At all the main stations and within the Railway Museum
Museum: Adjacent to Port Erin station, first opened in 1975, is situated in part of the original train storage shed, holding restored locomotives and carriages. A section of the building is still used for the maintenance of trains running on the line. It is possible to look into the blacksmith's workshop
Depot: Douglas

Locomotives – 3ft gauge

Name	No	Builder	Type	Built
Loch	4	B/Peacock (1416)	2-4-0T	1874
G. H. Wood	10	B/Peacock (4662)	2-4-0T	1905
Maitland	11	B/Peacock (4663)	2-4-0T	1905
Hutchinson	12	B/Peacock (5126)	2-4-0T	1908
Kissack	13	B/Peacock (5382)	2-4-0T	1908
Caledonia	15	Dubs & Co (2178)	0-6-0T	1885
Viking	17	Schottler (2175)	0-4-0DH	1958
Ailsa	18	Hunslet (22021)	4wDM	1994

Locomotive note: All operational, all other rolling stock stored off the line

On display in museum at Port Erin

Name	No	Builder	Type	Built
Peveril	6	B/Peacock (1524)	2-4-0T	1875
Mannin	16	B/Peacock (6296)	2-4-0T	1926

Rolling stock
16 coaches, 20 runners, 1 van, 2 open wagons, 1 well wagon, 1 track tamping machine

Length of line: 15.75 miles, 3ft gauge
Passenger trains: Douglas-Port Erin
Period of public operation: February to November
Special events: Held throughout the year
Facilities for disabled: Level access throughout Douglas and Port Erin stations including refreshment area. Carriages able to carry wheelchairs, ramps provided. Advance notice helpful
Special facilities: Parties or events can be accommodated; it is possible to book private carriages, trams or an entire train, or a special package to fit in with the hirer's requirements. Call 01624 697473 or e-mail david.thornton@gov.im for group bookings and availablity. Group discounts of 25% off bookings for 20 or more are available on timetabled services.

Island explorer tickets are also available, providing unlimited travel on the railways, horse trams and buses

---

Timetable Service | Manx Electric Railway | Isle of Man

Member: HRA

The 3ft gauge Manx Electric Railway is a unique survivor of Victorian high technology. A mixture of railway and tramway practice, it was built in 1893 and was a pioneer in the use of electric traction. It illustrates an example of a true electric interurban line. Two of the original cars are still in service, making them the oldest tramcars still in operation on their original route in the British Isles. After leaving Douglas, the railway passes the Groudle Glen Railway before reaching the charming village of Laxey, for the Snaefell Mountain Railway. The line continues over some of the most breathtaking coastal scenery in the Island before reaching its terminus at Ramsey nearly 18 miles from Douglas. Special events are held throughout the year, such as A Victorian Extravaganza, Manx Heritage Transport Festival and winter photography.

The line is owned and operated by the Isle of Man Government
Head of Railways: Ian Longworth
Chief Engineer: Peter Maddocks
Headquarters: Department of Tourism & Leisure, Heritage Railways, Public Transport Directorate, Transport Headquarters, Banks Circus, Douglas, Isle of Man IM1 5PT
Telephone: Douglas (01624) 663366
Fax: (01624) 663637
Internet address: *E-mail:* heritagerailways@gov.im
Main stations: Douglas (Derby Castle), Laxey and Ramsey
Other public stations: Groudle, Dhoon Glen, Ballaglass and numerous wayside stops
Car parks: Douglas, Laxey, Ramsey (nearby)
Access by public transport: Isle of Man Transport buses to main centres. Douglas Corporation Horse Tramway to Derby Castle in summer
Depots: Douglas and Ramsey
Refreshment facilities: Laxey Station café is situated within the

MER station building, a short way from the Rose Gardens in the centre of the village. Light snacks and homemade cakes are available throughout the railway's operating season

Length of line: 17.5 miles, 3ft gauge

Passenger service: Douglas-Ramsey

Period of public operation: March to November

Special events: Held throughout the year

Special notes: Folded wheelchairs can be carried. Please notify in advance. One trailer with disabled access used on advance request

Special facilities: Parties or events can be accommodated, it is possible to book private carriages, trams or an entire train, or a special package to fit in with the hirer's requirements. Call 01624 697473 or e-mail david.thornton@gov.im for group bookings and availablity. Group discounts of 25% off bookings for 20 or more are available on timetabled services

Motor cars — 3ft gauge

Nos	Type	Seats	Body	Built
1, 2	Unvestibuled saloon	34	Milnes	1893
5, 6, 7, 9	Vestibuled saloon	32	Milnes	1894
16	Cross-bench open	56	Milnes	1898
19-22*	Winter saloon	48	Milnes	1899
26	Cross-bench open	56	Milnes	1898
32, 33	Cross-bench open	56	UEC	1906
34	Engineer's Car	—	IoMT	2004

*22 rebodied 1991, McArd/MER

Trailers – 3ft gauge

Nos	Type	Seats	Body	Built
36, 37	Cross-bench open	44	Milnes	1894
40, 41, 44	Cross-bench open	44	EE Co	1930
42, 43	Cross-bench open	44	Milnes	1903
45-48	Cross-bench open	44	Milnes	1899
49-51, 53, 54	Cross-bench open	44	Milnes	1893
56*	Cross-bench open	44	ERTCW	1904
57, 58	Saloon	32	ERTCW	1904
59	Special Saloon	18	Milnes	1895
60	Cross-bench open	44	Milnes	1896
61, 62	Cross-bench open	44	UEC	1906

*rebuilt as disabled access trailer in 1993

Note: Other rolling stock stored off the line

Museum — Pallot Steam, Motor & General Museum — Channel Islands

Postal address: Rue de Bechet, Trinity, Jersey, Channel Islands

SatNav postcode: JE3 5BE

Tel: 044 1534 865307

Internet addresses:
E-mail: info@pallotmuseum.co.uk
Web site: www.pallotmuseum.co.uk

Access by public transport:
By bus: Route 25 with 0.5-mile walk, Route 4 with 1-mile walk

Access by car: A8 or A9, free parking

On site facilities: Train rides on Thursdays

Souvenir shop: On site

Length of line: 0.33-mile circuit

Period of public operation:

Locomotives

Name	No	Builder	Type	Built
La Meuse	—	La Meuse (3442)	0-6-0T	1931
Foles Hill	—	Peckett (2085)	0-4-0ST	1948
Kestrel	—	Peckett (2129)	0-4-0ST	1952
J. T. Daly	—	Bagnall (2450)	0-4-0ST	1931
—	D1	NBL (27734)	0-4-0DH	1958
—	—	M/Rail (11143)*	4wDM	1960

*2ft gauge

Monday to Saturday — 2 April to 2 November, 10.00-17.00. Closed Sundays. Winter visitors welcome by appointment

Facilities for disabled: Disabled-friendly museum with toilet and ramp access to upper galleries

Special events: Steam & Motor Fayre to be held in May and September

Snaefell Mountain Railway

Member: HRA

The 3ft 6in gauge Snaefell Mountain Railway is unique. It is the only electric mountain railway in the British Isles. Almost all the rolling stock is original and dates back to 1895. The railway begins its journey at the picturesque village of Laxey where its station is shared with the Manx Electric Railway. The climb to the summit of Snaefell (2,036ft) is a steep one and the cars travel unassisted up gradients as severe as 1 in 12. From the summit, on a clear day, it is the only place in the British Isles where you can see the seven kingdoms just by turning round; England, Ireland, Scotland, Wales, Mann, the Kingdom of Neptune and the Kingdom of Heaven.

The line is owned and operated by the Isle of Man Government

Head of Railways: Ian Longworth

Chief Engineer: Peter Maddocks

Headquarters: Department of Tourism & Leisure, Heritage Railways, Public Transport Directorate, Transport Headquarters, Banks Circus, Douglas, Isle of Man IM1 5PT

Telephone:

Trams – 3ft 6in gauge

Nos	Type	Seats	Body	Built
1-4, 6	Vestibuled saloon	48	Milnes	1895
5 (rebuild)	Vestibuled saloon	48	MER/Kinnin	1971

Douglas (01624) 663366

Fax: (01624) 663637

Internet address: *E-mail:* heritagerailways@gov.im

Main station: Laxey

Other public stations: Bungalow, Summit

Car parks: Laxey, Bungalow (nearby)

Access by public transport: Manx Electric Railway or Isle of Man Transport bus to Laxey

Depot: Laxey

Refreshment facilities: At the top of the island is the newly refurbished Snaefell Summit Hotel, which is open during the railway's operating season. A range of hot and cold food is available with superb views across the whole island. The Summit Hotel is the venue for the popular Sunset Dinners, available from 9 May to 21 September and offers a great Sunday lunch. Stargazing evenings

'Pie in the Sky' are also available

Souvenirs shops: None

Length of line: 4.5 miles, 3ft 6in gauge

Passenger service: Laxey-Snaefell Summit

Period of public operation: April to November

Special notes: Elderly and/or disabled passengers may find the access and egress steps narrow and steep

Special facilities: Parties or events can be accommodated; it is possible to book private carriages, trams or an entire train, or a special package to fit in with the hirer's requirements. Call 01624 697473 or e-mail david.thornton@gov.im for group bookings and availablity. Group discounts of 25% off bookings for 20 or more are available on timetabled services

---

Downpatrick & County Down Railway

Member: HRA

The railway museum is the only preserved Irish standard gauge (5ft 3in) railway operating in Ireland. It is a representative of the former Belfast & County Down railway terminus in Downpatrick, which closed in 1950, two years after being taken into state ownership

Location: The Railway Station, Market Street, Downpatrick, Co Down BT30 6LZ

OS reference: J483444

Operating society/organisation: Downpatrick & County Down Railway Society

Diesel locomotives and multiple-unit

Name	No	Origin	Class	Type	Built
W. F. Gillespie OBE	E421	CIE	421	C	1962
—	E432	CIE	421	C	1962
—	G611	CIE	611	B	1962
—	G613	CIE	611	B	1962
—	G617	CIE	611	B	1962
—	RB3	BRE-Leyland	—	4wDM	1981

Name	No	Origin	Class	Manufacturer	Type	Built
—	712	CIE	—	Wickham (8919)	4wDH	1962

Steam locomotives

Name	No	Builder	Type	Built
—	1*	O&K (12475)	0-4-0T	1934
—	3	O&K (12662)	0-4-0T	1935

*at Railway Preservation Society of Ireland at Whitehead for overhaul

Telephone: 028 4461 5779
Internet address: *Web site:*
www.downrail.co.uk
Car park: Free parking adjacent to station
Access by public transport: A regular service is operated by Ulsterbus from Belfast Europa bus centre (next to Great Victoria Street railway station).
Tel: (028) 9032 0011
Refreshment facilities: Buffet carriage open on operating days
On site facilities: Souvenir shop, toilets
Length of line: 4 miles open to public traffic. Current terminus: King Magnus's Halt. Track was extended southwards to Ballydugan and north to a new station at Inch Abbey
Public opening: Special events (see web site) and weekends 9 June-2 September
Journey time: 45min return journey from Downpatrick town to Downpatrick Loop Platform and King Magnus's Halt and Inch Abbey
Facilities for disabled: Toilets, shop, platform and trains accessible

Rolling stock
2 CIE Brake open standards (Nos 1918 & 1944); CIE Travelling Post Office (No 2978); 1 CIE Brake open standard generating steam van (No 3223); CIE Buffet open standard (No 2419); NIR '70' class railcar brake open standard intermediate (No 728); B&CDR 'Royal Saloon' (No 153); B&CDR 1st/2nd composite (No 152); B&CDR 3rd open (ex-railmotor); B&CDR 6-wheeled 2nd (No 154); B&CDR 6-wheeled brake 3rd (No 39); GS&WR 3rd open (No 836); GSWR 6-wheeled brake first (No 69); Ulster Railway Family Saloon (No 33); GNR 6-wheeled third; 4 LMS (NCC) parcels vans; 2 LMS (NCC) open wagon; LMS (NCC) brake van; CIE closed van; 2 GNR closed vans; GNR brake van; GSWR ballast hopper; GSWR ballast plough; LMS (NCC) steam crane; 2 private oil company tankers, CIE track inspection vehicle No 712; selection of carriage and wagon underframes for internal use

Owners
712, G611 and G617 the Irish Traction Group
G613 and M&GW full brake privately owned
RB3 is owned by Translink
E421 and E432 the Downpatrick & County Down Railway Society

for disabled
Membership details: The Membership Secretary, Downpatrick & County Down Railway Society, The Railway Station, Downpatrick, Co Down BT30 6LZ

| Timetable Service | Giant's Causeway & Bushmills Railway | Co Antrim |

The GC&BR was opened in 2002 using the stock of the former Shane's Castle Railway on the last two miles of the site of the Portrush to Giant's Causeway electric tramway closed in 1949. The line runs between Bushmills and the Giant's Causeway with its charming views along the River Bush, and spectacular vistas across the sea to Donegal
Location: The railway links the distillery (open to visitors) in the village of Bushmills to the entrance of the Giant's Causeway. Follow the signs to either Bushmills or the Giant's Causeway and the railway is clearly signposted. Car parking is dedicated to railway passengers at both Bushmills and the Giant's Causeway
Operating organisation: Giant's Causeway & Bushmills Railway, Giant's Causeway Station, Runkerry Road, Bushmills, Co

Industrial locomotives – 3 ft gauge

Name	No	Builder	Type	Built
Tyrone	1	Peckett (2264)	0-4-0T	1904
Rory	2	Simplex (102T016)	4wDH	1976
Shane	3	Barclay(2281)	0-4-0T	1949
—	—	S/Lamb*	4wDE	2010

Rolling stock
3 S/Lamb-built trailer coaches to be used with powered carriage*

Antrim, Northern Ireland BT57 8SZ
Bushmills Platform: Ballaghmore Road, Bushmills BT57 8YS
Telephone/Fax: (028) 2073 2844
Internet addresses: *E-mail:*
infogcbr@btconnect.com
Web site:
www.freewebs.com/giantscauseway railway
OS reference: 943437 (Irish Grid)
Access by public transport:
Nearest Translink railway stations are Portrush (5 miles), Coleraine (7 miles). Various bus routes

(including an open topped vehicle on fine days in the summer) operate from either or both, depending on the route. For timetables either contact Translink enquiries on (028) 9066 6630 or www.translink.co.uk
Length of line: 2 miles, 3ft gauge
On site facilities: Souvenir shop, café, toilets and picnic tables at Giant's Causeway station. Free parking at both stations for railway passengers
Passenger trains: Bushmills-Giant's Causeway or vice versa

Public opening: St Patrick's weekend; daily at Easter; weekends from Easter until end of June; daily July and August; weekends September and October

Note: Trains will operate at other times for advance party bookings in excess of 20 persons
Facilities for disabled: Access available at Giant's Causeway

station and Bushmills platform. One coach has been adapted for wheelchair use

Steam Centre

Railway Preservation Society of Ireland

County Antrim

Members: HRA, TT

The RPSI was formed in 1964, making it one of the older preservation societies in these islands. It has always specialised in main line steam operations, and runs an intensive summer programme of trips out of both Belfast and Dublin. The main maintenance base is situated at Whitehead, 15 miles north of Belfast on the NIR route to Larne Harbour. Here not only are the traffic locomotives shedded but the locomotive shed is also used for heavy maintenance; currently the society is completing the full rebuilding of its sixth boiler 'in-house'. A large engineering workshop has just been constructed for the Locomotive Department, with the 100-year-old overhead crane which was originally in the Belfast & County Down Railway Locomotive Erecting Shop at Queen's Quay in Belfast. This workshop, which will undertake all heavy engineering for the society, is currently being fitted out. A large carriage shed is also on site where traffic vehicles are maintained and coaches are fully rebuilt. There are also heavy lifting facilities on site, and access may occasionally be limited for safety reasons when these are in use. Annual operations commence with 'Easter Bunny' trains out of Belfast, usually on Easter Monday. In May the 'International Railtour' is the main event, a three-day steam extravaganza. During June there are main line trips out of both Belfast and Dublin (steam and jazz). July and August see the 'Portrush Flyers' from Belfast to Portrush and back, around 180 miles of main line steam, as well as the 'Sea Breeze' excursions from Dublin to Rosslare and back, covering 205 miles.

Locomotives

Name	No	Origin	Class	Type	Built
Merlin	85†	GNR(I)	V	4-4-0	1932
—	131**	GNR(I)	Q	4-4-0	1901
Slieve Gullion	171†	GNR(I)	S	4-4-0	1913
—	4§§	LMS (NCC)	WT	2-6-4T	1947
—	184†	GS&WR	J15	0-6-0	1880
—	186§	GS&WR	J15	0-6-0	1879
—	461††	D&SER	K2	2-6-0	1922
Lough Erne	27	SL&NCR	Z	0-6-4T	1949
Falcon	102	NIR	DL	Bo-Bo	1969
—	B141	CIE	GM	Bo-Bo	1963
—	B142	CIE	GM	Bo-Bo	1963

Industrial locomotives

Name	No	Builder	Type	Built
Guinness	3	H/Clarke (1152)	0-4-0ST	1919
R. H. Smyth	3	Avonside (2021)	0-6-0ST	1928
—	23	Planet (3509)	0-4-0DM	1951
—	1	R/Hornsby	0-4-0DM	1954

*on loan from Ulster Folk & Transport Museum
**frames and boiler only
†awaiting restoration
††undergoing restoration
§returned to traffic in 2004
§§returned to traffic in 2011

Stock

The society also owns some 20 operational coaches, normally divided between Whitehead and Dublin. Further coaches are awaiting restoration and a small number of freight wagons are also preserved, as well as a steam crane. A serious fire due to vandalism a couple of years ago destroyed several vehicles, and any rebuilding is likely to be some years in the future at best. The society has purchased a variety of Mk 2 coaches which are undergoing major overhaul and six of which returned to traffic in 2004 with a diner/bar coming into servive in 2008. The society's secondary maintenance base is at Mullingar, Co Westmeath, but there is **no** access to the public.

During July and August there are steam train rides on site at Whitehead on Sunday afternoons, and at the end of July there will be an Open Day in conjunction with the Whitehead Community Association when there will be access to the workshop areas. The season usually ends with Halloween and Christmas trains in Belfast and

Dublin
Location: Whitehead Excursion Station, Co Antrim, Northern Ireland
Operating society: Railway Preservation Society of Ireland, Castleview Road, Whitehead, Carrickfergus, Co Antrim BT38 9NA
Telephone/fax:

From UK (028) 9337 3968 (answerphone only)
Eire (01) 480 0553
Internet addresses: *E-mail:* rpsitrains@hotmail.com
Web site: www.steamtrainsireland.com
Car park: Public car parking is readily available adjacent to the premises, with a further large car park less than 5min walk away on the sea front. Both car parks are normally free
Access by public transport: Translink/NI Railways or Ulsterbus to Whitehead
On site facilities: Souvenir shop (operating days only)
Public opening: Visitors welcome

most weekends. Site not open during the week (except public holidays) or when main line trains are operating from Whitehead or Belfast. Special opening for parties, or in the evening, may be arranged by telephoning in advance
Special notes: The RPSI is noted for its main line excursions and traditional rolling stock. For details: www.steamtrainsireland.com
Facilities for disabled: Please note that wheelchair facilities can be provided on trains, with advance notice if possible. A dedicated coach for carrying wheelchairs operates on some Dublin-based trains. Wheelchair access around the workshops at Whitehead is possible,

but difficult, and advance warning is requested of any visitors who may need special facilities
Membership details: Membership Secretary, 148 Church Road, Newtownabbey, Co Antrim BT36 6HJ
Future developments: Completion of a new museum facility is planned, as well as a projected extension to the Carriage Shed and additional stores and maintenance areas, and there are further developments in the pipeline which will hopefully improve access. Additional locomotive and coach restoration is proposed. Construction of a new station will commence during 2012

Ulster Folk & Transport Museum

Museum **County Down**

Member: HRA

Forty-five acres are devoted to the Transport Galleries. Permanent exhibitions include the earliest forms of transport, horse-drawn vehicles, bicycles, motor cars and the Museum's *Titanic* exhibition.

The Irish Railway Collection is displayed in an award-winning purpose-built gallery — the largest Transport Museum gallery in Ireland.

The collection features *Maedb* — the largest locomotive run in Ireland. The display includes narrow gauge and standard gauge rolling stock, locomotives, carriages, goods wagons, railcars and railbuses along with memorabilia
Location: Ulster Folk & Transport Museum, Cultra, Holywood
Operating organisation: Ulster Folk & Transport Museum, Cultra, Holywood BT18 0EU
Telephone: (028) 9042 8428
Fax: (028) 9042 8728
Internet address: *Web site:* www.magni.org.uk
Access: By car or bus the museum is about 7 miles from Belfast city centre on the A2 Belfast-Bangor road. You can also reach the museum by train
Car park: Extensive free parking
On site facilities: Shops, toilets, tea room

Locomotives – 5ft 3in

Name	No	Origin	Class	Type	Built
—	93	GNR(I)	JT	2-4-2T	1895
—	30	BCDR	I	4-4-2T	1901
Dunluce Castle	74	LMS(NCC)	U2	4-4-0	1924
Maedb	800	GSR	B1A	4-6-0	1939
—	1	R/Stephenson (2738)	—	0-6-0ST	1891
Merlin*	85	GNR(I)	V	4-4-0	1932
—	1	GNR(I)	—	Railbus	1932
—	B113	IR	B / 113	Bo-Bo	1950
—	102	NIR	101	Bo-Bo	1970

*on loan to Railway Preservation Society of Ireland at Whitehead

Locomotives – 3ft gauge

Name	No	Origin	Class	Type	Built
Blanche	2	CDRJC	5A	2-6-4T	1912
Kathleen	2	CLR	—	4-4-0T	1887
Phoenix	11	CVR	—	4wD	1928
—	20	Industrial	—	0-4-0	1905
—	2	Industrial	—	0-4-0	1907

Stock

1 Dublin, Wicklow & Wexford Railway coach; 1 Dundalk, Newry & Greenore Railway coach; 1 Midland & Great Western Railway director's saloon (ex-private vehicle); 1 Electric tramcar of Bessbrook-Newry Tramway; 2 trams from Giant's Causeway Tramway, Great Northern Railway Ireland Fintona tram, Great Northern Railway Ireland Hill of Howth electric tramcar, 1 Cavan-Leitrim Railway coach; 2 County Donegal Railway railcars; 1 County Donegal Railway director's coach; 1 County Donegal Railway trailer coach (bodywork ex-Dublin & Lucan Railway coach); 1 Giant's Causeway (P&BVR) saloon trailer; 1 Castlederg & Victoria Bridge Tramway 1st/3rd coach; 1 County Donegal Railway 7-ton open wagon, 3 Belfast trams, 1 Belfast trolleybus, 1 Belfast double-deck bus. Extensive collection of cars, motorcycles, bicycles, commercial vehicles, horse-drawn vehicles, fire-fighting equipment and industrial railway vehicles

Cavan & Leitrim Railway

Steam Centre | County Leitrim

Restoration work commenced in June 1993 and to date some half-mile of line has been rebuilt, water tower and engine shed refurbished and new workshops and carriage shed constructed. The ultimate objective is to rebuild a further 5.75 miles of line to Mohill

Location/headquarters: The Narrow Gauge Station, Dromod, Co Leitrim, adjacent to the Irish Rail station

General Manager: Michael Kennedy

Telephone/Fax: 071-9638599

Internet addresses:
E-mail: info@irish-railway.com
Web site: www.irish-railway.com

Main station: Dromod

Car park: Dromod terminus

Access by public transport: Rail service to Dromod (Irish Rail) on the Dublin-Sligo line. Bus Éireann and Ulsterbus routes also call at Dromod

Refreshment facilities: Tea room open by arrangement. Full meals available at nearby bars

Souvenir shop: Dromod

Length of line: Half-mile (3ft gauge)

Museum: Large collection of locomotives, rolling stock, road vehicles and aircraft, many still awaiting restoration

Period of public operation: Closed 23 December to 2 January, otherwise every Saturday, Sunday and Monday. Diesel trains run on demand

Contact address: The Cavan & Leitrim Railway Co Ltd, Station Road, Dromod, Co Leitrim, Republic of Ireland

Locomotives – 3ft gauge

Name	No	Builder	Type	Built
Dromod	1	K/Stuart (3024)	0-4-2ST	1916
Nancy*	1	Avonside (3024)	0-6-0T	1908
Dinmor	F511	Fowler (3900011)	4wDM	1947
—	LM11	Ruhrthaler (1082)	4wDM	1936
—	9	M/Rail (115U093)	4wDH	1970
—	LM350	Simplex (60SL748)	4wDM	1980
—	LM91	R/Hornsby (371962)	4wDM	1952
—	LM131	R/Hornsby (379086)	4wDM	1955
—	LM87	R/Hornsby (329696)	4wDM	1952
—	LM131	R/Hornsby (382809)	4wDM	1955
—	LM260	Deutz (57841)	0-4-0DM	1965
—	LM180	Deutz (57122)	0-4-0DM	1960
—	LM186	Deutz (57132)	0-4-0DM	1960
—	—	Hunslet (6075)	4wDM	1961

*Nancy under restoration at Alan Keef Ltd, Ross-on-Wye

5ft 3in gauge

Name	No	Builder	Type	Built
—	SZA 979	Scammel lorry	2-2wDM	1959

2ft gauge

Name	No	Builder	Type	Built
—	D5	H/Hunslet (2659)	4wDM	1942
—	1	H/Hunslet (7340)	4wDM	1940
—	2	H/Hunslet (7341)	4wDM	1940
—	3	H/Hunslet (7341)	4wDM	1943
—	LM198	R/Hornsby (398076)	4wDM	1954

1ft 10in gauge (ex-Guinness locomotives)

Name	No	Builder	Type	Built
—	22	Spence	0-4-0T	1912
—	31	Planet (3446)	4wDM	1950
—	36	Planet (3447)	4wDM	1950
—	26	Planet (3255)	4wDM	1948

Railcars

Name	No	Builder	Type	Built
—	*5	Drewry Car (1945)	4wDMR	1927
—	C11	Bord na Móna	4wDMR	–
—	C42	Wickham (7129)	4wPMR	1955
—	C47	Bord na Móna	4wPMR	1958
—	C56	Wickham (7681)	4wPMR	1957
—	W6/11-4	Wickham (9673)	2-2-0PM	1964

*built as 5ft 3in gauge inspection car for Great Southern Railway, regauged in 1994
C42 used as unpowered p-way trolley

Rolling stock
Tralee & Dingle coaches 47C (6T), 45C (7T), 48C (8T) and 44C (10T) all
built 1890; Great Northern Railway (Ireland) AU345 built 1955 as motor
bus; Alan Keef-built No 13, (built 1997)
GNR Gardiner Bus No 389, built Dundalk 1951

Museum — County Donegal Railway Restoration Society — County Donegal

Member: HRA
Old Station House opened as a
permanent Railway Museum &
Heritage Centre from Easter 1995.
There are numerous outside exhibits
ranging from *Drumboe* to a garden
railway. Inside attractions include a
video-viewing room, railway
pictures and railway memorabilia
Location/Headquarters: Old
Station House, Tírchonaill Street,
Donegal Town, Co Donegal, Ireland
Telephone: (00353-7497 [from
UK]) (07497 [from Ireland]) 22655
Fax: (00353-7497 [from UK])
(07497 [from Ireland]) 23843
Internet addresses: *E-mail:*
donegalrailway@gmail.com
Web site:
www.countydonegalrailway.com
Contacts: Ann Temple
On site facilities: Video/DVD
viewing room, Donegal Railway

Locomotives – 3ft gauge

Name	No	Origin	Class	Type	Built
Drumboe*	5	CDR	5	2-6-4T	1907

*undergoing restoration at RPSI, Whitehead

Stock
1 CDR brake/third coach No 28
1 CDR railcar No 14
1 CDR trailer No 5
1 CDR combined goods/cattle and horse van (247 of 1893)
1 goods van

Viewing of all rolling stock is by arrangement only

memorabilia, shop, hot & cold
drinks, snacks, toilet
Public opening: Monday-Friday
10.00-17.00
Weekends in July and August
14.00-17.00.
Please ring to check weekend
opening

Access for disabled: Disabled
friendly
Membership details: From above
address
Membership journal:
The Phoenix

Railway Centre — Fintown Railway — County Donegal

This stretch of track has been laid
on the formation of the Fintown-
Glenties line and is the only
operational railway in Co Donegal.
The railway runs along the shore of
Lough Finn and it is planned to
have a dual ride, out by rail and
return by boat. The rolling stock
presently used consists of an ex-
mining Simplex locomotive with
three turn of the 19th/20th century
passenger tramcars from Charleroi
(Belgium)
Location/headquarters: Fintown
Railway Station, Fintown,
Co Donegal, Eire
Tel: 00353 (0)74 9546280
Internet addresses:
E-mail: info@antraen.com
Web site: www.antraen.com

Locomotives – 3ft gauge

Name	No	Builder	Type	Built
—	LM77	R/Hornsby (329680)	4wDM	1952
—	—	M/Rail (102T007)	4wDM	1974

Railcar

Name	No	Origin	Class	Type	Built
—	19	CDRJC	—	Diesel railcar	1940

Rolling stock
3 Belgian tramcars

Main station: Fintown Station
Car park: Located at station area
Access by public transport: Local
buses
Refreshment facilities: Local café
at top of station lane

Souvenir shop: Located at station
area
Length of line: 2.5 miles
(3ft gauge)
Museum: Not in operation but a
collection of antiquated farm

machinery is being restored
Period of public operation:
June — Monday/Friday
13.00-16.00, Sunday 13.00-17.00;
July-September —Monday/Friday
11.00-17.00, weekends 13.00-18.00.

Departures from Fintown every half hour
Special events: Halloween Ghost Train, Santa Specials in December
On site facilities: Toilet, it is also hoped to have a playground in

operation
Membership details: Bernadette McGee (Membership Secretary), c/o above address
Membership journal: *An Mhuc Dhubh* — annually

Steam Centre — Irish Steam Preservation Society — County Laois

Member: HRA, NTET
Location: Stradbally Hall, eight miles from Athy, six miles from Portlaoise (on N80 road).
Telephone (regarding steam trains): 00353 86 3890184 (from UK)
Telephone (regarding steam museum): 00353 57 8641878 (from UK)
Internet addresses: *E-mail:* rallysec@eircom.net or madigan.pauline@gmail.com *Web site:* www.irishsteam.ie
Access by public transport:
By rail: Irish Rail train to Athy or Portlaoise.
By bus: Kavanagh's Bus Portlaoise-Stradbally-Carlow (Monday-Saturday), also Bus Éireann Waterford-Kilkenny-Stradbally-Portlaoise-Athlone (one daily service including Sunday)
On site facilities: 3ft gauge railway
Catering facilities: None on site

Industrial locomotives – 3ft gauge

Name	No	Builder	Type	Built
—	2	Barclay (2264)	0-4-0WT	1949
Nippy	—	Planet (2014)	4wDM	1936
—	4	R/Hornsby (326052)	4wDM	1952

Stock
1 passenger coach; 2 ballast wagons; 1 brake van

but town centre quarter-mile away
Length of line: 1km
Public opening: Easter Sunday and Monday; May Bank Holiday weekend; June Bank Holiday weekend Sunday & Monday; National Steam Rally — first Sunday and Monday in August every year; October Bank Holiday weekend Sunday & Monday. Trains run as required 14.30-16.45 on all dates except National Steam Rally then 13.30-17.30
Any additional operating dates which may be arranged will be

shown on the web site
Special notes: This is the longest established heritage railway in Ireland. The Steam Museum (00353 57 8641878) is also now open, making Stradbally the real home of steam in Ireland.

Please contact Rally Secretary, for further details or telephone numbers shown or visit web site. Trains are operated by a steam locomotive; however, diesel locomotives are also used

---

Museum — Irish Traction Group — County Tipperary

Member: HRA
The Irish Traction Group was formed in 1989 with the objective of preserving at least one of each class of diesel locomotive to have operated on the Irish railway system. The ultimate aim of the group is to restore its collection of locomotives to operational condition.
Location: The former goods store adjacent to Carrick-on-Suir railway station
Operating society/organisation: Irish Traction Group, 31 Hayfield Road, Bredbury, Stockport,

Locomotives/Railcar

Name	No	Origin	Class	Manufacturer	Type	Built
—	A3R	CIE	001/A	M/Vickers (889)	Co-Co	1955
—	A39	CIE	001/A	M/Vickers (925)	Co-Co	1956
—	B103	CIE	101/B	BRCW (DEL22)	A1A-A1A	1956
—	124	CIE	121/B	GM (26274)	Bo-Bo	1960
—	146	CIE	141/B	GM (27472)	Bo-Bo	1962
—	152	CIE	141/B	GM (27478)	Bo-Bo	1962
—	190	CIE	181/B	GM (31257)	Bo-Bo	1966
—	226	CIE	201/C	M/Vickers (972)	Bo-Bo	1957
—	C231	CIE	201/C	M/Vickers (977)	Bo-Bo	1957
—	G601	CIE	601/G	Deutz (56119)	4wDH	1956
—	G611	CIE	611/G	Deutz (57225)	4wDH	1962
—	G616	CIE	611/G	Deutz (57227)	4wDH	1962
—	G617	CIE	611/G	Deutz (57229)	4wDH	1962
—	712	CIE	–	Wickham (8919)	4wDH	1962

Republic of Ireland

Cheshire SK6 1DE, England
Telephone: 07713 159869 (Mon-Sat 09.00-18.00 only)
Internet addresses: *E-mail:* info@irishtractiongroup.com
Web site: www.irishtractiongroup.com
Car park: Available in station goods yard
Access by public transport: Infrequent train service. Services operated by Bus Éireann from Dublin, Limerick and Waterford
Facilities: Toilets on IE station. Site is located quarter-mile from town

Notes:
A3R is stored at the West Clare Railway, Moyasta, Co Clare
A39 is currently on loan to Downpatrick & Co Down Railway
G611 and G617 are currently on loan to Downpatrick & Co Down Railway
C231 is stored at the West Clare Railway, Moyasta, Co Clare
124 is stored at the West Clare Railway, Moyasta, Co Clare
146 is currently on loan to Downpatrick & Co Down Railway
152 is stored at the West Clare Railway, Moyasta, Co Clare
190 is stored at the West Clare Railway, Moyasta, Co Clare
712 is currently on loan to Downpatrick & Co Down Railway

centre
Special events: Operation of railtours over IÉ/NIR systems

Opening times: Premises not open to the public; locomotives B103 and G601 are both stabled outside

---

Timetable Service — Tralee & Blennerville Steam Railway — County Kerry

The Tralee & Blennerville Steam Railway is Europe's most westerly line and as part of the former Tralee & Dingle Light Railway (1891-1953) it has folklore and tradition stretching back over 100 years. The railway links the town of Tralee with Blennerville on the coast.

The Tralee Town Council hopes to have the railway back in service for 2012, with No 5 returned to traffic by the autumn.
Location: Tralee (Ballyard) station is situated near the Aqua Dome; Blennerville station is adjacent to the windmill, 1 mile to the west of town on the main road to Dingle (N86)
Headquarters: Tralee & Blennerville Steam Railway, Tralee, Co Kerry, Republic of Ireland
General Manager: Nora Teahon
Telephone: 066 7121288 (Tralee Tourist Office)

Locomotives – 3ft gauge
3ft gauge

Name	No	Builder	Type	Built
—	5*	Hunslet (555)	2-6-2T	1892
—	LM92L	R/Hornsby (371967)	4wDM	1954

*an original Tralee & Dingle Railway locomotive

Rolling stock
A selection of passenger coaches and works wagons

Internet address: *E-mail:* blenmill@eircom.net
Car park:
At Tralee (Ballyard) station. Blennerville Windmill car park
Access by public transport:
By rail service to Tralee (Irish Rail).
By air to Kerry airport (10 miles) (car hire available).
By Bus Éireann to Tralee
Refreshment facilities: Restaurant at Blennerville in windmill complex

Length of line: 3km (3ft gauge)
Period of public operation: Daily June to September (subject to confirmation)
Passenger service: Trains operate from Blennerville 10.30-16.30 (17.30 in July and August); from Tralee at 11.00-17.00
Facilities for disabled: Toilets and wheelchair access, museum and catering facilities available at Blennerville windmill

---

Timetable Service — Waterford & Suir Valley Railway — Co Waterford

This heritage narrow gauge railway has been operating since 2003 and follows over 8.5km of the route of the abandoned Waterford-Dungarvan line. The line runs mostly along the picturesque banks of the River Suir between Kilmeadan and Waterford City. It offers views of the Mount Congreve Gardens and the recently discovered

Industrial locomotives – 3ft gauge

Name	No	Builder	Type	Built
—	LM179	Deutz (57121)	0-4-0DM	1960
—	LM183	Deutz (57127)	0-4-0DM	1960
—	—	M/Rail (60SP382)	4wDM	1969

Stock
Two carriages built specially for the railway. The steel coaches have approximately two-thirds of the accommodation in open toastrack seating, the remainder being an enclosed saloon, accessed from an end veranda

site of a Viking settlement at Woodstown. This is an area rich in history and only accessible by train. The ticket office/shop/coffee shop are in a former Irish Rail, ex-BR Mk 2, carriage

Location: Kilmeadan station, Kilmeadan, Co Waterford on the R680.

Contact: Maria Kyte, Business Development Manager, Waterford & Suir Valley Railway Co, Kilmeadan Station, Kilmeadan, Co Waterford

Telephone: 00353 (0) 51384058

Internet addresses: *E-mail:* info@wsvrailway.ie

Web site: www.wsvrailway.ie

Charity number: CHY 13857

Access by public transport: Suirway bus service to Kilmeadan (schedule can vary)

Access by road: From Waterford City take the R680 to Kilmeadan (10km). Drive through the village following signs for Cork. Drive through the Carrick Road roundabout, Kilmeadan station is on the left.

Alternatively take the N25 towards Cork. At Carrick Road roundabout take the last exit on to R680. Kilmeadan station is on the left. From the Cork direction at Carrick Road roundabout turn left on to the R680. Kilmeadan station is on the left.

Length of line: 8.5km, 3ft gauge. Round trip approximately one hour

Catering facilities: Coffee shop at station

Souvenir shop: Kilmeadan

Car parking: On site

Length of track: There is 10km of track laid from Kilmeadan to Carriganore. The summer schedule offers a 17km round trip between Kilmeadan and Gracedieu Junction

Public opening:

April and September — Monday to Saturday 11.00-15.00, Sunday 12.00-16.00. Trains depart on the hour

May to August — Monday to Saturday 11.00-16.00, Sunday 12.00-17.00. Trains depart on the hour

February and October /November — Mid term break 12.00-14.00. Trains depart 12.00, 13.00, 15.00. Children travel free

December — Santa Express

Special events: Halloween Ghost Trips — 27 October; Santa Trips — 1/2, 6, 8/9, 15/16, 22/23 December (must be pre-booked). Please contact to confirm dates and train times (051 384058)

Special facilities: Children's birthday parties (ride and refreshments).

Gift vouchers available for tickets, special events, Friends membership

Facilities for disabled: Train carriages accessible to wheelchairs, ticket office, shop and toilets

West Clare Railway (The Percy French Line)

Steam Centre · County Clare

The WCR expanded rapidly in 2010 and intends further major expansion of track as well as rolling stock for 2012. Soon a new museum building to house the new stock will be erected and readers are warned that the information given here could be out of date rapidly as further ex-Bord na Móna rolling stock is arriving at a rapid rate and a major expansion of 5ft 3in gauge rolling stock will occur as soon as a museum can be built to house it.

The WCR operates steam whenever it can justify the expense. All holidays and the months of July and August will see steam in operation most of the time. At all other times, the steam locomotive can be put into steam by prior arrangement for groups of 10 or more people and is always available for inspection and photography. The railway is open every day between April and September when diesel locomotives are otherwise used, and a new feature wil be the demonstration of Irish narrow gauge 'industrial' trains in action. At all other times, visitors are welcome if staff happen to be on site or, again, by prior arrangement. This, of course will alter when the museum is built; a telephone call is always advisable.

Rightly famous not only for the song 'Are ye Right, There, Michael' but also for its guided tours of its station house museum, the WCR has recently expanded its customer facilities by opening an ex-BR Mk 2 dining carriage as a cinema/lecture theatre capable of sitting up to 40 people where films are normally shown explaining Ireland's railways and the former WCR in particular and where school classes can also be held for the many school trips that visit. Coach trips of all types are particularly welcome.

New events are being planned including vintage days and Halloween along with the popular Santa Specials

Location/headquarters: West Clare Railway, Moyasta Junction, Kilrush, Co Clare, Republic of Ireland

Telephone: 00353 (0) 65 905 1284

Internet addresses: *E-mail:* info@westclarerailway.ie

Web site: www.westclarerailway.ie

Chief Executive: Jackie Whelan

Access by public transport: On N67 main coast road between Kilrush and Kilkee.

By rail — Ennis (then by bus).

By bus — from Ennis.

By air — Shannon airport, 1 hour drive

Main station: Moyasta Junction

Car park: Space for 50 vehicles on site

Length of line: 4km (3ft gauge), currently being extended

On site facilities: Refreshment coach, cinema/lecture theatre, station house museum

Period of public operation: Every day April to September, and each weekend other months, but always prepared to open by arrangement. Open 10.30-17.00, and 12.00-17.00 on Sundays

Special events: Vintage days and Halowe'en, plus Santa Specials in December

Facilities for disabled: All areas fitted for access by wheelchair

Locomotives – 3ft gauge

Name	No	Builder	Type	Built
Slieve Callan	5*	Dübs (2890)	0-6-2T	1892
—	101L	RFS	4wDH	1989
—	—	Huwood/Hunsley	0-6-0DH	c1949
—	LM25	R/Hornsby (244871)	0-4-0DM	1946
—	LM60	R/Hornsby (259738)	0-4-0DM	1948
—	LM64	R/Hornsby (259745)	0-4-0DM	1948
—	LM69	R/Hornsby (259755)	0-4-0DM	1948
—	LM98	R/Hornsby (375335)	0-4-0DM	1954
—	LM133	R/Hornsby (379090)	0-4-0DM	1955
—	LM136	R/Hornsby (382815)	0-4-0DM	1956
—	LM146	R/Hornsby (394024)	0-4-0DM	1956
—	LM147X	R/Hornsby (394025)	0-4-0DM	1956
—	LMQ168	R/Hornsby (402980)	0-4-0DM	1956

*an original West Clare Railway locomotive
LM number series are ex-Bord na Móna (some stored off site)

Rolling stock
2 carriages, with extra vehicles currently under construction

Locomotives/Railcar – 5ft 3in gauge

Name	No	Origin	Class	Manufacturer	Type	Built
—	A3R	CIE	001/A	M/Vickers (889)	Co-Co	1955
—	A015	CIE	001/A	M/Vickers (901)	Co-Co	1955
—	124	CIE	121/B	GM (26274)	Bo-Bo	1960
—	146	CIE	141/B	GM (27472)	Bo-Bo	1962
—	190	CIE	181/B	GM (31257)	Bo-Bo	1966
—	C231	CIE	201/C	M/Vickers (977)	Bo-Bo	1957

Note:
All locomotives are owned by the Irish Traction Group

Main Event Diary

Please see individual entries for events such as Easter specials, Teddy Bears', Mother's/Father's Day, Wine & Dine, real ale trains (except beer festivals), Halloween, Santa Specials, etc.

March

3/4	Diesel Weekend	East Lancashire
10/11	Half-Price Weekend	Bodmin
17	DMU Theme Day	East Lancashire
17/18	Steam Gala	Battlefield
17/18	Spring Gala	Chasewater
17/18	Spring Steam Gala	West Somerset
17/18	Kent Great Day Out	Romney, Hythe & Dymchurch
18	Spring Locomotive Steam Gala	Eastleigh Lakeside
22-25	Spring Steam Gala	West Somerset
23-25	Great Spring Steam Gala	Mid-Hants
23-25	Spring Steam Gala	Severn Valley
24/25	Half Price Weekend	South Devon
24/25	Railway at Work Weekend	Swanage
25	Volunteer Day	Avon Valley
25	Diesel gala	Colne Valley
25	Steam Day	East Anglian Railway Museum
25	Volunteering Open Day	Embsay & Bolton Abbey
25	Stirling Air Engine Rally	Kew Bridge
25	Railway Open Day	Moors Valley
29	Honda Goldwings Day	Ribble
30-1 April	Steam Weekend	Great Central

| 30-1 April | Spring Diesel Gala | Mid-Norfolk |
| 31 | Diesel Day | Llangollen |

April

1	Friendly Engines Day	West Lancashire
3-12	Easter Steaming	Avon Valley
4	Kids' Workshop at Bury Transport Museum	East Lancashire
6	Bygone Branchline Day	Dean Forest
6/7	Relaunch Event	Rocks by Rail (Rutland)
6-9	Easter Heritage Gala	South Devon
7-9	Ivor the Engine	Cholsey & Wallingford
7-9	Easter Steam Gala	Lincolnshire Wolds
7-9	Visit by *Tornado*	Nene Valley
7	Steam Toy Rally	Old Kiln
8	Vintage Car Show	Amberley
8	Classic Bike Rally	East Lancashire
11	Kids' Workshop at Bury Transport Museum	East Lancashire
14/15	Grandparents' Weekend	Kent & East Sussex
14/15	Vintage Bus Running Days and Rally	North Norfolk
14/15	Spring Steam Gala	Spa Valley
15	Hobbies & Pastimes Steam Day	Abbey Pumping
15	Post Office Vehicles and Industrial Trains Day	Amberley
15	Spring Steam Up & Country Fair	Bursledon
20-22	Spring Steam Spectacular	Bodmin
21	Bug Club Day	Romney, Hythe & Dymchurch
21/22	Macmillan Charity Walk	Bure Valley
21/22	Vintage Vehicle Rally	Colne Valley
21/22	Magic of Meccano	Kew Bridge
21/22	Spring Diesel Gala	Pontypool
21/22	Light Railway Weekend	Tanfiled
21-29	Steel, Steam & Star	Llangollen
28	Toy and Rail Collectors' Fair	Bluebell
28	Spring Diesel Day	Bodmin
28	Great Western Branch Line Day	Dean Forest
28/29, 2 May	1940s Weekend	Churnet Valley
29	Members' Day	Northampton & Lamport
29	50th Anniversary, Last Passenger Train to Blaenavon	Pontypool
30-5 May	Spring Art Week	Beer Heights

May

1	140th Anniversary of opening of Buckfastleigh, Totnes & South Devon Railway	South Devon
2	1940s Weekend	Churnet Valley
5	Recycling Railway Day	Abbey Pumping
5	Bygone Branchline Day	Dean Forest
5	Model Railway Exhibition	Old Kiln
4-7	Spring Steam Gala	North Yorkshire Moors
5/6	Calling Junior Trainspotters	Bure Valley
5/6	Miniature Railway Weekend	Foxfield
5/6	Gala Weekend	Kent & East Sussex
5/6	Tinkerbell Rally	Moors valley
5-7	Steaming Thru' the 40s	Bodmin
5-7	Branchline Weekend / Mixed Trafic Event	Embsay & Bolton Abbey
5-7	Spring Gala	Ffestiniog
5-7	Railway Children Weekend	Keighley & Worth Valley
5-7	Stratford Depot Weekend	Mid-Norfolk
5-7	Puffing Billy at the Children's Weekend	North Norfolk
5-7	Gala Weekend	Didcot
5-7	Vintage Train Weekend	Midland Railway
5-7	Friendly Engines Day	Ribble
6	Veteran and Classic Motorcycle Show	Amberley
6/7	Vintage Transport Weekend	East Anglian Railway Museum
6/7	Bluebell Walk	Middleton
9	History Day	North Norfolk
11-13	Spring Steam Gala	North Yorkshire Moors
11-13	Diesel gala	Swanage

Event Diary

12/13	Tractor Weekend	Battlefield
12/13	Southern at War	Bluebell
12/13	Steam in Miniature Weekend	Hollycombe
12/913	Village at War	Old Kiln
13	Vintage Agricultural Vehicles and Woodland Crafts	Amberley
13	Vintage Car Event	Bursledon
13	Morris Minor Event	Crich
13	Alresford Watercress Festival	Mid-Hants
19	Murder Mystery Evening	Avon Valley
19	Railway Open Day	Chinnor
19	Diesel Gala	Dean Forest
19/20	Volunteers' Weekend	Churnet Valley
19/20	Classic Motorbike Weekend	Crich
19/20	Spring Ale & Steam Weekend	Gloucestershire Warwickshire
19/20	Diesel gala	Great Central
19/20	1940s weekend	Kent & East Sussex
19/20	Haworth Village 1940s Weekend	Keighley & Worth Valley
19/20	Southern Gala Weekend	Mid-Norfolk
19/20	SVR Celebrates 125 Years	Severn Valley
19/20	1960s BR Mixed Traffic Weekend	South Devon
20	Military Vehicle Show	Amberley
20	Classic Car Rally	East Kent
20	Diesel & Electric Day	Groudle Glen
20	Historic Fire Engine Rally	Kew Bridge
25-27	Bodmin Branch 125th Anniversary Gala	Bodmin
25-27	Heritage Diesel Weekend	Keighley & Worth Valley
26/27	The World in Miniature	Battlefield
26/27	CV&HR 150 Weekend	Colne Valley
26/27	Hollycombe Steam Weekend	Hollycombe
26/27	Days Gone By	Old Kiln
26/27	Vintage Train	Welshpool & Llanfair
27	PECO Annual Vintage/Classic Vehicle Rally	Beer Heights
26-29	Tornado	Ribble
27	Toy & Train Fair	Great Central
27	Big 30th Birthday	Groudle Glen
31-31 July	Jack Boskett Photographic Exhibition	Gloucestershire Warwickshire

June

2	Bygone Branchline Day	Dean Forest
2/3	1940s Event	Avon Valley
2-4	Road and Rail Steam Traction	Chasewater
2-4	Blues and Beer Festival	Cholsey & Wallingford
2-4	1940s Wartime Weekend	East Lancashire
2-4	Family Weekend	Middleton
2-4	Branch Line Experience	Northampton & Lamport
2-5	Everything Goes	Bure Valley
2-5	Beer Festival	Foxfield
2-5	Grand Summer Steam Up	Kew Bridge
2-5	Kids for a Quid	Mid-Norfolk
2-5	Queen's Diamond Jubilee	Romney, Hythe & Dymchurch
2-5	Real Ale and Cider Festival	Swindon & Cricklade
2-5	Diamond Jubilee Weekend	South Devon
2-10	Railway Children theatrical on site	Mid-Norfolk
3	Harrington Vehicle Gathering	Amberley
3	Fifties Day	East Anglian Railway Museum
3/4	Peppa Pig	Bodmin
3/4	Beside the Seaside	Crich
3/4	Little Chuffer's Bank Holiday	Leighton Buzzard
3-5	Jubilee Weekend	Tanfield
5	Jubilee Street Party	Churnet Valley
5	Jubilee Celebration	Kent & East Sussex
6	Kids' Workshop at Bury Transport Museum	East Lancashire
7	Children's *Duncan* Day	Talyllyn
8/9	Bitton Beer Festival	Avon Valley
8-10	Wartime Evemnt	Great Central
8-10	Diesel Gala	North Norfolk

Event Diary

9/10	Mid Summer Steam Weekend	Amberley
9/10	Alf Tunstall Classic Bus Rally	Churnet Valley
9/10	Swap Meet	Churnet Valley
9/10	War on the Line	Mid-Hants
9/10	Grand Summer Gala	Moors Valley
9/10	'60s Weekend	North Yorkshire Moors
9/10	kids for a Quid	Ribble
10	Beer & Jazz	Bursledon
10	Classic Vehicle Day	Gloucestershire Warwickshire
15-17	Mixed Traffic Weekend	West Somerset
16	CAMRA Beer Festival	Kent & East Sussex
16	125th Anniversary of the Poppy Line	North Norfolk
16/17	Summer Steam Gala	Amerton
16/17	Heritage Transport Festival	Bodmin
16/17	Olly Owl's Family Fun Day	Kirklees
16/17	David Shepherd's Wildlife Weekend	North Norfolk
16/17	Railway Weekend	Hollycombe
16/17	Bridgnorth Station Gala	Severn Valley
17	Electric Vehicle Show	Amberley
17	Coal Train Day	Chasewater
17	Buses and Commercial Vehicles	East Kent
17	Morris Minor Rally	Foxfield
17	GWR Sponsored Walk	Gloucestershire Warwickshire
17	Classic Car Day	Lincolnshire Wolds
17	Classic Cars	Ribble
21-24	Made @ Kew	Kew Bridge
20	Vintage Nostalgia	Groudle Glen
22-24	Titfield Thunderbolt Live	North Norfolk
22/23	Heritage Railcar Gala	Llangollen
22-24	Steaming Through the '40s	Spa Valley
23	Murder Mystery Evening	Avon Valley
23	World Heritage Day	Pontypool
23/24	Leicester Vintage Festival	Abbey Pumping
23/24	1940s Weekend	Battlefield
23/24	Sussex Food Fair	Bluebell
23/24	Senior Citizen Weekend	Cholsey & Wallingford
23/24	1950s Weekend	Crich
23/24	Steam and Diesel Together	Mid-Norfolk
23/24	200th Anniversary of Steam	Middleton
23/24	1940s Weekend	Severn Valley
23/24	Vintage Train	Welshpool & Llanfair
24	Fire Show and Commercial Vehicles	Amberley
24	Model Railway Exhibition	Colne Valley
24	Bus Rally	Hollycombe
24	Vintage Trains Day	Perrygrove
24	Garn Lakes Day	Pontypool
24	Dreamcatcher Fundraising Day	Groudle Glen
24	Summer Locomotive Steam Gala	Eastleigh Lakeside
22	Vintage Nostalgia	Groudle Glen
30	Symphony Concert (evening)	Chasewater
30	Great Western Branch Line Day	Dean Forest
30	National Garden Scheme Open Garden Days for charity	Beer Heights
30-1 July	Model Railway Exhibition	Middleton
30-1 July	1940s Weekend	Severn Valley
30-1 July	Have-a-go and Garden Railway Gala	Talyllyn

July

1	Consall Garden Party	Churnet Valley
1	Dunstable Dasher 50	Leighton Buzzard
1	Vintage Transport Festival	North Norfolk
1	Great Western Branch Line Day	Dean Forest
1	National Garden Scheme Open Garden Days for charity	Beer Heights
1-8	Quad-Arts Week	North Norfolk
6/7	Indietrucks	Midland Railway
6-8	Summer Diesel Weekend	East Lancashire
7	Railway Gala Day	Abbey Pumping

Event Diary

7/8	Model Railway Weekend	Chasewater
7/8	Ale on Rail Weekend	Cholsey & Wallingford
7/8	Wartime Weekend	Pontypool
7/8	Military Weekend	South Devon
8	12th National Railway Velocipede Rally	Churnet Valley
8	Colne Valley at War	Colne Valley
8	London 60	Crich
8	Keighley Festival of Transport	Keighley & Worth Valley
13-15	Steam Gala	Mid-Norfolk
13-15	11th North Norfolk Railway Beer Festival	North Norfolk
14/15	Railway Gala Weekend	Amberley
14/15	Rails & Ales	Battlefield
14/15	China Clay Weekend	Bodmin
14/15	Edwardian Weekend	Crich
14/15	Wickham Rally Weekend	Foxfield
14/15	Narrow Gauge Railway Gala	Midland Railway
14/15	Garden Railway, Modellers' Weekend	Midland Railway
14/15	Garden Railway Event	Midland Railway
14/15	Vintage and Rail Mail Weekend	Nene Valley
14/15	Vintage Vehicle Weekend	North Yorkshire Moors
14/15	Teddy Bears' Olympics	South Downs
14/15	Friendly Engines	Ribble
15	Victorian Day	Bursledon
15	Senior Citizens' Day	Chinnor
15	Classic Car Rally	East Kent
15	Walkers' Sunday	Gloucestershire Warwickshire
15	MG Car Club Rally	Hollycombe
15	Alton Bus Rally and running day	Mid-Hants
15	Road Rally	Midland Railway
15	RH&DR 85th Anniversary	Romney, Hythe & Dymchurch
15	Model Gala	Telford
20-22	2nd Rail Ale Trail Beer Festival	Churnet Valley
21	Bygone Branchline Day	Dean Forest
21/22	Toy and Rail Collectors' Fair	Bluebell
21/22	Visiting Locomotives Weekend	Eastleigh Lakeside
21/22	Fairground Weekend	Hollycombe
21/22	Model Railway Weekend	Moors Valley
21/22	Riversway Festival	Ribble
21/22	Peep Behind The Scenes	Severn Valley
21/22	Vintage Train	Welshpool & Llanfair
22	Classic Microcars and Scooters	Amberley
22	Bus and Commercial Vehicle Rally	Colne Valley
22	Classic Bus Rally	Gloucestershire Warwickshire
22	Jester Express	Groudle Glen
25	25th Anniversary of Re-opening	East Lancashire
25	Kids' Workshop at Bury Transport Museum	East Lancashire
28/29	Diesel Gala	Bo'ness
28/29	Mixed Traction Weekend	Dean Forest
28/29	Guiness Weekend	Cholsey & Wallingford
28/29	Family Fun Weekend	Corris
28/29	Models and Miniatures	East Somerset
28/29	1960s Weekend	Llangollen
28/29	Vinatge Vehicles	Northampton & Lamport
29	Vintage Austin Car Rally	Avon Valley
29	Mini Meet	Crich
29	Rustic Sunday	Old Kiln
29	Toy and Collectors' Fair	West Somerset

August

1	Kids' Workshop at Bury Transport Museum	East Lancashire
3-5	Paddington Bear	Bodmin
3-5	Diesel Gala	Spa Valley
4	Animal Rescue Railway Day	Abbey Pumping
4	Bygone Branchline Day	Dean Forest
4/5	Edwardian Street Fair	Amberley
4/5	1960s Weekend	Kent & East Sussex

4/5	Railway at War Weekend	Mid-Norfolk
4/5	Preston Dock Event (tbc)	Ribble
4/5	Tom Rolt Steam Rally	Talyllyn
4/5	Steam Fayre & Vintage Rally at Bishops Lydeard	West Somerset
5	Steam & Diesel Gala	Chinnor
5	Emergency Vehicles Day	Crich
5	War on the Line with Dad's Army	East Anglian Railway Museum
5	Toy & Train Fair	Great Central
5	Ford Mk II Car Rally	Old Kiln
5	RNLI Dungeness Lifeboat Station Open Day	Romney, Hythe & Dymchurch
8	Kids' Workshop at Bury Transport Museum	East Lancashire
11	Bygone Branchline Day	Dean Forest
11/12	Vintage Transport Weekend	Bluebell
11/12	1940s Weekend	Crich
11/12	Vintage Weekend	Swindon & Cricklade
11/12	Vintage Train	Welshpool & Llanfair
11/12	Summer Gala Weekend	West Lancashire
12	Vintage Bus Rally	Avon Valley
12	Annual Charity Day	Chasewater
13/14	Ivor the Engine	Pontypool
14	Craft Fair at Abergynolwyn	Talyllyn
15	Kids' Workshop at Bury Transport Museum	East Lancashire
16	Craft Fair at Abergynolwyn	Talyllyn
18	Race the Train	Talyllyn
18/19	Steam Gala	Devon Railway
18/19	GWR C&W Dept Open Weekend	Gloucestershire Warwickshire
19	Harley Davidson Day	Amberley
19	Railway Event	Bursledon
22	Kids' Workshop at Bury Transport Museum	East Lancashire
23	Children's *Duncan* Day	Talyllyn
24-27	Rails and Ales	South Devon
25	Bygone Branchline Day	Dean Forest
25	Volunteers' Showcase Gala	Talyllyn
25/26	Classic Transport Weekend	Llangollen
25-27	Bank Holiday weekend of special events	Beer Heights
25-27	Model Railway & Toy Exhibition	Corris
25-27	Beer Festival	East Kent
25-27	The Way We Were 1930s-1950s	East Somerset
25-27	Steam and Diesel Mixed Traffic Event	Mid-Norfolk
25-27	Beer Festival	Mid-Norfolk
25-27	Vintage Train Weekend	Midland Railway
25-27	Seaside Specials	Northampton & Lamport
25-27	Friendly Engines	Ribble
25-27	Dymchurch Day of Syn	Romney, Hythe & Dymchurch
26	Series One Land Rover Gathering	Talyllyn
26/27	Fireman Sam	Bodmin
26/27	Teddy Bears' Weekend	Cholsey & Wallingford
26/27	Alice in Woodland	Crich
26-27	Children's Treasure Hunt	Swindon & Cricklade
26/27	Tenth Transport Rally	Pontypool
29	Bygone Branchline Day	Dean Forest
29	Kids' Workshop at Bury Transport Museum	East Lancashire
30-1 Sept	Ale at Amberley	Amberley
31	Grand Steam Gala	North Norfolk
31-2 Sept	Autumn Steam Gala	Llangollen

September

1	Bygone Branchline Day	Dean Forest
1/2	Craft and Food Fair	Amberley
1/2	BunkFest	Cholsey & Wallingford
1/2	Sweet Music	Corris
1/2	Grand Steam Gala	North Norfolk
1/2	Infernal Combustion	Kew Bridge
1/2	Steam Gala	Welshpool & Llanfair
1/2	Late Summer Weekend	West Somerset
2	Railway Relics Valuation Day	Avon Valley

Date	Event	Venue
2	Toy & Train Fair	Great Central
4-8	26th Chappel Beer Festival	East Anglian Railway Museum
6	Heritage Open Day (free admission)	Bursledon
6-9	Bridgnorth Beer Festival	Severn Valley
7	Photographic Evening	Tanfield
7-9	Steam Gala and Real Ale Festival	Bodmin
8/9	Eastern European Car Rally	Foxfield
7-9	Autumn Steam Gala	Mid-Hants
7-9	Grand Steam Gala & Vintage Transport Rally	Swanage
8/9	Heritage Open Day (free admission)	St Albans Signal Box
8/9	Mendip Steam Dream	East Somerset
8/9	1940s Weekend	Embsay & Bolton Abbey
8/9	Hoppickers' Weekend	Kent & East Sussex
8/9	Friends of Kirklees Light Railway 7th Annual Steam and Diesel Gala	Kirklees
8/9	1940s Weekend	Lincolnshire Wolds
8/9	Autumn Steam Gala	Nene Valley
8/9	Wartime Weekend	Swindon & Cricklade
8/9	Legends of Industry Weekend	Tanfield
8/9	CAMRA Real Ale Festival at Minehead	West Somerset
9	Seaside Special Steam Day	Abbey Pumping
9	Bus Show and Riders' Day	Amberley
9	Grandparents' Day	Avon Valley
9	Kit Car Display	Beer Heights
9	Annual Gala Day	Chinnor
9	Classic Ford Day	Crich
9	Vintage Transport Gathering	East Lancashire
9	Bus Rally	Romney, Hythe & Dymchurch
9	On The Buses	Severn Valley
10-27 Oct	FREE entry to gardens	Beer Heights
14/15	Diesel Gala	Dean Forest
14-16	Heritage Diesel Gala	North Yorkshire Moors
14-16	Annual Steam Gala	Pontypool
15/16	Miniature Steam Weekend	Amberley
15/16	Enthusiasts' Tram Event / Glasgow 50	Crich
15/16	Gala Weekend	Didcot
15/16	EMU Weekend	East Kent
15/16	Autumn Ale & Steam Weekend	Gloucestershire Warwickshire
15/16	Welsh Steam Up	Leighton Buzzard
15/16	Autumn Gala	Middleton
15/16	The Famous '40s Weekend	North Norfolk
15/16	Steam Gala	Ribble
15/16	Heritage Transport Gala and Behind the Scenes	South Devon
15/16	Swinging '60s Weekend	Spa Valley
16	Craft Fair	Colne Valley
16	Classic Vehicle Day	Gloucestershire Warwickshire
16	Classic Vehicle Gathering	Old Kiln
18-20	Pensioners' Treat	Kent & East Sussex
20/21	Sussex Branch Line Weekend	Bluebell
21-23	Beer Festival	Great Central
21-23	Class 47 50th Anniversary	Mid-Norfolk
21-23	Autumn Steam Gala	Severn Valley
22	Murder Mystery Evening	Avon Valley
22	Diesel Day	Llangollen
22	Open Day (Members and Shareholders)	Mid-Hants
22/23	Steam Gala	Rudyard Lake
22/23	Diesel Gala	Churnet Valley
22/23	Military Weekend	Dean Forest
22/23	Everything Goes	Devon Railway
22/23	Railway at War	Northampton & Lamport
22/23	South Downs Gala	South Downs
22-26	Autumn Gala	Perrygrove
23	Big American Wing Ding	Bursledon
28-30	Diesel Gala	Nene Valley
29	Autumn Diesel Day	Bodmin
29/30	History Down The Line	Bure Valley

Event Diary

29/30	Family Fun Weekend	Great Central
29/30	Waterworks at War	Kew Bridge
29/30	Super Power Weekend	Eastleigh Lakeside
29/30	Vintage on the Railway	Romney, Hythe & Dymchurch
30	Motorcycle Rally	Leighton Buzzard
30	Mixed Traction	Lincolnshire Wolds

October

4/5	Autumn Steam Gala	West Somerset
4-6	Diesel Enthusiasts' Gala	Severn Valley
4-7	Autumn Steam Gala	Great Central
5-7	Autumn Gala	Ffestiniog
6	Scarecrow Railway Day	Abbey Pumping
6	Model Railway Express	Bure Valley
6	Model Rail Day	Swindon & Cricklade
6/7	Small Engines Event	East Anglian Railway Museum
6/7	1940s Weekend	Nene Valley
6/7	Diesels Weekend	Ribble
7	Senior Citizens' Day	Chinnor
7	Folk Festival and Classic Cars	Churnet Valley
7	Autumn Steam Gala	West Lancashire
12-14	Railmotor Weekend	Bodmin
12-14	Steam Gala	Keighley & Worth Valley
12-14	Railway in Wartime	North Yorkshire Moors
13	Race the Train	Gloucestershire Warwickshire
13/14	Austin Counties Car Rally	Kent & East Sussex
13/14	Diesel Gala	East Lancashire
13/14	Big Four Weekend	Eastleigh Lakeside
13/14	Autumn Diesel Gala	Pontypool
14	Autumn Vintage Vehicle Show	Amberley
14	Victorian Sunday	Colne Valley
20	Diesel Locomotive Day	Corris
20/21	End of Season Gala	Avon Valley
20/21	Models Weekend	Crich
20/21	Steam Gala	Foxfield
20/21	Autumn Steam Gala	East Lancashire
20/21	Lancashire and Yorkshire Bus Gathering	East Lancashire
20/21	Transport Collectors' Fair	East Lancashire
20/21	21st Anniversary Weekend	Kirklees
20/21	Multiple Matters Weekend	Mid-Norfolk
20/21	CAMRA Beer Festival	Spa Valley
21	Autumn Industrial Trains	Amberley
21	Traction Engine Event	Bursledon
21	Red Oktober Day	Crich
24	Kids' Workshop at Bury Transport Museum	East Lancashire
25-28	Beer & Music Festival	Keighley & Worth Valley
27	Murder Mystery Evening	Avon Valley
27	Industrial Gala	Chasewater
27	The Jazz Train	Severn Valley
27-4 Nov	Family Fun Week	Swanage
28	Postman Pat	Bodmin
28	Enthusiasts' Day	Bredgar
28	Small Engines Miniature Steam Gala	Eastleigh Lakeside
29	Peppa Pig	Mid-Hants
29-3 Nov	Rides on the Beer Heights Frights Ghost Train	Beer Heights

November

3	Diesel Railway Day	Abbey Pumping
3	Diesel Theme Day	East Lancashire
3/4	Half Price Weekend	Bodmin
3/4	Modelling Mayhem	Kew Bridge
3/4	Poppy Train	Llangollen
3/4	Half Price Weekend	South Devon
10	Walk the Line	Mid-Hants
11	Tank Engine Day	Moors Valley
11	Remembrance Service	Great Central

11	Remembrance Sunday Service	Severn Valley
11	BBC Children in Need	West Lancashire
17/18	Steam Enthusiasts Event	Great Central
25	Winter Festival	Bursledon

December

4-6	Carols Down the Line	South Devon
7/8	Dunster by Candlelight	West Somerset
10/11	Carol Trains	West Somerset
28-31	Post Christmas Blues	Kent & East Sussex
29-31	Grand New Year Steamup	Kew Bridge
29-31	Kids for a Quid	Spa Valley

January 2013

| 1 | Grand New Year Steam-up | Kew Bridge |
| 13 | Magnificent Meccano | Abbey Pumping |

February 2013

| 3 | Steam Toys in Action | Abbey Pumping |

Days out with Thomas

March

3/4	Didcot
10/11	Midland Railway
17/18	Kirklees

April

6-9	Embsay & Bolton Abbey
6-9	East Anglian Railway Museum
6-9	Gwili
6-15	Mid-Hants
14/15	Dean Forest
21/22	Battlefield
28/29	Battlefield

May

5-7	South Devon
5-7	East Lancashire
5-7	East Somerset
12/13	Avon Valley
12/13	Spa Valley
18/19	Spa Valley
19/20	Bo'ness
19/20	Kirklees
26/27	Eastleigh Lakeside
26/27	Gloucestershire Warwickshire

June

2-5	Embsay & Bolton Abbey
7-10	Midland Railway
9/10	Dean Forest
23/24	Gwili
23/24	Nene Valley
29/30	Romney, Hythe & Dymchurch
30	Gwili

July

1	Gwili
1	Romney, Hythe & Dymchurch
7/8	Gwili
7/8	Eastleigh Lakeside
7/8	West Somerset
14/15	Gwili
14/15	Kirklees
22	Nene Valley

August

3-5	Bo'ness
3-5	East Lancashire
4-7	Midland Railway
4/5	Llangollen
4/5	Nene Valley
9-12	Llangollen
10-12	East Somerset
17-19	Dean Forest
17-20	Kirklees
18/19	Nene Valley
18-27	Mid-Hants
25-27	East Anglian Railway Museum
25-27	Embsay & Bolton Abbey
25-27	Churnet Valley
29	Churnet Valley

September

10/11	Kirklees
15/16	Eastleigh Lakeside
22/23	Bo'ness
22/23	Gloucestershire Warwickshire
22/23	Kent & East Sussex
29/30	Kent & East Sussex

October

6/7	East Lancashire
6/7	Spa Valley
13/14	Spa Valley
20/21	Llangollen
27/28	Nene Valley
25-28	Llangollen
31	Nene Valley

December

1/2	Didcot (to visit Father Christmas)
2	East Anglian Railway Museum
8/9	Didcot (to visit Father Christmas)
9	East Anglian Railway Museum
13	East Anglian Railway Museum
15/16	Didcot (to visit Father Christmas)
22/23	Didcot (to visit Father Christmas)
23	East Anglian Railway Museum
27-31	Midland Railway

Heritage Railway Association

www.heritagerailways.com

Company Limited by Guarantee and not having a share capital.
Registered in England No 2226245
(Registered Office: 2 Littlestone Road, New Romney, Kent TN28 8PL
President: Lord Faulkner of Worcester
Vice Presidents: Ian Allan OBE, Allan Garraway MBE, Brian Simpson MEP
Patron: Dame Margaret Weston DBE

Friends of HRA Membership Secretary:
Dr Alan Saunders, 31 Cedar Avenue, Malvern Link, Malvern, Worcs WR14 2SF
Tel: 0800 756 5111 (ext 423)
E-mail: alan.saunders@hra.gb.com

Corporate Membership Secretary:
Steve Wood, 15 Croftlands Drive, Ravenglass, Cumbria CA18 1SJ
Tel: 0800 756 5111 (ext 421)
E-mail: steve.wood@hra.gb.com

Heritage Railway Association

Anyone interested in nationwide railway preservation can become a Friend of the Heritage Railway Association.

Benefits include receiving a copy of the Annual Report, which details the work of the Association during the year. There is the opportunity of attending various business meetings, weekend meetings, which include visits to member railways, and seminars. This gives an opportunity to learn more about the preservation movement.

There is the opportunity to purchase *Railways Restored* at a reduced price and to purchase an Inter-Rail pass which allows visits to member railways at a concessionary price.

Current annual subscription is
£17.63 (non UK £17.63),

For further information, please contact the *Friends of HRA Membership Secretary:*
Dr Alan Saunders, 31 Cedar Avenue, Malvern Link, Malvern, Worcs WR14 2SF.
E-mail: alanhra@waitrose.com

Application Form to become a Friend of the Heritage Railway Association

Name
....

Address
....
....
....

Post Code
....

Telephone
....

Subscription enclosed
....

Donation enclosed
....

Members of the Heritage Railway Association

UK Affiliate Members (not in the main part of the book)

Association of Community Rail Partnerships: Neil Buxton, The Rail and River Centre, Canalside, Huddersfield, West Yorkshire HD7 5AB

Brookes No 1 Locomotive Co: Mr D. R. C. Moncton, 10 Blenheim Terrace, Woodhouse Lane, Leeds LS2 9HX

DB Schenker: Mr P. Johnson, Locomotive Engineer, Toton TNMD, Toton Sidings, Long Eaton, Nottingham NG10 1HA

Doppelmayr Cable Car UK Ltd (Birmingham Airport): Alan Kingsland, Air Rail Maintenance Shop, Birmingham International Airport B26 3QJ

Edmondson Ticket Printing Co: The Pighte, Dervaig, Tobermoray, Isle of Mull, Argyll PA75 6QN

R. E. V. Gomm Ltd: Mr M. J. Tyler, R. E. V. Gomm Ltd, Winster Grove, Great Barr, Birmingham B44 9EG

Guild of Railway Artists: Mr F. Hodges, Chief Executive Officer, 45 Dickins Road, Warwick CV34 5NS

Hastings Borough Council (Cliff Railway): Nick Sangster, Aquila House, Breeds Place, Hastings, East Sussex TN34 3UY

HIT Entertainment: Maple House, 149 Tottenham Court Road, London W1T 7NF

Invensys Rail: Helen Webb, PO Box 79, Pew Hill, Chippenham, Wiltshire SN15 1JD

Irish Railway Record Society: PO Box 9, Heuston Station, Dublin 8

Lloyd's Railway Society: Mr Douglas Cooper, 24 Yew Tree Road, Southborough, Tunbridge Wells, Kent TN4 0BA

Loco RH 200 DE No 424839: Brian Cunningham, 20 Ladybrook, Chapel Park, Newcastle, Tyne & Wear

Locomotive Club of Great Britain: Mr R. L. Patrick, 8 Wolviston Avenue, Bishopgate, York YO1 3DD

Marsh (UK) Ltd: Mr A. J. C. Brown, No 1, The Marsh Centre, London EC1 8DX

New Europe Railway Heritage Trust: Frank Cooper, Maple Lodge, Chapel Lane, Sibsey, Boston, Lincs PE22 0SN

Normanhurst Enterprises Ltd: Peter Brewer, 9 Burscough Street, Ormskirk, Lancs L39 2EG

Transport Trust: 202 Lambeth Road, London SE1 7JW

Overseas Affiliate Members

Australian Railway Historical Society: Mr R. Jowett, New South Wales Division, 67 Renwick Street, Redfern, NSW 2016, Australia

Fronz: Paul Dillicar, PO Box 13-771, Onehunga, Auckland, New Zealand

Puffing Billy Railway: Mr John Hoy, PO Box 451, Belgrave, Victoria 3160, Australia

Stoomcentrum Maldegem: Rik Degruyter, De Streep 19, B-8340 Damme-Sysele, Belgium

Additional Corporate Members not listed in the main part of the book

Aberystwyth Cliff Railway: Alun Davies, General Manager, Cliff Railway House, Cliff Terrace, Aberystwyth SY23 2DW

Aln Valley Railway Society: Mark Hayton, 7 Lower Barrasdale, Alnwick, Northumberland NE66 1DW

Anglesey Railway (2006) Ltd — Lein Amlwch: Robert Diddo, 12 Balmoral Crescent, Dronfield Woodhouse, Dronfield, Derbyshire S18 8ZY

Altrincham Electric Railway Preservation Society: Mr A. D. Macfarlane, 25 Prestbury Avenue, Timperley, Altrincham, Cheshire WA15 8HY

Babbacombe Cliff Railway: David Cooper, Kestrel House, Marine Road, Eastbourne BN22 7AU

Battle of Britain Locomotive Preservation Society: Les Mitchell, 30 Hilton Way, Sible Hedingham, Essex CO9 3JW

Bridgend Valleys Railway: Mr J. Leach, 10 Y-Wern, Bettws, Bridgend, Mid Glamorgan CF32 8RR

Bridgnorth Castle Hill Railway: Malvern Tipping, 6A Castle Terrace, Bridgnorth, Shropshire WV16 4AH

Britain's Great Little Railways: Mr M. B. Beevers, 64 Bullar Road, Southampton SO18 1GS

Britannia Locomotive Society: Mr A. Sixsmith, 6 Vermont Grove, Peterborough PE3 6BN

Bulleid Society Ltd: Mr A. J. Fry, 28 Houndean Rise, Lewes, Sussex BN7 1EQ

Burry Port & Gwendraeth Railway Co Ltd: Mr Stuart Thomas, Wellfield, Yrecor Lane, Ferryside, Carms SA17 5UT

Caerphilly Railway Society Ltd: Mr A. Smith, 51 Worcester Crescent, Newport NP9 7NX

Camelot Locomotive Society: Mr P. W. Gibbs, 13 Clarendon Road, High Wycombe, Bucks HP13 7AW

Central Tramway Scarborough: Jim Dungey, Upper Station, Marine Parade, Scarborough, North Yorkshire YO11 2ER

Class 40 Preservation Society: Martin Walker, c/o Beaver Sports (YOMO) Ltd, Flint Street, Fartown, Huddersfield HD1 6LG

Class 45/1 Preservation Society: Mr N. Burden, 97 Richmond Park Crescent, Handsworth, Sheffield S13 8HF

Class 56 Group: Alan Flockhart, 3 Bainbridge Drive, Selby, North Yorkshire YO8 4QN

Clwyd & District Railway Heritage Trust: Arfryn, 13 Pen-y-maes Avenue, Rhyl LL18 4ED

Cornish Steam Locomotive Preservation Society Ltd: Mr M. Orme, 3 Jubilee Terrace, Goonhavern, Truro, Cornwall TR4 9JY

Cravens Heritage Trains: Robert Ward, 29 Carlton Avenue, Hertford SG14 2GR

Darlington Railway Preservation Society: Mr M. Bentley, 64 Dimsdale View East, Porthill, Newcastle under Lyme ST5 8HL

Dean Forest Locomotive Group: Mr J. S. Metherall, 15 Sudbrook Way, Gloucester GL4 4AP

Darjeeling Himalayan Railway Society: Mr P. D. Whittle, 8 Broadwater Close, Woking, Surrey GU21 5TW

Deltic Preservation Society: Nigel Paine, 49 Woodgate Road, Wootton Fields, Wootton, Northants NN4 6ET

Devon Diesel Society Ltd: Steve Squires, 15 Springfield, Acle, Norfolk NR13 3JW

Diesel and Electric Group: Mr J. E. Cronin, The Old Goods Shed, Williton Station, Williton, Somerset TA4 4RQ

Diesel Unit Preservation Associates Ltd: Mr M. Cornell, 24 Ashbury Drive, Marks Tey, Colchester, Essex CO6 1XW

Dolgarrog Railway Society: Mr P. Smith, 84 Gorlan, Conwy LL32 8RR

East Essex Locomotive Preservation Society: Mr R. Moore 7 Woodbine Grove, Enfield, Middx EN2 0EA

Eastleigh Railway Preservation Society Ltd: Neil Kearns, 38 Arundel Road, Boyatt Wood, Eastleigh, Hants SO50 4PQ

Eden Valley Railway Trust: Ms G. Boyd, 1 Victoria Road, Barnard Castle, Co Durham DL12 8HW

EPB Preservation Group: Mr R. Baines, 73 Woodhurst Avenue, Petts Wood, Orpington, Kent BR5 1AT

Firefly Trust: Mr S. Bee, 9 Shenstone, Lindfield, West Sussex RH16 2PU

The Flour Mill: Mr W. A. Parker, Stowe Grange, St Briavels, Lydney, Glos GL15 6QH

Folkestone Leas Lift: Terry Begent, 24 Harbour Way, Folkestone, Kent CT20 1NF

Foxcote Manor Society: Mr G. Heddon, 31 Lordsmill Road, Shavington, Crewe, Cheshire CW2 5HB

Furness Railway Trust: Tim Owen, Meadowside, 105 Station Road, Cark in Cartmel, Grange over Sands, Cumbria LA11 7NY

Gloucester Railcars Trust Ltd: John Bull, 61 Walsingham Gardens, Stoneleigh, Epsom, Surrey KT19 0LT

Glyn Valley Tramway & Industrial Heritage Trust: David Norman, 4 Yew Tree Court, Gresford, Wrexham LL12 8ET

Glyn Valley Tramway Trust: D. Cooper, Pentre Garth, Pentre Cilgwyn, Llwynmawr, Glyn Ceriog, Llangollen LL20 7BG

GWR 813 Preservation Fund: Mr P. Goss, 23 Hatchmere, Thornbury, Bristol BS35 2EU

Hampshire & Sussex Units Preservation Society: Mr C. Dann, 48 Hollybrook Park, Bordon, Hants GU35 0DL

Hampshire Narrow Gauge Railway Trust: Mark Arnold, 61 Havendale, Hedge End, Southampton SO30 0FD

Hastings Diesels Ltd: Mr J. White, The Rail Engineering Centre, Bridgeway, St Leonards on Sea, East Sussex TN38 8AP

Headhunters Barber Shop & Railway Museum: Selwyn Johnson, 5 Darling Street, Enniskillen, Co Fermanagh, Northern Ireland BT74 7DP

Heaton Park Electric Tramway: Roger Morris, 38 Wolsey Road, Sale, Cheshire M33 7AU

Holden F5 Steam Locomotive Trust: Steve Cooper, 49 Beech Avenue, Halstead, Essex CO9 2TT

Hull & Barnsley Railway Stock Fund: Mr A. E. Hallman, 6 Chequerfield Court, Pontefract, West Yorkshire WF8 2TQ

Kingdom of Fife Railway Association (The): Steve Dewar, 1 Castle View, Aberdour, Fife KY3 0UF

Lambton No 29 Syndicate: Mr J. M. Richardson, 509 Westgate Apartments, York YO26 4ZF

Lancashire & Yorkshire Railway Preservation Society:
Eric Ring, 29 Shelley Close, Newport Pagnell
MK16 8JB

Lartigue Monorail: Jimmy Deeniham TD, Listowel,
County Kerry, Eire

*Lincolnshire Coast Light Railway Historical Vehicles
Trust:*
Mr Frederick Ellis, Chairman, c/o Ellis Bros
(Contractors), 7 Lansdowne Road, Skegness,
Lincolnshire PE25 2DJ

Llangollen Railway Great Western Locomotive Group:
David Clark, 10 Cleveland Grove, Lupset Park,
Wakefield WF2 8LD

LMS Carriage Association: David Winter,
42 Tandlewood Park, Royton, Oldham OL2 5UZ

LMS Patriot Co Ltd: Richard Saint, PO Box 3118,
Hixon, Staffordshire ST16 9JL

Locomotive Owners Group (Scotland) Ltd:
Mr H. Stevenson, 28 Hazeldean Avenue, Bo'ness,
West Lothian EH51 0NJ

London & North Western Society: Martin O'Keeffe,
36 Martony Court, 21-35 Dane Road, Margate, Kent
CT9 1SG

Lynton & Barnstaple Light Railway: Mr D. Hill,
8 Long Lakes, Williton, Taunton, Somerset TA4 4SR

Lynton & Lynmouth Lift Co: Ceri Hughes, The Cliff
Railway, The Esplanade, Lynmouth, Devon
EX35 6EQ

Maid Marian Locomotive Fund: Mr H. Johns,
139 Stoops Lane, Doncaster DN4 7RG

Market Drayton Railway Preservation Society:
Glyn Rowe, Shakeford Mill House, Hinstock, Market
Drayton, Shropshire TF9 2SP

Maunsell Locomotive Society:
Mr J. S. Pilcher, 312 Riverside Mansions,
Garnett Street, Wapping, London E1 9SZ

Merchant Navy Locomotive Preservation Society Ltd:
Howard G. Reynolds, 4 Ash Grove, Liphook, Hants
GU30 7HZ

Merseyside Tramway Preservation Society:
Robert Jones, 103 Grove Road, Wallasey, Merseyside
CH45 3HG

Modern Railway Society of Ireland: Ken harte,
12 Orken Lane, Aghalee, Craigavon, Co Armagh
BT67 0ED

National Museums Scotland: Alistair Dodds, Principal
Curator of Transport, Chambers Street, Edinburgh
EH1 1JF

NER 1903 Electric Autocar Trust: Stephen Middleton,
Rose Lea House, 23 Brunswick Drive, Harrogate
HG1 2QW

North Eastern Locomotive Preservation Group:
Mr C. Hatton, 20 Sorrell Court, Marton,
Middlesbrough TS7 8RZ

North Gloucestershire Railway Co Ltd:
Mr R. H. Wales, 'Wellesbourne', Oakfield Street,
Tivoli, Cheltenham, Gloucestershire GL33 8HR

Ongar Railway Preservation Society:
Mr David Rumble, c/o Bywaters Ltd, Lea Riverside,
Twelvetrees Crescent, London E3 3JG

Poulton & Wyre Railway Trust: Richard Rossall,
c/o The Print Room, Hillhouse Business Park,
Thornton, Lancashire FY5 4QD

Princess Royal Locomotive Trust Ltd: PO Box 6233,
The West Shed, Ripley, Derbyshire DE5 4AD

Project 62 Locomotive Group:
Richard White, 45 Cedar Crescent, North Baddesley,
Southampton SO52 9FU

Railway Vehicle Preservations Ltd:
Mr Gordon Maslin, 14 Lawson Avenue, Stanground,
Peterborough PE2 8PA

Red Rose Society: Mr G. Jones, Astley Green Colliery
Museum, Higher Green Lane, Astley, Tyldesley,
Manchester M29 7JB

Rushden, Higham & Wellingborough Railway:
Dave Clipstone, Rushden Station, Station Approach,
Rushden, Northamptonshire NN10 0AW

Scarborough Cliff Railway: Alan Dargue, Town Hall,
St Nicholas Street, Scarborough YO11 2HG

Scottish Locomotive Preservation Trust Fund:
Mr J. Shepherd, 29 Earlspark Avenue, Glasgow
G43 2HN

Shipley Glen Tramway: Councillor Dean Smith,
10 Craven Park, Menston, Ilkley, West Yorkshire
LS29 6EQ

Sir Nigel Gresley Locomotive Preservation Trust Ltd:
Peter Travis, 26 Cheltenham Gardens, Halifax, West
Yorks HX3 0AN

Southend-on-Sea Cliff Railway: Shane Bartley,
Visitor Services Manager, Central Museum, Victoria
Avenue, Southend-on-Sea, Essex SS2 6EW

Southern Electric Group:
Mr B. Cakebread, 41 The Drive, Shoreham by Sea,
West Sussex BN43 5GD

Southern Locomotives Ltd:
Mr S. Troy, 16 Arcadia Road, Istead Rise, Meopham,
Kent DA13 9EH

Southwold Railway Society (The):
Mr J. Bennett, 1 Barnaby Green, Southwold, Suffolk
IP15 6AP

Stanier 8F Locomotive Society Ltd: John Peddar, 87 Broadway, Erdington, Birmingham B24 0AH

Steam Power Trust '65: Mr A. R. Thompson, The Station House, Penshaw, Houghton le Spring DH4 7PQ

Steeple Grange Light Railway: Martin Smith, 187 Chesterfield Road, Matlock, Derbyshire DE4 3GA

Stephenson Locomotive Society: Mr M. A. Green, 3 Cresswell Court, Hartlepool TS26 0ES

Stratford on Avon, Broadway Railway Society: Mr Roland Hill, 10 Garard Close, Salford Priors, Evesham, Worcs WR11 5XG

Suburban Electric Railway Association: Mr R. Davidson, 6 Coombfield Drive, Darenth, Dartford, Kent DA2 7LQ

Underground Railway Rolling Stock Trust: Mr D. C. Alexander, 13 Irvine Drive, Stoke Mandeville, Aylesbury HP22 5UN

Urie Locomotive Society: Mr A. Ball, 'Lavenham', Adams Lane, Selborne, Alton, Hants GU34 3LJ

Wainwright 'C' Preservation Society: Mr I. A. Demaid, 69 Bromley Gardens, Bromley, Kent BR2 0ES

Waverley Route Heritage Association: Ian Macintosh, Signal Box Cottage, Whitrope, Hawick, Roxburghshire TD9 9TY

Weardale Railway Trust: Mr G. Chatsfield, Stanhope Station, Bondisle, Bishop Auckland, Co Durham DL13 2YS

Western Locomotive Association: Mr H. Coates, 5 Rake End Court, Ridware, Rugeley, Staffs WS15 5RW

Wisbech & March (Bramley Line): Simon King, Waldersea Depot, Long Drove, Waldersea, Friday Bridge, Wisbech PE14 0NP

Worcester Locomotive Society Ltd: Brian Thomas, 158 Cromer Road, Saint Johns, Worcester WR2 5JD

Yorkshire Wolds Railway Restoration Project: Ivan Merino, 95 Westgate, Driffield, East Yorkshire YO25 6TA

1857 Society: Mr G. West, 21A Broad Street, Brigtown, Cannock, West Midlands WS11 3DA

35006 Locomotive Co Ltd: Nigel Hills, Flat 1, 55 Holland Park, London W11 3RS

4247 Ltd: Mr N. Powles, 15 Claydon Close, Washford, Watchet, Somerset TA23 0PQ

45163 Ltd: Jeremy Dunn, Chairman, 4 Whitlock Drive, Great Yeldham, Halstead, Essex CO9 4EE

48624 Locomotive Soc: Keith Godley, 11 Cobnar Drive, Newbold, Chesterfield S41 8DD

5 BEL Trust: Gordon Rushton, 15 Ryecroft, Furzton, Milton Keynes MK4 1AH

6201 Princess Elizabeth Society Ltd: Mr A. Harries, 1 Ormerod Close, Sandbach, Cheshire CW11 4HA

71000 Duke of Gloucester Steam Locomotive Trust Ltd: D. J. Brown, 11 Stirling Close, Woolston, Warrington WA1 4DW

8E Railway Association: Roger Moris, 38 Wolseley Road, Sale, Cheshire M33 7AU

LM2MT 46464 Trust: Mr I. Hopley, 53 Redmoss Road, Nigg, Aberdeen AB12 3JJ

Beer Heights Light Railway: (see main section)

Bekonscot Light Railway:
Bekonscot Model Village, Warwick Road,
Beaconsfield, Bucks HP9 2PL
www.bekonscot.co.uk

Bentley Miniature Railway:
Bentley Wildflower & Motor Museum, Halland,
Nr Lewes, East Sussex BN8 5AF
www.bentleyrailway.co.uk

Bickington Steam Railway: (see main section)

Bolebroke Castle & Lakes Steam Railway:
Bolebroke Castle, Edenbridge Road, Hartfield,
East Sussex TN7 4JJ
www.bolebrokecastle.co.uk

Brookside Miniature Railway: (see main section)

Cleethorpes Coast Light Railway: (see main section)

Cuckoo Hill Railway:
Avon Valley Nurseries, South Gorley, Fordingbridge,
Hants SP6 2PP

Dragon Miniature Railway:
Wyevale Garden Centre, Dooley Lane, Marple,
Cheshire SK6 7HG
www.freewebs.com/dragonrailway

East Herts Light Railway:
The Van Hage Garden Centre, Pepper Hill,
Great Amwell, Ware, Herts SG12 9RP
www.ehmr.co.uk

Eastleigh Lakeside Railway: (see main section)

Evesham Vale Railway: (see main section)

Exbury Gardens Steam Railway: (see main section)

Exmoor Steam Railway:
Cape of Good Hope Farm, Bratton Fleming,
Barnstaple, Devon EX32 7JN

Fairbourne Railway: (see main section)

The Fancott Miniature Railway:
Fancott, Nr Toddington, Dunstable, Beds LU5 6HT
www.fancottrailway.tk

Great Laxey Mine Railway: (see main section)

Grosvenor Park Miniature Railway:
Grosvenor Park, Park Road, Chester, Cheshire
CH1 1QQ
www.gpmr.co.uk

Lappa Valley Railway: (see main section)

Moors Valley Railway (see main section)

Mortocombe Railway:
Wyevale Garden Centre, Newbury Road, Chilton,
Oxon OX11 0PG
www.mortocombe-railway.co.uk

North Bay Railway: (see main section)

Perrygrove Railway & Treetop Adventure:
(see main section)

Porthmadog Woodland Railway:
Tremadog Road, Porthmadog, LL49 9DY

Rhyl Miniature Railway: (see main section)

Romney, Hythe & Dymchurch Railway:
(see main section)

Rudyard Lake Railway: (see main section)

Sherwood Forest Railway:
Lambs Pen Lane, Edwinstowe, Nr Mansfield, Notts
NG21 9HL
www.sherwoodforestrailway.com

Shibden Miniature Railway:
Shibden Park, Listers Road, Halifax, W. Yorks
HX3 6XG

South Downs Light Railway: (see main section)

Stansted Park Light Railway:
Stansted House, Rowlands Castle, Hants PO9 6DX
www.splr.info

Strawberry Line Miniature Railway:
Avon Valley Country Park, Pixash Lane, Keynsham,
Bristol BS31 1TS
www.strawberryminirail.co.uk

Swanley New Barn Railway:
Mr P. Jackson, New Barn Lane, Swanley, Kent
BR8 7PW
www.snbr.co.uk

Weston Miniature Railway:
Marine Parade, Weston-super-Mare, Somerset
www.westonminiaturerailway.co.uk

Caledonian Railway No 828 and LMS Ivatt Class 2
'make smoke' for the photographer as they traverse the
Strathspey Railway with a train from Broomhill.*SR*

INDEX

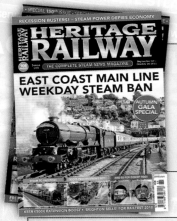
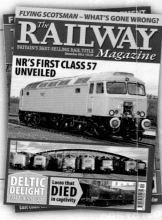
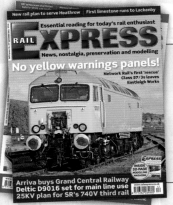

Join today for 6 months half price

To celebrate the launch of our new Essential and Premiere Collections, we're offering new customers **half price for 6 months**. Choose from over 175 digital TV channels including HD ones; keep up to speed on everything with superfast fibre optic broadband; and enjoy unlimited weekend calls to UK landlines. Prices start from just **£3.50 a month** for 6 months, then £7 a month after that (when you take a Virgin Phone line for £13.90 a month).

Now with up to 30Mb

HD box | **Talk Weekends**

£3.50 a month
for 6 months, then £7 a month after that

Digital TV

✓ Over 75 channels including Sky1, Sky Living and Discovery.

✓ 6 HD channels including Film4 HD.

✓ Catch Up TV – Sky Anytime, ITV Net Player, BBC iPlayer, 4oD and Demand 5.

✓ TV On Demand – instant access to a vast library of entertainment.

Calls

✓ Unlimited weekend calls to UK landlines△, 0870 numbers and Virgin Mobile numbers.

✓ Free calls to Virgin Media Directory Enquiries on 118 180.‡

Up to 30Mb | **Talk Weekends**

£7.25 a month
for 6 months, then £14.50 a month after that

Fibre optic broadband

✓ Up to 30Mb – 4x faster than UK average.ˣ

✓ Download and browse as much as you like, no caps, no hidden charges.◇

✓ Wireless Super Hub included.

Calls

✓ Unlimited weekend calls to UK landlines△, 0870 numbers and Virgin Mobile numbers.

✓ Free calls to Virgin Media Directory Enquiries on 118 180.‡

Want our TiVo® service? If you're not taking a Collection, you can add TiVo for just £5 a month.

Want more Premium channels? Add more channels, like Sky Sports or Sky Movies, even in HD, for a bit more each month.

sky SPORTS 1 HD   sky SPORTS 1   sky SPORTS 3   sky SPORTS NEWS   sky SPORTS F1
sky SPORTS 2 HD   sky SPORTS 2   sky SPORTS 4   sky MOVIES HD   sky MOVIES

Already a customer? Give us a call to upgrade to TiVo, with HD as standard, and our latest broadband speeds and wireless Super Hub, in one of our new Collections. Also, don't forget we are doubling your broadband speed.

Call 0800 052 0824

Visit virginmedia.com/bundles or pop in store today

Introducing our new Collections

Half price

for 6 months

Save up to **£135**

A League of Their Own
Fridays, 9pm

Bear Grylls:
Born Survivor

TV, broadband and calls.
Pick 2 or 3.
Prices start from £3.50 a month.
When you take a Virgin Phone line for £13.90 a month.

Keep up

Ben 10:
Ultimate Alien
Saturdays, 10am

Nikita

TiVo included

TiVo included

Essential Collection

TiVo | Up to 30Mb | Talk Weekends

£12.50 a month
for 6 months, then £25 a month after that

Digital TV

✓ TiVo 500GB – record, pause and rewind live TV, up to 250 hours recording space, record three shows and watch a fourth you recorded earlier.

✓ Over 75 channels including Sky1, Sky Living and Discovery.

✓ 6 HD channels including Film4 HD.

✓ Catch Up TV – Sky Anytime, ITV Net Player, BBC iPlayer, 4oD and Demand 5.

✓ TV On Demand – instant access to a vast library of entertainment.

Fibre optic broadband

✓ Up to 30Mb – 4x faster than UK average.ᵛ

✓ Download and browse as much as you like, no caps, no hidden charges.^

✓ Wireless Super Hub included.

Calls

✓ Unlimited weekend calls to UK landlinesᴬ, 0870 numbers and Virgin Mobile numbers.

✓ Free calls to Virgin Media Directory Enquiries on 118 180.†

Premiere Collection

TiVo | HD Extra box | Up to 60Mb | Talk Weekends

£22.50 a month
for 6 months, then £45 a month after that

Digital TV

✓ TiVo 500GB – record, pause and rewind live TV, up to 250 hours recording space, record three shows and watch a fourth you recorded earlier.

✓ Over 175 channels including Sky1, Sky Living, Discovery, Nickelodeon and FX.

✓ ESPN channels included.

✓ 23 HD channels included.

✓ Catch Up TV – Sky Anytime, ITV Net Player, BBC iPlayer, 4oD and Demand 5.

✓ TV On Demand – instant access to a vast library of entertainment.

✓ Music On Demand – watch thousands of music videos whenever you want.

✓ **Plus – extra HD box for another room.**

Fibre optic broadband

✓ Up to 60Mb – 7x faster than UK average.ᵛ

✓ Download and browse as much as you like, no caps, no hidden charges.^

✓ Wireless Super Hub included.

Calls

✓ Unlimited weekend calls to UK landlinesᴬ, 0870 numbers and Virgin Mobile numbers.

✓ Free calls to Virgin Media Directory Enquiries on 118 180.†

Introducing our new Collections

Half price

for 6 months

Save up to £135

sky 1

A League of Their Own
Fridays, 9pm

A LEAGUE OF THEIR OWN

Bear Grylls:
Born Survivor

TV, broadband and calls.
Pick 2 or 3.
Prices start from £3.50 a month.
When you take a Virgin Phone line for £13.90 a month.

Virgin media

Keep up